# General Course of Study

for

# Lutheran Elementary Schools

## With Supplement

Published under the Auspices of
THE BOARD OF CHRISTIAN EDUCATION
Evangelical Lutheran Synod of
Missouri, Ohio, and Other States

St. Louis, Mo.
CONCORDIA PUBLISHING HOUSE
1943

# FOREWORD

**The Basis for the Lutheran School**

The Lutheran elementary school is a church institution. It has been found to be the most efficient agency by means of which the local congregation may meet its obligation to teach and train children according to the solemn charge of Christ to His disciples of all times in the Great Commission: "Go ye, therefore, and teach all nations (including the young) . . . teaching them to observe all things whatsoever I have commanded you." Matt. 28:19, 20. It is an institution at the same time by means of which the called servant of the congregation or any of his official associates or assistants carry out the obligation of the congregation summarized by Christ in His word to Peter: "Feed My lambs!" John 21:15. This agency of Christian training is therefore rightly called a parochial school, that is, a school of a parish, of a congregation. It is also owned and operated by the congregation as a corporate body, not by the parents, not by private persons, not by the State or the civic community, not by Synod.

The parents have their own particular obligations toward the children, regardless of what the congregation may or may not do by way of educating children. Their obligations parallel those of the congregation so far as religious and spiritual education is concerned, as will be seen from the command of Scripture: "Ye fathers, provoke not your children to wrath, but bring them up in the nurture and admonition of the Lord." Eph. 6:4. But parental obligations go farther in that they include the child's entire education, also for the common requirements of life. In the case of the Christian child or Christian parents, all of education is Christian education.

Holy Scripture recognizes no dual education; neither does the Christian Church nor the Christian parent. Hence, while the Church as such has no command to teach anything but the Word, it undertakes a full educational program in its parochial school for these reasons: 1. The Church has the example of the Old Testament Church. 2. A Christian congregation bears a definite responsibility toward all the baptized children in its midst in keeping with Scriptural injunctions, e. g., Matt. 28:20. 3. The Word of God is taught not only during the so-called religious hour, but also in the form of practical application throughout the entire school day and the entire course. 4. In order to have the children present for continued observation, guidance, and training, the church school is made to substitute for the public school in general education. 5. Since education is never really non-religious, and since, because of its moral objectives, it is as personal as religion itself, the Lutheran Church holds that the education of a Christian child should be wholly in the hands of his parents and the church of his faith.

### The Need for a Manual and Course of Study

While substituting for the public school in the sense that it provides its pupils with the same general education, the Lutheran school is not a dual institution, say in part like a Sunday school and in part like a public school. It is a religious school throughout. The whole educational program is aimed at Christian training, though the particular subject taught may be geography, history, or music. This unity is often overlooked, however, or the teacher is misled by textbooks not written from the Christian viewpoint. A manual should, therefore, be a welcome guide and reminder. It aims to present a uniformly Christian course of instruction and training in all branches of learning, one which takes into account all of the child's needs of body, soul, and mind, a course that aims to accomplish the objectives of temporal Christian living and the one great objective of eternal life.

The present Course of Study with its Supplement is meant to be:

1. A general guide to the Lutheran instructor.

2. A basis upon which local schools or the school systems of synodical Districts may write their more specific courses.

3. A means to maintain the unity of the widely scattered schools of the Lutheran Church, particularly those of the Evangelical Lutheran Synod of Missouri, Ohio, and Other States.

4. A manual of information for local boards of education, church members, parents, or anyone else desiring information about the'Lutheran school and its educational program.

5. An instrument which sets forth the theory of Christian education in its practical application.

## The Nature of the Course

The Course is primarily one of school subjects. The course in religion lays the foundation for all other subjects and forms the center of the curriculum. Each of the other subjects is presented from the Christian viewpoint and made to serve as a course in Christian training. This is particularly true of the content subjects. At the same time no common school branch is turned into a course of religious teaching. Its primary purpose is nowhere disturbed, but its religious significance and viewpoint are set forth.

## Authorship

This Manual and Course of Study was largely written by William A. Kramer, an associate in the School Office. Several sections of the manuscript were prepared by others, as indicated in the acknowledgments. The work is based upon numerous courses of study, upon the principles underlying the latest textbooks, theoretical books, and scientific findings, and upon the principles of Lutheran pedagogy and the best thought in Christian education.

May this book lead to intensified efforts in behalf of the Christian education and training of increasingly larger numbers of children.

May 15, 1942    A. C. STELLHORN, *Secretary of Schools*

# ACKNOWLEDGMENTS

To acknowledge every assistance received in the preparation of this Manual and Course of Study is impossible. Assistance came from many sources and many persons. First among these is A. C. Stellhorn, Secretary of Schools, whose advice, encouragement, and constructive criticism have been invaluable. He has taken a deep interest in the project from the beginning and has helped to shape it in form and content.

Among those who have furnished sections of the manuscript the following deserve special mention for work in the areas listed:

Dr. Paul Bretscher — A Christian Teacher's Philosophy of Education; Arthur L. Miller — Arithmetic; A. H. Stellhorn — Language, Geography, Music; Professor Alfred Schmieding — Fusion-Units Course in Religion; Wm. W. Bloom — Art Education; G. H. Reifschneider — General Science; Professor A. V. Maurer — Educational Guidance; E. R. Lindemann, E. H. Hafner, E. H. Brockmann, A. C. Richter, A. Boehme, Carl E. Freudenburg, and Rev. W. Griesse — Time Allotment and Daily Programs.

Grateful acknowledgment is made also of the services of many others who rendered various assistance: The Superintendents' Conference — advice and suggestions; The South Wisconsin Board of Christian Education — permission to adapt its Bible Reading schedules; The Minnesota Committee on Christian Education — permission to use some of its schedules in Religion; Concordia Publishing House — permission to quote at length from the Texas *Educational Guide and Course of Study;* The Board of Christian Education — constant encouragement while the manuscript was in preparation; representatives of the Theological Seminaries and Teachers Colleges and a committee of the Board of Christian Education — critical reading of the manuscript and suggestions for improvement;

and others who read parts of the manuscript or assisted in other tangible ways.

May God, under whose gracious protection Lutheran elementary education has grown and flourished, be pleased to bless this volume for a better understanding of Christian educational principles and a more diligent and efficient practice in their application. May He make it an aid to the thousands of consecrated Christian teachers whose service to the youth is an essential part of the Church's ministry.

May 15, 1942                                    WM. A. KRAMER

---

# TABLE OF CONTENTS

# Supplement

# I. A CHRISTIAN TEACHER'S PHILOSOPHY OF EDUCATION

"There is in each of us a stream of tendency, whether we call it philosophy or not, which gives coherence and direction to our thoughts and action." This observation by Justice Cardozo hardly requires proof. The normal mind is so constituted that it attempts, however feebly, to co-ordinate and systematize empirical data and to react to, and to interpret, new data in the light of the organized body of experiences which it already possesses.

Largely as a result of the ever-growing multitude and complexity of experiential data which are available in our day but which the limited mind of man finds precariously difficult to integrate into a comprehensive system of thought, leaders in various fields of human endeavor have found it desirable to formulate philosophies of segments of human interests. Thus there have come into being within the past half century philosophies of religion, of science, of the fine arts, of history, of education, and of other cultural pursuits. Philosophies of education, in particular, have poured from the presses in large numbers. We have arrived at the point where it would be a hazardous, if not fruitless, undertaking to discriminate sharply and justly between all of them were it not for the consideration that their basic assumptions are for the most part easily recognizable.

By far the greater number of modern philosophies of education rest their case on the findings of scientific investigation. Others, even in this scientific age, still proceed from unproved postulates of human reason with little or no regard for the deductions of modern science. A Christian teacher's philosophy of education, however, is rooted in divine revelation, to wit, the Bible, though it grants suffrage to those findings of science and to those postulates of reason which are not at variance with the pronouncements of divine revelation.

The answer to the question which philosophy of education an educator will adopt obviously depends on his attitude toward scientific investigation, toward reason, and toward divine revelation as sources of knowledge. Educators who believe that there are at best two sources of knowledge, scientific investigation and reason, will not allow in their philosophy of education data which are implicit only in divine revelation. The Christian educator, on the other hand, who believes the fact of divine revelation, acknowledges the Bible as a primary source of knowledge. He by no means disparages evidences of science and postulates of reason, but he grants them a place only in those areas of human interests whose exploration divine revelation has left to the mind of man, and he fearlessly objects whenever these evidences and postulates presume on holy ground.

The Christian educator not only admits divine revelation as a source of knowledge; he regards it as the only absolutely reliable, inviolable source of knowledge. He believes that God, who speaks in the Bible, cannot err, that, however, the evidences of science and the postulates of reason are subject to error. Therefore he makes the truths of divine revelation and their applications the fundamental premises in his philosophy of education.

What are these truths? They are, briefly summarized, the following: There is a God, and only *one* God, all the vagaries and vaporings of many scientists and rationalists notwithstanding. This God is three Persons in one essence. He created man and the universe by His almighty power, and He willed that man should make the earth subservient to himself. God created the first human beings, Adam and Eve, in His own image, that is, in perfect holiness and righteousness. But Adam and Eve disobeyed God's will and sinned. God punished them and their descendants with death and the countless evils which since the fall of Adam and Eve attend every human life from the cradle to the grave. Every descendant of Adam and Eve is born in sin, is under the wrath of God, and is not, as Rousseau and his disciples maintain, "perfect as he comes from the hand of the Creator." Moved by His grace through the sacrifice of His own Son, Jesus Christ, God pardoned the transgressions of the entire human family, and He grants that pardon to everyone who believes and is baptized and thus by faith accepts the merits of Jesus Christ. Such a person is a new creature. He is eager to live close with God and with the Savior. He leads a life of prayer and reads and meditates on God's revealed Word. He frequently attends and liberally supports a church in which the truths of divine revelation are taught in their purity, he often partakes of Holy Communion, and he helps to spread the Gospel of Jesus Christ throughout the world. The assurance that God is his loving Father buoys him up even in the darkest moments of life, for it holds out to him the hope of eternal life in the presence of his Savior and a glorious resurrection of his mortal body. Such a child of God strives also to live in God-pleasing relationship with his fellow men, regardless of their race, color, and social status. Love is the basic principle in these relationships. Love, not friendship, as Aristotle held; not duty for duty's sake, as Kant reasoned; not utilitarian considerations, as Mill urged; but love, love which at least faintly approximates in purity and selflessness the love which Jesus manifested in His life and by His death.

The Christian educator makes these divine truths and their applications to the lives of men the terminus to which he daily directs the thought and activities of his pupils; they constitute the basis of his instruction in religion; they are the incentive which cause him to go about his tasks ungrudgingly even though his philosophy of education does not achieve the acclaim of other educational leaders, even though he does not realize his aims in the lives of all his pupils, and even though he often meets with ignorance and disapproval of his views on the part of parents whose children he educates; they enable him to see in every child a sinner whom he must on occasion admonish, warn, or punish, but also a saint whom it is his privilege to encourage and to comfort; they are, finally, the vantage point from which he evaluates all knowledge made available by scientific investigation and by reason.

And since the secular activity of a Christian does not constitute a life apart from his Christianity, this philosophy not only allows for, but imposes on, the Christian educator the duty and responsibility of preparing his pupils adequately for the common requirements of life on earth, in order that they may accomplish their divinely intended purposes also in secular affairs and promote the best interests of their community and of human society in general. The Christian educator therefore aims to safeguard and improve the physical health of his pupils, to sharpen their intellect, to stimulate their emotional life, to direct their will, to discover and to develop native skills and interests, and to enrich their minds and memories with knowledge indispensable for successful living in this world and with a deep appreciation of the culture which past ages have bequeathed to the present generation. As he prepares the child to assume duties and responsibilities in this life, his major concern is always that the child will incorporate the teacher's philosophy of education into his philosophy of life and thus go through life with eyes focused on heaven.

A Christian educator finds, whether incidentally or upon investigation, that his philosophy of education works, that it produces the blessed results which he aimed to achieve on the basis of that philosophy. He finds that his pupils, by and large, grow into strong Christian men and women, whose lives reflect the love which God and their Savior showed them, who are a tribute to their community, who are able to overcome the fears arising from an accusing conscience, and who look forward to the glories of heaven in times of peace, economic security, and glowing health as well as in times of war, economic instability, dire want, and in the hour of death.

## II. DISTINCTIVE OBJECTIVES OF THE LUTHERAN ELEMENTARY SCHOOL

1. Diligent teaching of God's Word in obedience to divine command. Deut. 6: 6, 7.

2. Provision for both the temporal and eternal welfare of the child by means of an integrated Christian education in a single environment, which is substituted for the combination of the public school and part-time agencies of religious instruction.

3. Thorough indoctrination of the pupil in the fundamentals of Christianity.

4. Protection of the pupil against the dangers of a purely secular schooling.

5. Daily Christian pupil-fellowship as one of the most powerful factors in building character and training in Christian living.

6. Support of parenthood and home life for the purpose of strengthening the very base of human society.

7. Stabilization and strengthening of the congregation and the Church generally through the training of a well-grounded, discerning laity and youth.

8. The maintenance of a single-minded, faithful ministry and teaching profession within the Church.

9. Christian citizenship grounded in obedience to God and His Word.

---

## III. RELIGION

### 1. Religion in General

Christian religious convictions must permeate all life relationships and all fields of knowledge. They give a particularly Christian viewpoint to educational thought and theory, and affect all subject matter in purpose or content. The Christian religion, correlated and applied to all situations, purifies the motives for all school activity and gives a complexion to learning which lifts it out of the realm of the purely secular and makes for a distinctively Christian education.

The various subjects under the heading of *Religion* are the heart of the Lutheran school curriculum. *Bible History, Catechism, Memorizing,* and *Bible Reading* are primary subjects, which deal directly and systematically with the inculcation of Biblical truth. *Church History* (including church customs and practices, mission study, and the like) and *Church Music* occupy a secondary, supplementary position. Though not a school subject, the *Devotions* provide opportunities for worship and constitute an important part of the religious program in a Christian school.

The means of religious instruction is the Word of God, the Bible. Such books as the Bible History texts, the Catechism, the Hymnal, and others contain the Word of God either directly quoted from Scripture, or their content throughout is based on the teachings of Scripture.

The purpose of all religious instruction is to bring the child into the right relationship with God. The objectives may be stated correctly in various ways, but fundamentally they contain the elements listed below.

### General Objectives in the Teaching of Religion

I. Full realization of mankind's sinfulness and the fearful consequences of sin.

    A. The total depravity of mankind through the fall of man.

    B. The absolute inability of natural man to fulfill the Law.

    C. The certain damnation of those who do not believe.

    D. The imperfect fulfillment of the Law even on the part of the regenerated.

    E. Full realization of one's own utter unworthiness, hopelessness, and helplessness.

II. Implicit faith in the grace and mercy of God.

    A. His goodness and mercy as revealed in the creation and preservation of the world.

    B. His grace and mercy manifested in the work of redemption through Christ Jesus.

        1. Realization of the all-sufficiency of the work of Christ.

            a. In fulfilling the Law for sinful mankind.

            b. In making atonement for the sins of all mankind.

        2. Faith in Christ as one's personal Savior.

    C. His grace and mercy bestowed through the sanctifying work of the Holy Spirit.

        1. Saving faith in Christ in the hearts of the believers.

        2. A sanctified Christian life on the part of the believers.

        3. Eternal salvation.

III. The earnest desire and spiritual strength required for a sanctified Christian life.

    A. Grateful and diligent use of the Word and Sacraments as means of grace for the sustaining and nurturing of spiritual life.

B. Daily communion with God in prayer.

C. In general, consecrated Christian life which seeks the glory of God and the welfare of one's fellow man in thought, word, and deed.

D. Zeal for the promotion and extension of the kingdom of God in the home, in the local congregation, in the community, and in the world at large.

E. The willingness and strength required to bear the cross of Christ.

    1. Patience in tribulation: sickness, bereavement, shame, grief, loss of property, and the like.

    2. Strength to confess Christ in the face of ridicule and persecution.

F. Strength and courage when the devil, the world, and one's flesh tempt to evil.

G. Joyful anticipation of the bliss of heaven and a constant readiness to depart and to be with Christ.

## 2. School Devotions

### Purpose of the Devotions

The school devotions do not constitute a separate school subject, but they are a definite part of the course in religion. They provide an opportunity for worship and communion with God and are, therefore, not a teaching exercise, but an expression in practical application of many truths learned in the study of religion. They help to develop in the pupil the habit of worship and prayer.

### Nature of the Devotions

The purpose of the devotions determines their nature. All the elements of worship will occur, depending upon the time, the particular need, or the spirit of the lesson to which the devotions may be adapted. The devotions will take the teacher and pupils before God in penitent confession of their sins, in praise and adoration of God, or in joyful thanksgiving for His blessings. At other times the devotions will center about a petition for temporal or spiritual blessings, or they may be a meditation upon the beauty and comfort of Scripture. They are always an act of worship performed in reverence, awe, and humility.

### Variety to Avoid Mechanical Performance

School devotions demand variation to avoid the danger of reducing them to mere mechanical exercise. The devotions may be centered about the central thought or the specific aim of the religion lesson of the day; the church year may be taken into account; civic holidays may be considered; or they may concern a morning worship. Generally speaking, a hymn and a brief Bible reading are part of the morning devotions. The teacher will preferably read the Scripture lesson, though occasional pupil reading is proper. Psalms may occasionally be read in unison or responsively. The Creed or other parts of the Catechism may be recited. A variety of prayers is available for use in school devotions, but the teacher will also prepare his own. Prayers should be short and to the point.

Some schools conduct a weekly liturgical service for all children attending school, usually in church.

### Conditions Necessary for Proper Devotions

The same care that is required in all teaching must mark the preparation of the devotions. Haphazardness destroys the spirit of reverence and defeats the purpose of the devotions. There must be no haste; worship is deliberate and unhurried. The sincere and wholehearted entry of the teacher into the spirit of the occasion will almost invariably assure the same attitude on the part of the pupils. The material must be on the level of the group; therefore no set of prepared devotions will serve all teachers and all classes alike. The devotions must be thought of as prepared to meet the needs of the individual class. Ordinarily they should not exceed ten minutes in length.

Reverence is not dependent upon any particular position. Pupils may stand, bow their heads, and fold their hands, or they may pray while seated. The kneeling position is probably not practical in the schoolroom, but the children should be encouraged to kneel at their bedside while saying their evening prayers at home and be taught that the kneeling position indicates penitence and humility.

### Worship Opportunities

The devotions at the opening of school are the most important. They indicate that all the Christian's work is begun in the name of God, and they may be thought of as providing a theme for the day. Other opportunities for brief prayers offer themselves before and after the noon recess. Table prayers are spoken under the supervision of the teacher before and after the children eat their lunch at school. At the close of school the class is dismissed with a hymn or prayer. This may be of a general nature; it may be a prayer for safety on the homeward way or through the night; some special school problem may be presented to God, or thanksgiving for a special blessing may be brought. In addition there will be special occasions when the class will seek comfort, strength, and spiritual growth in hymns and prayers. Memorized hymns, Scripture passages, and portions of the Catechism provide a rich store of materials for this purpose.

## SAMPLES OF MORNING DEVOTIONS

### A. The Pharisee and the Publican (Topic of Religion Lesson)
#### (*Adv. B. H., N. T.*, No. 34)

1. Hymn: *Lutheran Hymnal*, No. 324: 1—5.
2. Scripture Reading: John 1: 8, 9 or Psalm 30.
3. Prayer: General Confession.

### B. First Day of School in Calendar Year

1. Hymn: *Lutheran Hymnal*, No. 118.
2. Scripture Reading: Psalm 90.
3. Prayer: Dear Father in heaven, Thou hast been good to us in permitting us to begin another new year. We pray Thee, be with us every day of the year. Help us always to think and say what is right. Help us to remember that time passes swiftly and that the end of the world is near. Make our faith stronger. Bring more and more people to repentance and faith.

Give us also food and clothing and whatever else we need. O Lord, make an end of the war, and help everyone to live in peace and safety. Thou knowest what things are best for us. Give them to us for Jesus' sake. Amen.

### C. Last Day of School before Christmas
#### (Also suitable for primary grades)

1. Hymn: *Lutheran Hymnal*, No. 85: 1-3.
2. Scripture Reading: Luke 2: 1-20 (Ordinarily the Scripture reading for the primary grades is shorter). •
3. Hymn: *Lutheran Hymnal*, No. 85: 13.
   For the devotions at the close of the last school day before Christmas; Hymn No. 97.

### D. Peter's Confession. Christ's Transfiguration (Topic of Lesson)
#### (*Adv. B. H., N. T.*, No. 26)

1. Hymn: *Lutheran Hymnal*, No. 346.
2. Scripture Reading: Luke 12: 1-9.
3. Confession of Faith: Apostles' Creed.

### E. Fourth Petition (Topic of Lesson)

1. Hymn: *Lutheran Hymnal*, No. 458: 1, 5.
2. Scripture Reading: Matthew 6: 24-34.
3. Confession of Faith: First Article with explanation.

**The Bible.** **Selected References**

Glawe, H., "The Devotional Exercise in School." *Lutheran School Journal,* June, 1938, pp. 451—454.

Kramer, Wm. A., *Devotions for Lutheran Schools.* Concordia, 1934.

*Lutheran Hymnal.* Concordia, 1941.

Luther's Small Catechism. Concordia.

Rupprecht, F., *Bible History References,* Volumes I and II. Concordia, 1934.

Local or District Course of Study.

# 3. Catechism

## A. OBJECTIVES

It is difficult to formulate a set of distinctive aims for each of the religious subjects because of overlapping. This is particularly true of Catechism, which is the comprehensive study of Christian doctrine. The following statement by A. C. Stellhorn [1] might be classed as a general statement of aims in religion as well as of Catechism instruction.

**General Objectives**

To speak in the most general terms, the instructor should try to achieve in his pupils a saving, active, growing, and steadfast faith in the Triune God, through an orderly study, knowledge, understanding, and application of the Christian doctrine, to the end that the Christian may be brought to, and kept in, the right relationship with his God, have forgiveness of his sins, lead a holy life, and be eternally saved.

More specifically stated, we should have the following aims:

1. Knowledge of God as He has revealed Himself.
    a. His being and attributes.
    b. His works, past, present, and future.
    c. His Word.
    d. His holy will concerning man.
2. Knowledge of self, according to Scripture.
    a. As the foremost visible creature, made in the image of God, and destined for eternal life.
    b. As totally depraved as a result of the Fall, a lost and condemned sinner, altogether unable to change his condition, and wholly dependent upon the mercy of the Lord.
    c. As one of the redeemed — called, enlightened, sanctified, and kept in the true faith, and thus saved by the grace of God in Christ Jesus.
    d. As one who, if he believes and is baptized, will be saved, but if he believes not, will be damned.

---

1) *Manual for Lutheran Saturday Schools,* p. 20.

3. A saving faith in the Triune God.
   a. A growing 'knowledge of, and sorrow over, sin, despair of meriting God's grace through personal righteousness, and a desire for mercy.
   b. Acceptance of the grace of God and reliance thereon alone in life and death. (Regeneration, justification.)
4. Sanctification of life.[2)]
   a. An ever-increasing spiritual enlightenment of the mind (growth in understanding and faith and of power to fight victoriously against the spiritual enemies).
   b. An ever-increased cleansing and renewal of the heart (daily repentance and abounding more and more in holiness).
   c. An ever-increasing eagerness to be fruitful in good works.
5. A Christian death.
   a. A realization and daily consciousness of the fact that death or the Judgment may come upon us at any moment.
   b. A true estimate of the vanity, instability, and transience of the things of this world and an avoidance of all that draws the heart away from our eternal home.
   c. A constant readiness, also in youth and while enjoying good health, to depart this life at the will and call of the Lord.
   d. Peace and joy in the hour of death.

## B. CATECHISM INSTRUCTION IN THE LUTHERAN SCHOOL
Scope.

Fundamentally, the content of Bible History and Catechism is the same, inasmuch as the Bible supplies the basis for both subjects. The difference lies in the approach and emphasis. In Bible History historical fact and the story element predominate, and systematic doctrine is taught by way of the Bible story and its application; in the Catechism instruction the doctrine is presented in a logical, systematic arrangement, but with the Bible and Bible History still the source.

The instruction in the Catechism does not aim at the development of a comprehensive system of dogmatics. The content of the instruction is found within the limits of the Small Catechism, which Luther wisely restricted to the essentials of Christian faith and life. The clear, simple, positive, unpolemic presentation of Luther's Small Catechism is based on sound pedagogical prin-

---

2) After a definition of sanctification by Dr. C. F. W. Walther.

ciples. It meets the needs of the youth of the Church and the common people, who "require brief compact sentences in which the most important elements of what they may and should believe are summarized and which may serve at any time as a medium of orientation." [3]

## The Instruction

The doctrines in the Catechism are taken from Scripture and are God's Word. The instruction must emphasize the authority of Scripture at all times and train for its frequent and intelligent use. "The Word of God is quick and powerful." Heb. 4:12. The instruction in the Catechism ceases to be abstract and becomes alive and vital in the measure in which the "quick and powerful" Word is applied properly "for doctrine, for reproof, for correction, for instruction in righteousness." 2 Tim. 3:16, 17.

This implies that the Word must be used to influence the emotions and will of the pupils for right behavior in all situations of life. This is the area of Christian training, the most difficult of the teacher's tasks. To achieve Christian training, the teachings of Scripture must be made concrete to the child first of all. Illustrations from the Bible and from life will help to clarify abstract definitions and open the way for intelligent Christian practice. Projects in which Christian life and service find expression increase the understanding of Biblical teachings and help in achieving the transfer of Christian precept into practice. [4] To fail in Christian training means to reduce Catechism to a subject of mere content and knowledge of doctrine and thus to defeat its prime purpose.

## The Teacher of the Catechism

It is certainly true that the power of the Word resides in the Word itself and that faith is kindled and sustained by the working of the Holy Spirit, and not by any earthly person or power. Yet it is equally true that proper teaching and application of the Word are essential, and that the teacher's neglect or inefficiency may serve as an obstruction to the Holy Spirit. The effectiveness of John the Baptist, Paul, and Peter was no doubt partly due to their manner of teaching as well as to the content of their message. This points to the importance of the teacher's position.

---

3) M. Reu, *Catechetics*, pp. 310, 311.

4) For a fuller discussion of the problem of securing transfer in religious instruction see J. M. Runge, "Integrating Religious Truths with the Experiences of Life," *Lutheran School Journal*, Vol. LXXV, No. 1 (September, 1939), pp. 18—21; and Alfred Schmieding, "Evaluation of Christian Life and Service Projects," *Lutheran School Journal*, LXXVII, No. 7 (March, 1942), pp. 300—302.

The teacher must have a comprehensive Biblical background to be able to make the most of his instruction opportunities. He needs to be a humble Christian, who has experienced in his own heart and soul the depth of God's grace and the merciful guiding hand of God. His personal faith and devotion must be evident at all times. Extensive knowledge of Scripture, efficient method, pleasing personality, will fail if there is the slightest reason to suspect that the teacher is not sincere about his message. A deep love for God and His Word, for his work, and for the redeemed souls under his care must be the foremost qualification of the Christian teacher.

## C. METHOD IN CATECHISM [5]

### The Catechetical Method [6]

Skillfully handled, this method is effective for all ages of children. It consists in the main of a progressive, interesting, and sympathetic exchange of ideas in questions and answers between teacher and pupils according to a carefully prepared plan and in pursuit of a definite aim. Properly used, it stimulates thought and judgment and provides for a high type of mental activity.

The plan should include the following features:

1. A brief survey of the previous lesson or lessons in a few well-directed questions.
2. The approach to the new lesson (introduction):
    a. A statement of its need, value, importance.
    b. A statement of topic and aim of the new lesson.
    c. Briefly, any plan of the teacher which will immediately and reverently direct the pupil's thinking into the lesson.
3. The lesson proper:
    a. Taught in a conscious pursuit of the aim.
    b. Drawn from, and impressed by, the Word of God (Bible passages, Bible stories).
    c. Taught for the purpose of direct application.
    d. Illustrated and made clear by examples from Scripture and (sparingly) from life.
4. A brief summary and emphasis in accordance with the previously stated aim.

---

5) For a detailed discussion of method in religious instruction see P. E. Kretzmann, *The Teaching of Religion*, pp. 114—137; and M. Reu, *Catechetics*, pp. 435—612. See also *Method in Bible History*, pp. 24—29.

6) A. C. Stellhorn, *op. cit.*, pp. 22, 23.

**Steps in the Preparation of the Lesson**

In preparing the individual lesson, four steps are necessary: 1. Study of the materials to be taught: 2. Consideration of the child's needs; 3. Formulation of the aim; 4. Planning of the lesson. The aim "should be conceived in terms of spiritual advancement and not merely as a knowledge aim." [7] The lesson is outlined with the purpose in mind of achieving the aim. This requires that the points which must be emphasized to bring out the real importance and consequence of the lesson are selected and arranged in orderly sequence, together with the Bible passages, Bible stories, hymn stanzas, or other materials that are to be used. With these well in mind, there is little danger that essentials will be omitted or that extraneous nonessentials will obscure the real purpose of the lesson.

An outline illustrative of these suggestions is added herewith:

### Christ Will Come to Judge the World

(Schwan, Question 166)

a. **Aim:** To realize the necessity of constant readiness for Christ's appearance.

b. **Devotion:** Hymn 552:1-5. Bible Reading: The Judgment, Matt. 25:31-46. Morning prayer, special prayer, confession of the Creed, or confession of the Second Article with explanation.

c. **Review of Previous Lesson:** Christ Ascended on High and Sitteth at the Right Hand of God. (Schwan, Ques. 164, 165.) The leading thoughts will be recalled on the basis of a few questions.

d. **Introduction to the New Lesson:** Example: This same Christ who has ascended on high to prepare a place for us and who rules all things, especially His Church, will appear visibly on this earth again. He will come at the Last Day in all His glory to judge the quick and the dead. As we study the circumstances surrounding Christ's coming, let us heed particularly His admonition to constant readiness for His appearance.

e. **The Lesson in Outline:**

1. *We confess* that Christ at the Last Day will come to judge the quick and the dead. When He had ascended to heaven, the two angels who appeared to the disciples foretold His return. Acts 1:11. Also Acts 17:31; Acts 10:42.

2. The *manner* of His coming indicates the *importance* of the event.
    a. He will appear *visibly* in the heavens "in like manner as ye have seen Him go." Acts 1:11.
    b. He will come in the *full glory* of the Son of God. Matt. 25:31.
    c. He will come *unawares*. He is the Son of God, who has redeemed us and given us His Word that we may be prepared, and He owes us no specific announcement of His coming. 2 Pet. 3:10.

---

7) *Ibid.*, p. 23.

3. In view of Christ's coming to Judgment *everything else is unimportant.*

    a. His coming marks the *end of the universe* of time and all earthly life, of riches and honor. 2 Pet. 3:10.

    b. *All people,* the quick and the dead, *will be judged* according to the standards of God's Word. The Judgment will decide whether the eternal abode of a person will be heaven or hell. 2 Cor. 2:10; John 12:48; The Final Judgment, Matt. 25:31-46.

4. The imminence of the Judgment (either Judgment Day or death) calls for *constant readiness and watchfulness* on our part (use of God's Word, repentance, faith, prayer). Mark 13:32-37; Rev. 2:10; Rev. 3:11.

f. **Summary:** The lesson is summed up on the basis of a few leading questions and answers which center around the points emphasized.

g. **Closing Hymn (or Prayer):** Hymn 552:7.

h. **Assignment:**

1. The assignment may call for pupil presentation of the Biblical teaching regarding the Judgment on the basis of an outline. Proof for every statement made by the pupil is important.

2. The pupils may be asked to write a paper which contains the essential teachings of Scripture in regard to the Judgment, either in the form of an essay, an outline, or questions and answers.

3. Preparation for an oral review discussion of the subject may be assigned.

In either of the above plans a proper understanding of the aim is required.

## D. COURSE SUGGESTIONS

### Primary Grades (1—3)

In the primary grades the Catechism truths are taught largely in connection with the Bible stories and memory material. If Catechism is taught as a separate subject, the lessons should be brief, perhaps no longer than 20 minutes. Doctrinal teaching is made clear and simple, and Bible truths are liberally illustrated with Bible stories. The teachings of the Catechism are applied to the life problems of the primary age group.

In four-room schools, or under any other division of grades in which the third grade is in the same room with older pupils, regular Catechism instruction begins in the third grade.

### Intermediate Grades (4—6)

In the intermediate grades separate Catechism lessons are a part of the course in religion. The instruction follows closely the text of Luther's Small Catechism and is illuminated with Bible texts, illustrations from Bible History, and illustrations from life. The functional aim is prominent in the instruction.

Reference materials are valuable for the teacher but, as a rule, are too difficult for children of this age.[8]

Two out of every five religion periods per week (or two fifths of all religion periods during the year) are generally devoted to Catechism instruction where the intermediate grades are in one room. In case of a division of grades, three Catechism periods as against two Bible History lessons may be begun in the sixth grade.

## Upper Grades (7—8)

An extended course in Catechism is given in the upper grades. Also here the text of Luther's Small Catechism, the Bible texts, and the Bible stories are the basic materials, but the exposition is used more liberally than in the lower grades. Never, however, must the Catechism instruction develop into a course in dogmatics. Luther's Small Catechism, which has been memorized and reviewed repeatedly, should be part and parcel of the pupils mental and spiritual equipment by this time.

The instruction is designed to deepen Christian conviction, to strengthen faith and Christian life, and to fortify the pupil with the ability to defend his faith against those who seek to destroy his confidence in God. The teaching of positive truth is of foremost importance, but false doctrine must also be pointed out and condemned as error.

Three out of five religion periods are devoted to Catechism instruction, except in confirmation class, where the Catechism forms the basis of the entire course.

## Schedules for Religion in General

One method is to alternate Catechism and Bible History instruction daily, or to schedule three Bible History and two Catechism periods weekly in the lower grades and three Catechism and two Bible History periods in the upper grades. Or Catechism and Bible History may be taught in units. Thus the lessons in Old Testament Bible History belonging to the Primeval Period (Advanced Bible History, Nos. 1—6) might be taught successively at the beginning of the school year and followed by the First Chief Part of the Catechism. This, in turn, might be followed by the Bible stories belonging to the Period of Patriarchs (Nos. 7—23), and so on.

Whether Catechism and Bible History are alternated from day to day or by units, certain divisions for the year will have to

---

8) Geo. Mezger, *Lessons in the Small Catechism*, is suggestive of material on the intermediate grade level.

be observed. If three out of five lessons are devoted to Catechism instruction in the upper grades, approximately 108 lessons a year are available for the Catechism. The Synodical Catechism may be divided conveniently into approximately this number of lessons including tests and reviews, as shown under Catechism schedules. This makes possible the teaching of the entire Catechism in one year if that is thought desirable. In a one-year course of confirmation instruction this must be done.

Where the number of periods is evenly divided between Catechism and Bible History, some of the Chief Parts are taught intensively one year, and the others are surveyed according to the so-called survey-penetration plan.

In the lower grades, where the ratio of Bible History to Catechism is three to two, or even two to one, only 72 or 60 periods are available for Catechism, and the latter will have to be divided on a survey-penetration basis. The survey of Chief Parts may well be undertaken on the basis of the text of Luther's Small Catechism rather than the Exposition.

In Bible History a yearly alternation between the Old and the New Testament is recommended. When the Old Testament is taught, the New is briefly surveyed at the end of the school year; when the New is taught, the Old Testament is briefly reviewed at the beginning of the year to provide a proper setting for the New. To cover the material, a few lessons have to be combined.

The schedules below indicate how these plans may be carried out. They are not intended as a hard and fast rule.

### Sample Schedule for Grades III and IV

(Ratio: B. H. 2; Catechism 1)

*I Year Bible History* (120 lessons). *Elementary Bible History*

Old Testament penetration — 100 lessons. (Some stories receive two-day treatment. Reviews are also included.)
New Testament survey — 20 lessons

*II Year Bible History* (120 lessons)

Old Testament survey — 20 lessons
New Testament penetration — 100 lessons

*I Year Catechism* (60 lessons). Simple presentation of Small Catechism

| | *II Year Catechism* (60 lessons) |
|---|---|
| I Chief Part — 25 lessons | I Chief Part — 5 lessons |
| II Chief Part — 10 lessons | II Chief Part — 32 lessons |
| III Chief Part — 14 lessons | III Chief Part — 4 lessons |
| IV Chief Part — 3 lessons | IV Chief Part — 10 lessons |
| V Chief Part — 3 lessons | V Chief Part — 6 lessons |
| VI Chief Part — 5 lessons | VI Chief Part — 3 lessons |

## Sample Schedule for Upper Grades

### (Semester Plan)

*I Year Bible History* (90 lessons). *Advanced Bible History*

 Old Testament penetration — 78 lessons
 New Testament survey — 12 lessons

*II Year Bible History* (90 lessons)

 Old Testament survey — 10 lessons
 New Testament penetration — 80 lessons

| *I Year Catechism* (90 lessons) | *II Year Catechism* (90 lessons) |
|---|---|
| I Chief Part — 35 lessons | I Chief Part — 15 lessons |
| II Chief Part — 19 lessons | II Chief Part — 45 lessons |
| III Chief Part — 17 lessons | III Chief Part — 7 lessons |
| IV Chief Part — 5 lessons | IV Chief Part — 10 lessons |
| V Chief Part — 4 lessons | V Chief Part — 8 lessons |
| VI Chief Part — 10 lessons | VI Chief Part — 5 lessons |

### Catechism Schedules [9]

#### Schedule A (One-year course. 108 lessons)

| | |
|---|---|
| I Chief Part — 33 lessons | IV Chief Part — 7 lessons |
| II Chief Part — 40 lessons | V Chief Part — 6 lessons |
| III Chief Part — 13 lessons | VI Chief Part — 9 lessons |

## Synodical Catechism Divided into Lessons

This division of the Catechism for a one-year course is based on the New Synodical Catechism.[10] The revision of the book may necessitate minor changes in the schedule.

1. *Luther's Small Catechism.* Ques. 1—6.
2. *The Bible, the Inspired Word of God.* Ques. 7—11.
3. *Purpose and Use of the Bible.* Ques. 12, 13.
4. *Law and Gospel.* Ques. 14—17.
5. *The Ten Commandments in General.* Ques. 18—23.

 *The First Commandment*

6. (The Existence of God.) Ques. 24.
7. (Attributes of God.) Ques. 25.
8. (The Trinity.) Ques. 26, 27.
9. (What God Forbids.) Ques. 28, 29.
10. (What God Commands.) Ques. 30—33.

 *The Second Commandment*

11. (Misuse of God's Name in General.) Ques. 34—37.
12. (Cursing and Swearing.) Ques. 38—41.
13. (Witchcraft, Lying and Deceiving.) Ques. 42, 43.
14. (Proper Use of God's Name.) Ques. 44.

---

9) Minnesota Course of Study in Religion. Used by permission.

10) Proof Print, October 1, 1940.

*The Third Commandment*

15.      (Sabbath and Sunday.)  Ques. 45—48.
16.      (What God Commands and Forbids.)  Ques. 49—52.
17. *Review*. Lessons 1—16.

*The Fourth Commandment*

18.      (Summary of Second Table and What God Forbids in Fourth
              Commandment.)  Ques. 53—57.
19.      (What God Commands.)  Ques. 58, 59.

*The Fifth Commandment*

20.      (What God Forbids.)  Ques. 60.
21.      (What God Commands.)  Ques. 61.

*The Sixth Commandment*

22.      (What God Forbids.)  Ques. 62, 63.
23.      (What God Commands.)  Ques. 64—66.

*The Seventh Commandment*

24.      (What God Forbids.)  Ques. 67.
25.      (What God Commands.)  Ques. 68.

*The Eighth Commandment*

26.      (What God Forbids.)  Ques. 69.
27.      (What God Commands.)  Ques. 70.

*The Ninth and Tenth Commandments*

28.      (What God Forbids.)  Ques. 71, 72; 75, 76.
29.      (What God Commands.)  Ques. 73, 74; 77, 78.
30. *The Close of the Commandments*. Ques. 79—86.
31. *Purpose and Fulfillment of the Law*. Ques. 87—90.
32. *Sin*. Ques. 91—99.
33. *Review*. Lessons 18—32.

*The First Article*

34.      (The Creed — Faith.)  Ques. 100—104.
35.      (God the Father Almighty.)  Ques. 105—107.
36.      (The Good Angels.)  Ques. 108—110.
37.      (The Evil Angels.)  Ques. 111.
38.      (Man.)  Ques. 112—115.
39.      (Divine Preservation.)  Ques. 116, 117.
40.      (God's Goodness and Mercy.)  Ques. 118—120.
41. *Review*. Lessons 34—40.

*The Second Article*

42.      (The Names of Jesus Christ.)  Ques. 121—124.
43.      (The Divine Nature of Christ.)  Ques. 125, 126.
44.      (The Human Nature of Christ.)  Ques. 127, 128.
45.      (The Personal Union.)  Ques. 129.
46.      (The Necessity of the Personal Union.)  Ques. 130—132.
47.      (Christ Our Prophet.)  Ques. 133A.

### The Sacrament of Holy Baptism

87.      (Sacrament in General.) Ques. 243, 244.
88.      (What Baptism Is.) Ques. 245—249.
89.      (Infant Baptism.) Ques. 250—253.
90.      (The Benefit of Baptism.) Ques. 254—257.
91.      (The Power of Baptism.) Ques. 258, 259.
92.      (What Baptism Signifies.) Ques. 260—267.
93. *Review.* Lessons 87—92.

### The Office of the Keys

94.      (What the Office of the Keys Comprises.) Ques. 268, 269.
95.      (The Power of the Office of the Keys.) Ques. 270—275.
96.      (Public Administration of the Office of the Keys.) Ques. 276—284.

### The Confession

97.      (Confession and Absolution I). Ques. 285—289.
98.      (Confession and Absolution II). Ques. 290—295.
99. *Review.* Lessons 94—98.

### The Sacrament of the Altar

100.      (The Character of the Lord's Supper I.) Ques. 296, 297.
101.      (The Character of the Lord's Supper II.) Ques. 298—301.
102.      (The Character of the Lord's Supper III.) Ques. 302—312.
103.      (The Benefits of the Lord's Supper.) (Ques. 313—315.
104.      (The Power of the Lord's Supper.) Ques. 316—318.
105.      (The Salutary Use of the Lord's Supper.) Ques. 319—325.
106.      (Who May or May Not Attend the Lord's Supper.) Ques. 326.
107.      (Confirmation.) Ques. 327—331.
108. *Review.* Lessons 100—108.

**Schedule B (Two-year course. 72 lessons per year) 11)**

*First Year*

I Chief Part — 22 lessons
II Chief Part — 25 lessons
III Chief Part — 13 lessons
IV Chief Part — 7 lessons
V Chief Part — 5 lessons

*Second Year*

I Chief Part — 28 lessons
II Chief Part — 36 lessons
VI Chief Part — 8 lessons

**Schedule C (Two-year course. 72 lessons per year) 12)**

*First Year — Intensive Study*

I Chief Part — 25 lessons
First Article — 13 lessons
Second Article — 14 lessons
Third Article — 6 lessons

*Second Year — Intensive Study*

Third Article — 14 lessons
III Chief Part — 13 lessons
IV Chief Part — 7 lessons
V Chief Part — 5 lessons
VI Chief Part — 8 lessons

11) Minnesota Course.
12) Minnesota Course.

*First Year — Extensive Study*          *Second Year — Extensive Study*
   III Chief Part — 4 lessons             I Chief Part — 12 lessons
   IV Chief Part — 2 lessons             First Article — 5 lessons
   V Chief Part — 2 lessons             Second Article — 8 lessons
   VI Chief Part — 3 lessons

Note: The combination of lessons is left to the planning of the individual teacher.

## E. CORRELATION POSSIBILITIES

The intimate relation that must exist between the instruction in religion and all other teaching is so fundamental to the success of the Christian school and so obvious throughout this entire Course of Study that little need be said on the subject at this point. Every lesson which indicates a spiritual or temporal blessing, a duty, or a moral teaching of any kind suggests reference to Scripture or the Catechism.

However, one phase is easily overlooked and deserves special mention, namely, the frequent opportunity provided by the Catechism for correlation between its own different parts. Examples: First Article and Fourth Petition; Second Commandment and First Petition.

## F. EVALUATING OUTCOMES

Because of the nature of the subject of Catechism, as of all subjects in the field of religion, it is difficult to evaluate achievements accurately. Knowledge of doctrine and memory materials is subject to measurement by means of oral and written tests, but the elements of spiritual advancement, faith and Christian life, are intangibles which cannot always be measured accurately.

Evaluation of Christian behavior is made by observation. The behavior of the school as a whole, the attitude of the individual toward sin, his attitude when he has committed a wrong, his willingness to confess his Savior by word and deed, his trust in God in the time of trouble and need, his prayer-life, his desire in general to lead a Christian life, his love toward the Word of God, all these to a certain degree are measurable elements for the observant teacher, especially for the teacher who meets his pupils outside of the classroom as a counselor and friend.

The teacher who takes time to look for and record achievements along these lines eventually develops a useful set of standards and finds himself well repaid, both because of the satisfaction that results and of the wholesome effect upon the work of the school.

### Selected References

Beck, Walter H., "Visual Materials, Handwork, and Activities in Religious Education." *Lutheran School Journal*, March, 1942, p. 295.

*Course of Study in Religion.* Minnesota District, 1939.

Fehner, H. B., *Outlines for Catecheses and the Technique of Questioning.* Concordia, 1926.

Graebner, A. L., et al., *Proof Texts of the Catechism with a Practical Commentary.* Concordia, 1927.

Jesse, F. W. C., and Appelt, T. C., *Catechetical Preparations*, Parts I, II, III.

Koehler, E. W. A., *A Summary of Christian Doctrine.* River Forest, Ill.: Koehler Publishing Co., 1939.

Kraeft, W. O., *Religion for the Primary Grades in Units of Learning.* Concordia, 1926.

Kretzmann, P. E., *The Teaching of Religion.* Concordia, 1925.

Lee, Murray J., *A Guide to Measurement.* D. Appleton Century, 1936.

Lindemann, F., *Scholia.* Concordia, 1903.

Luther, Martin, Small Catechism. Also Large Catechism.

Luther's *Katechetische Schriften*, Vol. X. Concordia.

Meibohm, D., *Catechizations.* Concordia.

Reavis, Wm. C., *Evaluating the Work of the School.* University of Chicago Press, 1940.

Reu, M., *Catechetics.* Wartburg, 1931.

Schmieding, Alfred, "Courses in Religion for the Lutheran Elementary School." *Lutheran School Journal*, December, 1931, pp. 145—153.

Schmieding, Alfred, *Teaching the Bible Story*, Chapters III and IV. Concordia, 1935.

Schwan, H. C., *A Short Exposition of Dr. Martin Luther's Small Catechism.* Concordia.

Stellhorn, A. C., *Manual for Lutheran Saturday Schools.* Concordia, 1935.

Synodical Catechism, 1942.

## 4. Bible History

### A. GENERAL OBJECTIVES

The general objectives of religious instruction apply also to Bible History, though this subject has its own peculiar aims, as is apparent in the statement of objectives below:

1. In general, an elementary knowledge of Biblical history with its practical spiritual benefits.

2. A saving knowledge of the true God as He has revealed Himself — His being, His works, His will, and particularly His plan of salvation through Jesus Christ.

3. A knowledge of man and self as portrayed in Bible history and the ability and habit of applying to himself and others what God has thus revealed.

4. A truly penitent and believing heart, a sanctified, spiritual life, and preparation for a Christian death. (Salvation now and forever.)

5. An understanding of the doctrinal meaning of individual Bible stories and the ability to use these stories in fixing the teachings of the Catechism in the mind of the child.

6. An enduring interest in Bible history and the desire and habit to read, study, and contemplate the Bible itself.

## B. DISCUSSION OF THE OBJECTIVES

### A Historical Subject

Bible history is the connected chronological account of sacred history as recorded in the Bible. The textbooks used in the Lutheran schools contain selections that preserve the continuity of Biblical history from the Creation to the establishment of the New Testament Christian Church, covering a period of about 4,000 years.

### More Than History

A knowledge of Biblical history is considered part of a well-rounded general education, but Bible history is not taught merely for the sake of history; rather because Christ and His work of redemption as well as all the works of God and the will of God are more readily understood in their historical setting. "Whatsoever things were written aforetime [including the historical sections of Scripture] were written for our learning." Rom. 15:4. "All Scripture . . . is profitable for doctrine, for reproof, for correction, for instruction in righteousness." 2 Tim. 3:16.

Biblical history, as a whole, centers about God's plan of salvation, the Christian's faith, and his God-pleasing life. In addition, every period of sacred history teaches its own lesson. For example: The life of Abraham illustrates what is meant by a life of faith and shows how God accomplishes His purpose in His elect through a life of joy and tribulation. The history of Israel teaches that "righteousness exalteth a nation: but sin is a reproach to any people." Prov. 14:34.

In the same manner every narrative carries its own doctrinal import and has its individual application according to which the aim of the lesson is determined. Thus, for example, the feeding of the five thousand shows the power and providence of Christ; God's promise of a Savior shows His love for sinful man; the Good Samaritan teaches love and neighborliness; the publican in the story of "The Pharisee and the Publican" illustrates true penitence, etc.

The child learns that many Bible histories have to do with the God-pleasing life of the Christian. This is made clear to him, and he is taught and trained to apply them effectively to life situations. The power of the Word, the obvious Christian humility and sincerity of the teacher, and the effective presentation of the lesson will work together to impress the emotions and the will of the child, so that knowledge will be accompanied by attitudes and acts. However, the instruction is not complete with the mere teaching of the lesson, but constant guidance in Christian living accompanies the daily religious instruction in order to make it function in the life of the child.

It is obviously impossible to give the child practice in the thousands of situations in which Christian judgment must function, neither is it necessary. Religious instruction is generally effective when the child is brought thoroughly to understand the precepts of God's Word; is shown how these precepts apply in typical situations; is taught how to solve individual problems in accordance with God's will and by the strength of the Holy Spirit, who works through the Word; and is given constant training and guidance in Christian conduct.

### Divine Authority of Bible History

The pupil must understand that Bible history is Bible instruction.[1] The fact that Bible history is the Word of God gives authority to the instruction which the nonreligious subjects lack. Full appreciation of the authority and importance of the Word of God on the part of the pupil encourages enduring interest in the Bible and its diligent use. Where faithful reading and study of the Bible results, it is probable that all other objectives of the instruction are likewise achieved.[2]

### C. METHOD IN BIBLE HISTORY [3]

### Method in General

To teach a Bible story effectively, the following fundamental principles must be kept in mind:

    a. Have a definite aim.

    b. Adhere to the story facts and, as much as possible, to Bible language.

    c. Show how the lesson applies in the life of the pupil.

    d. Vary the approach and procedure according to the type of story and the age of the pupils.

---

1) Suggestions for putting the Bible to more extensive use are given by Herbert Jaeger in "A Series of Bible History Lessons." *Lutheran School Journal*, April, 1933, pp. 337—345.

2) See also Course in Bible Reading.

3) For a detailed discussion of method in religious instruction, see M. Reu, *Catechetics*, pp. 435—612. For methods in Bible History, see Alfred Schmieding, *Teaching the Bible Story*.

A consecrated teacher, filled with his subject, and earnestly desiring to lead his class on the way to salvation, is vastly more important than any specific method. Religious leaders of great influence proclaimed truths, not methods. This realization assures proper perspective as the teacher decides upon his method of instruction.

A method by which children are induced to think and talk freely about religious truths, to repeat them, and to study and practice them, is likely to be effective. To achieve such desirable response, the method must provide for self-activity, mental or physical, on the part of the pupils; for the impression of concepts; for expressions on the subject matter under discussion; and for social situations that stimulate expression and practice.

Activities in religious instruction are more mental than physical, except possibly in the case of very young children. Besides being purposeful and pertinent, activities in religious instruction must meet the requirements of reverence. The child shoulders responsibility for any activity engaged in, but he remains under the guidance and direction of the teacher at all times.

Telling the Bible story is essential in the primary grades. It precedes pupil expression and discussion. In the higher grades, also, the telling of Bible stories has its place, though there are other approaches to the lesson. As the understanding of pupils increases, discussion plays an increasingly important part.

**Specific Methods**

A modified form of the socialized recitation provides a practical procedure for instruction in Bible history. C. H. Meier [4] fully outlines this method and its application to religious instruction.

H. H. Gross [5] discusses the possibilities of the project method in religious instruction, concluding that its use is practical only when utilized as a supplementary device.

Suggestions for procedure in the primary grades, especially where a three- or four-day treatment of the Bible story is desired, are found in an article by Herbert Brummer.[6]

---

4) "Socializing Religious Instruction." *Lutheran School Journal*, Sept., 1935, pp. 4—12; Oct., 1935, pp. 56—64; Nov., 1935, pp. 99—108. Stenographic reports of religion classes conducted by means of the Socialized Recitation are reprinted in the *Journal*, Dec., 1933, pp. 165—169; and June, 1934, pp. 455—463.

5) "The Project in Teaching Religion." *Lutheran School Journal*, May, 1935, pp. 385—391.

6) "Procedure in Religion Lessons in the Primary Grades." *Lutheran School Journal*, Mar., 1932, pp. 308—311.

A. C. Stellhorn [7] suggests the following as an effective method of teaching a Bible story:

1. The instructor asks a few well-directed summary questions about the foregoing story and states the introduction, topic (heading), and aim of the new story.

2. Then he tells the story in Bible language, but with brief explanatory remarks where necessary and with natural applications leading to the achievement of his aim anywhere in the story, in the form of a remark or a question. The object is to present the story in as brief and clear a form as possible and to apply it. Wordiness must be avoided.

3. He asks a few summary questions in a quick recall.

4. He retells the story, this time using Bible language only, without explanations or applications. If the story is not too short, he tells it this second time in parts, in natural divisions, perhaps paragraphs.

5. After each paragraph or other division he questions the pupils on the contents, including the explanations and applications made in the first telling.

6. At the end he summarizes the main story facts and the chief applications with pupil participation.

7. He makes sure throughout, in relating the story, in his remarks, applications, and review questions, that he is following the aim he has set for himself.

8. The teacher gives specific directions for reviewing the lesson. This may include the telling of the story on the part of the pupils, outlining, workbook activities, additional Bible reading, or such other activities as appear necessary to fix the aim and the subject matter permanently in the minds of the pupils.

### Steps in the Preparation of the Lesson

See suggestions under Catechism, p. 13.

Below is added an outline illustrating an effective use of materials in the pursuit of an aim in Bible History:

### The Unmerciful Servant

(*Adv. B. H., N. T.,* No. 27)

a. **Aim:** To create in the hearts of the pupils a readiness to forgive those who sin against them.

b. **Devotions:** Hymn 196:6. Scripture Reading: Joseph Forgives His Brethren, Gen. 45:1-8; or Col. 3:12-17. General Confession used as a joint prayer.

---

7) *Manual for Lutheran Saturday Schools,* p. 45.

c. **Review of the Previous Lesson:** This consists of a few well-directed questions to summarize the previous story and to state the lesson to be derived from it in terms of the aim according to which it was taught. If possible, connect the previous story with the new lesson.

d. **Introduction (Approach):** *Sample 1:* One of the most troublesome problems is the right treatment of those who sin against us. Joseph, for example, had to face this problem when his brothers dealt cruelly with him. Some of you have had to deal with the problem.

In the present story, "The Unmerciful Servant," Jesus teaches us how to deal with those who sin against us. It is a matter of life and salvation that we learn the right answer; therefore let us give our undivided attention to what He has to say.

*Sample 2:* Peter once came to Jesus with a question which also troubles us at times: "Lord, how often shall my brother sin against me and I forgive him? Till seven times?"

What would you have answered Peter?

Probably none of us would have thought of the reply which Jesus gave. He answered, "Seventy times seven." (490 times.) What did Jesus mean by setting this high figure? (That we must forgive again and again, no matter how often.)

In order to make His meaning clear and unmistakable, Jesus told the story of "The Unmerciful Servant." Let us learn from Him the importance of forgiving our neighbor.

e. **Presentation (Telling) of the Story.** *Note:* It is understood that the presentation must provide for pupil participation. This ouline indicates merely the points that require emphasis if the aim of the lesson is to be achieved.

1. *Parable:* Point out that this is a parable which speaks of the Christian and God in a picture. A king took account of his servants even as God takes account of everything we do. He observes all our deeds and judges them.

2. *God's boundless mercy:* This must be emphasized. When the servants were brought before the king, there was one who owed 10,000 talents, which is at least $10,000,000. The poor man had nothing with which to pay; therefore he and his family were ordered sold that the king might realize at least something in payment of the debt. However, upon the servant's plea and good promises the king had compassion and forgave him the debt. *Through the mercy of the king a hopelessly indebted slave became a free man, who could face the king without fear.* The two facts that the man was hopelessly indebted and that he was absolutely freed through the mercy of his master must stand out; also that this servant is a picture of every sinner whose sins are forgiven and who therefore stands perfectly righteous before God. *The servant is a picture of us — us Christians;* this must be impressed. *We were lost, but God in His mercy freed us from all our sins. It is by His mercy that eternal life is ours.*

3. *The servant's unfathomable ingratitude:* When this same servant, who had experienced infinite mercy, went out and found a fellow servant who owed him the small sum of an hundred pence ($16.00),

he was unwilling to show the same consideration which he had received. He did not heed his fellow servant's pleas for patience and forgiveness, and refused to believe his promises, though there was much greater possibility of fulfillment than there had been in his own case, and he cast the unfortunate man into prison. Have children consider, "What should he have done?" or "What would we naturally expect of a man who himself had experienced the great mercy of his master?" or "How many of us would expect him to show mercy and cancel the small debt of his fellow servant?"

The example of Joseph (read in the devotion) may be used to illustrate the right spirit. Use also the Fifth Petition in this connection (an example of correlation between Bible History and Catechism): We are worthy of none of the things for which we pray; we daily sin much and indeed deserve nothing but punishment; God forgives us; therefore we must also heartily forgive and readily do good to those who sin against us.

Bring out how difficult it is for us to do God's will in this respect and how very much like the wicked servant we are. Ask the class for a few situations in which various individuals have found it difficult to "make up" or forgive (without mentioning names) and point out that the Word of God in the matter of forgiving applies in just such cases (correlating the teaching with the experiences of the pupils). *Impress the pupils with the fact that the same unfathomable ingratitude to which the wicked servant succumbed can come also over us, for we are all similarly inclined.*

4. *Eternal punishment for those who do not forgive:* When the unmerciful servant's action became known to the king, he immediately called the offender to account. The king did not trifle with sin. He withdrew the promised mercy and cast the wicked servant into prison. So also God does not trifle with sin. If we act like the wicked servant, we shall receive eternal damnation. What effect should this have upon us? Emphasize the statement: *"So likewise shall my heavenly Father do also unto you if ye from your hearts forgive not everyone his brother their trespasses."* Show that this word of Jesus answers Peter's question and our questions in the matter of forgiving those who have offended us. Make it clear that this statement applies in all cases where our neighbor has harmed us, or where we think he has harmed us, and we are unwilling to forgive. It applies in the quarrels of children as it applies in the quarrels of adults. Emphasize that the forgiveness must be real, that is, *from the heart.*

**f. Summary:** There are three high points about which the parable centers, and about these the questions of the summary must be built. These points are:

a. The king's limitless mercy toward the hopelessly indebted servant (God's boundless mercy toward us).

b. The unfathomable ingratitude of the wicked servant (our lack of appreciation of the mercy which God shows in forgiving our sins and the resultant lack of mercy for the neighbor).

c. The sure and unending punishment of the unforgiving servant (eternal damnation for us if we refuse to forgive our fellow men, fellow pupils, etc.).

g. **Conclusion:** After the summary, close with a suitable hymn stanza, sung or prayed, or with a brief prayer in which we thank God for His mercy toward us in forgiving our sins though we daily sin much, and in which we ask Him to create in us a forgiving heart toward others. For example: *Lutheran Hymnal*, No. 458:6.

h. **Assignment:** This may include activities such as the following:

1. Thorough study of the content of the story for the next day.
2. Telling of the story.
3. Working out of Mertz and Siems, *Exercises in Bible History, N.T.*, p. 55, No. 27.
4. Reading of Gen. 45:1-8; Luke 23:33, 34; Acts 7:59, 60.

## D. COURSE SUGGESTIONS

### Lower Grades (1—4)

During the first two years of school the religious instruction consists largely of Bible history and of memory work. Even after the Catechism is introduced, usually in the third grade, Bible history predominates. A text is introduced in the second grade. Pictures are used freely to aid the instruction in the lower grades.

Pending the publication of a simpler textbook for the primary grades, the text used up to the fourth or fifth grade, depending on the division of grades, is the *Elementary Bible History*. The instruction is adapted to the age level of the class, but Bible language is used as much as possible.

In schools consisting of two or more rooms all grades are ordinarily combined in one class in religion. In one-room schools they are separated, grades 1—3 in the primary group and grades 4—8 in the advanced group. After the lesson has been taught in all grades, a ten- or fifteen-minute period is devoted to the primary grades, while the older pupils prepare their assignment. The lesson is reviewed with the younger pupils and applied to their particular needs. If preferred, the first period in the afternoon may be set aside for primary religion.

Suggestions for arrangement of the material appear under schedules for Bible History and for religion in general.

### Upper Grades (5—8)

The textbook in the upper grades is the *Advanced Bible History*, in which the material of the *Elementary Bible History* is enlarged upon. It contains more stories, and they are more complete.

The upper-grade teacher faces the problem of re-teaching Bible stories previously learned and making the instruction profitable. The repetition of stories every two years by a plan of alternation as suggested in the schedules is based on sound pedagogical principles. Though often repeated, Biblical material gains in value and appreciation when properly presented, and becomes the more firmly fixed in the mind. The better it is learned through frequent repetition, the greater will be its influence upon the heart and will of the child. In these repetitions the emphasis is not so much mere story fact as the larger setting of the story and its value as spiritual food for teacher and pupil. The Bible itself is used to provide the larger setting and background for the stories in the *Advanced Bible History.*[8]

Thorough inculcation of the Bible text is important for these reasons:

1. In spite of some uncommon expressions, the Bible as a whole contains clear and simple language.

2. The Bible is the religious handbook of the Christian, and he must be familiar with its language.

3. Quotations and readings from the Bible are heard frequently in sermons and in daily life, and a knowledge of the Bible text facilitates appreciation and understanding.

4. Departure from the Bible texts opens the way for false interpretation and false impressions.

5. A fixed form of phraseology is a valuable aid to the memory.

### Bible History Schedules [9]

**Schedule A.** *Elementary Bible History*

*First Year* (72 lessons), *Old Testament*                      Lessons

   *First Period:* Primeval History (4000—2000 B. C.) ................10

   *Second Period:* The Patriarchs (2000—1600 B. C.) ................15

   *Third Period:* Moses and the Giving of the Law (about 1500 B. C.)  8

   *Fourth Period:* The Occupation of Canaan (about 1460 B. C.) ....  3

   *Fifth Period:* The Time of the Judges (1440—1100 B. C.) ..........  6

   *Sixth Period:* The Undivided Kingdom (1100—975 B. C.) ..........  7

   *Seventh Period:* The Divided Kingdom (975—588 B. C.) ..........  8

   Review of one or more units of New Testament ..................15

                                        —

                                       72

8) See Footnote 1.

9) Minnesota Course of Study in Religion (reprinted by permission).

*Second Year* (72 lessons), *New Testament*

*Note:* A separate lesson should be allowed for the review of each period. The periods may be arranged in any order for a two-year course.

*Example: First Year:* O.T., Periods 2 and 3; N.T., Periods 1 and 2.
*Second Year:* O.T., Periods 3, 4, 5, 6, and 7; N.T., Periods 3, 4, and 5.

**Schedule B.** *Elementary Bible History*

*One-Year Course* (108 lessons)

*Old Testament*

### Suggested Combinations

1. The Call of Abraham and the Promise of Isaac.

2. Isaac Blesses Jacob and Jacob's Ladder.

3. The Second Journey of Joseph's Brethren and Joseph Makes Himself Known.

*New Testament*

## Suggested Combinations

The Birth of Jesus Christ and the Announcement of the Savior's birth.

*Note:* A separate lesson period should be allowed for the review of each larger unit of the Old and the New Testament.

Teachers of the primary grades may wish to follow the above schedule but find it too much to cover in one year. In that case two periods may be spent on each lesson and the work covered in two years, making it a two-year course.

**Schedule C.** *Advanced Bible History*

*First Year* (72 lessons), *Old Testament*

Old Testament Introduction                             Lessons

| | |
|---|---|
| *First Period:* Primeval History | 7 |
| *Second Period:* The Patriarchs | 12 |
| *Third Period:* Moses and Joshua | 17 |
| *Fourth Period:* The Judges | 6 |
| *Fifth Period:* The First Three Kings | 11 |
| *Sixth Period:* From the Division of the Kingdom to the Babylonian Captivity | 11 |
| *Seventh Period:* From the Babylonian Captivity to the Birth of Christ | 8 |
| | 72 |

## Suggested Combinations

1. The Call of Abraham and Abraham's Faith.
2. Isaac's Marriage and Isaac Blesses His Children.
3. Jacob's Ladder, Jacob and Laban, Jacob's Return.
4. Joseph in Egypt and Joseph Before Pharaoh.
5. The First and Second Journeys of Joseph's Brethren.

*Second Year* (72 lessons), *New Testament*             Lessons

New Testament Introduction

| | |
|---|---|
| *First Period:* The Childhood of Jesus | 9 |
| *Second Period:* The Public Ministry of Christ | 35 |
| *Third Period:* The Passion of Our Lord Jesus Christ | 8 |
| *Fourth Period:* The Glorified Lord | 7 |
| *Fifth Period:* The Founding and Growth of the Christian Church | 13 |
| | 72 |

## Suggested Combinations

1. Jesus in Gethsemane and Jesus Taken Captive.
2. The Crucifixion, Parts I and II.
3. Paul's Second and Third Missionary Journeys.

*Note:* The periods may be arranged in any order.

*Example: First Year:* O.T., Periods 1, 2, 3; N.T., Period 2.
                 *Second Year:* O.T., Periods 4, 5, 6; N.T., Periods 1, 3, 4, 5.

## E. CORRELATION POSSIBILITIES

The following examples are suggestive of the almost limitless opportunities for natural correlation between Biblical history and other school subjects:

*Catechism.* Biblical historical material is constantly used to prove and give basis for the teachings of the Catechism. See suggestions in Catechism.

*Bible Reading.* Bible reading is a natural sequence to the course in Bible History.

*Geography.* The geography of Asia and Africa is not complete without a study of the movement of the patriarchs and the children of Israel; the establishment of the early Christian Church also receives attention.

*History.* Provides opportunities for drawing lessons from Biblical history: the punishment of unjust governments by the examples of Ahab, Herod, and Pilate; or the destruction of godless nations by the example of Israel. The Old World Background course is properly taught against the background of Bible History.

*Civics.* Good citizenship is illustrated by accounts from Scripture, such as the Good Samaritan, Jesus' submission to civil authority, His payment of tribute, and others.

*Reading.* The reading period is at times devoted to selections from the Bible.

*Health and Safety.* The healings of Jesus, protection of the disciples in the storm, and similar selections are used as illustrations of divine aid and protection in sickness and danger.

*Science.* God, not chance and man's skill, created and preserves the world; the achievements of science are the fulfillment of Genesis 1:28 ("and subdue it").

*Child Training in General.* Training is made effective by the use of Bible stories which illustrate the traits that are to be developed. *Examples:* Purity in thought, word, and deed by the example of Joseph; love of the Word of God by the example of Mary.

## F. EVALUATING OUTCOMES

The teacher will frequently stop to evaluate his work on the basis of the aims. As in Catechism, the knowledge of subject matter is easily tested. Objective tests of single stories, of periods of Biblical history, or of an entire Testament are not difficult to construct and should be used. In this manner historical knowledge, familiarity with the doctrine taught, and, in general, the intellectual knowledge of God's plan of salvation may be measured. Over a period of time, tests will be developed which

may be used repeatedly, and a definite standard of achievement
for the various grades of the school will result.

Other aspects will require evaluation by observation. The
interest in Bible history may be seen from the attitude evidenced
in the instruction. The desire and habit to read the Bible itself
is not easy to determine, but discussion with the pupils of this
point and occasional questioning will indicate the progress.

The effect of the instruction upon the heart and will of the
pupils must be judged by the outward behavior of the pupils.
"Ye shall know them by their fruits." Matt. 7:16. At the same
time it must always be remembered that also the sanctified children
remain sinners. But the "new man" will show himself in many
observable ways. Special occurrences which indicate the religious
influence upon children should be noted and preserved, both for
encouragement at times when all instruction seems fruitless and
for the compilation of a definite standard of behavior which might
be expected as a result of constant Christian instruction and
training.

## Selected References

### PROFESSIONAL BOOKS

Avent, Joseph Emory, *Beginning Teaching*. Knoxville: University of
Tennessee, 1926.

Beck, Walter H., "Visual Materials, Handwork, and Activities in Religious
Education." *Lutheran School Journal*, March, 1942, p. 295.

*Course of Study in Religion*. Minnesota District, 1939.

Koehler, E. W. A., "Is Our Method of Teaching Religion as Effective as It
Might Be?" *Lutheran School Journal*, May, 1929, pp. 161—166; June,
1929, pp. 203—209; July, 1929, pp. 241—247; Aug., 1929, pp. 281—286.

Kraeft, W. O., *Religion for Primary Grades in Units of Learning*. Concordia, 1926.

Kramer, Wm. A., *Bible History Outlines*. Concordia, 1939.

Kretzmann, P. E., *The Teaching of Religion*. Concordia, 1925.

Reu, M., *Catechetics*. Wartburg, 1931, pp. 289—296.

Rupprecht, F., *Bible History References*, Vols. I and II. Concordia, 1935.

Schmieding, Alfred, *Teaching the Bible Story*. Concordia, 1935.

Stellhorn, A. C., *Manual for Lutheran Saturday Schools*. Concordia, 1935.

### TEXTBOOKS AND HELPS

*Advanced Bible History*. Concordia, 1936.

*Elementary Bible History*. Concordia, 1935.

Mertz, H. A., and Siems, W. A., *Exercises in Bible History*. Concordia, 1937.

Schmidt, W. A., Weber, F. H., and Roth, S. J., *Working with God's Word*.
Saginaw: Lutheran School Service, 1941.

*Concordia Picture Rolls*. Concordia.

A good map of Biblical lands.

# 5. A Fusion-Units (Correlated) Course in Religion

The traditional method has been to divide the Catechism, Bible History, and Bible Reading into separate courses. Each of the three fields of study provides sufficient material for well-organized courses as indicated in the various outlines under these subjects. At times the teacher may desire to combine all of them in a single course, including also memorizing. This enables teacher and pupil to see the entire field from a new point of view. Such a fused course might be taught every third year in a one- or two-room school. In a four- or eight-room school it might be taught once in the middle grades and once in the upper grades.

The outline for the fusion-units course reprinted below was prepared by Professor Alfred Schmieding of Concordia Teachers College, River Forest, Illinois, and is used with his permission. It supplies sufficient material for an entire year. The course is based on the Christian Church Year. It is divided into units and each unit into lessons. Each unit is taught under the guidance of a general objective and each lesson under a specific aim, or central thought, making an important contribution to the attainment of the general objectives.

References to the Catechism are to the Proof Print of the revised Catechism dated October 1, 1940. The hymn selections are from the *Lutheran Hymnal*. The abbreviations *ABH* and *EBH* are used to designate the *Advanced* and *Elementary Bible Histories*.

## Units of Study

For the sake of compactness many of the obvious details have been omitted. As outlined, the course is suitable for the middle or upper grades. Adjustment to grade level is one of the teacher's problems. It may also be suggested that in the upper grades the lessons be based on Bible reading and Bible study as often as possible.

### Unit I: God's Word (September)

**General Approach:** Explanation of the course for the entire year (one lesson with pupil co-operation).

**Unit Approach:** The importance of God's Word for all people.

**Objectives:** Understanding and appreciation of the Bible as God's Word which shows us the way to salvation in Jesus.

*Lesson Materials*

Catechism Lesson: What is the Bible? Why has God given us the Bible? Exposition questions 7—13.

Bible Lesson: Review and extension of previous lesson and informal examination of the Bible. Finding books; simple classification of books.

Bible Story. Jesus about His Father's Business. *ABH*, New Testament, No. 7. *EBH*, N. T., No. 9.

Bible Story: One Thing is Needful. *ABH*, New Testament, No. 29. *EBH*, N. T., No. 23.

Catechism Lesson: The Third Commandment (two lessons).

Catechism Lesson: The Law and Its Purpose. Exposition, questions 14, 15.

Catechism Lesson: The Law and Its Purpose. Exposition, questions 87—90.

Bible Story. The Giving of the Law. *ABH*, O. T., No. 30. *EBH*, O. T., No. 28.

Catechism Lesson: Survey Discussion of Ten Commandments (two lessons).

Catechism Lesson: The Gospel and Its Relation to the Law. Exposition, questions 15, 16, 17, 165, and 166.

Bible Lesson: Jesus, the Center of the Entire Bible. Read and discuss Matt. 18: 11; Is. 53: 4, 5; John 11: 25, 26; John 3: 16.

Bible Lesson: Luke 15.

Bible Lesson: Matt. 13 (selected portions if desirable).

Functional Lesson: How and where we may hear and learn the Word of God. Discussion by children guided by teacher.

Functional Lesson: First Petition.

Mission Lesson (Functional): Recitation and discussion of Hymn No. 496.

Oral review, test, re-teaching.

## Unit II: Prayer (October)

**Approach:** Importance of prayer in the life of a Christian.

**Objective:** A ready willingness to carry everything to God in prayer.

*Lesson Materials*

Exploratory Approach: Under teacher's guidance children find materials on prayer in Catechism, Bible History text, Bible, and Hymnbook (1 lesson).

Bible Story: The Centurion (2 lessons). *ABH*, N. T., No. 21; *EBH*, N. T., No. 18.

Bible Story: The Faith of a Woman (2 lessons). *ABH*, N. T., No. 25; *EBH*, N. T., No. 154.

Catechism Lesson: What is Prayer? What should induce us to pray? Exposition, questions 202 and 204.

Catechism Lesson: How Christians should pray. Exposition, questions 207—213 (2 lessons).

Catechism Lesson: Survey discussion of the Lord's Prayer (1 or 2 lessons).

Catechism Lesson: Discussion of the Morning and Evening Prayers as given in Small Catechism.

Catechism Lesson: Discussion of the Table Prayers as given in Small Catechism.

Functional Lesson: Discussion of situations in which Christians may pray and the content of such prayers (1 or 2 lessons).

Functional Lesson: Brief review of previous lesson, each child then writing a prayer for a given occasion.

Bible Story: How Stephen Prayed for His Enemies. *ABH*, N. T., No. 61; *EBH*, N. T., No. 49.

Functional Lesson: Critical but sympathetic discussion of the prayers written previously.

Bible Story: Jesus in Gethsemane. *ABH*, N. T., No. 43; *EBH*, N. T., No. 36.

Functional Lesson: Discussion of Hymn No. 457.

Oral review, test, re-teaching (if necessary).

(If no other provision is made for a study of the Reformation, the last days of October may be devoted to a brief unit leading up to the Reformation Festival.)

### Unit III: God Made and Preserves Me and All Creatures (November)

**Approach:** Harvest Festivals as celebrated by the Jews in the Old Testament and later by the Christians (much interesting material). Note harvest in community (a concrete discussion).

**Objective:** Understanding and appreciation that God is a good and gracious God. He has created me and all creatures, and He provides me with all that I need and protects me against all danger.

*Lesson Materials*

Bible Story: The Creation Story as Told in the Bible. *ABH*, O. T., No. 1; *EBH*, O. T., No. 1.

Bible Story: Jesus Feeds the Five Thousand. *ABH*, N. T., No. 23; *EBH*, N. T., No. 20.

Bible Story: The Savior's First Miracle. *ABH*, N. T., No. 11; *EBH*, N. T., No. 13.

Bible Story: How God Provided for Elijah in Time of Need. *ABH*, O. T., No. 56; *EBH*, O. T., No. 44.

Bible Story: How God Protected Daniel against Danger. *ABH*, O. T., No. 68; *EBH*, O. T., No. 50.

Catechism Lesson: The First Article (Penetration according to Exposition in the Catechism (5 to 10 lessons).

Bible Story: The Poor Widow's Mite. *ABH*, N. T., No. 38; *EBH*, N. T., No. 33.

Bible Study: Study of Ps. 104 (selected parts).

Functional Lesson: How Christians Celebrate Thanksgiving.

Oral review, test, re-teaching.

### Unit IV: The Coming of the Lord (December)

**General Approach:** The Christian Church Year and its significance to the Christian (spend at least one whole lesson on this important topic).

**Special Approach:** Advent and its threefold meaning to the Christian.

**Objective:** Strengthening of faith in Jesus, the promised Messiah, who came to save me from sin and damnation.

*Lesson Materials*

Bible Lesson: Important Prophecies (either presented by the teacher in narrative form or read in the Bible by the pupils (1 lesson).[1]

Bible Story: Announcement of the Forerunner. *ABH*, N. T., No. 1; *EBH*, N. T., No. 1.

Bible Story: Announcement of the Savior. *ABH*, N. T., No. 2; *EBH*, N. T., No. 2.

Bible Story: The Birth of John the Baptist. *ABH*, N. T., No. 3; *EBH*, N. T., N. 3.

Bible Story: The Birth of Jesus. *ABH*, N. T., No. 4; *EBH*, N. T., No. 4.

Catechism Lesson: Study of applicable part of the Second Article with the aid of Luther's Small Catechism and the Exposition. Exposition questions 121—132 (3 to 5 lessons).

Appreciation Lesson: Study of one or several Christmas hymns.

Bible Lesson: Study of Ps. 72 (or How Christians Celebrate Christmas).

Oral review, test, re-teaching.

### Unit V: Jesus the Great Prophet (Epiphany)

(Arrange according to the time available)

**Approach:** The meaning of Epiphany; sometimes called the Christmas of the heathen.

**Objective:** Functional appreciation that Jesus came to save *all* people.

*Lesson Materials*

Bible Story: The Presentation of Jesus in the Temple. *ABH*, N. T., No. 5; *EBH*, N. T., No. 6.

Bible Story: The Coming of the Wise Men. *ABH*, N. T., No. 6; *EBH*, N. T., No. 7.

Bible Story: Jesus about His Father's Business. *ABH*, N. T., No. 7; *EBH*, N. T., No. 9.

Bible Story: The Baptism of Jesus. *ABH*, N. T., No. 9; *EBH*, N. T., No. 11.

Catechism Lesson: The Prophetic Office of Our Savior (Catechism question No. 133, A).

Bible Stories: (Parables and miracles of our Lord.) Select according to time available.

Catechism Lesson: Baptism (Study of Fourth Chief Part — 3 to 8 lessons).

Functional Lesson: The Second Petition according to Luther's Small Catechism and the Exposition with special emphasis on mission work.

Functional Lesson: Our opportunities to do mission work today.

Oral review, test, re-teaching.

---

1) See course in Bible Reading, p. 64.

### Unit VI: The Suffering of Our Lord (Lent)

**Approach:** Review of the Christian Church Year with special reference to Ash Wednesday, Lent, Palm Sunday, Holy Week, Maundy Thursday, and Good Friday.

**Objective:** A strengthened and growing faith in Christ who redeemed me, a lost and condemned creature, purchased and won me from all sins, from death and the power of the devil, not with gold or silver, but with His holy, precious blood and with His innocent suffering and death.

*Lesson Materials*

Catechism Lesson: The Priestly Office of Christ (Catechism question 133, B).

Bible Lesson: Prophecy concerning the Suffering of Jesus according to Isaiah 53.

Bible Story: Jesus Celebrates the Passover and Institutes the Lord's Supper. *ABH*, N.T., No. 42; *EBH*, N.T., No. 35.

Bible Story: Our Savior's Suffering in Gethsemane. *ABH*, N. T., No. 43; *EBH*, N.T., No. 36.

Bible Story: Jesus is Taken Prisoner. *ABH*, N.T., No. 44; *EBH*, N. T., No. 37.

Bible Story: Jesus is Condemned before the High Priest. *ABH*, N. T., No. 45; *EBH*, N.T., No. 38.

Bible Story: Jesus Suffers under Pontius Pilate. *ABH*, N. T., No. 47; *EBH*, N.T., No. 40.

Bible Story: Jesus is Crucified. *ABH*, N.T., Nos. 49 and 50; *EBH*, N. T., No. 41.

Bible Story: Jesus is Buried. *ABH*, N. T., No. 51; *EBH*, N.T., No. 42.

A survey study of the events during the Holy Week.

Catechism Lesson: Christ's State of Humiliation (according to Luther's Catechism and Exposition, questions 135—148. 5 to 8 lessons).

Appreciation Lesson: Study of one or several Passion Hymns.

Bible Reading: (If time permits.) A brief study of the entire life of Christ on the basis of carefully selected portions from the Gospels. (5 to 10 lessons.)

Oral review, test, re-teaching.

### Unit VII: The Victorious Christ (Easter to Ascension)

**Approach:** Discussion of Hymn: "I Know That My Redeemer Lives," *Lutheran Hymnal*, No. 200.

**Objective:** Appreciation that Christ's victory is my victory.

*Lesson Materials*

Bible Story: Our Savior Rises from the Dead. *ABH*, N.T., N. 52; *EBH*, N.T., No. 43.

Bible Story: Jesus is Seen by the Women. *ABH*, N.T., No. 53; *EBH*, N. T., No. 44.

Bible Story: Jesus Reveals Himself to the Two Disciples. *ABH,* N. T., No. 54.

Catechism Lesson: Christ's Kingly Office (Catechism, question 133, C).

Catechism Lesson: Christ's State of Exaltation (according to Luther's Small Catechism and Exposition, questions 149—160. 5 to 8 lessons).

Catechism Lesson: Study of the Lord's Supper (Sixth Chief Part. 4 to 8 lessons).

Bible Story: The Ascension of Our Lord (close of the Easter Cycle). *ABH,* N.T., No. 57; *EBH,* N.T., No. 46.

Appreciation Lesson: "Jesus! and Shall It Ever Be." Hymn 346.

Oral review, test, re-teaching.

## Unit VIII: The Founding and Work of the Christian Church

### (Pentecost and Trinity)

(Arrange according to the time available)

**Approach:** The importance of Pentecost as a festival. Why the Trinity Festival brings to a fitting close the half of the Christian church year which contains the great festivals.

**Objective:** Understanding and appreciation of Christ's words: "Lo, I am with you alway even unto the end of the world." Matt. 28:20.

*Lesson Materials:*

Bible Story: The Pentecost Story. *ABH,* N. T., No. 58; *EBH,* N. T., No. 47.

Bible Story: How Peter Heals a Lame Man. *ABH,* N. T., No. 59; *EBH,* N. T., No. 48.

Bible Story: Stephen. *ABH,* N. T., No. 61; *EBH,* N. T., No. 49.

Catechism Lesson: Faith in the True God (Exposition, questions 24—27; 103, 104).

Bible Lesson: Division of Trinity Sundays (develop according to time available).

| | | |
|---|---|---|
| The call of the Holy Ghost through the Gospel | Trinity Sundays 1 to 5 | Use Epistle and Gospel Lessons |
| Enlightenment | Trinity Sundays 6 to 14 | |
| Sanctification | Trinity Sundays 15 to 23 | |
| Preservation of Faith | Trinity Sundays 24 to 27 | |

Catechism Lesson: Penetration of Third Article (on the basis of Luther's Catechism and the Exposition. 5 to 10 lessons).

Catechism Lesson: The Office of the Keys (Fifth Chief Part, 3 to 5 lessons).

Bible Lesson: Important Events in the Founding of the Church.

Functional Lesson: Christ's Great Command according to Matt. 28:19-20. Mission work.

Appreciation Lesson: Hymn (No. 496), "Hark, the Voice of Jesus Crying."

Oral review, test, re-teaching.

**Unit IX: Review of Important Doctrines According to the Church Year Arrangement; Test, Re-Teaching**

*Note:* The foregoing material may be expanded or contracted. It is assumed that the Catechism lessons and the Bible stories given will be taught in the usual way. Bible stories may each be given a one- or two-day treatment. Each lesson is taught under the control of a single aim or central thought. The memory work, which may be correlated, may be much or little, according to the time available and the ability of pupils. Bible reading may be made an integral part of each unit. If desirable, the Sunday Gospel and Epistle Lessons may also be read during the week.

In order further to illustrate the course, the first unit has been worked out in greater detail. The lessons given indicate the approximate amount which may be taught each day.

**Unit I. God's Word**

**Level:** Middle grades.

**Objective:** An understanding and appreciation that the Bible is God's Word which shows us the way to salvation in Jesus.

### Lesson I

**Devotion:** Hymn No. 285; Scripture Reading, 2 Tim. 3:15-17; Creed.

**Overview:** Brief presentation of the entire unit by the teacher, giving the children definite indications of the materials to be studied.

**Catechism Lesson:** What is the Bible? Why has God given us His Word? Exposition, questions 7—13.

**Central Thought:** A personal acquaintance with the greatest of all books.

**Memory Work:** Assign John 5:39 (No. 10); Luke 11:28 (No. 11).

### Lesson II

**Devotion:** Hymn No. 292; a specially prepared prayer; Creed.

**Bible Lesson:** Review, and if thought necessary, extend the first lesson. Pupils examine the Bible informally. Name the two parts. Find and name some of the books. Considerable explanation by the teacher.

**Central Thought:** A personal acquaintance with the greatest of all books.

**Memory Work:** Texts assigned in Lesson I assignment: Learn to read the names or titles of the books of the Old Testament.

### Lesson III

**Devotion:** Hymn No. 281; prayer by teacher; Creed.

**Bible Story:** Jesus About His Father's Business. *ABH*, N. T., No. 7; *EBH*, N. T., No. 9.

**Central Thought:** Gladly hear and learn the Word of God.

**Memory Work:** Read the titles of the books of the Old Testament. Discuss their order and grouping. Also review texts 10 and 11. Assign the reading of the titles of the books of the New Testament.

### Lesson IV

**Devotion:** Hymn No. 16 or 366; responsive reading of Psalm 84; Creed.

**Bible Story:** One Thing Needful. *ABH*, N.T., No. 29. *EBH*, N.T., No. 23.

**Central Thought:** Seek ye first the kingdom of God.

**Memory Work:** Read the titles of the books of the New Testament; find each book in the Bible; classify them.

### Lesson V

**Devotion:** Hymn No. 286; Bible Reading, Luke 2:41-52; Creed.

**Catechism Lesson:** The Third Commandment (First Lesson, questions 45—48).

**Central Thought:** The main purpose of our festivals and holidays is to provide opportunities for hearing and learning the Word of God.

**Memory Work:** Further discussion of the classification of the books of the New Testament; finding chapters and passages in the New Testament (drill). Assignment of Acts 2:42 (108).

### Lesson VI

**Devotion:** Hymn No. 286; Luke 2:36-38; Creed.

**Catechism Lesson:** The Third Commandment (Second Lesson, questions 49—52).

**Central Thought:** We should gladly hear and learn God's Word.

**Memory Work:** Discussion and recitation of Acts 2:42.

**Assignment:** Reading of the Ten Commandments as given Ex. 20:1-17.

### Lesson VII

**Devotion:** Hymn No. 295; prayer by teacher; Morning Prayer.

**Catechism Lesson:** The Law and Its Purpose (questions 14, 15 in Exposition).

**Central Thought:** An understanding of the nature of the Law.

**Memory Work:** Reading of the Law as given in Ex. 20. Discussion.

### Lesson VIII

**Devotion:** Hymn No. 295; prayer by teacher; Morning Prayer.

**Catechism:** The Law and Its Purpose (Second Lesson, questions 87—90).

**Central Thought:** Man's helplessness because of sin and his need for a Savior. (Point to Gospel briefly.)

**Memory Work:** Assignment of Psalm 14:3 (210); Is. 64:6 (212); Psalm 143:2 (214); Romans 10:4 (239).

### Lesson IX

**Devotion:** Hymn 291; responsive reading, Psalm 5; Morning Prayer.

**Bible Story:** The Giving of the Law. *ABH*, O.T., No. 30; *EBH*, O.T., No. 28.

**Central Thought:** The importance of the Law for man.

**Memory Work:** Recitation of texts 210, 212, 214, 239.

Assignment of Commandments 1 to 3 for memory work.

### Lesson X

**Devotion:** Hymn No. 295; Morning Prayer.

**Catechism Lesson:** Survey Discussion of Commandments 1 to 3 as given in Luther's Small Catechism.

**Central Thought:** Our duty toward God as God's children justified by grace.

**Memory Work:** Commandments 1 to 3. Assignment of Commandments 4 to 10 (text only if necessary).

### Lesson XI

**Devotion:** Hymn No. 295; Morning Prayer.

**Catechism:** Discussion of Commandments 4 to 10 as given in Luther's Small Catechism.

**Central Thought:** Our duty toward our neighbor as God's children justified by grace.

**Memory Work:** Commandments 4 to 10 (text only if necessary).

*Note:* In Lessons X and XI knowledge of sin, the all-sufficiency of God's grace in Jesus, and the consequent consecration to do God's will should be the underlying thought of the entire treatment. Thus the way will be prepared for a more detailed study of the Gospel. (Teacher must carefully distinguish in the use of Law and Gospel. In the previous lessons the Law is discussed more fully, and the Gospel message is pointed to briefly.)

### Lesson XII

**Devotion:** Hymn No. 297; Luke 14:16-23; Lord's Prayer.

**Catechism:** The Gospel and Its Relation to the Law (questions 15, 16, 17, 165, and 166 in Exposition).

**Central Thought:** The Holy Ghost called me by the Gospel, enlightened me with His gifts, sanctified me, and kept me in the true faith.

**Memory Work:** Assignment of 1 Cor. 12:3 (421); John 3:16 (18).

### Lesson XIII

**Devotion:** Hymn No. 349; Romans 5:1-11; Creed.

**Bible Lesson:** Jesus as the Center of the entire Bible.

Review purpose of the Law; the work of Holy Ghost by the Gospel. Read in Bible and discuss Matt. 18:11; Is. 53:4, 5; John 11:25, 26; John 3:16.

**Central Thought:** Jesus has redeemed me from sin and damnation without the works of the Law.

**Memory Work:** Texts 421 and 18. Assignment of texts studied in this lesson.

### Lesson XIV

**Devotion:** Hymn No. 354 or 324; Creed.

**Bible Lesson:** Luke 15.

**Central Thought:** There is joy in heaven over one sinner that repents.

**Memory Work:** Texts assigned in previous lesson.

### Lesson XV

**Devotion:** Hymn No. 292; Creed.

**Bible Lesson:** Matthew 13 (select parts if necessary).

**Central Thought:** Who hath ears to hear, let him hear, Matt. 13:9.

**Memory Work:** Assignment of books of Bible or such portions as can be memorized by the class.

### Lesson XVI

**Devotion:** Hymn No. 291; Luke 12:16-31; Creed.

**Functional Lesson:** How and where we may hear and learn the Word of God. (Children list and discuss the many opportunities.)

**Central Thought:** Blessed are they that hear the Word of God and keep it.

**Memory Work:** Recitation of such portions of the titles of the Books of the Bible as the children can learn.

### Lesson XVII

**Devotion:** Hymn No. 328; Col. 3:1-17; Lord's Prayer.

**Catechism Lesson** (Functional): The First Petition.

**Central Thought:** Pray to God to keep us from false doctrine and ungodly life and to give us pure doctrine and holy life.

**Memory Work:** Assignment of Hymn No. 496.

### Lesson XVIII

**Devotion:** Hymn No. 496; Acts 20:16-24; Creed.

**Mission Lesson** (Functional): Recitation and discussion of Hymn No. 496.

**Central Thought:**

> "You can tell the love of Jesus,
> You can say He died for all."

### Lesson XIX

Test and Oral Review.

### Lesson XX

Such re-teaching as the test and the oral review show to be necessary.

*Note:* The teacher may plan the other units in a similar manner. Most of them will give fewer difficulties than the foregoing unit. In the work from day to day it is important that the whole unit is unified by the introductions, approaches to, and the conclusions of, the daily lessons. Pausing to recall is an essential element of good teaching. Reviewing must not be overdone, however. If the interest of the children is to be maintained, the unit should move forward in a fairly rapid stride. The Scripture lessons given for devotion may be used as brief Bible reading lessons leading to the lesson for the day. If they are so used, only the most necessary explanation should be made, keeping the Bible reading mainly devotional. (See the author's *Teaching the Bible Story*, pp. 129—133, for a similar lesson outline of the unit on Prayer. Unit II.)

# 6. Memory Work

## A. OBJECTIVES

1. Knowledge by memory of the essential elements of the Christian faith and doctrine.

2. Acquisition of a store of religious memory material adequate for the Christian's needs.

3. Intimate acquaintance with gems of religious literature as a means of sympathetic contact between Christians.

4. The ability and habit of putting memorized materials to practical use.

5. The ability and habit of exact memorizing and quotation.

6. Stimulation of a love and desire for memory work through a realization of its present and future usefulness.

## B. DISCUSSION OF OBJECTIVES

Before Scripture was recorded, the only possibility of religious instruction was by means of memory work. A certain amount of it is necessary today for every Christian "to be ready always to give an answer to every man that asketh you a reason for the hope that is in you." 1 Pet. 3:15. Full agreement on the selections to be memorized or on the exact amount to be memorized is not necessary, and these will vary somewhat from school to school and from pupil to pupil. All teachers should make sure that the essential elements of Christian faith and doctrine are covered thoroughly. This requires memorization of all of Luther's Small Catechism, brief passages of Scripture as well as longer portions (especially Psalms), and a selection of Christian hymns (*Note:* The Scripture passages in the Catechism are not all intended for memorization; many of them are to be used merely as proof texts in the Catechism instruction).

### Choice of Selections to Meet Needs

Acquisition of a rich store of religious memory material is desirable for purposes of meditation and edification; prayer; admonition; comfort and consolation; confession of faith; instruction of others; effective statement of a point in argumentation; and ready and exact quotation of authority, or beauty of expression. These purposes determine the choice of selections. The wealth of material from which the choice must be made and the purposes for which it is to be used call for careful and discriminative selection.

## Benefits and Proper Use of Memorized Materials

"Memory is your best library. It goes with the persecuted into exile; with the soldier into the battle and 'over the top'; with the sick into the hospital and to the operating table. Who will estimate the value of a memory filled with Bible verses and hymns in the hour of temptation, sorrow, trouble, sickness, and death?" [1]

Some pupils will automatically put to use the material they learn, as the following experience illustrates: "One Thanksgiving we were using some of the Psalms for our festival. Some of the children's fathers were out of work, and there was grief and anxiety in many homes. A child whispered to me one day, 'You know what? Those Psalms are nice to say when you go to bed. They make me feel kind of safe.' " [2]

The benefit to the child is much greater, however, when the teacher makes a conscious effort to show the particular use of each selection that is learned. Practical use is demonstrated by quoting the memorized materials in the instruction, using them in the school devotions or in conversation where they apply, singing the memorized hymns, and in other ways. The close and opening before and after the noon hour, and the close of school, alone provide three times one hundred and eighty opportunities for utilizing memorized materials and for exercising children in the proper use thereof.

## Forgetting

The fact that much of the material that is memorized, especially that which is not frequently used, is later partially forgotten need not be unduly alarming. The child who is taught how to utilize memorized materials properly will certainly retain those parts which most adequately serve his needs. In testing an adolescent several years after confirmation the teacher may be shocked at the discovery that his former pupil is unable to repeat a certain Scripture passage or hymn stanza which he once knew perfectly; but he may find that the same boy or girl remembers other selections and uses them constantly. People sick in bed and unable to read have been found to recite to themselves long hymns like "If Thou But Suffer God to Guide Thee" or "Commit Whatever Grieves Thee," which they learned in childhood. Others have used similar selections when long sleepless nights threatened,

1) Herman Voigt, *Graded Memory Material*, p. 5.

2) May Hill Arbuthnot in "Reading Can Be Fun." *School Briefs*, Scott Foresman and Company, October, 1940.

and found peace, comfort, and rest. There is no record of what they have forgotten. Yet their memory work in school has been to them a source of inestimable blessing, because they were able to recall selections, or quickly to re-learn them, when they were needed.

From such facts the teacher must take his cue. He must teach a variety of religious memory material that meets all spiritual needs, show how to apply it, and make sure that his pupils are able to put their knowledge to practical use. He must not concern himself with the fact that some of it will be inevitably forgotten. Knowledge of two or three hymns of comfort, for example, is desirable; but the retention' and use of one when needed is sufficient. Teaching the pupils something worth while together with the ability to use it provides ample assurance to the teacher that some of it will be used. Occasional inquiry regarding the practical use of the memorized materials helps to keep the children impressed with its importance and usefulness.

### Memory Gems as a Means of Sympathetic Contact between Christians

This objective is achieved both with the material that is perfectly remembered and that which is partially forgotten. How often is not a worshiper in church edified, strengthened, comforted, admonished, or otherwise benefited by the citation of a familiar Scripture passage or hymn stanza or one which had once been memorized though now partially forgotten. Immediately there is established a point of contact and sympathy which wholly new material does not ordinarily produce. The pastor finds the same sympathetic response in the private ministry to his members in times of need and trouble and at the sickbed. Christians find the mutual acquaintance with identical religious material a bond of fellowship in many situations. All this is putting memorized material to practical, beneficial use. This benefit the teacher must keep in mind personally and convey to his pupils by means of concrete explanation and examples.

### Habit and Skill of Memorizing

By-products of religious memory work are the ability and habit of economical and exact memorizing and of accurate quotation. These are not spiritual objectives, since they can be achieved equally well through the memorization of nonreligious material, but their incidental attainment through the memorization of religious material is to be sought consciously and systematically.

## Love and Desire for Memory Work

Love and desire for religious memory work is important for success. Too often pupils, as also some parents, regard memorizing as an unnecessary burden. One reason for this view may be that they do not recognize the benefits of memory work indicated above. The practical, beneficial, and devotional use of memorized materials in school, and suggestions and guidance for similar use out of school, should overcome this obstacle and bring about a greater appreciation of the value of memorizing.

A second reason for a lack of interest is occasionally found in ill-adapted assignments. A pupil of low learning capacity, finding the daily assignment consistently beyond his ability, is likely to lose all love and desire for further memorizing. This is doubly disastrous because his dislike involves religious material. The teacher must make sure, therefore, that the assignments are adapted to the capacity of the individual pupils and that they are understood. In the ordinary class, pupils of average, above-average, and below-average ability are found. This calls for an average and a minimum assignment and for additional materials for the highly gifted child. Thus favorable conditions for study and Christian growth are created.

## C. METHOD IN MEMORIZING

### How to Memorize: Suggestions to the Pupil

1. Be sure you know exactly what and how much you are to memorize before you begin.

2. Make every effort to understand the material that is to be memorized.

    a. Read the entire lesson several times and see its meaning as a whole. Reading aloud will help.

    b. State the meaning in your own words. If necessary, outline the lesson.

    c. Try to see the memory gem in your book with your eyes closed.

    d. Write the lesson if you have difficulty in learning it from the printed page.

3. Think of the benefit of the material you are learning.

4. Memorize in a quiet place, where you can concentrate on the lesson.

5. Memorize short selections as wholes rather than as parts.

6. Memorize long selections by parts which have a single general thought; then memorize the connections between the parts. But read the entire selection carefully and thoughtfully several times before studying the parts.

7. Memorize exactly (carelessly memorized material is quickly forgotten; exactness in all things aids character growth).

8. Begin early and memorize in short periods, avoiding a last-minute cramming effort.

9. Review frequently the material you have memorized, even after you know it perfectly ("overlearning" aids the retention of memorized materials).

10. Let someone test you before you recite in school, or test yourself by writing the lesson from memory.

**General Suggestions to the Teacher**

1. Teach the pupils how to memorize, giving them practice in the procedure until it becomes automatic with them.

2. Place the suggestions for memorizing on the blackboard to be copied, or hand duplicate copies to the children.

3. Make sure that the pupils understand the assignment and know precisely what and how much to memorize.

4. Know the material by memory yourself.

5. Help pupils understand the material. Young children especially should know from one half to three fourths of the selection before it is assigned as memory work. Beginners should do all their memorizing in school.

6. Show the class the benefits to be derived from the material and how to apply it practically.

7. Help the pupils develop a general "place memory" of a small number of important Scripture passages. [3] This will require a measure of drill.

8. Do not threaten or in other ways make the work unpleasant. This may create a dislike for religion. Impress upon pupils who refuse to study their assignments the benefits of religious memory work and the duty of Christian children.

9. Make the course adequate without permitting it to become a burden to any child. Evaluate the course on a qualitative, not a quantitative basis.

10. Make ample allowance for individual differences. (Class work is necessary for economy in assignment, but the class assignment is likely to be inadequate for the highly gifted and excessive for the poorly gifted child.)

11. Provide opportunity for frequent review of the materials learned. Make the review thought provoking. Ask: Which text proves . . . etc.?; From which text do we learn that . . . etc.?; Which text ascribes . . . etc.?

---

3) See also course in Bible Reading, p. 57.
General Course of Study 4

## Suggestions for the Recitation

1. If at all possible, have all pupils recite the entire assignment. Or the lesson may be written, the papers exchanged and corrected by the pupils. Occasional recitation in chorus is permissible for a saving of time.

2. Do not make a practice of prompting or assisting the pupil.

3. Require thoughtful and expressive recitation. (Proper demeanor, good posture, clear enunciation, correct phrasing.)

4. Aim at a perfect recitation.

5. Give the pupil ample time for reciting.

6. Do not, as a rule, require pupils who have failed to recite as a punishment at recess or after school. All pupils need the rest and recreation of free periods. Rather inquire into their mode of learning and show them how to study.

7. Give pupils who have failed in their recitation another opportunity at the end of the period.

8. If the class recitation has been a failure, assign for a second time.

9. Speak as little as possible during the recitation.

10. Have all pupils in the room, also those in other grades, listen while the recitation is in progress. They will learn from one another; the higher grades by way of repetition, the lower grades by way of preparation for assignments that are to follow.

## Aids in Studying a Lesson [4]

The average child should be shown various ways of committing things to memory and advised as to when and how often to study.

The breaking up of the material into logical units is one substantial help. Classes that have failed on certain long passages have shown uniform perfection of recitation after the teacher had analyzed the passage into its various parts.

Let the instructor read such a passage to the class or diagram it on the board. Articulate clearly. Emphasize properly. Let children repeat the passage. Insist on clear articulation and proper expression.

Accustom children to speak deliberately and distinctly. The common tendency is for them to "rattle off" what they have learned. Check this. Remember, children who articulate. care-

---

[4] These suggestions are taken from the *Manual for Lutheran Saturday Schools*, by A. C. Stellhorn, pp. 36—38.

fully and phrase properly can be well understood in their recitations in public, though they may not be speaking loud. Herein lies the secret of making themselves understood.

Pay close attention to the enunciation of consonants and endings of words. Do not let them say: "Wesh'd fea'n love God," but insist on "We should fear and love God." Watch the phrasing. Not: "God is a spirit, and they that worship Him must worship Him in spirit and in truth"; but: "God is a *spirit* — and they that *worship* Him — must worship Him in *spirit* — and in *truth.*" A child who stresses the italicized words in the recitation a few times with proper phrasing and proper emphasis should know it by memory; he will not know it if he tries merely to repeat the string of words.

It is profitable occasionally to assist the memory also by writing. Let the instructor try this at the blackboard (once the method is learned, children will do it automatically on paper):

> Let me be — —,
> Thou faithful God — —;
> Let me — — never
> Nor wander — — Word.

With these lines at the board, the instructor, pointing at the words and dashes, says the stanza as it should be; children repeat. Should a dash cause trouble, insert the word. Also have individuals repeat. Then erase other words, as, for example:

> Let — — — —,
> Thou — — — —;
> Let — — — —
> Nor wander — — —.

Repeat the foregoing process. Erase the last line; children recite. Erase the second-last line; children recite. And so on. If difficulties develop, insert the troublesome words again. Continue with the rest of the stanza. There will be very few children who do not know their stanza perfectly before the lesson is over. This need not be done every time; just often enough for the class to realize the helpfulness of it.

The same may be done with difficult Bible or Catechism passages.

Why do children stumble so much in reciting the Catechism, especially the Ten Commandments? One chief reason is, of course, mechanical memorizing without attention to content; another is poor phrasing and poor emphasis. An explanation of a commandment is boldly and fluently started: "We should fear and love God that we may — may not —," and there the child is stuck.

Another chief reason is that the teacher has always helped from there on. But a third and probably the main reason is that the child has never been given an overview of the Commandments for the express purpose of distinguishing one explanation from the other. Such a special exercise is important. Have children quickly run through all the explanations and recite only the beginning words after "We should fear and love God," like this: —

> "that we may not curse, swear . . .".
> "that we may not despise preaching . . .".
> "that we may not despise our parents . . .".
> "that we may not hurt nor harm . . .".
> "that we may lead . . ." etc.

Children may be told that all explanations outside the First and Sixth Commandments contain the words "that we may not"; furthermore, that they must judge the following words by the commandment itself. Similar exercises should be conducted with the Petitions and other parts of the Catechism.

### Division of Time and Materials

Ordinarily 20 to 25 minutes are available for memory work. This is little time for the work that is to be done, especially where the classes are large.

Grades 3 and 4 may be combined in one class, grades 5 and 6 likewise, and the work for grades 3 and 5 may be taught the first year and that for grades 4 and 6 the second. This eliminates two classes and provides additional time for discussing and explaining assigned material. Grades 7 and 8 may be similarly combined and the work alternated where both are in the same room during instruction in religion.

Instruction in correct study methods and training in good study habits may often be given to a number of classes at once for a saving of time. Written or (rarely) chorus recitation may be used occasionally to provide time for such instruction or in cases where the assignment calls for a greater amount of discussion and explanation than usual.

The time element will rarely present difficulties if the suggestions for a systematic and economical recitation are followed.

### D. COURSE SUGGESTIONS

The publication of the new *Lutheran Hymnal* and the proposed new Synodical Catechism will make necessary a revision of all existing courses. Voigt's *Graded Memory Material for Lutheran Schools* and District Courses of Study may serve as guides until a course based upon the new books is published.

## E. CORRELATION POSSIBILITIES

It would be ideal if all memory work could be combined with the regular course in religion (Catechism and Bible History). That may be impossible or at least impractical at times. Teachers who have tried the plan state two difficulties: 1. Uneven lesson assignments (too much material for one lesson, not enough for another); 2. Difficulty in arranging for systematic review. This is especially true in the intermediate and higher grades with the greater amount of memory material.

Still there are many opportunities for correlation:

*Catechism:* The Commandments and Scripture passages are repeated from memory as far as they have been learned. Fitting hymn stanzas are cited.

*Bible History:* In the stories many Scripture passages that have been previously memorized occur, and suggestions for appropriate Catechism selections, Scripture passages, and hymn stanzas appear under the story. These are reviewed and recited as far as they have been learned from memory.

*Bible Reading:* Provides many opportunities for reviewing memory gems, for calling attention to context, and for stressing "place memory" of selected passages.

*Music:* Memorized hymns are sung in the music period for their devotional benefit and for a closer association between the music and words (Christian people are often found humming hymn tunes while they "think" the words of the hymn. This is worship, and acquaintance with the music provides an additional point of contact for the recall of memorized materials).

Additional hymns and songs are memorized in the process of learning the music.

*Devotions:* Memorized hymns, prayers, and parts of the Catechism are used in the school devotions.

*General:* The quoting of memory gems or the singing of memorized hymns may often be combined with instruction in the common school branches as indicated also in the Discussion of Aims. Think, for example, of the opportunities that geography and nature study offer for singing hymn No. 43 of the *Lutheran Hymnal.*

For effective correlation the teacher needs to have rather clearly in mind what the children have memorized and himself know the selections from memory, and the opportunities to use the material will crowd in upon him. See Discussion of Objectives for suggestions.

## F. EVALUATING OUTCOMES

The outcome of Memory Work can be judged under a number of larger questions which, however, offer suggestions for the construction of a more detailed evaluation scale. Examples: Nos. 2, 4, 5, and 7 below may be subdivided into many specific statements or questions.

1. The course in Memory Work defines the subject matter standards that are to be attained. Has the average child mastered the memory material adopted as standard for his grade? Has the superior child done additional work? Has the poorly gifted child learned well at least a minimum of choice selections?

2. Do the pupils know how to memorize economically and exactly? Has the proper manner of study become habitual with them?

3. Do they recite thoughtfully and expressively?

4. Do the pupils recognize the value of learning a large variety of religious memory gems?

5. What evidence is there that the pupils use the memorized materials for practical purposes?

6. What is the attitude of the pupils toward memory work? Do they seemingly find pleasure in studying their assignments, or do they consider the work a burden?

7. Does the teacher succeed in the correlation efforts outlined above?

### Selected References

The Bible (King James Version).

Graded Memory Course for Lutheran Sunday Schools. Concordia, 1937.

Koehler, Ed., "The Value of Memorizing." Lutheran School Journal, December, 1925, pp. 460—465.

Lutheran Hymnal. Concordia, 1941.

"Memory Work." Course of Study in Religion. Minnesota District.

"Regarding Memorizing." Lutheran School Journal, February, 1914, p. 42.

Rommelmann, H. C., "Memory Work in Our Religious Instruction, with Special Reference to the Functional Viewpoint." Lutheran School Journal, February, 1931, pp. 246—257.

Stellhorn, A. C., Manual for Lutheran Saturday Schools. Concordia, 1935, pp. 33—39.

Stellhorn, A. C., "Observations on Memory Work." Lutheran School Journal, April, 1937, pp. 366, 367.

Synodical Catechism. Concordia, 1942.

Voigt, Herman, Graded Memory Material for Lutheran Schools. Concordia, 1928.

Weber, F. H., and Schmidt, William A., "Correlating the Contents of the Catechism and Hymn Book with the Bible History." Lutheran School Journal, September, 1941, pp. 11—17.

Local or District Course of Study.

# 7. Bible Reading

## A. OBJECTIVES

1. Acquaintance with the arrangement and content of the Bible, and the ability to locate passages or parts from source indications..

2. The conviction that the Bible is the source of all Christian doctrine and the absolute standard of faith and conduct.

3. Holy regard and awe for the Word of God.

4. Diligent reading and searching of the Scriptures as the source of all spiritual knowledge.

5. The habit of frequent meditation upon the Word of God for personal edification, comfort, and strength.

## B. DISCUSSION OF OBJECTIVES

### The Importance of Bible Study

The Bible is the source of all Christian doctrine and spiritual knowledge, the absolute standard of faith and conduct, and, therefore, the foundation of all religious instruction. The instruction in Catechism, Bible History, and Memory Work is actually Bible study, but a more extensive acquaintance with the Bible itself is essential if the Bible is to be used profitably.

### Holy Regard and Awe for the Word of God

The pupil is kept aware of the fact that God speaks through the Bible and that every part of it is the inspired, absolute truth. Snickering at the accounts of sin or at certain expressions used in the Bible cannot be tolerated under any circumstances. There will be no difficulty on this point if the teacher exercises care in the choice of readings, handles them discreetly, and uses them to demonstrate the complete sinfulness of human nature and the mercy of a forgiving God.

Because the Bible is God's Word, Bible reading can never be a mere mechanical study of a book. Even when the organization of the Bible, the classification of content, or the chronologies of the Bible are studied, Scripture is still handled with reverence. "To this man will I look, even to him that is poor and of a contrite spirit, and *trembleth* at My Word." Is. 66:2.

Instruction alone is not sufficient for the development of a holy regard and awe for the Word of God, but it must be accompanied by constant training and exercise in right behavior. Here the example of parents, teachers, and 'friends is of greatest importance. The teacher, in addition to setting an example of reverence, assists in keeping his pupils on the right path. If he

observes jesting in sacred matters, irreverence on the part of
pupils in the divine services, during the school devotions, or in
the religious instruction, he earnestly, yet with Christian love
and patience, rebukes the offense and shows its sinfulness. At the
same time he encourages and strengthens the pupils in a God-
pleasing attitude and in right action by pointing them to the Word
of God as the source of all strength. Ps. 119:9;  James 1:21.

## Use of the Bible

The pupil is taught to read and search the Scriptures for
information and instruction, for proof of doctrine, for historical
confirmation, and for other purposes of an intellectual nature. More
important than these is the reading of the Bible for personal edification, comfort, and strength, and it is the teacher's task to assist
the pupil in the use of Scripture for the attainment of these
spiritual values. This requires that he be made intimately
acquainted with Scripture readings particularly appropriate for
thanksgiving, comfort, encouragement, and other common needs.
It requires also that he learn the purpose and benefits of, as well
as ways of procedure in, individual and family worship, since the
objectives of Bible reading cannot be achieved except by frequent
communion with God in prayer and in meditation upon His Word.

## Types of Bible Reading

Sometimes Bible reading is distinguished as being either
devotional, instructional, or cursory, though in reality these classi-
fications overlap. This is seen in the Bible History instruction,
which falls into all three classes.

*Devotional reading* is designed for edification, application to
the problems of life, and appreciation of the beauty, comfort, and
power of the Word of God. It is designed to strengthen the Christian in his faith and life. The Scripture readings in the morning
devotions offer one of the best means of teaching children how to
use the Word of God for devotional purposes. Bible reading in
the family devotion is another example.

*Instructional reading* aims more toward knowledge of the Bible.
The Bible stories listed in the Catechism, used to clarify and
illustrate the Catechism teachings, are examples of this type of
reading. The reading of Scripture to find answers to specific
questions and the practice of reading the Gospel and Epistle lessons
for the following Sunday also fall into this classification.

By *cursory reading* is meant the reading of an entire book
or section of a book giving the connected story of an event or
period or person, such as the story of Abraham, Joseph, etc.

A report in writing in a few short sentences, or a few leading questions after the pupil has read the assignment, may be part of this study. Cursory reading may be done individually or in the class period.

## C. METHOD

**General Suggestions**

The study of the organization and arrangement of the Bible is necessary, but is not to be overstressed. Frequent Bible reading, with appropriate suggestions from time to time, will bring about a ready familiarity with the Book. Mechanical drill is reduced to a minimum, though a certain amount of it is necessary to enable the pupil to use the Bible intelligently and efficiently.

Drill helps to establish the division between the Old and the New Testament, to fix the names, location, and approximate length of the various books, and other matters of a purely mechanical nature. Important among these is the development of a "place memory" for outstanding passages, among which those listed below deserve consideration:

The Creation, Genesis 1 and 2; The Fall of Man, Genesis 3; The Giving of the Law, Exodus 20:1-17; The Aaronitic Blessing, Numbers 6:24-26; Penitential Psalms (choose a favorite), 6, 32, 38, 51, 102, 130, 143; Main Prophecies of Christ's Death, Psalms 22 and 69, Isaiah 53; Christ's Birth, Luke 2:1-20; Christ's Passion, Matthew 26 and 27, Mark 14 and 15, Luke 22 and 23, John 18 and 19; The Sermon in the Mount, Matthew 5—7; Christ's Intercessory Prayer, John 17; Joy in Heaven, Revelation 7:9-17.

Two extremes are to be avoided in Bible reading: extensive reading with little understanding, and too limited reading with excessive expository comment. Both are likely to defeat the purpose of the lesson. The reading should be reasonably extensive, with enough explanation and questioning interposed to make the lesson clear. It is the teacher's task to find the right balance in his own class.

To be effective, the reading must be deliberate and unhurried. It is better to reduce the length of the selections than to render them ineffective by haste.

The method of reading may be varied to provide for individual, responsive, chorus (rarely), silent, or oral reading. Map studies or question periods may be used occasionally for variety. The Socialized Recitation lends itself well to Bible reading. See Footnote 4 under Bible History, p. 25.

The use of cross references, commentaries, concordances, and Bible dictionaries is taught incidentally in the Bible reading period, or at such times as the need or opportunity for their use arises.

In every case the teacher must make every effort for maximum interest and instruction that a lively and lasting love for the Bible and its contents may result.

## Time

As a rule, Bible reading is begun in the fifth grade and continued through the eighth. In addition to the short readings in the morning devotions and the correlation with other school subjects, two separate periods of from 15 to 20 minutes each per week are generally set aside for this subject. The time available depends largely upon the number of teachers in the school.

In one-room schools only a single period is available, and more of the regular reading periods may be set aside for Bible reading. Or time may be gained by assigning portions of Scripture for silent reading. For maximum benefit to the pupil, this requires a clear assignment which indicates the purpose of the selection. A subsequent brief class discussion is necessary to make sure that the reading has been completed and understood.

## Materials

Careful selection of materials is made from the voluminous content of the Bible. Entire books or selections from books may be read. When entire books of the Bible or longer sections of books are read, it is important to discuss the specific purpose and content, and the writer of the book when he is known. Knowledge of the setting of the book makes for greater interest and better learning.

Readings may be adapted to the church year in as far as that is possible. Lessons may be made up of parallel passages showing prophecy and fulfillment. Series of readings of the miracles of the Old or the New Testament may be arranged. A concordance will supply suggestions for arranging similar units.

The fact that there is considerable repetition of materials studied in Bible History, especially when the Gospels and Acts are read, helps to fix these accounts the more permanently in the minds of the pupils.

## D. COURSE SUGGESTIONS [1]

The schedules below are arranged for two lessons per grade per week. With more than one grade in the room, the work is alternated. In one-room schools a four-year alternation plan provides a satisfactory arrangement. If the material is too extensive, the quantity, not the quality of instruction, is to be reduced.

---

1) *Note:* Some of the schedules under *Course Suggestions* are patterned largely after the Wisconsin Course of Study for Lutheran Schools, 1928. Used by permission.

### Fifth Grade

*Schedule I:* This schedule, intended for the first Bible-reading period of the week, is based principally on Matthew and the church year. The order of readings will vary somewhat with the church year.

Lessons 1—14: Matt. 3—16 (one chapter each lesson).

Lesson 15: *Christmas:* Matt. 1:1, 17-25; Matt. 2.

Lessons 16—20: Matt. 17—21 (one chapter each lesson).

Lesson 21: *Lent:* Matt. 26:1-46.

Lesson 22: *Lent:* Matt. 26:47-75; Matt. 27:1-10.

Lesson 23: *Lent:* Matt. 27:11-66.

Lesson 24: *Lent:* Ps. 22.

Lesson 25: *Lent:* Ps. 69.

Lesson 26: *Lent:* Is. 53.

Lesson 27: *Easter:* Matt. 28.

Lessons 28—31: Matt. 22—25 (one chapter each lesson).

Lesson 32: *Ascension:* Ps. 47; Ps. 110.

Lesson 33: *Pentecost:* Gal. 5; Gal. 6:1-10.

Lesson 34: *Penitence:* Ps. 6; Ps. 32.

Lesson 35: *Comfort:* Ps. 23; Ps. 126.

Lesson 36: *Praise:* Ps. 100; Ps. 103.

*Schedule II:* This schedule is intended for the second period of the week. It provides guidance in reading the Bible for specific purposes and for the solution of specific problems.

Lesson 1: When discouraged: Is. 40; Ps. 43.

Lesson 2: When the world is good to you: Deut. 8.

Lesson 3: When your faith wavers: Heb. 11.

Lesson 4: When things go against you: Ps. 27.

Lesson 5: To find joy for church attendance: Ps. 84.

Lesson 6: When sins trouble you: Ps. 51.

Lesson 7: When you become indifferent toward God: Rev. 3.

Lesson 8: When seeking forgiveness: Ps. 32.
When you travel: Ps. 121.

Lesson 9: When you feel blue: Ps. 34.

Lesson 10: Same as 9: John 14.

Lesson 11: When you are lonely and fearful: Ps. 23; 1 Pet. 5:7.

Lesson 12: When God seems far away: Ps. 42; Ps. 139.

Lesson 13: When you are in danger: Ps. 91.

Lesson 14: When you are tempted: Matt. 4:1-11.

Lesson 15: Same as 14: Rom. 6.

Lesson 16: When you are sick: Matt. 9:1-8; Ps. 39; Ps. 91.

Lesson 17: In times of severe trial: Rom. 8; 1 Pet. 4:12, 13.

Lesson 18: When in sorrow over death: John 11.

Lesson 19: Same as 18: John 14.

Lesson 20: Same as 18: 1 Cor. 15.

Lesson 21: When you worry: Matt. 6:19-34.

Lesson 22: When you are angry: Matt. 6:14, 15; Col. 3:12-17.

Lesson 23: When you grow bitter and critical: 1 Cor. 13.

Lesson 24: When weary and heavy laden: Is. 55; Matt. 11:28-30.

Lesson 25: Encouragement to pray: Luke 11:1-13.

Lesson 26: The Gospel in brief: John 3:16; Rom. 3:19-28; Rom. 1:16, 17.

Lesson 27: Assurance of conversion: Eph. 2.

Lesson 28: If you want your life to be fruitful: John 15.

Lesson 29: Same as 28: Jas. 1.

Lesson 30: Same as 28: Jas. 2.

Lesson 31: Same as 28: Rom. 12.

Lesson 32: When you forget your blessings: Ps. 103.

Lesson 33: For strength against worldliness: 1 John 2:15-17; 1 Tim. 6.

Lesson 34: To get enjoyment out of church work: Gal. 6:9; Jas. 5:20; Dan. 12:1-3; Hag. 1:2-8.

Lesson 35: For the assurance that Christ intercedes for you: John 17.

Lesson 36: For a description of heaven: Rev. 7:9-17; Rev. 21.

## Sixth Grade

In the sixth grade the Gospel according to St. Luke is read in its entirety. The books of the Bible are studied and memorized, and brief selections from each book are read. This must not develop into mechanical exercise or speed contests. One period a week is devoted largely to the reading of passages appropriate to the church year. The last two weeks are spent in reading parallel passages of prophecy and fulfillment.

### First Week

*First Period:* The Bible (The Book); Old Test., New Test. (Covenant); Language: Old Test. in Hebrew, New Test. in Greek; Translations: Authorized (King James) Version in English, Luther's in German, hundreds of others; Old Test.: 39 books, New Test.: 27 books. *Put necessary data on the blackboard.*

*Second Period:* Read Luke 3.

### Second Week

I. Books of Old Testament: a. 17 historical; b. 5 poetic (Job, Psalms, Proverbs, Ecclesiastes, Song of Solomon); c. 17 prophetic. — The five books of Moses (Pentateuch): Genesis (origin), Exodus (departure), Leviticus (worship), Numbers (Moses numbered the people), Deuteronomy (repetition of the Law); Joshua (brings Israel into Canaan); Judges (deliverers); Ruth (a Gentile, an ancestress of Christ). Spend some time drilling names of books.

II. Read Luke 4.

### Third Week

I. Review the lessons of the first period in the two previous weeks. Read: Gen. 1:1-3; Gen. 6:13-15; Gen. 50:24; Ex. 6:6-8; Ex. 20:12; Lev. 1:1-4; Num. 1:45-47; Deut. 28:1, 2; Josh. 4:1-7; Judg. 7:5-8; Ruth 1:16-18.

II. Read Luke 5.

### Fourth Week

I. Two books of Samuel (a prophet); Two books of Kings (first kings: Saul, David, Solomon); Two books of Chronicles (records); Ezra and Nehemiah (under whom the Jews returned from the Babylonian captivity after 70 years); Esther (a Jewess who saved her people from destruction). Read: 1 Sam. 3:1; 1 Sam. 9:1, 2; 1 Sam. 16:1; 2 Sam. 16:5, 6; 1 Kings 2:1-3; 2 Kings 5:1-3; 2 Chron. 2:1, 2; Ezra 7:27, 28; Neh. 9:6.

II. Read Luke 6.

### Fifth Week

I. Review books up to Esther. Poetic books: Job (a great sufferer); Psalms (sacred songs); Proverbs (wise sayings); Ecclesiastes (a guide to a pious and happy life); Song of Solomon (a song concerning Christ, the Bridegroom, and the Church, His bride). Read: Job 1:20-22; Job 19:25-27; Ps. 25:8, 9; Ps. 90:2; Ps. 150:1; Prov. 14:34; Prov. 24:21, 22; Eccl. 12:13, 14; Eccl. 9:11.

II. Read Luke 7.

### Sixth Week

I. Four major prophets; Isaiah, Jeremiah (Lamentations), Ezekiel, Daniel. Twelve minor prophets: Hosea, Joel, Amos, Obadiah, Jonah, Micah, Nahum, Habakkuk, Zephaniah, Haggai, Zechariah, Malachi. Spend some time drilling names of prophets. If time permits, read: Is. 5:20; Dan. 12:3; Lam. 3:22, 23; Zech. 9:9; Mic. 5:2; Ezek. 36:26, 27; Jer. 33:16; Hos. 13:14; Amos 8:11; Joel 2:13; Mal. 3:1; Zeph. 3:9.

II. Read Luke 8.

### Seventh Week

I. Review names of the books of the Old Testament and classify them, viz.: 17 historical, 5 poetic, 17 prophetic books. Read: Ezra 3:10; Mal. 3:1; Neh. 9:6; Jer. 33:8; Job 27:4; Ps. 25:7; Prov. 23:26; Is. 61:10; Jonah 3:10; Eccl. 12:13; Ps. 34:8; Is. 12:2.

II. Read Luke 9.

### Eighth Week

I. Four Gospels (life of Christ): Matthew (a publican); Mark (a Levite); Luke (a physician); John (whom Jesus loved especially); The Acts (deeds of the apostles), by Luke. Read: Luke 22:22; Acts 11:18; Mark 1:35; Matt. 10:28; John 9:2, 3; Acts 15:1; Luke 8:12; Mark 13:27; Matt. 21:15; Acts 5:19, 20; Luke 10:41, 42; John 14:21.

II. Read Luke 10.

### Ninth Week

I. Thirteen Epistles (letters) of St. Paul: Romans, 2 Corinthians, Galatians, Ephesians, Philippians, Colossians, 2 Thessalonians, 2 Timothy, Titus, and Philemon; Hebrews, Epistle of James, 2 Peter, 3 John, Jude, Revelation (prophecies of the future of the Church). Drill names. Read: Heb. 1:9; Rom. 8:16, 17; 1 Tim. 3:16; Rev. 1:18; 1 Cor. 13:13; Eph. 6:1, 2; Rom. 8:32; Heb. 7:26; Gal. 4:4, 5; 1 Pet. 2:24; 1 John 2:1, 2; Col. 2:9.

II. Read Luke 11.

### Tenth Week

I. Review books of the New Testament. Read: John 1:29; Rev. 5:9; 2 Pet. 2:1; Rom. 4:25; John 11:25, 26; 2 Cor. 5:21; 1 John 3:8; Matt. 17:5; Heb. 13:8; Acts 4:12; Eph. 4:24; Jas. 2:19.

II. Read Luke 12.

### Eleventh Week

I. Discuss briefly the church year.[2]

II. Read Luke 13.

---

2) See course in Church History, p. 80; also *Lutheran Hymnal*, pp. 3, 158—161.

### Twelfth Week

I. Discuss the church year.

II. Read Luke 14.

### Thirteenth Week

I. Read Advent texts: Gen. 3:15; Gen. 12:1-3; Gen. 49:8-10; Num. 24: 17:19; Deut. 18:15; 2 Sam. 7:12, 13; Ps. 24; Ps. 50:1, 2; Ps. 118:24-26.

II. Read Luke 15.

### Fourteenth Week

I. Advent texts: Is. 7:14; Is. 11:1, 2; Jer. 23:5, 6; Micah 5:2; Hag. 2: 6-9; Zech. 9:9; Mal. 3:1.

II. Read Luke 1.

### Fifteenth Week

I. Christmas texts: Is. 9:6, 7; Matt. 1:18-25; Titus 2:11-14; 1 John 4:9; Heb. 1:1, 2.

II. Read Luke 2.

### Sixteenth Week

I. Epiphany texts: Ps. 72:8-11; Is. 40:9-11; Is. 60:1-3; Zech. 8:22; Matt. 2:1, 2; Matt. 28:18-20; Luke 14:23; Rom. 10:14, 15; Rev. 7:9, 10.

II. Read Luke 16.

### Seventeenth Week

I. The Bible, God's Word: The writers, men, but the author, God. Thus we read 100 times: "God spoke to Moses." Read: Ex. 9:1; Ex. 20:1-6; Lev. 20:1, 2; Deut. 10:1, 2; God spoke to Isaiah: 1:1-3; to Jeremiah: 1:1, 2; to Ezekiel: 1:1-3; to Paul: 1 Cor. 11:23; 1 Cor. 15:3; Gal. 1:11, 12.

II. Read Luke 17.

### Eighteenth Week

I. The Bible, God's Word: Given by inspiration: 2 Pet. 1:20, 21; 1 Cor. 2:13. Purpose of Bible: 2 Tim. 3:15-17. Our duty toward the Word of God: Rev. 22:18, 19; John 5:39; Luke 11:28.

II. Read Luke 18.

### Nineteenth Week

I. Family Devotions: Spend the first periods of the nineteenth and twentieth weeks in discussing the why and how of family worship. Plan with the children a number of family devotions. Select Scripture readings, hymns, and prayers that might be used. Let them examine various books intended for family devotions. Call their attention to the suggested daily Bible readings in the *Lutheran Hymnal*.[3] Urge them to discuss the question of family devotions with their parents.

II. Read Luke 19.

### Twentieth Week

I. Family devotions: See above.

II. Read Luke 20.

### Twenty-first Week

I. Lenten texts: Gen. 3:15; 1 John 1:7; Eph. 1:7; Heb. 9:12-14; Heb. 9:18-22; Heb. 9:27, 28; Rev. 12:10, 11.

II. Read Luke 21.

### Twenty-second Week

I. Lenten texts: Is. 43:24, 25; Hos. 13:14; 1 Pet. 2:21; 1 Pet. 3:18.

II. Read Luke 22.

---

3) Pp. 161—164.

### Twenty-third Week

I. Lenten texts: 2 Cor. 5:21; 1 Pet. 1:18. 19; 1 Pet. 2:21-25; Heb. 10:12-18.

II. Read Luke 23.

### Twenty-fourth Week

I. Lenten reading: Is. 53.

II. Read Luke 26.

### Twenty-fifth Week

I. Lenten reading: Psalm 22.

II. Read Matt. 27.

### Twenty-sixth Week

I. Seven words of Christ on the cross: (1) Luke 23:34; (2) Luke 23:43; (3) John 19:26, 27; (4) Matt. 27:46; Mark 15:34; (5) John 19:28; (6) John 19:30; (7) Luke 23:46.

II. Read John 19.

### Twenty-seventh Week

I. Easter reading: Ex. 12:1-27.

II. Read Luke 24.

### Twenty-eighth Week

I. Easter texts: Job 19:25-27; Ps. 16:9, 10; Is. 26:19, 20; Matt. 28:1-10.

II. Read 1 Cor. 15:1-28.

### Twenty-ninth Week

I. Easter texts: Mark 16:1-6; 1 Cor. 15:35-37.

II. Read John 20:1-18.

### Thirtieth Week

I. Easter texts: Rev. 1:17, 18; Ezek. 37:1-14.

II. Read John 11:1-45.

### Thirty-first Week

I. Appearances of Christ after Resurrection: John 20:11-17; Matt. 28:9, 10; 1 Cor. 15:5; Luke 24:13-31; Luke 24:36-43.

II. Appearances: John 20:24-29; John 21:1-19; 1 Cor. 15:6; 1 Cor. 15:7; Acts 9:1-5.

### Thirty-second Week

I. Ascension texts: Matt. 28:16-20; Mark 16:15-20; Luke 24:50-53; Acts 1:9-12.

II. Election of another apostle: Acts 1:15-26.

### Thirty-third Week

I. Pentecost texts: Joel 2:28-32; John 14:25, 26; Acts 2:1-16.

II. Review the books of the Bible. Practice the finding of passages, perhaps the following: 2 Tim. 1:12; Gen. 15:6; Rom. 4:5; Phil. 3:21; Dan. 12:2; Rev. 14:13; Matt. 7:13; John 10:27, 28; 1 John 3:2; Is. 63:16; Eph. 3: 14, 15; Ezek. 22:26; Luke 12:32; 1 Pet. 1:5; Ps. 145:15, 16; James 1:13, 14; Prov. 1:10; Job 5:19; 2 Tim. 4:18; Amos 9:11.

*Caution:* The practice of finding Bible passages should not become a speed contest. All children are to find the passage, and one is called upon to read while the rest follow the reading in their Bibles.

### Thirty-fourth Week

I. Trinity texts: Gen. 1:26; Num. 6:24-27; Matt. 3:14-17; Matt. 28: 18-20; 2 Cor. 13:14.

II. Trinity texts: Is. 6:1-8; John 16:5-7; John 16:12-15.

### Thirty-fifth Week

I. Prophecy and fulfillment. Parallel texts: Born of a virgin: Is. 7:14 — Matt. 1:23; in Bethlehem: Micah 5:2 — Matt. 2:5 ff.; called out of Egypt: Hos. 11:1 — Matt. 2:13-15; preceded by John: Mal. 3:1 — Mark 1:1-3; a true Shepherd of His flock: Ezek. 34:11,12 — John 10:11-16.

II. As above: Rides into Jerusalem: Zech. 9:9 — Matt. 21:5-7; sold for thirty pieces of silver: Zech. 11:12,13 — Matt. 26:15; betrayed: Ps. 41:9 — Luke 22:47, 48; spit upon: Is. 50:6 — Matt. 26:67; mocked: Ps. 22: 7, 8 — Matt. 27:39-44; smitten on the cheek: Micah 5:1 — John 18:22.

### Thirty-sixth Week

I. Prophecy and fulfillment: Given gall to drink: Ps. 69:21 — Matt. 27:34; crucified: Num. 21:9; John 3:14 — Luke 23:33; garments divided: Ps. 22:18 — John 19:23, 24; pierced: Zech. 12:10 — John 19:32-35; divine person: Ps. 2:7 — Acts 13:33.

II. As above: A king's Son: Is. 9:6, 7 — Matt. 28:18; carried our griefs: Is. 53:4 — John 1:29; not to be left in the grave: Ps. 16:10 — Acts 13:35; to come again in the clouds: Dan. 7:13 — Luke 21:27; to reign forever: Dan. 7:14, 27 — Luke 1:33.

## Seventh Grade

The Gospel according to St. Mark and Paul's Epistle to the Romans are read in their entirety in the seventh grade.

Four periods are devoted to a review of Schedule II under the Fifth Grade. The purpose is to emphasize the value of the Bible in the solution of life's problems. Copies of the schedule should be in the hands of the pupils. These may be duplicated or written on the blackboard and copied by the pupils on the flyleaf of their Bibles. As far as time permits, selections of this schedule should be read and discussed.

The second period of each week is devoted to the reading of varied portions of Scripture with which the pupils ought to be acquainted. Some adaptations to the church year are made in the outline below.

| First Period of Week | Second Period of Week |
| --- | --- |
| 1. Mark 1. | Ex. 20: Law of God. |
| 2. Mark 2. | Ex. 40: Tabernacle of God. |
| 3. Mark 3. | Lev. 16: Feast of Atonement. |
| 4. Mark 4. | Deut. 34: Moses' death. |
| 5. Mark 5. | Josh. 24: Joshua's death. |
| 6. Mark 6. | Judg. 13: Samson's birth. |
| 7. Mark 7. | Judg. 14: Samson's marriage. |
| 8. Mark 8. | Judg. 15: Samson's revenge. |
| 9. Mark 9. | 2 Thess. 2; Ps. 46: Reformation. |
| 10. Mark 10. | 2 Kings 23:1-28: Reformation under Josiah. |
| 11. Mark 11. | Is. 35: Church of the New Testament. |
| 12. Mark 12. | Is. 54: Comfort of the Church. |
| 13. Mark 13. | Is. 55; Deut. 8: Thanksgiving. |
| 14. Mark 14. | Ps. 24: Advent. |

| First Period of Week | Second Period of Week |
|---|---|
| 15. Mark 15. | Is. 9:1-8; 40:1-11: Advent. |
| 16. Mark 16. | 1 Sam. 1: Birth of Samuel. |
| 17. Rom. 1. | 1 Sam. 10: Saul anointed king. |
| 18. Rom. 2. | 2 Sam. 1: David mourns Saul's death. |
| 19. Rom. 3. | 1 Kings 3: Solomon's prayer and wisdom. |
| 20. Rom. 4. | 1 Cor. 13: Praise of charity. |
| 21. Rom. 5. | Prov. 4: A guide to a happy life. |
| 22. Rom. 6. | Eccl. 1: All earthly things are vanity. |
| 23. Rom. 7. | Is. 53: Prophecy of Christ's Passion. |
| 24. Rom. 8. | Ps. 38 and 143: Penitential psalms. |
| 25. Rom. 9. | Ps. 20 and 130: Penitential psalms. |
| 26. Rom. 10. | John 17: Christ's high-priestly prayer. |
| 27. Rom. 11. | 1 Cor. 15:1-28: Resurrection of the dead. |
| 28. Rom. 12. | 1 Cor. 15:29-58: Resurrection of the dead. |
| 29. Rom. 13. | Matt. 5: Sermon in the Mount. |
| 30. Rom. 14. | Matt. 6: As above. |
| 31. Rom. 15. | Matt. 7: As above. |
| 32. Rom. 16. | Eph. 6: Table of Duties and weapons of the Christians. |
| 33. Review Schedule | 1 Thess. 5: Description of last days. |
| 34. II under Fifth | Rev. 2: Letters to churches in Asia Minor. |
| 35. Grade. See intro- | Rev. 3: As above. |
| 36. duction above. | Rev. 21: The eternal city. |

### Eighth Grade

The eighth-grade schedule provides for the reading of the Gospel according to St. John, the Acts, and Galations in full. A number of additional topical selections serve either to review portions previously read, or to widen the pupil's acquaintance with the Bible and thereby to nurture his spiritual life.

| First Period of Week | Second Period of Week |
|---|---|
| 1. John 1. | John 2. |
| 2. John 3. | John 4. |
| 3. John 5. | John 6. |
| 4. John 7. | John 8. |
| 5. John 9. | John 10. |
| 6. John 11. | John 12. |
| 7. John 13. | John 14. |
| 8. John 15. | John 16. |
| 9. John 17. | John 18. |
| 10. John 19. | John 20. |
| 11. John 21. | Acts 1. |
| 12. Acts 2. | Acts 3. |
| 13. Acts 4. | Acts 5. |
| 14. Acts 6. | Acts 7. |

| First Period of Week | Second Period of Week |
|---|---|
| 15. Acts 8. | Acts 9. |
| 16. Acts 10. | Acts 11. |
| 17. Acts 12. | Acts 13. |
| 18. Acts 14. | Acts 15. |
| 19. Acts 16. | Gen. 14: Abraham rescues Lot. |
| 20. Acts 17. | Gen. 21:9-21: Hagar cast forth. |
| 21. Acts 18. | Gen. 23: Sarah's death. |
| 22. Acts 19. | Gen. 48: Jacob adopts and blesses Ephraim and Manasseh. |
| 23. Acts 20. | Ex. 15:1-21: Song of Moses. |
| 24. Acts 21. | 2 Pet. 3:3-14: The last days. |
| 25. Acts 22. | Heb. 10:14-39: Christ's blood cleanses, but beware of sin. |
| 26. Acts 23. | Eph. 5:1-21: Exhortation to lead a godly life. |
| 27. Acts 24. | Is. 1:1-20: Exhortation to repentance. |
| 28. Acts 25. | Ps. 22 and Ps. 69: Messianic psalms. |
| 29. Acts 26. | Is. 53: Messianic prophecy. |
| 30. Acts 27. | Rev. 22: The eternal city. |
| 31. Acts 28. | Josh. 2: Rahab hides the spies. |
| 32. Gal. 1. | 1 Sam. 6—7:1: The Ark returned. |
| 33. Gal. 2. | 1 Kings 12:26—13:10: Jeroboam's idolatry. |
| 34. Gal. 3. | 2 Kings 6:1-23: The Syrians blinded. |
| 35. Gal. 4. | 2 Kings 10:1-28: Ahab's sons and Baal's worshipers destroyed. |
| 36. Gal. 5 and 6. | Dan. 4: Nebuchadnezzar's fall. |

## E. CORRELATION POSSIBILITIES

*Religion.* The content of the Catechism and Bible History is taken directly from Scripture; generally speaking, the morning devotions are incomplete without a Scripture reading; Church history can be understood only against its background of Biblical history; memory material is selected largely from the Bible.

*Reading.* Entire reading periods may be devoted occasionally to Bible reading, this especially in one-room schools where time is at a premium.

*Spelling.* Biblical terms and names may be studied in a spelling lesson.

*Language.* Biblical events may serve as topics for language exercises and compositions. The writing of original religious verse based on Bible texts is encouraged.

*Arithmetic.* Biblical weights and measures may be studied.

*Geography.* Reference is made to the Creation and other works of God as recorded in the Bible. Pertinent passages of the Bible are read.

*History.* Biblical history is used to illustrate how God rules in the affairs of men (Israel, Balaam, David), how He blesses righteous and punishes disobedient nations and rulers, and how He can preserve whole nations against famine and enemies (Israel).

*Civics.* References such as the Decalog, Rom. 13, 1 Tim. 2, Matt. 22, Titus 3, and 1 Peter 2 are adduced.

*Science.* Ps. 148 or similar passages are read.

*Health and Safety Education.* Passages such as Ps. 91 may be read.

*Music and Art.* Passages which have inspired hymns or masterpieces of art are read as the latter are studied.

*Note:* These suggestions are merely illustrative, but they indicate that in the Christian school the Bible finds daily use as a guide and handbook in many situations apart from the regular religion lesson. It should be remembered that it is largely this use of the Bible, together with the natural references to Bible facts in the conversation between teacher and pupils, which distinguishes the Lutheran school from the purely secular institution.

## F. EVALUATING OUTCOMES

In evaluating the success of his instruction, the teacher will readily note how well his pupils know the arrangement and order of the Bible. He will check their skill in locating books, chapters, and verses, and their ability to use the cross references, the concordance, and the Bible dictionary.

More difficult to evaluate, but of much greater importance, is the attitude which his pupils take toward the Bible and the use they make of it. The following questions will aid in checking this phase:

Is there any evidence that the pupil appreciates the Bible as a gift of God?

Is he reverent when the Word of God is read, studied, or preached?

Does he understand that the entire Bible centers about Christ?

Does he treat the Bible as a book reverently?

Is he able to comfort himself with Scripture passages and to make application of Scripture to other problems of life?

It is evident that it will be difficult, often impossible, to determine the answers to these questions accurately, but the teacher will observe, admonish, instruct, and train his children with these standards in mind and note carefully the progress along these lines. A check list for the class or for the individual pupils with space for plus or minus marks to indicate positive or negative behavior will be useful.

## Selected References

The Bible (King James Version; one with cross references, concordance, and Bible dictionary preferred, also for pupil use).

*Advanced* and *Elementary Bible History*. Concordia.

*Course of Study in Religion*. Minnesota District, 1939.

Davis, John D., *Dictionary of the Bible*. Philadelphia: Westminster Press, 1925. (Available at Concordia.)

Drewes, Chr. F., *Introduction to the Books of the Bible*. Concordia, 1929.

*Manual and Course of Study for the Lutheran Schools of Wisconsin*. South Wisconsin District, 1928.

Schaller, John, *The Book of Books*. Concordia, 1924.

Stellhorn, A. C., *Manual for Lutheran Saturday Schools*. Concordia, 1935.

Walker, J. B. R., *Comprehensive Concordance to the Holy Scriptures*. Macmillan, 1941. (Available at Concordia.)

## 8. Church History [1]

### A. GENERAL OBJECTIVES

1. The realization that the world continues to exist solely for the expansion of Christ's Church on earth and that God guides its history in accordance with this purpose.

2. Knowledge of a connected chain of the main events which make up the history of the Church.

3. The ability to understand the present and to plan the future on the basis of the lessons which Church History teaches.

4. An understanding and appreciation of the history, organization, practices, and literature of the Lutheran Church, especially of the Missouri Synod.

5. Grateful appreciation of the benefits and willing acceptance of the duties which Church membership implies.

### B. CHURCH HISTORY IN THE LUTHERAN SCHOOLS

#### Fundamental Concepts

Fundamental to the study of Church History in the Lutheran School is the realization that it centers about Christ, that the Church is the Lord's institution, and that for its sake the world still continues to exist. From the time of Adam, God has guided the affairs of the world with the ultimate welfare of the believers in view, as Biblical history clearly indicates. All secular history eventually "works together for good to them that love God" (Rom. 8:28) and cannot be properly interpreted without a knowledge of Church History.

---

1) *Note:* Though Church History appears in the group of religious subjects, it occupies merely a related, supplementary position. Church History is not religion unless it is Biblical History.

## The Function of Church History

The study of subject matter in Church History cannot be overemphasized. The period covered by Biblical history, the Reformation, and Missouri Synod history receive special emphasis, but these must be adequately linked with the intervening periods to provide a connected chain of events. The history of the early Christian Church and its growth amidst persecution, the spiritual decline of the Lutheran Church in the centuries after the Reformation, and the immigration of the Saxons in 1839 and of the Bavarians in 1845 occupy important places as connecting links. American Lutheran history in general is of necessity considered only briefly.

A knowledge of the heroic struggles of our spiritual forefathers, of their trials and tribulations, will serve to strengthen the Church of the present in its difficulties. The fact that the Church survived under the most violent attacks and persecutions and always returned with renewed strength bears out the word of God "The gates of hell shall not prevail against it" (Matt. 16:18) and establishes it as an institution of God. It inspires with courage in days of adversity and makes for joyful and hopeful labor in the kingdom of God. It is important that the child acquire this confidence in the future of the Church.

Church History is a story of continuous cause and effect. The child must learn that the Church's prosperity has always depended upon its faithfulness to the divine commission to teach all nations. Periods in which interest in the salvation of others waned were periods also of internal disintegration, because seeking one's own salvation cannot exist apart from concern for the souls of others. Similarly, failure to join the future generations to the present by neglecting to indoctrinate the children in the Word of God invariably led to decay and corruption. Periods of zeal in spiritual matters, on the other hand, brought renewed strength and made the Church an important factor in the lives and affairs of men. An understanding of these truths on the part of its members will help to determine the right course for the Church of the present and future, and it is therefore one of the chief aims of the Church History course in school.

Study of the Reformation and of distinctively Lutheran Church history and practices, especially Missouri Synod history, practices, and organization, will establish the necessity of maintaining a separate Church body for doctrinal reasons and lead to an appreciation of the Lutheran heritage of purely Scriptural doctrine and practice. Acquaintance with the history and contents of Lutheran literature, the Catechism, hymns, and confessional writings leads to a greater appreciation of the heritage of the fathers.

The history of the local congregation and school is always an interesting chapter in the course, and also contributes its part toward training in intelligent and willing participation in the work of the Church.

The end and aim is always a grateful appreciation of the benefits and a willing acceptance of the .duties which Church membership implies and a consecrated zeal in the work of the Church.

## C. METHOD. TIME DIVISION

**Method**

The method of teaching Church History may well be the same as that for any other content subject as long as it provides for class discussion, individual reading and study, and oral and written reports.

Important for the successful use of any method is the arousing and sustaining of interest. This is not difficult in Church History. The heroic struggles of the Church in the face of persecution and adversities, the inspiring lives of prominent individuals, such as Luther, Walther, Wyneken, and others, and the constant effort of the Church to reach as many people as possible with the Gospel of salvation — these can be made to appeal to the fancy of boys and girls as much as stories of adventure.

To make the most of any method in Church History instruction, the school library must contain a wealth of biographical and other Church History material for use as collateral reading or reports of various types.

### Division of Time

The amount of time to be set aside for this subject on the school program depends largely upon the type of school and the extent to which Church History is correlated with other subjects. A school of three or more rooms will have more time available than smaller schools. A school in which a systematic plan of correlation with other school subjects has been devised will need less time for the treatment of Church History as an individual subject than where this is not the case.

A twenty- or thirty-minute period four or five times a week during a quarter or semester of the school year is preferable to one period a week throughout the year, because concentration upon a subject makes for better learning. In some cases the regular history course may be arranged to allow for a quarter of Church History each year.

The regular religion period is not to be used except for the study of purely Biblical history.

## D. COURSE SUGGESTIONS

Several factors combine to make the arrangement of a course in Church History difficult. The lack of a definite text is keenly felt; the wealth of varied materials on Church History, biography, and missions requires careful consideration and selection; and the difference in the amount of time available in various schools demands utmost flexibility. Until the proposed text in Church History appears, the following outline is suggested.

### Lower Grades (1—4)

The course consists largely of the inspired history (Bible History). The festivals of the Church within the comprehension of the children receive special attention in the Bible History period. The stories of the Reformation and the Saxon immigration are related or read. *The Life of Luther,* by Albert H. Miller, may be used as a text by those who are able to read. Congregational and general church activities, the mission festival and the like, as far as they affect the children of this age group, receive attention. Simple biographical materials and mission stories may be selected to create an interest in, and understanding of, important phases of Church history. The children are given an opportunity to contribute for mission purposes.

### Grades 5 and 6

One 20-minute period per week throughout the year, two periods per week for one semester, or four periods per week for a quarter of nine weeks should be allowed in these grades. Preferably the formal study is confined to one quarter, and correlation is carried on throughout the year.

*The Life of Luther,* by Gustav Just, may be used as a text, with chapters 1—10 providing the basis for instruction in even-numbered years (1942—1943; 1944—1945), and chapters 11—20 in odd-numbered years (1943—1944; 1945—1946).

In addition the history of the local congregation and school may be studied the first year, while literature pertaining to Synod and District may be read in connection with the study of the District the second year. For suggestions and outlines see *Guide in the Study of Missions.*

The *Church History Inserts,* available to teachers and pupils free of charge, are used as part of the regular history course.

### Grades 7 and 8

Except where each grade has its own teacher, grades 7 and 8 are combined in one class, and the work is alternated.

If possible, 36 periods of 20 or 30 minutes each are devoted to the study of Church History each year, preferably in one quarter to preserve the continuity of the subject.

Current church events and directed reading of the *Lutheran Witness* and *Concordia Messenger* provide opportunity for the incidental study of Church History throughout these grades.

The *Church History Inserts* are used in the regular history course.

### Even-Numbered Years (1942—1943; 1944—1945)

Synodical history is studied in even-numbered years. The history of the Reformation is briefly reviewed at the beginning of the course and the connection between the Reformation and American Lutheran history shown. The *Guide in the Study of Missions* offers suggestions for supplementing the textbook. Suggested text: W. G. Polack, *The Building of a Great Church;* or Theo. Graebner, *The Story of Our Church in America.*

### Odd-Numbered Years (1943—1944; 1945—1946)

Study of the Confessions, the Common Service, common customs and practices of the Lutheran Church, and the church year is alternated with Church History in odd-numbered years. The *Educational Guide and Course of Study* of the Texas District [2] is recommended as a handbook for the second year's work. The division of lessons may well be observed. Certain sections may be supplemented from the *Concordia Cyclopedia* and other sources. The outline below is reprinted for the benefit of those to whom the Texas Course is not available. It is used by permission.

### The Lutheran Church

*Lesson 1*        **A. The Confessions of Our Lutheran Church**

**WHY OUR PUPILS SHOULD BE FAMILIAR WITH THE CONFESSIONS**

a. Our Confessions show that our Lutheran Church has plainly and consistently adhered to the clear and truthful teaching of God's own revelation and that many of the errors which have sprung up in modern times are simply a repetition of old heresies.

b. Every member of our Lutheran Church is expected to accept not only the Bible, but also the Confessions.

c. Our children will not only pledge themselves to adhere to the Lutheran Confessions (Confirmation), but, in later years, will exact such a pledge of their ministers and teachers.

d. Allegiance to our Lutheran Church ought to be a matter of intelligence and conviction, and not merely of custom.

---

2) Pp. 67—76.

*Lesson 2*.

## LUTHERAN CONFESSIONS

Our Lutheran Confessions, or Creeds, show how we understand and interpret the Bible. They are the presentation of the teachings of the Holy Scriptures and therefore the voice of the Christian Church, repeating what Christ and the Apostles have taught. They are also known as symbols, *i. e.,* marks or signs by which the followers of the Christian religion and the Lutheran Church are distinguished from the followers of other religions and denominations.

In their order of succession these Confessions are:

a. The Apostles' Creed.
b. The Nicene Creed.
c. The Athanasian Creed.
d. The Unaltered Augsburg Confession.
e. The Apology.
f. The Smalcald Articles.
g. Luther's Small Catechism.
h. Luther's Large Catechism.
i. The Formula of Concord.*

*Lesson 3*

## THE APOSTLES' CREED

The Apostles' Creed bears this name because it is a clear and condensed summary of the doctrine of the apostles as found in the New Testament. It had its origin in the formula of Baptism.

Though containing expressions which were in use in the time of the apostles and existing in a shorter form before the year 150 A.D., the Apostles' Creed in its present form was not completed before the end of the fifth century.

In the Third Article, Luther substituted the word *Christian* for *catholic* (universal) to obviate the misconception that reference is here made to the Roman Catholic Church.

*Lesson 4*

## THE NICENE CREED

The Nicene Creed received its name from the Council (general convention) of Nicea, Asia Minor (325 A.D.). Its present form it received from the Second Ecumenical Council, held at Constantinople (381 A.D.). The Third Ecumenical Council at Toledo, Spain (589 A.D.), inserted the phrase *and the Son* in the statement concerning the Holy Ghost.

The Nicene Creed was adopted by the Council of Bishops as a symbol against the Arian heresy, which denied that Christ is true God. The chief and successful opponent of Arius was Athanasius, a young deacon, also of Alexandria.

*Lesson 5*

Devote this lesson to the reading and a brief discussion of the Nicene Creed. *Lutheran Hymnal,* p. 22.

---

* Of these nine Confessions the first three existed before the Reformation and are known as Ecumenical (general, universal) Symbols because the truths which they contain are believed and confessed by all Christians.

*Lesson 6*
### THE ATHANASIAN CREED

The Athanasian Creed is said to be the most explicit statement of the doctrines of the Trinity to be found in the literature of the Church. Luther says of it: "I doubt if since the days of the apostles anything more important has ever been written in the Church of the New Testament."

Since this Creed was formulated not earlier than the year 450, Athanasius cannot be the author. He died in the year 373. It is called Athanasian because it embodies his teachings.

*Lesson 7*

Devote this lesson to the reading and to a brief discussion of the Athanasian Creed. *Lutheran Hymnal*, p. 53.

*Lesson 8*

Review briefly Lessons 1—7.

*Lesson 9*
### THE AUGSBURG CONFESSION

This confession was presented to Emperor Charles V at the Diet, or Reichstag (imperial diet), of Augsburg in the year 1530. Acting upon the proclamation of the emperor, Elector John of Saxony, on March 14, requested Luther, Jonas, Bugenhagen, and Melanchthon to draw up a document treating especially of "those articles on account of which division, both in faith and in other outward church customs and ceremonies, continues." Melanchthon wrote the Confession, basing it on material prepared by Luther. It was written in the German and Latin languages. The German copy was read publicly by Chancellor Beyer on June 25, 1530.

The Augsburg Confession is divided into two parts:
1. The chief articles of faith (1—21);
2. Articles in which are reviewed the abuses which have been corrected (22—28).

In 1540 Melanchthon published a Latin text, with some alterations, making concessions to the Reformed Church, especially in the article on the Lord's Supper. We hold to the Unaltered Augsburg Confession (U. A. C.).

*Lessons 10 and 11*

Devote these two lessons to the reading and to a brief discussion of a number of articles, and encourage the pupils to read the entire Augsburg Confession. Concordia Tract, No. 83.

*Lesson 12*
### THE APOLOGY

On the day after the Augsburg Confession had been read, the emperor instructed the papists to prepare an answer, a confutation. On July 12 or 13, 1530, they presented an answer which was returned to them as a "miserable, bulky botch," a "bungling document," to be rewritten. After five such attempts their "Confutation" was read before the Diet, August 7, 1530.

Melanchthon and others took notes when the "Confutation" was read and prepared a reply, a defense of the Augsburg Confession, known as the Apology. The Diet, on September 22, refused them permission to read it. — Rewritten and enlarged, it was adopted as a confession by the Lutheran princes and theologians.

Only those articles which the "Confutation" rejected are discussed extensively.

*Lesson 13*
#### THE SMALCALD ARTICLES

Because the Pope had called a general council to meet on May 8, 1537, at Mantua, Italy, to attempt "the utter extirpation of the poisonous, pestilential Lutheran heresy," Elector John Frederick of Saxony requested Luther to draw up a confession in which the attitude of the Protestants towards Rome should be re-stated. In 1537 the chief Lutheran theologians signed these articles in the city of Smalcald.

The Smalcald Articles consist of three main parts:
1. Four articles on the divine majesty;
2. Four articles on the office and work of Jesus Christ;
3. Fifteen articles of doctrine "to be discussed with reasonable men (not the papists, for they do not care about them)."

Furthermore, they contain a "Treatise on the Power and Primacy of the Pope," drawn up by Melanchthon at Smalcald at the suggestion of the Lutheran princes.

*Lesson 14*
#### THE SMALL AND THE LARGE CATECHISM OF LUTHER

Both the Small and the Large Catechism of Luther, written in 1529, treat the chief parts of the Christian doctrine.

The Small Catechism, intended primarily for children and the uninformed, renders service also to parents, teachers, and ministers for their own instruction and edification and serves in an admirable manner as a textbook for the successful instruction of those entrusted to their care. It presents the great vital truths of the Bible in such a simple but clear way that every child is able to grasp them.

Some interesting facts concerning it:
a. It is now 400 years old as a textbook.
b. In 1929 (its four-hundredth anniversary) it had been translated into 137 languages.
c. Only the Bible exceeds it in the number of copies sold.

*Note.* Here cite a few well-chosen quotations about the value of the Small Catechism.

The Large Catechism, intended particularly for teachers and ministers, is a more detailed and exhaustive discussion of the Chief Parts of the Christian doctrine.

*Lesson 15*
#### THE FORMULA OF CONCORD

After Luther's death, in 1546, bitter controversies arose. Prominent Lutheran clergymen sought to settle them. This resulted in the writing of the Formula of Concord, completed in 1577.

It is essentially a restatement of the principal Lutheran doctrines discussed in the other confessions. Its purpose called for very explicit and complete statements of the doctrines at issue.

Our Lutheran Church possesses a treasure of inestimable value in these Confessions, collected and published in 1580 (Book of Concord).

*Lesson 16*

Review briefly Lessons 9—15.

## B. LITURGICS [3)]

*Lesson 17*

### THE COMMON SERVICE

The Common Service is the official form of worship for our divine services. It is a reproduction of the Lutheran liturgies of the sixteenth and seventeenth centuries.

This matchless Common Service with its wonderful harmony, its beautiful significance, and its remarkable unity is a work of highest art. But it must be understood to be appreciated. Therefore we should lead the pupils of the upper grades to understand the significance of the various parts. Ignorance on this point is one of the causes why we have so little uniformity in the liturgical part of our services. Though "no church should condemn another because one has less or more external ceremonies not commanded by God than the other" (Form. Conc., Art. X), yet we should strive for uniformity of liturgy "that the unity of the Christian people may be affirmed also by such external things as otherwise are not necessary of themselves" (Luther). This is especially desirable today because of much travel, many joint services, conventions, etc.

*Lesson 18*   THE CONFESSION

The Confession, at the beginning of the service, should "prepare the hearts of both minister and congregation for communion with God." If our worship is to be acceptable to God, we must be truly penitent.

### THE INTROIT

The Introit dates back to the services in the Temple, where two divisions of singers would sing psalms responsively.

With the Introit the congregation enters on the service proper. It consists of the Antiphon, one or more verses of a psalm, and the Gloria Patri. These verses are a summary of the Scripture lessons and the sermon; the Gloria Patri is the grateful response of the congregation.

### THE KYRIE

When the congregation begins to worship and praise God, it realizes that it must cry for help: "Lord, have mercy upon us." This is not a cry for forgiveness, but of lamentation and a cry for help on account of the many miseries attending this earthly life, to render acceptable worship to God.

---

3) See *Lutheran Hymnal,* pp. 5—31, 168. If preferred, study of the Common Service may be undertaken as part of the Music Course, pp. 232—239.

*Lesson 19* THE GLORIA IN EXCELSIS

God hears His people's cry. But all help must come through Christ Jesus. Therefore they are directed to Him by the Gloria in Excelsis, in which they also express their joy over the fact that their prayer is heard.

### THE SALUTATION

After such assurance of forgiveness and of God's merciful assistance in their worship, the pastor salutes the congregation ("The Lord be with you"), and in turn receives its salutation ("And with thy spirit").

### THE COLLECT

The congregation and the pastor now collect their desires into one short petition unto God, which is therefore called the Collect.

Since the Collect is to contain the joint desires of the congregation on one particular occasion, the Common Service has a different Collect for every Sunday of the year.

*Lesson 20* THE EPISTLE AND THE GOSPEL

In the Epistle and in the Gospel, God gives what He promised in the Introit and what the congregation asked in the Collect.

The Epistle is principally the reading of a doctrinal portion of Scripture, which the congregation acknowledges by an utterance of praise, "Hallelujah," or a Hallelujah sentence.

The Gospel presents the Savior. Therefore, as soon as it has been announced, the congregation — like the angelic messengers of old — breaks forth into a shout of joy: "Glory be to Thee, O Lord!" Since Christ Himself comes in the sacred Gospel, the congregation responds to its reading with the words, "Praise be to Thee, O Christ."

### THE CREED

The congregation responds to the reading of the Epistle and the Gospel by confessing the Apostles' Creed. Christ having spoken, we answer at once, *I believe.* Therefore, if the Creed is sung, the prelude and interludes should be omitted.

The Nicene Creed is used on festivals and Communion days.

### THE SERMON

The sermon is the climax of the entire service. It is so indispensable that without it the service would fail of its purpose. Therein God speaks to His people. The congregation, like Mary, is sitting at Jesus' feet, hearing His Word.

*Lesson 21* THE OFFERTORY

The Offertory has its origin in the offerings brought by the first Christians for the support of the ministry and for benevolent purposes to express also in a material way their gratitude for God's blessings.

Before these offerings are collected, the words "Create in me a clean heart, O God," etc., or other suitable words are sung; for the heart must first be cleansed if the gift is to be acceptable.

### The General Prayer and the Lord's Prayer

Before going home the worshipers bring all their petitions before God in the General Prayer and in that most excellent of all prayers, The Lord's Prayer.

### The Benediction

The worshipers who have partaken of God's goodness take His blessings on their way.

*Lesson 22*

Review the lessons on the Common Service.

*Lesson 23*        **THE HOLY COMMUNION SERVICE**

#### Introduction

The Holy Supper is properly celebrated in the main service. The Communion Service is introduced by the singing of a suitable hymn.

*The Preface.* The Salutation and Response open the new part of the service. The prefatory sentences are eucharistic, or thanksgiving prayers, culminating in the Sanctus.

*The Sanctus* (Holy, etc.), Is. 6:3; Ps. 118:26, is an exalted hymn of glorification of the Trinity and of Christ as the Messiah.

*Lesson 24*          Administration

*The Lord's Prayer* is especially fitting at the celebration of Communion since believers thereby become conscious of their adoption and their fellowship as members of the same body.

*The Consecration.* By means of the words of institution the bread and wine are consecrated, or set apart for sacred use, and the eating and drinking is distinguished from ordinary use, thus becoming a Sacrament.

*The Pax Domini* (Peace be with you) is the risen Christ's greeting to the believers about to commune.

*The Agnus Dei* (Lamb of God) is a plea that Christ would grant His mercy and peace to the communicants.

*The Distribution.* With the words "Take, eat," etc., "Take, drink," etc., distribution is made. The word *true* has been inserted before *body* and *blood* in the formula of distribution to prevent the intrusion of Reformed errors.

*Lesson 25*           Conclusion

*The Nunc Dimittis* ("Now lettest Thou depart"). The communicants give expression to the assurance that they may now "depart in peace" since they have received the seal of forgiveness, and they praise the *Triune* God for it.

*The Thanksgiving.* The Thanksgiving collect, preceded by the thanksgiving versicle, is an expression of gratitude for the grace received and a prayer that it may redound unto true sanctification.

*The Benedicamus* ("Bless we the Lord") is an exhortation to praise the Lord.

*The Benediction.* This imparts the blessings of the Triune God and closes the service.

*Note.* The sainted Rev. F. Lochner was a pioneer in bringing about correct liturgical forms in our Synod. See his book *Der Hauptgottesdienst.*

*Lesson 26*

Review the lessons on the Holy Communion Service.

The teacher may devote the remaining periods to some other subject, *e. g.,* to some of the time-honored customs and practices of our Lutheran Church. Thus we shall lead our children to a greater appreciation of such practices and help preserve them.

## C. COMMON CUSTOMS AND PRACTICES OF OUR LUTHERAN CHURCH

(Baptism in the Presence of the Congregation)

Baptism should not be a mere family affair, but part of the service because —

a. This Sacrament deserves such high distinction;

b. It reminds the hearer of the heavenly gifts he received in Baptism.

*Suggestion.* Admonish pupils to be attentive during the administration of Holy Baptism.

### THE CLERICAL GOWN·

The gown is worn to signify that the preacher is set apart as the messenger of Christ.

### ALTAR, CRUCIFIX, CANDLES, PULPIT, BAPTISMAL FONT

The altar occupies the most prominent position because it symbolizes God's presence. In prayer, therefore, the pastor turns toward it, while in addressing the congregation and pronouncing the benediction he faces the congregation.

The crucifix is a continuous reminder of Christ's great sacrifice on Calvary.

The lighted candlesticks recall "the night in which He was betrayed."

The pulpit, usually boxed in, is designed to divert the attention of the hearer from the person of the preacher.

The baptismal font is rightly placed at the foot of the chancel steps or in a similar position and in view of the congregation. (See first paragraph of this section.)

### THE SIGN OF THE CROSS

The sign of the holy cross is not a sort of charm, but a mere reminder of Christ's redemptive suffering and death on the cross.

### TOKENS OF REVERENCE

The Bible does not command any special posture in prayer, but it does mention and recommend several, *e. g.,* kneeling and "lifting up holy hands."

Those commonly used in our Lutheran Church — and their meaning — are: *kneeling* as an acknowledgment of unworthiness; *standing* as a mark of reverence; *folding of hands* as a token of helplessness and dependence on God.

Other expressions of reverence are: the *bowing of the head* during the benediction, the *genuflection* and the bowing of the head at the approach to the Lord's Table.

### RINGING THE CHURCH BELLS

The ringing of the bells at the beginning of the service is, so to speak, a call from heaven: "Come and worship!" * The ringing on Saturday evenings should remind the members to prepare by meditation and prayer for the worship of the approaching Sunday. Tapping the bells three times or three times three after the ringing on Saturday indicates that the members of that church worship the Triune God. The tapping of the bells during the Lord's Prayer should remind people within reach — and particularly Christians who were unable to attend church — that now the congregation raises its hands and hearts in prayer to the Lord.

## D. THE CHURCH YEAR 4)

The church year is divided into two periods, the festival and the non-festival period. The first begins with the first Sunday in Advent and closes with Trinity Sunday. It embraces the three great festivals, Christmas, Easter, and Pentecost, which emphasize the great facts of our salvation through Christ Jesus. The second period begins with the first and ends with the last Sunday after Trinity.

The four Sundays in *Advent* should prepare the Church for the advent of Christ, His coming into the flesh, celebrated on the joyous Christmas festival. Eight days later, on *New Year's Day*, the Church commemorates the circumcision of the Christ Child. Six days later the Epiphany festival commemorates the manifestation of the new-born King of the Jews to the Gentiles. (*Christmas Cycle:* from the first Sunday in Advent to the last Sunday after Epiphany, inclusive.)

On the Sunday after the first vernal full moon comes the oldest of all church festivals, *Easter*, the festival of Christ's resurrection. This is preceded by *Good Friday*, the day of the Lord's crucifixion and death; by *Maundy Thursday*, when the Lord's Supper was instituted and the Savior was betrayed; by *Palm Sunday*, when He made His last, triumphal entry into the city of Jerusalem and the multitude spread palm branches on His path. This week is known as *Holy Week*. The six weeks before Easter, beginning with *Ash Wednesday*, are observed as the season of *Lent*. Forty days after Easter occurs the *Ascension* festival, commemorating Christ's visible ascension to heaven. (*Easter Cycle:* from Septuagesima, seventieth day before Easter, to Ascension.)

One week after *Pentecost*, which commemorates the outpouring of the Holy Spirit, the Church observes *Trinity Sunday*, the festival of the "Trinity in Unity," of the Triune God.

---

* *Admonition for Pupils.* One who without a good reason comes too late or leaves before the service is over commits an act of irreverence, disturbs his fellow worshipers, and thus gives offense.

4) See also *Lutheran Hymnal*, pp. 3, 158—161.

Some Sundays of the church year have special names, such as "Judica," "Rogate," etc. Others are numbered backward from Easter, such as "Quinquagesima," i. e., the fiftieth day before Easter; "Sexagesima," sixtieth; "Septuagesima," seventieth. Still others are numbered forward from a special Sunday (Sundays in Advent, Epiphany, and after Trinity).

**The One-Room School**

There are two alternatives in the case of the one-room school:

1. If two periods per week throughout the year can be made available for Church History instruction, the room may be divided into two classes, "Intermediate Grades" and "Upper Grades," and the course taught as outlined for Grades 5 and 6 and for Grades 7 and 8. The primary grades will. learn what they can from the intermediate group.

2. When it is necessary to combine Grades 5—8 in one class, as in many instances it will be, the material for both groups may be condensed, so that the entire course for intermediate grades is taught in one year and the entire course for the upper grades the second. Under this plan the work of the fifth grade is repeated in the seventh, and the work of the sixth in the eighth grade. Additional work is required of the older pupils.

## E. CORRELATION POSSIBILITIES

The teacher with a good background of Church History will find many opportunities to correlate in the various school subjects, thus supplementing the organized course in Church History and relating it to all fields of knowledge. A few possibilities are indicated.

*Bible History* and *Bible Reading.* Much of Bible history is Church history. This should be understood by the pupils. Refer to events in Church history which illustrate the truth of Scripture. Examples: The seven thousand in Israel at the time of Elijah (1 Kings 19) to prove that the gates of hell shall not prevail against the Church (Matt. 16:18); the growth of the Nigerian and other missions to show that God's Word does not return void (Is. 55:11).

*Catechism.* Discussion of Luther's Catechism will necessitate reference to the Reformation; study of the Lord's Supper will require reference to the division in Protestant circles after the Reformation.

*Children's Services.* These feature the subject matter of Church history, but primarily they serve the purpose of expressing gratitude for God's mercies.

*Reading.* The Concordia Edition of the *Bobbs Merrill Readers* contains many selections from the history of the Church. Where another text is used, supplementary readings in Church history may be provided. The school library is used for individual reading, book reports, summaries, or oral class reports.[5]

*Language* or *Social Studies.* Oftentimes the local community is studied as part either of the language or social studies course. The history of the local church and school should be included; in larger centers, Lutheran history in the community in general.

*Geography.* The history of the Church comes constantly into play, for there is no continent, and hardly a country, where the Church has not left its marks. Church activities, missions, educational institutions, statistics, and landmarks correlate naturally and interestingly with geographical facts.

*History.* Church and secular history are inseparably interrelated, and each supplements the other. The *Church History Inserts,* published by Synod's Publicity Office, and supplied free to schools, contain suitable material for correlation.

*Civics.* The Reformation as the source of civil and religious liberty is given due attention; the relation between Church and State is brought out.

*Science.* The use of inventions in the service of the Gospel, *viz.,* printing, radio, etc.

*Music and Art.* Events in Church history that inspired musical gems, as Luther's "A Mighty Fortress Is Our God"; works of art depicting church-historical scenes, as "Luther at Worms" and "The Great Supper"; creative art activity dealing with Church history events, perhaps during Reformation season.

*Visual Education: Lectures.* Motion pictures, lantern slides, and lectures by foreign and home missionaries offer opportunities for supplementing the ordinary school instruction.

## F. EVALUATING OUTCOMES

When the child leaves the elementary school, he should have a reasonably clear picture of the history of God's people from the Creation of Adam and Eve to the present.

In addition to the historical account he should be able to see the relation between cause and effect, the prosperity of the Church in times of obedience and zeal, and its decline and punishment during periods of indifference and disobedience to God's commands. He should see the permanence of the Church both in view of God's promise and of His preservation of a small remnant of faithful believers even in the darkest periods of Church history.

---

5) See School Reference Catalog (Concordia) for suggestions of titles.

The pupil should appreciate the struggles and sacrifices of the Apostles and Prophets, of Luther and other leaders in the Reformation, of the founders of the true Lutheran Church in America, and, above all, the supreme sacrifice of the Savior, Jesus Christ. He should have a good understanding of the history of the Lutheran Church, and of the organization and practices of the Missouri Synod, for a sound basis of intelligent church membership.

There should be noticeable in the pupils a general interest in the activities of the Church and its welfare, a desire to learn more about it by reading the Church periodicals, and appreciation of, and love for, the divine services of the Church and the Christian instruction in school, a desire to serve wherever possible, an effort to be a credit to the Church under all circumstances, and a willingness to proclaim its teachings by word and example.

These standards are ideals which should be recognizable in greater or lesser degree in the individual pupils. There will be disappointments in spite of the best efforts, because the functional aims of education are always the most difficult to achieve. But if the history of the Church has been taught properly, every child should show some measure of achievement along the lines suggested.

### Selected References

#### BOOKS FOR THE TEACHER

Beck, Walter H., *Lutheran Elementary Schools in the United States.* Concordia, 1939.

Bente, F., *American Lutheranism* (2 vols.). Concordia, 1919.

*Course of Study in Religion.* Minnesota District, 1939.

Dobberfuhl, M. E., *Curriculum in Church History.* Concordia, 1932.

*Educational Guide and Course of Study* (Texas District). Concordia, 1930.

Finck, William J., *Lutheran Landmarks and Pioneers in America.* Philadelphia: General Council Publication House, 1917.

Fuerbringer, L., *Men and Missions* Series. Concordia.

Hageman, G. E., *Sketches from the History of the Church.* Concordia, n. d.

Kretzmann, P. E., *Christian Art in the Place and in the Form of Lutheran Worship.* Concordia.

Krauss, E. A. W., *Lebensbilder.* Concordia, 1911.

*Lutheran Hymnal.* Concordia, 1941.

Polack, W. G., *Fathers and Founders.* Concordia, 1939.

Polack, W. G., *The Story of Luther.* Concordia, 1931.

Polack, W. G., *The Story of C. F. W. Walther.* Concordia, 1935.

*Statistical Yearbook.* Concordia.

Stellhorn, A. C., *A Century of Lutheran Schools in America.* St. Louis: Department of Publicity and Missionary Education, Missouri Synod, 1939.

Stellhorn, A. C., *Guide in the Study of Missions.* St. Louis: Department of Publicity and Missionary Education, Missouri Synod.

Wegener, W., *The Great Reformer.* Concordia, 1917.

*Lutheran Annual,* Church periodicals, and other current publications.

**TEXTBOOKS**

*Advanced Bible History.* Concordia, 1939.

The Bible.

*Church History Inserts.* St. Louis: Department of Publicity and Missionary Education, Missouri Synod, 1941.

*Elementary Bible History.* Concordia.

Graebner, Theo., *The Story of Our Church in America.* Concordia, 1935.

Just, Gustav, *Life of Luther.* Concordia, 1903.

Miller, Alb. H., *The Life of Luther.* River Forest, Illinois; Miller Publishing Co.

Polack, W. G., *The Building of a Great Church.* Concordia, 1941.

Stellhorn, A. C., *Children's Centennial Service* (History of the Saxon Immigration). Concordia, 1939.

Wegener, W., *The Great Reformer.* Concordia, 1917.

---

# IV. LANGUAGE ARTS

## 1. Reading

### A. OBJECTIVES IN READING

1. Mastery of the mechanics necessary for good oral and silent reading.

2. The desire to read well.

3. Development of a taste for good literature, particularly for the periodicals, books, and other Christian literature of the Church.

4. The desire and habit to read for spiritual enlightenment and edification, particularly in the Bible; for general information; for wholesome enjoyment; and for vicarious experiences in the various phases of human life.

5. Christian standards of judgment and discrimination in the choice of reading materials.

6. The ability and habit to use the library, reference sets, dictionaries, indexes, table of contents, and the like, economically and efficiently.

### B. DISCUSSION OF OBJECTIVES

**Mastery of Mechanics**

The child with a mental age of six years is believed ready for instruction in reading. If he has had good home environment, he has the foundation of experience and sound images upon which visual language can successfully be built and is therefore able to acquire reading ability as the tool for independent learning.

Many specific abilities are necessary before a person can

become a good reader. The knowledge of words, phonetics, letters, and punctuation is fundamental.

Oral reading requires interpretation and thought-sharing. These are possible only when the child has learned proper enunciation, clear articulation, correct pronunciation, rhythmical expression, and proper emphasis. To achieve good oral reading, correct reading habits must be stressed from the beginning, and practice in interpretive and audience reading must be provided. Selections that are used for this purpose must be interesting and on the child's reading level, since materials which lack appeal and which present too many mechanical difficulties make interpretive reading impossible.

Efficient silent reading requires the ability to read rapidly without lip movement or other vocalization, the ability to get the thought clearly, and the ability to reproduce what has been read. When a person apprehends the thought faster than he can pronounce the words, he has become a good silent reader. A large amount of interesting material on the level of the child's reading ability must be readily available if the pupil is to develop into a good silent reader.

The mechanics of reading cannot be learned once and for all, but constitute a cumulative ability. They will be mastered adequately only when the ability to read is fostered in all subjects from the first grade throughout. This teaching must include the analysis of any reading difficulties and such remedial work as may be indicated in each individual case. The different abilities and the varied methods and rates of learning, different backgrounds and interests, and the state of physical fitness and emotional stability must all be considered in determining the procedures and the materials to be used.

## The Desire to Read Well

The child will not learn to read well unless he has the desire for it. The mere desire to please the teacher is insufficient, while the idea of self-glorification is sinful. The highest type of motivation for learning to read resides in the material itself. The teacher will, therefore, endeavor to find each child's interest, cultivate it by careful guidance, and supply the child with carefully graded materials that appeal to him.

Reading to the children or otherwise introducing them to suitable material that they can read themselves, including Bible stories and other religious material, is a basic way of creating interest, for it opens to them a world of fascinating experience in which every normal child will wish to share. The reading ability of children of elementary school age often lags several years behind their ability to enjoy; therefore the selections read by the teacher may be of considerably greater difficulty than those read by the children and yet provide enjoyment and stimulate the desire to read themselves.

Pointing out the usefulness of reading for the interpretation of signs, warnings, instructions, and for the acquisition of useful information in general, especially for an acquaintance with the Word and will of God, helps in creating a desire to read. Some pupils may be inspired by the mere pleasure of overcoming obstacles, but the number subject to this influence is comparatively small. For small children the play motive is important. With them seat work with paper, paste, colors, and classroom games may be employed to stimulate interest and facilitate learning.

In the case of the poorly gifted child it is important to avoid as much as possible the discouragement of failure, and in the case of the exceptionally gifted child to prevent the boredom which accompanies a progress too slow for his ability. A feeling of inferiority, fear, lack of interest, or complete aversion to school easily follows the continued use of reading material unsuited to the intellectual and emotional level of the child. It is the teacher's task to provide material which will stimulate interest and the desire to read on the part of the child.

### Types of Reading Material

It must be remembered that reading is never an end in itself; it must have a definite and worth-while purpose. The type of reading engaged in exerts an important influence on the child's Christian character and life. The most important purpose of reading for the Christian is spiritual enlightenment and edification. Therefore it is necessary constantly to lead children by actual experience to appreciate the value of the Bible as a true source of information, comfort, and strength, and to the periodicals, books, and other Christian literature of the Church written on their level of understanding.[1]

The child is led to develop a taste for good literature in general: literature useful in the mastery of school subjects or in the solution of the everyday problems in home or vocation; literature offering vicarious emotional experiences that release tension or aid in the formation of Christian character; and literature supplying clean enjoyment for leisure time.

With respect to leisure-time reading it is important that it be not regarded only as a harmless occupation of time for want

---

1) The *Juvenile Literature Catalog* of Concordia Publishing House will be of value to the teacher in this phase of the work.

of something better to do. Leisure-time reading is justified only in so far as it contributes to the development of reading skills, to spiritual edification, clean enjoyment, thinking about worth-while things, familiarity with current events and current trends, or to a broadening of the general outlook upon life.

It is never enough merely to point out good literature for the present needs of the child, or to warn against that which is harmful. It is much more necessary on the basis of God's Word to teach the child Christian standards of judgment and discrimination and habits of correct thinking, which he may apply also in unsupervised situations. The Christian character and conviction developed in the religion period and in all Christian instruction and training furnishes the basis for these standards. The application is made in the reading for all subjects. The child leaving the elementary school should have reached the stage where he refuses to accept conclusions blindly, having acquired the ability to judge common reading matter according to the standards of the Bible and common decency.

### Special Abilities

In addition to the ability to read for thought and interpretation and to select materials that serve a legitimate use, certain special mechanical abilities are necessary for an efficient reader. Pupils must learn where to find information they desire. Thus they are taught to use the library, reference sets, dictionaries, indexes, tables of contents, and the like. The careful direction and supervision in the use of these helps is designed to train the pupils in their habitual, economic, and efficient use.

It is vital, though often neglected, that children learn the importance of title, author, and publication date of a book.

The proper care and handling of books; cleanliness of hands, proper turning of pages, the opening of a new book without breaking the binding, the proper position of the book with respect to light in reading — all such matters provide valuable lessons in cleanliness, neatness, health, and economy, and are by-products of the reading instruction.

## C. PRACTICAL SUGGESTIONS

### Method

The method or combination of methods to be used in the teaching of reading must be determined by the teacher after he has thoroughly informed himself on the latest findings relating to the subject. The bibliography, teacher's manuals or guidebooks, and educational journals should be consulted for suggestions dealing with the psychology and teaching of reading.

## Time Allotment

Reading in the first grade may properly occupy as much as 25 per cent of the entire school time, divided into two or three shorter periods a day. Long periods of concentration will fatigue the child, and fatigue makes sustained interest and attention difficult. An hour a day may be devoted to the subject in second grade. In third and fourth grades this amount of time will be somewhat reduced. In grades five to eight a half hour daily is sufficient. This half hour includes the time set aside for the study of literature in grades seven and eight.

Practical considerations will, in many cases, make this ideal schedule impossible. Especially in one- and two-room schools the time allotment for reading must be substantially reduced as for all subjects except Religion. In such cases some time may be gained by combining classes from the third grade up, but especially beginning with the fifth grade. In reducing the total amount of time, the number of periods devoted to the subject is reduced rather than the length of the periods. Time may be gained also by making one or the other content subject part of the reading course. Readings in the Bible, health and safety, general science, the social studies, or Church history are suitable especially for this purpose. Any possible grade combinations, either for one or more recitation periods, or for a semester or year at a time, will be utilized by the practical teacher to the fullest extent.[2]

### Materials and Equipment Helpful in the Teaching of Reading

1. A good basic text and several supplementary texts on the level of each grade in sufficient quantity for class use.

2. A selection of books on lower grade levels for those who have reading difficulties.

3. Several copies of good children's magazines. Recommended: *Child's Companion; Young Lutherans' Magazine; Concordia Messenger;* choice depending on age of children; a current events publication and a publication on children's hobbies or handicraft. (The latter must be carefully selected to avoid the introduction of material at variance with the aims of the Christian school.)

4. A library containing a standard reference set and books on many topics of interest, including the field of religion and Christian literature. Consult Concordia *Juvenile Literature Catalog.*

---

2) See: Herman W. Teske, "Conservation of Time in the One-Teacher School." *Lutheran School Journal,* November, 1938, p. 109; Fred H. Witte, "Organizing Instruction in the One-Teacher School." *Ibid.,* March, 1941, p. 305; Fred H. Witte, "The Reading Program in the One-Teacher School." *Ibid.,* May, 1941, p. 408.

5. A number of books beyond the children's own reading ability from which the teacher may read to the class.

6. Workbooks for the pupils.

7. A reading table.

8. Several good dictionaries in addition to those owned by the pupils themselves.

9. A hand printing press, charts, and flash cards for the primary room.

10. Bulletin board for notices, display of materials and pictures, and posting of children's papers.

11. Teacher's Manuals for basic text.

## D. COURSE SUGGESTIONS

It is neither necessary nor practical to outline a detailed course in reading. The adoption of a good basic text in all grades is required for best results, for these reasons:

1. A standard text is based upon the findings of experts in the field of reading, and their selection of materials is the result of careful study and judgment. A course planned by the average teacher is likely to be inferior to a good text.

2. Dependence upon the use of diversified materials would be costly, and lack of a sufficient number of books for large classes would likely be unavoidable.

3. The vocabulary of a good textbook series is carefully graded and controlled and provides for systematic and gradual development.

4. The manuals accompanying the series give detailed suggestions for basic, supplementary, and independent reading, and suggest related activities.

5. Often workbooks accompany the text and provide additional opportunity for guiding the learning activities toward definite goals.

The use of a basic text does not require following the sequence of the text. The seasonal use of material is recommended. To broaden the understanding of pupils and to give them extended vocabulary practice, the teacher will assign supplementary readings on the level of the pupils. They will be encouraged also to engage in independent reading for recreational purposes or problem-solving, and especially, for edification through the reading of Christian and Biblical materials.

The *Bobbs Merrill Readers* (Concordia Edition) are designed to lead the child into an appreciation of Christian literature in the reading program and are used in many Lutheran schools as the basic text. The *School Reference Catalog* and the *Juvenile Literature Catalog* of Concordia Publishing House contain suggestions for supplementary materials for all grades.

## Primary Grades (1—3)

` One or more pre-primers, a primer, and a first reader generally comprise the basic material for the first grade. The *Bobbs Merrill Readers* (Concordia Edition) lack pre-primer provisions. *Playmates* of the Baker and Reed Curriculum Series [3] will serve satisfactorily in this capacity. Fifty-four of its seventy-nine words are repeated in the *Bobbs Merrill Primer* (Concordia Edition), a better percentage than in the case of pre-primers of other series.

Standardized tests may be used as an aid in determining reading readiness, but their value must not be overestimated. Preparation for reading through wide language experience entitles the child to make an attempt at learning to read. If it develops that he is not prepared to learn, more preliminary work and simple, informal reading exercises are indicated, and the pre-primer period is prolonged.

Lack of reading readiness is often due to failure to make auditory and visual discriminations. *Building Word Power,*[4] by Durrell and Sullivan, and the accompanying workbook, *Ready to Read,* supply thirty-eight exercises for developing auditory and visual acuity. The books are intended chiefly for the primary grades, but they may be used to help also children in the intermediate grades to overcome reading difficulties. Full directions for use are given. Fifteen minutes to half an hour daily for about two months are required to complete the exercises.

Phonics are introduced after a sufficient vocabulary has been developed. They are an aid to reading, never a basic method of teaching.

The child reads silently from the beginning, but oral reading receives primary attention. As he grows in reading skill and overcomes mechanical difficulties, silent reading takes more and more of his time.

As the child enters a higher grade, supplementary readers on the previous grade level serve as an easy and pleasant introduction to the work.

Primary children show great interest in Bible stories written on their level, other factual material, folk tales, fables, and simple poetry. The simple material will be read by the children themselves, that which is more difficult by the teacher. Poetry has. a double appeal to children: a rhythm appeal which the child seems to enjoy apart from understanding, and a thought appeal where the poetry deals with experiences on the child's level of understanding, interest, and emotion. To create a permanent, vital interest in poetry, it is necessary to emphasize thought appeal.

---

3) Bobbs-Merrill Co., 1938.      4) World Book Co., 1941.

Egermeier's *Bible Story Book,* the *Child's Companion,* and Christian stories take care largely of the needs of Christian reading material. The *Juvenile Literature Catalog* should be consulted for suggestions.

Factual material of a secular nature is supplied by means of Science, Social Science, Health, Safety, or supplementary readers. The textbooks used in subjects other than reading are valuable, especially beginning with the third grade. — Stories of Luther, other Church leaders, and of American historical characters are read to the children or by them.

Among the fables and folk tales with which the children should become familiar in these grades those listed below deserve mention. They are read either by or to the class.

| | |
|---|---|
| Little Black Sambo | The Travels of a Fox |
| The Three Pigs | Thumbelina |
| The Gingerbread Man | The Cat and the Mouse |
| Cinderella | The Straw Ox |
| The Little Red Hen | The Wonderful Iron Pot |
| Chicken Little | The Ant and the Grasshopper |
| The Old Woman and Her Pig | How the Bear Lost His Tail |
| The Fox and the Little Red Hen | Why the Sea Is Salty |
| The Town Mouse and the Country Mouse | The Hare and the Hedgehog |
| | The Fox and the Stork |
| The Lion and the Mouse | The Frog and the Ox |
| The Dog and His Shadow | The Lark and Her Young |
| The Bremen Town Musicians | |

### Intermediate Grades (4—6)

The reading text, textbooks in other subjects, supplementary readers, and the school library supply the pupil with an abundance of literature on many topics. It is the teacher's task to lead him into these new reading adventures and to help him develop a strong and permanent interest in reading as useful and recreational. To accomplish this aim, the individual interest and ability are considered and suitable materials provided to fit each pupil's need.

The interest of pupils in these grades is directed toward Bible stories, hymns, and other Christian literature, including the periodicals for children published by the Church. In the fifth and sixth grades the Bible itself is read.[5]

Of particular interest to children in these grades are stories of adventure, travel, biography, and fiction. Both prose and poetry are included. Independent reading is encouraged and suitable material provided. If the child has developed a love for good books, uses them, and knows to some extent how to use the library, the course has been successful.

---

5) See course in Bible Reading, pp. 55—68.

## Upper Grades (7—8)

The reading text and the textbooks in all subjects form an important part of the reading material in these grades. Much time is devoted to the extension of literary appreciation by the study of some of the masterpieces of prose and poetry which have stood the test of time. In the study of these materials the informative and work-type purposes of reading are not stressed unduly, but the selections are treated particularly as materials for enjoyment and appreciation. To dissect beautiful selections of literature by laboratory methods, especially in the elementary school, often results in the loss of their beauty. The study of the structure of a literary selection is justified only to the extent to which it serves genuine enjoyment and appreciation.

As the child's reading horizon broadens, his judgment is strengthened. He learns to evaluate selections on the strength of their informative, entertaining, or edifying value. Diligent Bible reading, both in class and independently, helps to balance his sense of values.

Authors of appealing selections assume greater importance to pupils in these grades, and teachers provide for the study of the lives of important authors. The reading of current events is encouraged, and teachers stimulate this activity through the discussion of important church and secular events. In this connection economic habits of reading newspapers and magazines are taught. Church periodicals and local church bulletins constitute an important phase of the child's independent reading. Interest in church periodicals is fostered by calling attention to articles with special appeal to children. The teacher makes a conscious effort thus to interest the pupils in the *Lutheran Witness* and other church publications. Fiction and other materials with a Christian background are supplied by the school library.

### E. CORRELATION

In the matter of correlation, reading occupies a position different from other school subjects. Reading is the educational tool without which the child is helpless except in the acquisition of memoriter knowledge through the oral presentation of another. Reading is, therefore, taught throughout, the teacher realizing that he is an instructor in reading regardless of the subject he is teaching. The effective use of textbooks in all subjects is an important part of the reading problem. Any other view hampers the reading program in the elementary school.

As reading is taught in connection with all school subjects, so, in turn, every subject is correlated with the reading program, especially so the content subjects. Modern curriculum readers illustrate this point.

Reading, itself a language art, is important in all phases of the formal language program. It is used in securing information necessary in the preparation of reports, talks, programs, assemblies, and the like. Without the stimulation of reading and the drawing of knowledge from superior minds, creative language abilities would soon deteriorate. The cultivation of good silent and oral reading habits is necessary to enable the pupils to grasp and interpret the thoughts of superior minds.

The *Bobbs Merrill Readers* (Concordia Edition) show how Biblical and Church history may be integrated with the reading program. Where the basic textbook is lacking in this respect, the teacher supplies these supplementary materials. The same applies to Geography, History, Civics, Health, Safety, General Science, Art, and even to Music when it involves the content of hymns or information on lives of musicians in whom the class becomes interested.

In one-room schools with crowded programs it is frequently advisable to use the reading period in the study of content subjects as previously indicated. This accomplishes the purposes both of reading and of the subjects so studied and helps to avoid duplication of time and effort. Silent reading especially may be profitably directed toward topics that contribute to the achievement of the aims of the various areas in the school curriculum.

## F. EVALUATING OUTCOMES

Reading ability alone is not considered today as the criterion for promotion. The child's mental, social, and physical development and maturity is equally important. This means that comparatively wide variation in reading skill will exist in any reading group and that the teacher will adapt the difficulty and amounts of materials assigned to individuals in the class, or to divisions within a given grade group.

The teacher's records are supplemented by standard tests for purposes of evaluation. The test results do not serve primarily the purpose of determining promotion or non-promotion, but rather that of grouping pupils or adapting materials and methods to individual needs.

The following questions are suggested for the teacher as an aid in evaluating reading outcomes. A progress chart may be constructed for the class and an accurate check kept on the abilities of individual pupils.

**Grade 1**

1. Does the child love Bible stories and good reading in general?

2. Has he a desire to own books?

3. Does he handle books carefully and keep them clean?

4. Does he seek reading experiences of his own accord?

5. Has he an elementary acquaintance with the organization of a book: cover, title, story, illustrations?

6. Does he hold the book properly with respect to light and position while reading?

7. Can he find a story by page number?

8. Does he attack words from left to right?

9. Is he able to use context clues, similarity to other words, and phonics in recognizing new and unfamiliar words?

10. Can he answer fact questions on material read, follow simple printed instructions, read fluently orally, and reproduce the main thoughts of a selection on his grade level?

11. Does he read without finger pointing, lip or head movement?

12. Is he able to read silently material for first grade at the rate of between 85 and 100 words per minute?

**Primary Grades (1—3)**

1. Does the child love to read Bible stories?

2. Does he read other Christian material on his grade level, such as found in books or in the *Child's Companion*?

3. Is he able to distinguish between Christian and mere secular literature?

4. Does he indicate interest in books in general by independent reading?

5. Does he show a desire to own good books?

6. Does he distinguish between various types of reading material, such as stories, factual material, prose, poetry, fairy tales, and the like?

. 7. Is he able to employ context clues and phonics in reading new and unfamiliar words?

8. Has he overcome habits of finger pointing, and head and lip movement in reading?

9. Is he able to use efficiently the table of contents and to find stories or chapters by page reference?

10. Is he able to reproduce what he has read, and to show by oral reading that he has experienced the emotional meaning of a selection?

11. Does he show progress in correct pronunciation, clear enunciation, correct phrasing, and the use of a pleasant, well-modulated voice?

12. Is he able to read intelligently the materials assigned in connection with other school subjects?

13. Does he concentrate on the work at hand, participate in discussion, and listen courteously?

14. Can he follow reading directions in workbooks, drawing lessons, or games?

15. Can he answer questions based on the text?

16. Can he read silently from 120 to 140 words per minute at the end of the third grade?

17. Does he sit correctly with the book in proper position while reading?

18. Does he use books with little wear and tear, without defacing or damaging them?

### Intermediate Grades (4—6)

1. Has the pupil begun to form the habit of Bible reading?

2. Is he interested in Christian books and the Church periodicals suited to his ability?

3. Do his standards of Christian judgment and discrimination function in his choice of reading material?

4. Has he learned to use the dictionary in increasing his reading vocabulary?

5. Does he make use of the library and discuss his reading with others?

6. Is he willing to spend some of his own money on good books?

7. Has he, by the end of the sixth grade, overcome mechanical reading difficulties in silent reading?

8. Has he acquired clear enunciation, correct pronunciation, proper phrasing, good expression and interpretation, and a pleasing voice for oral reading?

9. Does he read to solve problems?

10. Can he follow written instructions or warnings?

11. Can he reproduce what he has read?

12. Is he able to use reference sets, indexes, tables of contents, and glossaries?

13. Is he able to read factual materials suited to his grade at the approximate standard rate of speed: fourth grade, 140—160 words; fifth grade, 160—200 words; sixth grade, 180—220 words per minute?

## Upper Grades (7—8)

1. Has the pupil a wide range of interests with the ability to enjoy different types of prose and poetry?

2. Is he able to distinguish between good and trashy literature, and does he habitually choose that which is good, both in Christian literature and in secular books and periodicals?

3. Is he able to express the real meaning and purpose of a selection in oral reading?

4. Does he use his Bible independently?

5. Has he the ability and habit to make economic and efficient use of the library, reference sets, dictionaries, indexes, tables of contents, and other helps?

6. Does he spend part of his leisure time in reading?

7. Do his reading tastes give promise of worth-while reading in the future?

8. Is he able to distinguish finer shades of meaning in words and sentences?

9. Has he developed the habit of wider reading in books, newspapers, and magazines when seeking the solution of a problem?

10. Can he read silently material suited to his age at the rate of 200—250 words per minute?

### Teachers' References for Reading

Betts, Emmett A., *The Prevention and Correction of Reading Difficulties*. Row, Peterson and Co., 1936.

Cole, Luella, *The Improvement of Reading*. Farrar and Rinehart, 1938.

Cram, Fred K., *A Course in the Study of the Dictionary, Encyclopedia, Indexes, Tables of Contents, Maps, Charts, Diagrams, and Vocabulary Building*. Follett Publishing Co.

Diesing, A. E., *Curriculum in Reading*. Published by the author, 1924.

Dolch, Edward W., *The Psychology and Teaching of Reading*. Ginn and Co., 1931.

Eastman, Max, *Discovering Poetry and Enjoyment of Poetry*. Charles Scribner's Sons.

Gates, Arthur I., *The Improvement of Reading*. The Macmillan Co., 1935.

Gray, William Scott, and Whipple, Gertrude, *Improving Instruction in Reading*. University of Chicago, 1933.

Harrison, M. Lucille, *Reading Readiness*. Houghton Mifflin Co.

*Manual and Course of Study for Lutheran Schools*. (Wisconsin Districts.) Section B, 1—29.

McCallister, James M., *Remedial and Corrective Instruction in Reading*. D. Appleton-Century Co., 1936.

McKee, Paul, *Reading and Literature in the Elementary School*. Houghton Mifflin Co., 1934.

*Missouri Course of Study in Reading for Elementary Schools*, 1937.

Monroe, Marion, and Backus, Bertie, *Remedial Reading*. Houghton Mifflin Co., 1937.

Monroe, Marion, *Children Who Cannot Read*. University of Chicago Press, 1932.

National Education Association, Department of Elementary School Principals, *Newer Practices in Reading in the Elementary School*. Seventeenth Yearbook, 1938.

National Society for the Study of Education, *The Teaching of Reading*. Thirty-sixth Yearbook, Part I. Public School Publishing Co., 1937.

N. E. A. *Research Bulletin*, November, 1935. "Better Reading Instruction."

Newmayer, S. Weir, M. C., *First Aids in Reading Difficulties*. Philadelphia: North American Printing Co., 1940. Emphasizes the significance of visual functions and defects as they apply to reading and suggests therapeutic and training measures.

Patterson, S. W., *Teaching the Child to Read*. Doubleday, Doran, and Company, Inc., 1930.

Smith, Nila Blanton, *American Reading Instruction*. Silver, Burdett, and Company, 1934.

Stone, C. R., *Silent and Oral Reading*. Houghton Mifflin Co., 1926.

Stone, C. R., *Better Advanced Reading*. Webster Publishing Co., 1937.

Witty, Paul A., and Kopel, David, *Reading and the Educative Process*. Ginn, 1939.

State, County, or City Course of Study.

### Selected References for Children's Books

The selection of suitable books for children will be simplified by the use of the *Juvenile Literature Catalog* (Concordia Publishing House), booklists released by State Departments of Education, and library lists of juvenile literature. The references below suggest additional sources of information:

Beust, Nora, *Graded List of Books for Children*. American Library Association, 1936.

Colburn, Evangeline. *A Library for the Intermediate Grades*. University of Chicago Press, 1930.

Mahoney, Bertha E., and Whitney, Elinor, *Five Years of Children's Books*. Doubleday, Doran, and Company, 1936.

National Education Association, Department of Elementary School Principals. *Elementary School Libraries*. Twelfth Yearbook, 1933.

Rawlinson, Eleanor, *Introduction to Literature for Children*. W. W. Norton and Co., 1931.

Sears, Minne E., compiler, *Children's Catalog*. H. W. Wilson Company, 1936.

Uhl, Willis L., *The Materials of Reading*. Silver, Burdett, and Co., 1924.

Wilkinson, Mary S., chairman, *Right Book for the Right Child*. Committee on Library Work with Children, American Library Association. John Day Company, 1936.

State, local, or District Course of Study.

# 2. Language

## A. GENERAL OBJECTIVES

1. A proper Christian understanding and use of language.
2. The desire for effective oral and written expression.
3. An adequate speaking and writing vocabulary.
4. The ability and habit of organizing thought and materials logically, effectively, and in accepted form.
5. Skill in the common language situations in life.
6. The ability and habit of self-criticism and self-help in language.

## B. DISCUSSION OF OBJECTIVES

### Christian Understanding, Attitude, Use

The Christian child learns that, historically, language is not an evolutionary development, but a gift of God and one of the marks which distinguishes man from the irrational creatures; that originally there was only one language, spoken and understood by all men; that the confusion of tongues followed as a punishment upon man for his arrogance and pride; that people of other nationalities love their mother tongue as much as we love ours; and that a sympathetic attitude toward other languages and toward those who speak them must be maintained.

He learns to realize that, in its moral aspect, language is a revelation of the thoughts that fill the heart (Luke 6:45) and that man must give an account to God for every idle word that he speaks or writes (Matt. 12:36, 37). Briefly, the child must learn to use his language ability in the service of God in prayer, praise, and thanksgiving; and in the service of man by proclaiming God's Word and will, by speaking well of the neighbor and assisting him with words of encouragement and advice, and the like. He must learn to observe the principles of Christian propriety and honesty in all language communication (Eph. 4:29). This is part of the instruction in religion, but it is repeated, emphasized, and extended in the language class.

Among the many passages of Scripture that will aid in the achievement of a God-pleasing use of languages are these: Ps. 34:13; 37:30; 109:2; 144:8; Prov. 4:24; 10:10, 19; 12:18; 15:4; 18:21; 19:28; Eccl. 10:12; Jer. 9:8; Rom. 3:14; Eph. 4:29; 5:4; Col. 3:8; 4:6; Tit. 2:8; James 3.

Special efforts are necessary to counteract the tendency toward profanity and obscenity of speech common also among many so-called Christians. The teacher must warn against these sins, observe the language habits of his class, admonish and correct when necessary, and, by all means, conform his own practice to the Word of God and thus serve as an example worthy of emulation.

### Desire for Correct Expression

Two conditions are likely to hinder the desire of pupils for clear, concise, grammatically correct, and interesting language expression. Some will feel that their own imperfect expression serves them well and that improvement is not worth the effort; others will be reluctant to surrender ungrammatical or slang forms because they do not want to be different from friends and relatives who use these expressions. The latter is the more important of the two, because common custom is a powerful factor, difficult for the best school to break down.

In trying to overcome these obstacles, the teacher must not immediately set his expectations too high, but remember that the child's habits of spontaneous expression are deeply intrenched and that progress in most cases will be slow at best.

Exercises that show the need for clear and correct expression, and that call for a great deal of speaking and writing, offer the best attack upon unsatisfactory language habits. The making of requests, writing orders for supplies, writing letters with a definite purpose, reporting facts accurately, and similar exercises train pupils in correct expression and help to convince them that much unnecessary explanation, misunderstanding, and loss of time can be avoided if the language is clear and to the point. Many will also be able to understand that their social and vocational progress is largely dependent upon their language ability. In addition to appropriate class exercises, it is necessary that the child be held to speak correctly on all other formal occasions.

If progress seems slow, and satisfactory practice does not accompany learning, the teacher will be encouraged by his own experience and that of others, which indicates that most pupils who have learned correct form in language find it easy to adjust their language practice to a higher standard without much difficulty when the evident need for it arises and is felt.

The incentive of careful, exact, and interesting speech on the part of the teacher is important as a means of inspiring pupils to greater effort. Appreciation lessons in which literary selections are studied for their simplicity and beauty of language are likewise useful in developing an appreciation of, and desire for, exact and pleasing expression.

### Vocabulary Development

Poverty of vocabulary may be due to a lack of experience, to a lack of word knowledge, or to a lack of choice and discrimination in the use of words. While vocabulary development goes on at all times, in and out of school, effectiveness and adequacy of

speech are learned ordinarily only by patient application and by
conscious practice of efficient reading and study habits. Among
these are: Listening carefully to others for new words and uses
of words; using the dictionary to find the meanings of unfamiliar
words one meets; using new words frequently until their use
becomes easy and natural; and judging words or word groups as
to their fitness and usefulness.

Incorrect and ineffective use of language is pointed out and
eliminated whenever it occurs; clear, exact, and economical expression of thought is commended, encouraged, and insisted upon.

### Ability to Organize Thought

. The child must learn that words have value only in so far as
they convey thought, and he must be trained in logical and effective
organization and expression. Logical expression grows out of clear
and logical thinking and is one of the highest language skills.
Among the exercises that aid thought and organized expression
are: Summarizing and arranging in logical sequence a number of
points in a given list; analyzing the thoughts of others as found
in print and recognizing them in their proper order; repeating
concisely and economically a thought that has been expressed
at greater length; expressing the same thought in various ways;
memorizing a thought or statement that has been particularly
well expressed. Some of these will be suggested by the textbook,
others will be supplied by the teacher. In these exercises it is
important that the child be given opportunity to think and express
his own thoughts. Thought implies a measure of originality, not
mere repetition of the ideas of others.

The training in thought and expression is accompanied by
instruction in sentence, paragraph, and theme forms, according
to the grade level, and the relation between logical thought and
these forms of organization is indicated.

### Skill in Common Language Situations

Narration, description, argumentation, illustration, quotation,
conversation, letter writing, and conveying messages are forms
of language communication most of which are used by the child
daily, and he must be trained in their use. Speaking and writing
for directly useful and practical purposes provides motivation,
calls forth the best efforts on the part of most pupils, and develops
the necessary skills. Examples: Writing prayers based on specific
situations and needs, and perhaps using the best of them in the
school devotions; writing letters that are actually sent; preparing
a debate as part of a school program; writing for the school paper;

story telling on the part of individual pupils; practice in natural conversation about a given topic; imaginary telephone conversations; and similar activities.

Good language usage implies good listening habits. The socialized recitation provides training in self-expression and in attentive listening and has its place in developing skill in common language applications.

### Self-Criticism and Self-Help

Play and games have their place in the lower grades as a means of language instruction. As the child grows older, he must realize that the people whom he admires for their gifts of speech and expression achieved this excellence only through hard labor; that they acquired the niceties of language form only by painstaking effort and self-criticism. He must learn to depend less on the teacher, to rely more on his own resources, and to make his own product as perfect as possible. The child must be exercised, therefore, in evaluating, criticizing, and improving his own work; he must be trained in the habit of self-discipline. At the same time he must learn to give charitable and grateful consideration to the constructive criticism of others.

### The Place of Grammar

Language proficiency is rare without the knowledge of grammar, because rules and accepted usage are based on grammatically correct form. The teaching of grammar has swung from one extreme to the other, and back again to a middle-of-the-road policy. Most modern textbooks can be safely followed in their degree of emphasis upon formal grammar.

## C. DIVISION OF TIME AND MATERIALS

Language belongs to the major subjects of the curriculum and occupies important time on the school program.

Language study is begun in the first grade, where the work is carried on informally. Where grades are combined, both the first and second grades are usually taught to express themselves simply in story telling and in the writing of very few sentences. Informally, language study is carried on in every school subject.

Systematic language study is necessary from grades three to eight. A definite time should be set aside every day for the particular development of oral and written expression. Twenty minutes daily is suggested as the minimum for each class or combination of classes. In one-room schools language work can very well be combined in as many as three or four grades. Constant repetition is an important factor in fixing correct language usage.

## D. COURSE SUGGESTIONS

### Primary Grades (1—2)

In the first grade the children will learn language by much speaking. Most of the language work is oral. Stories are repeated and personal experiences related. Children of primary age delight in telling stories and hearing them. Copy work and manual activities are useful.

In the second grade oral work continues, and writing is introduced. Systematic language exercises may be used if available; otherwise exercises prepared by the teacher that lead children to write briefly on a simple theme. Such written expression is limited to a very few thoughts. Composition work is usually begun with the writing on simple subjects: Religious experiences, pets, playthings, and the like. Story and composition subjects must be held within the child's interest.

### SUGGESTED CONTENT FOR GRADE 2

1. Writing Names
2. How We Talk to Each Other
3. How Sentences Begin
4. How Sentences End
5. The Word *I*
6. *Is* and *Are*
7. Writing Sentences
8. Asking Questions
9. Days of the Week: God-pleasing use of time; regular church and school attendance
10. *Was* and *Were*
11. *Were* Used with *You*
12. Using Capital Letters in Names: Include God, Jesus
13. *Has* and *Have*
14. Letter Writing (Very simple form)
15. *Saw* and *Seen*
16. Months of the Year
17. Writing Simple Rhymes
18. *Did* and *Done*
19. *I* and *We*
20. *Went* and *Gone*
21. *Isn't* and *Aren't*
22. Careful Speaking: No cursing, swearing, etc.
23. Choosing Words
24. Writing Stories; also Simple Bible Passages; Memory Material.
25. Reporting Experiences

Note: The outline above contains a few examples to indicate how spiritual and moral teachings can be woven into the language instruction. There are many other opportunities. When *was* and *were* are taught, the pupils may be asked to form statements or questions on church attendance; letters or compositions may tell in a sentence or two the reason for attending a Christian school; the Second Commandment may be briefly reviewed in connection with No. 22; etc. This will help the child in the realization that Christianity is a constant and all-pervading part of his life.

### Intermediate Grades (3—6)

Throughout these grades the children should learn to express themselves correctly and adequately in oral and written work. All phases of oral and written expression are developed in elementary form.

Economy of thought and expression are stressed from the beginning. Correct use of words and phrases is encouraged. Practical situations in oral work are provided constantly. The child is taught to address people, familiar or strange; speak correctly over the telephone; give proper directions; express himself distinctly and with emphasis; and listen attentively and respectfully to all persons with authority to speak. The socialized recitation provides an excellent medium for class participation, in which everyone speaks in turn and to the point.

In written expression the children are trained to write clearly and neatly what they intend to express. They become acquainted with the elementary forms of written expression, such as letter writing, theme writing, notes, and outlines. Pupils learn to organize thoughts and to eliminate waste of words and expressions. Through exercises provided by texts and workbooks they will become aware of common mistakes and correct usage.

In the fifth and sixth grades a beginning is made in the study of parts of speech and sentence structure. This will help the child still further to eliminate mistakes and make use of complete thoughts. Sentence study will help the child to analyze his own thoughts and the thoughts of others. He must always ask himself the question: "What am I told in that thought?" or "What am I trying to say to others?"

In composition work and story telling, religious topics, events from Church history, or current church events of local or synodical interest are utilized.

### Suggested Content for Grades 3 and 4 *

1. Sentence Recognition
2. Kinds of Sentences
3. Punctuation
4. Capitalization
5. Use of a and an
6. The Friendly Letter: Letters of Condolence, Encouragement, etc.
7. Addressing Envelopes
8. Their and There
9. There with Is and Are
10. Words Used in a Series
11. To, Too, Two
12. Writing Dates
13. Titles of Respect: Add Father, Mother, Pastor, Teacher to List in Textbook
14. May and Can
15. Writing Possessives
16. Contractions
17. Irregular Verbs
18. Arranging Words Alphabetically
19. Dividing Words
20. Teach and Learn
21. Writing Direct Quotations
22. Giving Talks
23. Writing Prayers, Playlets
24. Story Writing
25. Avoiding Unnecessary Words
26. Writing Poetry
27. Practice in Clear Enunciation and Pronunciation

* See note under Grade 2.

1. Good Usage (Verb forms)
2. Sentence Recognition
3. Capital Letters
4. Punctuation
5. End Punctuation
6. Recognizing Nouns
7. Letter Writing
8. Writing of Stories, Prayers, Memory Material
9. Recognizing Pronouns
10. Correct Use of Nouns and Pronouns .
11. Paragraphing
12. Theme Writing: Including Topics of Religious or Church Interest
13. Verbs and Verb Phrases
14. Choice of Verbs
15. Subject and Predicate
16. Choosing Suitable Adjectives
17. *This, That, These, Those*
18. *Lay* and *Laid*
19. *Lie, Lay, Lain,*
20. *Who's* and *Whose*
21. Direct Quotations
22. Use of Adverbs
23. Irregular Verbs
24. *Good* and *Well*
25. Prepositions
26. Conjunctions
27. Interjections
28. Double Negatives
29. Adjective and Verb Phrases
30. Business Letters
31. Interesting and Effective Speaking: Confession of Faith; Approaching Others with the Gospel
32. Clear Enunciation and Pronunciation
33. Criticizing Own Work

## Advanced Grades (7—8)

Practice in good language usage is continued in these grades. Exercises that train in good habits of speech and written work must be continued throughout. The elementary forms of speech are applied to advanced subjects and materials. The more formal types of social communication are practiced in addresses, debates, class discussions, and in meetings conducted according to the rules of parliamentary procedure.

Children in the advanced grades learn more of the possibilities of written expression. Theme work is developed in such types as essays, expositions, pleas, argumentations, and the like. There is a close correlation between written and oral procedure. Written work may be used as a preparation for oral presentation; oral presentation may provide a subject for a written assignment.

In these grades the scope of analytical language work should be enlarged. Based on elementary concepts of language forms, the work should prepare the pupils for analysis of sentence essentials and the recognition of parts of speech. This study receives parallel consideration with creative language work and exercises in correct usage. Care should be taken not to ignore one type in preference to the other. Practical application must be made of grammatical forms if their study is to be effective.

---

* See note under Grade 2.

As in the lower grades, topics centering in the religious and church life of the child should be substituted occasionally for others of lesser importance suggested by the textbook. The principles of honesty and Christian propriety of language communication must be stressed throughout.

SUGGESTED CONTENT FOR GRADES 7 AND 8

1. *Group Activity*
   - a. Prepared Speaking
   - b. Debates
   - c. Dramatizations
   - d. Holding Formal Meetings
   - e. Telephone Conversations
   - f. Making Appeals
   - g. Conferences, Reports
   - h. Planning a Project
   - i. Corrective Exercises

2. *Individual Exercises*
   - a. The Sentence
       1. Parts of Sentence
       2. Kinds of Sentences
       3. Punctuation
       4. Recognition and Classification of Sentences
   - b. Parts of Speech
       1. Substantives
       2. Verbs and Verbals
       3. Modifiers and Connectives
       4. Prepositions
       5. Phrases and Paragraphing
   - c. Composition
       1. The Outline
       2. Business Letters
       3. Friendly Letters
       4. Types of Letters
       5. Parapraph Writing
       6. Theme Writing
       7. Diction
       8. Correct Usage
       9. Synonyms, Antonyms

## E. CORRELATION

Language learning accompanies all school instruction. To become fully effective, the principles of language must be practically applied to all school situations. Christian understanding and use of language, clear enunciation and pronunciation, logical thinking and expression, correct and concise English, vocabulary growth, and all other language attitudes, habits, and skills must be practiced and improved in connection with every school subject.

This does not mean that every recitation is a language period, nor even that language emphasis is evident at all times to the casual observer, but the incidental teaching of language is present nevertheless. A new term learned in arithmetic, a report in geography, the spelling of a scientific term, the writing of memory work, or any thought expressed orally or in writing calls for correct language application. Conscious and planned use of these opportunities for correlation on the part of teacher and pupil makes language more profitable and interesting as a school subject.

## F. EVALUATING OUTCOMES

The questions below will help in evaluating the results of the language instruction:

1. Does the child recognize language as a gift of God and use it accordingly?

2. Is he guided in his speech by the principles of Christian propriety and honesty?

3. Does he show proper courtesy in his discussions with the teacher, classmates, and associates?

4. Does he indicate that he feels a need and desire for better speaking and writing?

5. Does the child show a tendency toward self-improvement and development of word usage in oral and written work?

6. Has he learned to express himself before an audience without fear and hesitation?

7. Does he carefully guard against the use of incorrect expressions?

8. Does he adhere to his topic in speaking and writing?

9. Can he analyze and summarize his own thoughts and the thoughts of others?

10. Can he speak or write on a topic or theme of his own selection?

11. Is his speech direct and to the point?

12. Does he offer constructive criticism to the fellow pupil who uses incorrect English? Is he willing to accept constructive criticism from others?

13. Is the child equipped to meet life's problems with a command of proper English and the ability to interpret the thoughts of his associates?

14. Can he write a good letter, correct in form and interesting in content?

### Selected References

Abney, Louise, and Miniace, Dorothy, *This Way to Better Speech.* World Book Co., 1940.

Brown, Dorothy Lathrop, and Butterfield, Marguerite, *The Teaching of Language in the Primary Grades.* Macmillan, 1941.

Certain, C. C., *Handbook of English for Boys and Girls.* Scott, Foresman and Co., 1939.

English: *A Handbook for Teachers in Elementary Schools*. Albany: University of the State of New York Press, 1940.

Kretzmann, P. E., *The Teaching of English*. Concordia, n. d.

Leiper, M. A., *Language Work in the Elementary Schools*. Ginn, 1916.

Locke, Anna, *Everyday Grammar and Composition*. Row, Peterson, and Co., 1928.

Morrison, Henry C., *The Curriculum of the Common School*. University of Chicago Press, 1940. Pp. 34—67.

Reed, H. B., *Psychology of Elementary School Subjects*. Ginn, 1938. Pp. 130—207.

Schmieding, A., *Curriculum in Language for Lutheran Schools*. Concordia, 1932.

*Twentieth Yearbook* of the Department of Elementary School Principals. Washington: National Education Association, 1941.

# 3. Spelling

## A. OBJECTIVES

1. The ability to spell the words commonly used in writing, including words peculiar to the Lutheran Church.

2. Chiefly, the desire and determination to spell correctly.

    a. Interest in words as words.

    b. The habit of observing new or troublesome words in ordinary reading, with a view to spelling them correctly.

    c. Exactness and self-criticism in all writing.

## B. SPELLING IN THE LUTHERAN SCHOOL

Spelling is primarily a skill subject. It calls chiefly for the ability to recognize, visualize, and reproduce the written or printed word.

Helpful, if not imperative, in the acquisition of this ability are: Methods of study, the proper analysis of words, the study of roots from which words are derived, syllabication, understanding the meaning and use of words, the dictionary habit, and the attitude of care and exactness.

But more important than these is the desire and determination to spell correctly. This is the actual key to success in spelling. Once that desire and determination has firmly taken hold of the learner, correct spelling and continued learning to spell will follow automatically, even without a formal course. The desire manifests itself particularly in the careful observation of words in ordinary reading, in the habit of adding to one's spelling vocabulary any new words encountered, and in keeping troublesome words correctly in mind; it also shows itself in exactness and self-criticism in all writing.

In all this there is nothing specifically Christian or Lutheran. Yet, in the Lutheran school, or with the Christian child, even such abilities and attitudes are acquired more readily, wholesomely, and thoroughly on the basis of Christian obedience and sense of duty. The Lutheran and Christian influence will make itself felt particularly in establishing and maintaining in the pupil the proper *motives*. This subject contributes nothing to the *Christian* training of the child if he is made letter-perfect and a winner of contests, so long as the driving force within him is selfishness or vainglory. On the other hand, even this skill subject can be made to contribute to such training if Christian motives are fostered and those not contrary to Scripture are approved. Among the motives to be encouraged is the desire of the Christian to use his spelling ability toward increasing his usefulness in this world.

The subject receives an additional Lutheran and Christian coloring by also dealing with a vocabulary that is peculiar to the religious subjects in our schools and to the Lutheran Church.

## C. METHOD OF TEACHING SPELLING

Spelling should be taught in a way that the pupil learns a system of study which will be useful to him throughout life. Any effective method of learning spelling resolves itself into systematic word study. The study includes hearing, pronouncing, seeing, and writing the word, both as a whole and in syllables; picking out the familiar, unfamiliar, and difficult parts of words and associating the difficult and unfamiliar parts with identical or similar letter groups or other words; and using the word in a sentence.

There is no single correct procedure of teaching a word, but all successful methods have similar elements. The suggestions given below may be helpful.

### Teacher Presentation

1. The teacher pronounces the word — if a long word, by syllables — and uses it in a sentence.

2. The teacher writes the word on the board and the class pronounces it.

### Pupil Study

1. Look at the word, pronounce it slowly and softly, and use it in a sentence.

2. Look at the word and spell it softly.

3. Close eyes and repeat.

4. Write the word and say the letters softly while writing. Consult the book if necessary.

5. Put a circle around any difficult part of the word.

6. Write the word without consulting the book.

7. Check and write again at least three times. Continue until the word can be written correctly without difficulty.

Authorities are fairly well agreed that in the lower three grades the "Study-Test Method" should be used to give young pupils the benefit of systematic study under the direction of the teacher. Beginning with the fourth grade the "Test-Study Method" may be profitably employed to avoid the spending of time on words that are already familiar.

The spelling class provides an ideal opportunity for teaching the use of the dictionary. As spelling consciousness, the awareness of the correctness or incorrectness of words, develops, the dictionary will become increasingly useful. This will be the case especially when the child or adult meets words of special or limited use, or words of unusual difficulty, which for obvious reasons have not been included in his spelling text.

Since only drill brings skill, it is evident that the school cannot depend wholly upon the incidental teaching of spelling. A systematic course, the discipline of drill, and attentive and frequent repetition are necessary to fix the desired skill and make correct spelling a permanent and natural part of the pupil. Nothing but a high standard of efficiency will suffice.

Additional suggestions for teaching spelling may be found in the helps suggested in the bibliography and in any good standard textbook.

### Time Devoted to Spelling

Time is not the most important factor in the effective teaching of spelling, but rather the way in which the time is spent. The daily program of the average school will allow 15 to 20 minutes per day for the teaching of spelling.

## D. THE COURSE

It is obvious that not all words that a child will ever use can be taught in the spelling course. Modern spellers generally include words that are of immediate use to the children and, in anticipation of their needs, a selected list of words from the adult vocabulary. They contain generally a minimum list of words and one or more supplementary lists, allowing for individual abilities of the pupils. It is advisable to adopt a standard text and to follow the course as outlined.

In all cases the text will need to be supplemented with words of local significance, the name of the city, village, and county, the names of important State officials, geographical and historical terms, etc., that are part of the vocabulary of the children.

In the Lutheran school, words peculiar to Christianity and the Lutheran Church must be added. The following list of supplementary words for Lutheran schools is essentially that recommended by Mertz and Siems [1] but with a number of additions. Since many of these words are found also in textbooks, the teacher and pupils may profitably check this list against their speller and eliminate such words as occur in the regular course. Whether the words are taught from the text or on the basis of this supplementary list, the specifically Christian or Lutheran connotation should be made clear.

### Supplementary Words for Lutheran Schools

#### PRIMARY GRADES

| | | | |
|---|---|---|---|
| angel | church | heaven | Savior |
| Bible | Easter | hell | sin |
| Christ | God | Jesus | soul |
| Christmas | godly | prayer | |

#### INTERMEDIATE GRADES

| | | | |
|---|---|---|---|
| Advent | elder | mercy | Satan |
| apostle | eternal | mission | service |
| article | everlasting | missionary | slander |
| baptism | faith | offering | stanza |
| baptize | faithful | offertory | synod |
| befriend | font | organist | teacherage |
| bliss | glorify | parish | temptation |
| catechism | Gospel | parsonage | Trinity |
| chimes | grace | Pentecost | triune |
| Christian | gracious | pew | virgin |
| Concordia | Holy Ghost | postlude | wafer |
| covet | human | preach | worship |
| creed | hymn | preacher | *Names of:* |
| deacon | Lent | prelude | Congregation |
| descend | liturgical | pulpit | School |
| despise | liturgy | Redeemer | Synod |
| devil | Luther | religion | Pastor |
| devotion | Lutheran | religious | Teachers |
| divine | merciful | saints | |

---

1) H. A. Mertz and W. A. Siems, *Curriculum in Spelling.*

UPPER GRADES

| | | | |
|---|---|---|---|
| absolution | congregation | install | sacrament |
| absolve | contribution | installation | salvation |
| admonish | covetous | institute | sanctification |
| adultery | covetousness | introit | sanctify |
| agenda | damnation | Jehovah | Scripture |
| almighty | deceitfully | justification | Seminary |
| altar | defame | Messiah | spiritual |
| anthem | desecrate | nave | stewardship |
| betray | doctrine | New Testament | synodical |
| bodily | doxology | omnipotent | temporal |
| budget | enlighten | omniscient | tidings |
| cancel | entice | ordained | transept |
| catechumen | Epiphany | parochial | trespass |
| chalice | estrange | pastor | trespasses |
| chancel | evangelical | penitent | vestibule |
| charity | evangelism | petition | vestry |
| chaste | evangelist | prophecy | Walther |
| circuit | excommunicate | prophesy | Walther League |
| choir | excommunication | reconciliation | worthily |
| choral | forgiveness | redemption | worthy |
| chorale | generation | Reformation | waver |
| commandment | hallowed | regeneration | wrath |
| Communion | humiliate | remission | |
| confess | humiliation | remit | *Names of:* |
| confession | humility | repentance | Societies in |
| confirm | idolatry | resurrection | Congregation |
| confirmand | inspiration | righteousness | President of |
| confirmation | inspire | Sabbath | Synod |

## E. CORRELATION

To develop a spelling conscience and consciousness, it is necessary to emphasize correct spelling in the written work of all subjects, for spelling is closely associated with success in nearly all learning. From every other school subject the regular list of 3,500 to 4,000 spelling words in the common course is supplemented. Proper names in history and geography, place names of local significance, the names of the local church and school and of the pastors and teachers are illustrations.

## F. EVALUATING OUTCOMES

The testing of the past has largely given way to better methods of teaching spelling. Still, testing is necessary from time to time.

Standard tests provide useful devices for comparing the achievements of different groups of children. They do not measure the direct results of class instruction, since many words in the test are not included in the word list of the spelling text for the respective grade, and some are not in the text at all. Therefore standard tests measure rather the sum total of spelling learning, including what has been learned incidentally. Unless given at regular intervals, they also fail to measure adequately the growth of efficiency in spelling.

The tests based upon the word lists of the textbook are of three kinds, pre-tests, main tests, and review tests. The pre-test eliminates from further study the words which the child already knows; the main test checks the immediate success of a lesson that has been taught; and the review test, given after a longer period of time, indicates which words have been retained, and which require further study and attention.

Tests consisting of written contextual exercises show more accurately than either oral or written column exercises which words the child is able to use correctly. However, column exercises may be used occasionally for a saving of time and for convenience.

For an accurate and constant evaluation of their own work, pupils should be held to keep a list of words that present particular difficulties and to keep a graph record of their weekly progress. Specific suggestions for these records will be found in most textbooks.

The pupil's desire and determination to spell correctly, and the motives which impel him to put forth his best efforts, are not subject to objective testing devices. They can be measured best by inference; by the pupil's *apparent* attitude and interest, by his application to the work, and by his achievements.

### Selected References

Mertz, H. A., and Siems, W. A., *Curriculum in Spelling*. Concordia, 1931.
Tidyman, W. F., *The Teaching of Spelling*. World Book Company, 1924.
Breed, F. S., *How to Teach Spelling*. F. A. Owen Publishing Co., 1930.
Pryor, H. C., and Pittman, M. S., *A Guide to the Teaching of Spelling*. Macmillan, 1921.
Reed, Homer B., *Psychology of Elementary School Subjects*. Ginn, 1938. Pp. 208—263.
State, local, or District Course of Study.

## 4. Handwriting

### A. GENERAL OBJECTIVES

1. The desire to write well.

2. Legibility, ease, and speed of handwriting for successful written communication and the proper recording of facts and ideas.

3. Neatness and good form in all written work, *e. g.*, margins, spacing, paragraphing; and habitually good practice in all writing situations.

4. The ability to study one's own writing critically with a view toward diagnosing and correcting difficulties.

## B. DISCUSSION OF THE OBJECTIVES

### The Desire to Write Well

A good handwriting is possible only where the desire for it exists. Establishment of this desire is a fundamental task of the teacher. Intrinsic or extrinsic motives may be used to stimulate the desire, the former being the more valuable. Of intrinsic value is the realization on the part of the child that he needs the skills of handwriting for the purpose of expressing his thoughts when oral communication is impossible. He must learn to see the relationship of writing to his home and school life and to apply it to subject matter within his grasp of understanding and interest. Also the desire to do a worth-while thing well is of intrinsic value. Here the Christian child will be aided by the realization that all good things are blessings of God, that they must be used in His service, and that their use and exercise must be improved to the greatest possible degree of perfection.

Approval, awards, and competition are extrinsic motives that may be utilized, but with proper precaution. Wrongly used, these may lead to pride and jealousy and counteract the school's efforts in Christian training. Rightly used, they may nurture a healthy desire to write well. Filing of handwriting specimens for future comparison, exchange of specimens between classes, rooms, or schools, and exhibition of work done according to a satisfactory standard may be utilized legitimately to stimulate interest and desire for improvement.

The teacher's own valuation placed upon a good handwriting as evidenced by his enthusiasm for the work and his own handwriting on the blackboard and in correcting pupil papers also has a strong influence upon pupil desire and attitude.

Less attention to prolonged formal drill and more attention to actual writing of a useful nature will help in the stimulation of interest, inasmuch as it stresses the utility of the work.

Concentration of attention is closely allied with interest. It reflects interest on the part of the class and is one of the essentials for success in handwriting.

### Legibility, Ease, Speed

Writing as a phase of language is a substitute for speech and has large social and business utility. As one of the purposes of language instruction is to lead the pupil to express himself clearly and correctly, so in handwriting he should be able to present facts and ideas clearly, legibly, and easily. The course in the elementary school is not intended to train for specialized vocational demands, but to meet the requirements of the ordinary man and woman. Vocational requirements are met by the vocational school. The writing objectives of ease, speed, and legibility are best attained by practice in ordinary purposeful writing.

Good form in writing depends upon three factors: 1. Recognition of the right letter or word form; 2. Visualization of the right form while writing; 3. Sufficient drill to achieve the right form.

The legibility and facility necessary for everyday purposes should be achieved by the end of the sixth grade. The arm, hand, and finger muscles all play their part in these skills, and as long as the movement is free and fairly rapid, the pupil should be permitted to make his own adaptations. He will thereby retain his individuality in writing. Blackboard writing is important in acquiring ease and rhythm in writing.

### Good Writing Habits in All Written Work

Good writing is a habit which should function at all times and in all writing situations. Therefore it must be emphasized in all subjects where any form of written expression is required. Systematic practice and repetition will finally fix the habit so that it will carry over into actual writing situations. It will be useful to include, in the daily practice, material from the subjects in which writing is required. For example: Spelling and language work may well form the basis of lessons in handwriting; or an exchange of letters with other schools, invitations to school functions, or similar practical situations may be utilized to stimulate interest and to relate the subject to the areas in which the skill is expected to function. Much actual writing under guidance is the important thing.

Besides neatness and correctness of letter form, the handwriting course must stress good form in larger units of written work: margins, spacing, paragraphing, and the like. With this emphasis, the writing lesson not only becomes interesting and purposeful, but it saves much time in language and composition instruction.

### Self-Criticism

No pupil will ever develop into a good writer unless he learns to appraise his own writing. His practice must be guided by close attention to correction and improvement of his work. For that reason he should be taught to compare his writing with a good standard sample and to judge his product according to it. See page 118 under *F. Evaluation* for more detailed suggestions on this point.

## C. PRACTICAL SUGGESTIONS
**Position**

*Light:* From left side; supplemented by artificial lighting if not bright enough.

*Seat:* Low enough to permit feet to rest comfortably on the floor.

*Desk:* Adjusted so that by placing the forearms on the desk the elbows rest two or three inches from side of body.

*Position:* Sit erect, with spine on a fairly straight line with the head, shoulders even, with body well balanced.

*Paper:* Directly in front of writer, the lower edge forming an angle of about 30 degrees with the edge of the desk.

*Hand:* Grasp pen or pencil lightly with fingers curved in natural position; hand not turned more than halfway to the side; rest and slide easily on third and fourth fingers; forefinger about an inch from pen point and thumb resting on penholder a little above the first finger.

*Blackboard:* Hold chalk between thumb and first and second fingers, the inner end pointing toward the palm of the hand. Stand an easy arm's length from the board. The hand must not touch the board. The eraser is held behind the back. Write on the level of the eye as much as possible.

### Movement

The writing movement consists of the combined action of arm, hand, and fingers. The arm provides the larger movement which carries the hand over the page. In addition the arm swings upward and downward somewhat as the up-and-down strokes are formed. The hand slides easily upon the third and fourth fingers. The movement of the fingers is utilized in forming the details of the letters.

The combined movement is more natural and more easy to learn than either the exclusive arm movement or the cramped finger movement. It allows for ease in the larger swinging strokes and for the speed and rhythm necessary in good writing. The pupil's adaptation of the combined movement will encourage and preserve his individuality in handwriting.

A free, easy, well-co-ordinated movement is necessary for fluency and speed in writing. In the broad sense of the term, such movement is rhythmical. This means that there is a certain regularity of movement, though the more complicated strokes will slow down the speed somewhat. Rhythm is taught most satisfactorily by means of simple exercises which are written to count.

For the more complicated strokes, letters and simple words are written to count. Good handwriting manuals explain in greater detail this phase of teaching and supply exercises for developing the desired fluency and speed. These should be consulted.

## Left-Handedness

The teacher will give special attention to the pupil who shows a tendency to write with the left hand. He will observe him at work and play to see which hand he uses in throwing a ball, driving a nail, or any similar activity. Unless he is very strongly left-handed, he may be taught to write with his right hand. If he is found to be definitely left-handed, he is permitted to write with his left hand but is held to the same position as the right-handed child — only in reverse. Five to six per cent of all children are thought to be left-handed.

## Manuscript Writing

Manuscript writing has the following advantages for beginners:

1. The use of one alphabet in reading and writing simplifies teaching.
2. The strokes are based on straight lines and circles. This makes for simplicity.
3. Small children find it more legible.
4. It is attractive.
5. A fair rate of speed is possible in manuscript writing.
6. The transfer to cursive writing presents little difficulty.

There is no full agreement as to the time when the transfer to cursive writing is most desirable, but, in general, authorities regard the latter part of the second grade or the first part of the third grade as the most suitable time.

Any good handwriting manual or text will contain the manuscript alphabet. For that reason it is not reproduced here.

## Individual Progress

Teaching is adapted to the need of the individual, and pupils are allowed to progress at their own rate of speed. The standards set for the individual pupil must be attainable. Pupils who have reached an adequate standard and maintain the standard may be excused from further handwriting instruction and practice.

## Time Division

It is not necessary to instruct each grade separately in handwriting. Combinations of classes are practical. In one-teacher schools only two classes are necessary, one class in manuscript and one in cursive writing. The group practice and instruction is supplemented by attention to individual needs.

Daily short periods are preferable to fewer longer class sessions. In the lower grades, ten minutes daily will be sufficient. In the higher grades, three to five 15-minute periods per week are suggested, depending upon the time that is available.

In one-room schools it will often be an advantage to send pupils, especially the primary children, to the blackboard, where the teacher may supervise them while he is conducting another class.

## D. COURSE SUGGESTIONS

An outline of course suggestions is unnecessary. For best results in handwriting it is desirable that a set of practice books be introduced and followed systematically. Directions will be contained in the accompanying teachers' manual. Texts are suggested in the bibliography.

## E. CORRELATION POSSIBILITIES

The standards set in the writing lesson must be insisted upon in all writing situations. Again, a large amount of work in other school subjects may be taken care of in the handwriting period. It is suggested especially that the following subjects be considered for their possibilities in this respect:

*Memory Work:* Occasionally write memory work, stressing especially the proper form of recording Bible passages, writing hymn stanzas, and the exact reproduction of material.

*Language:* Teach the proper form of compositions, itemized lists and orders, social and business letters, and provide practice in writing them.

Teach the proper forms of margins, spacing, indentations, paragraphing, punctuation, and the like, and have pupils write exercises in which these are practiced.

Teach capitalization and write words and sentences in which capitals are correctly and neatly used.

*Spelling:* Occasionally a spelling dictation may constitute a lesson in handwriting. Give consideration to correct spelling, column formation, and neatness in general.

*Arithmetic:* Write arithmetic examples, stressing form of numbers; neatness, exactness, and clarity of example form; and proper succession and continuity of steps in the solution.

*General:* In all written work stress proper identification of paper: Name, date, etc.

## F. EVALUATING OUTCOMES

Scales and score cards will help both teacher and pupil in evaluating the quality of handwriting.

### TESTS AND SCALES FOR MEASURING AND ANALYZING HANDWRITING

Ayers, L. P., *Measuring Scale for Handwriting: Elementary Grades.* Russell Sage Foundation.

Courtis, S. A., *Standard Practice Test in Handwriting,* Grades 3—8. World Book Co.

Freeman, F. N., *Chart for Diagnosing Faults: Elementary Grades.* Houghton Mifflin Co.

Freeman, F. N., *Handwriting Measuring Scale for Elementary Grades.* Zaner-Bloser Co.

Zaner-Bloser Staff, *Handwriting Faults and How to Correct Them.* Zaner-Bloser Co.

The pupil should learn to analyze his difficulties in handwriting under the direction of the teacher. Test papers should be preserved to facilitate comparison with earlier work. Special difficulties may be recorded on a chart in order that progress may be noted. The chart below is suggestive of what is meant.

### HANDWRITING CHART [1]

| Where to Improve | Test 1 | Test 2 | Test 3 | Test 4 |
|---|---|---|---|---|
| 1. Use correct position in all writing situations | ...... | ...... | ...... | ...... |
| 2. Use a freer movement | ...... | ...... | ...... | ...... |
| 3. Increase speed of writing | ...... | ...... | ...... | ...... |
| 4. Do not crowd letters | ...... | ...... | ...... | ...... |
| 5. Write letters closer together | ...... | ...... | ...... | ...... |
| 6. Write with lighter touch | ...... | ...... | ...... | ...... |
| 7. Write heavier | ...... | ...... | ...... | ...... |
| 8. Write letters the same size | ...... | ...... | ...... | ...... |
| 9. Slant all letters in the same direction | ...... | ...... | ...... | ...... |
| 10. Make a longer final stroke | ...... | ...... | ...... | ...... |
| 11. Keep margins straight | ...... | ...... | ...... | ...... |
| 12. Practice the following small letters | ...... | ...... | ...... | ...... |
| 13. Practice the following capitals | ...... | ...... | ...... | ...... |

*Directions:* 1. Check column where improvement is needed.

2. After first test use "+" sign to show improvement and "—" sign to indicate the lack of it.

3. For the last two items, insert the letters that most need improvement.

*Name* ............................................. *Grade* ..................... *Year* .............

1) Patterned somewhat after chart in Missouri *Course of Study* (1937), p. 773.

## Selected References

### BOOKS FOR THE TEACHER

Conrad, Edith Underwood, *Teacher's Guide. Manuscript Writing.* A. N. Palmer Co.

Freeman, Frank N., *Courses of Study in Handwriting.* Zaner-Bloser Company, 1928.

Freeman, Frank N., *Solving Handwriting Needs as We See Them Today.* Zaner-Bloser Co.

Freeman, Frank N., and Daugherty, Mary, *How to Teach Handwriting.* Houghton Mifflin Company, 1923.

Graves, Minnie B., *Muscular Writing.* W. S. Benson and Co., 1928.

Missouri *Course of Study*, 1937, pp. 767—774.

Morrison, Henry C., *The Curriculum of the Common School.* University of Chicago Press, 1940, pp. 40—48.

Reed, Homer B., *Psychology of Elementary School Subjects.* Ginn and Company, 1938, pp. 264—301.

West, Paul U., *Changing Practices in Handwriting Instruction.* Public School Publishing Company, 1927.

Wise, Marjorie, *Manuscript Writing: On the Technique of.* Charles Scribner's Sons. 1924.

### TEXTBOOKS

*Palmer Method of Business Writing.* A. N. Palmer Co.

*Zaner-Bloser Series.* By Frank N. Freeman. All elementary school grades. Manuscript writing in grades one and two, with transition during the latter part of the second grade. Teacher's manuals. Zaner-Bloser Company.

---

# V. ARITHMETIC

## A. OBJECTIVES *

1. Recognition of number and ability in its use as gifts of God which can and should be used to His glory.

    a. An appreciation of the meaning, use, and value of number in life.

    b. A growing understanding of ways in which number can be used in the service of God.

2. The ability to deal with the fundamental processes.

    a. Integers.

    b. Fractions.

    c. Denominate numbers.

---

* Objectives as stated in *Curriculum in Arithmetic for Lutheran Schools,* by Arthur L. Miller, Concordia, 1937. The objectives are there made the basis for suggested activities which illustrate how they can be made functional in the classroom.

3. The ability to deal with life situations involving number.

    a. The understanding and habitual use of an adequate number vocabulary.

    b. Understanding how to attack "thought problems."

    c. Ability to cope with typical problem situations.

    d. Measurement.

    e. Acquaintance with common business transactions and skill in performing the arithmetic involved in so far as this is useful for the average citizen.

    f. The habit of scrutinizing problem situations and business transactions in the light of God's Word.

4. The maintenance of understandings and skills.

5. The understanding and habitual use of economical habits of work in arithmetic.

    a. Estimating answers.

    b. Checking answers.

    c. Neatness.

6. The ability to think quantitatively and with precision.

    a. The ability to grasp the meaning of mathematical data found in other studies and in wide reading.

    b. The habit of inquiring after, and using, precise data in formulating judgment on any issue.

## B. DISCUSSION OF OBJECTIVES

Our number system is one of the greatest inventions of man. It would be extremely difficult, if not impossible, to imagine our civilization developing as it has without this tool of precision — the Hindu-Arabic number system. The contribution of arithmetic to science, industry, and commerce is incalculable.

The human origin of our number system is lost in obscurity, yet, like "every good and perfect gift," it comes from the Lord. Being a gift from God, the Christian child will be taught to appreciate arithmetic as such; will recognize how this tool makes easy many otherwise difficult aspects of human life; will recognize how it makes possible inventions that make our life more comfortable; and will appreciate that the scientific achievements made possible by our number system contribute to the extension of the Gospel.

Having recognized the number system as a gift from God, having appreciated its wide use and value in life, the Christian child will seek to grow proficient in its use. He will be stimulated to work up to the level of his ability in acquiring understanding and economical habits of work.

Along with proficiency in the fundamental processes, ability to cope with typical lifelike problem situations, and an understanding of common business transactions, the child is led to understand the ways in which numbers can be used in the service of God and also acquires the habit of scrutinizing problem situations and business transactions in the light of God's Word. Now, arithmetic, *per se*, is neither moral nor immoral, it is amoral; however, also during the arithmetic period, the child will be taught to think and to work as a Christian.

## C. METHOD

In asking children to master our complicated number system, we ask them to master one of the most wonderful and difficult intellectual inventions ever made. Proof of the complicated nature of the number system is seen in the accumulation of difficulties in the intermediate and upper grades of the elementary school. These difficulties are ascribed to the fact that our ideas are by nature concrete rather than abstract, which the teaching of arithmetic does not always recognize. To minimize the difficulty which children have with the abstract phases of arithmetic, we must first of all develop an adequate number concept. This is best developed by unhurried experience with concrete materials for the greater part of the first year, followed by a gradual introduction to the additive and subtractive combinations on the basis of objects and pictures.

Learning arithmetic is not memorizing facts, nor merely manipulating symbols, but the building up of ideas, of generalizations. What is needed in the teaching of arithmetic is broad experience from which generalizations can be developed.

Nor is such broad experience confined to the beginning pupil; at every new step in the study of arithmetic we should return to the fact that the processes of arithmetic are intellectual processes, not mere pencil and paper processes. Adequate initial teaching on the basis of concrete materials will make for understandings that make otherwise dark abstractions meaningful.

Three theories dominate current practice in the learning and teaching of arithmetic:

1. *The Drill Theory,* which conceives learning arithmetic as the acquisition of a host of abstract isolated statements of fact; which conceives teaching as administering drill; and which proposes that progress in the development of ability in arithmetic may be adequately measured by measuring either or both rate and accuracy.

2. *The Incidental Theory,* which holds that no systematic teaching of arithmetic is necessary and that children who learn arithmetic only as the need arises in an activity-child-centered curriculum learn quite as much arithmetic as those who have systematic instruction in the subject.

3. *The Meaning Theory,* which holds that in the learning of any new process there must be adequate objective experience, from which the correct principle, understanding, and method is extracted before drill takes place.

The Drill Theory has dominated arithmetic teaching in the elementary school for some time. Had this teaching been successful, there would be no cause for complaint, but it has not been successful, because it does not take into account the actual mental processes of children. While the procedure does succeed with some pupils, it neglects those pupils who do not immediately develop the specific, direct connections they are expected to develop.

The Incidental Theory is a reaction against the Drill Theory. As a reaction against the artificiality and formalism which so long dominated the teaching of arithmetic, it doubtless has some validity; certainly it has high motivation in its favor. Studies comparing the achievements of pupils studying arithmetic incidentally in activity programs with those having regular instruction in arithmetic, tentatively seem to show that the former did quite as well as the latter.

The Meaning Theory is a reaction against both the Drill Theory and the Incidental Theory. It suggests that the Drill Theory misplaced drill, giving it precedence over actual teaching and overestimating its importance. Certainly drill remains an essential part of good teaching procedure in skill-building and skill-holding; the former should follow adequate initial teaching; the latter is included in maintenance programs which seek by periodic recall and restudy to make retention permanent through longer periods. The Meaning Theory suggests that the Incidental Theory is also in error in maintaining that systematic arithmetic is naturally stilted and formal. The advocates of the Meaning Theory reject the idea that the choice must be made between the Drill Theory and the Incidental Theory. They realize that the entire school set-up is based on the idea that through organization the school can give the child what he cannot attain for himself, and therefore they believe in properly motivated systematic instruction, minus the objectionable elements of artificiality and formalism.

Systematic teaching, rich in concrete materials, rich in child-activity situations, rich in additional problem situations, and utilizing a testing program coupled with remedial measures, offers a program more likely to succeed in developing understandings, more likely to recognize interference factors and to eliminate them, than any program of incidental teaching, no matter how rich in motivation or how carefully planned.

## D. COURSE SUGGESTIONS

### Organization of Materials

The textbook has dominated arithmetic teaching to such an extent that attempts at individualizing instruction to take care of the particular needs of individual children have suffered. Adequate initial teaching will make unnecessary much of the elaborate remedial measures schools have frequently set up. The best of teaching, however, will fail to produce homogeneity in any school subject, and least of all in arithmetic. Systematic diagnosis of pupil difficulties coupled with appropriate remedial measures is absolutely necessary for effective teaching. Quite likely no wholesale individualization of the arithmetic program such as utilized under the Winnetka Plan will receive much support in our schools, but recognition of individual differences demands that we provide a set-up that takes these differences into account.

One method of accomplishing this is to set up three areas of work in arithmetic:

1. *Social arithmetic,* an understanding of how number is used in business and problem situations, with computational difficulties held to a minimum. This aspect of arithmetic should be developed with the entire class.

2. *Minimum essentials* in computational arithmetic, also developed with the entire class.

3. *Supplementary activities* including both additional topics and more difficult computation for those in the class who have satisfactorily finished the minimum essentials.

Such a program would permit each pupil to stress those aspects of arithmetic most difficult for him, whether in any of the fundamental processes in integers, fractions, or denominate numbers, or in some special phase of arithmetic, such as percentage, areas, volume, etc.

Obviously the textbook under such a program would be used differently than under a method that always dealt with the class as a unit. Different members of the class would be working on differentiated textbook materials, supplemented with other practice materials. Obviously, too, the method of assignment, of grading, and of recording would need to take into account this partially individualized program. The Unit Organization for the Grades suggested on page 69 of the Curriculum in Arithmetic,[1] would provide a start for such an organization, although many of the topics would need to be further detailed, particularly the fundamental processes.

## Problem Solving

The major function of work in arithmetic is to give the child ability to handle such problems as arise in life situations. Problems may be classified under three heads:

1. Those based upon situations which are actually present to the pupils' senses. Such problems must come from the immediate environment and experiences of the group and be initiated by the pupils and the teacher. Textbooks can not be expected to supply this type of problem, although they may give valuable suggestions as to projects and activities that require considerable use of number. Valuable as these problems are, a satisfactory course for children will require additional problem material.

2. Those based upon situations not actually present to the pupils' senses, but which they can readily imagine. Such problems can be quite as real as those encountered in an activity program, and they permit the use of a much wider range of material. There is no shortage of this desirable type of problem, for it includes planning for parties and excursions, saving money to buy something, trips, and other topics of interest to children.

3. Mere verbal descriptions of situations which the pupil can not readily imagine and in which he has little if any interest. Many difficulties in learning problem solving can be charged to this type of problem. Teachers will do well to substitute other problem material for any of this type encountered in their arithmetics.

Each new phase of a process should be introduced through the medium of a problem, and skills which pupils acquire should be put to use immediately in solving problems. Verbal statements which are all of the same pattern and which do not require the pupils to decide which operation or operations to perform are not really problems, for real problems require reasoning.

In testing the problems presented to the children in any arithmetic text it is well to keep in mind the following criteria:

1. Reality. Good problems are real. Problems that do not exist in practical life are all too frequent in children's assignments.

2. Interest. Good problems are derived from situations which make a strong appeal to the children.

---

1) Miller, Arthur L., *Curriculum in Arithmetic for Lutheran Schools.* Concordia, 1937.

3. Simplicity of language. Good problems are presented in language that the pupil understands, free from unnecessary unknown forms and unfamiliar words. Good problems read like stories and have an attractive style. Buswell and John's investigation of vocabulary difficulties in arithmetic indicated that most textbooks gave insufficient teaching to new concepts.

Where the textbook fails, the teacher must develop the concepts.

## Grade Placement of Topics in Arithmetic

A comparison of the more recent textbooks in arithmetic with those of a decade or more ago reveals that many topics have been shifted to a higher grade. This has been largely in response to the findings of the Committee of Seven, whose latest report is given in the *Thirty-Eighth Yearbook* of the National Society for the Study of Education.[2] Another change is the continuing of topics with actual teaching beyond the initial year of presentation, *e. g.*, long division was formerly completed rather thoroughly in the fourth grade, with reviews of the subject in later grades. The present tendency is to extend the teaching of this topic through several grades. This procedure is also followed in other topics.

## E. CORRELATION POSSIBILITIES

The teacher who is alert to catch the opportunities for problem-solving which come up in children's school and out-of-school affairs, will find much use for arithmetic in correlation with other school subjects. Such use of arithmetic will deepen the understanding of children in the other school subjects and will also have a reciprocal influence upon the children's abilities in arithmetic. So many correlations are possible that it is impossible to submit an exhaustive list. Some of the possibilities are:

*Religion*

1. Graphing church attendance.
2. Graphing the growth of the local church, school, and Sunday school.
3. Graphing the possibilities in Missions.
4. Problems about offerings and church attendance.
5. Budgets for Christian boys and girls, and for Christian families.
6. Budgets and contributions of congregation and District.[3]

---

2) See Selected References.

3) The *Statistical Yearbook* may be used as source. Some District publications also contain detailed contribution lists.

*Reading*

Teach the arithmetical concepts encountered. A vocabulary study of arithmetical terms should prove useful.

*Language*

The social aspects of arithmetic lend themselves to good oral and written theme topics:

1. The Metric System.
2. The Origin of our System of Weights and Measures.
3. Insurance.
4. Our Postal System.
5. Stocks and Bonds.
6. Banking.
7. Taxes.
8. Geometric Figures in the Home.
9. The Cost of Telephone and Telegraph Messages.
10. Meters (Gas and Electric).

*Spelling*

See the *Curriculum in Arithmetic* [4] for an arithmetic vocabulary.

*Geography*

1. Graphs of production, population, imports, and exports.
2. Latitude and longitude.
3. Figuring per capita wealth, trade, and production.
4. Drawing maps to scale.
5. Measuring distances on maps.
6. Figuring time intervals on map or globe.
7. Recognizing arithmetical meanings of dot maps, rainfall maps, etc.

*History and Civics*

1. Figuring intervals between dates.
2. Knowledge of the public debt and taxes.
3. Graphing population growth.
4. Graphing increase in area.
5. The history of Roman numerals.
6. The history of our Hindu-Arabic system of notation.

*Science and Health*

1. Graphing safety statistics.
2. Graphing data on the fight against disease.
3. Graphing data on food costs and food values.
4. Understanding the part played by number in the advance of science.

*Art*

Understanding the geometric figures used in designs and architecture.

---

4) Miller, Arthur L., *op. cit.*, pp. 40, 56, 57.

## F. EVALUATING OUTCOMES

In arithmetic we are concerned with three factors: rate, accuracy, and methods of procedure. Rate and accuracy are important measures of arithmetical ability, and both are measured by various types of achievement and diagnostic tests. Of more fundamental importance than either, however, is an evaluation of the methods of procedure used by the child or the teacher. The teacher asks: What is going on in the mind of the child? This can be ascertained by having the pupil think aloud. While the usual class load will not permit using this procedure with all children in the class, certainly those children who experience difficulty with one or the other phases of arithmetic should receive such individual diagnosis and remedial treatment.

### Selected References

Brownell, Wm. A., "Psychological Considerations in the Learning and the Teaching of Arithmetic." Ginn and Co. (Reprint from *The Tenth Yearbook* of the National Council of Teachers of Mathematics.)

Brownell, Wm. A., *The Development of Children's Number Ideas in the Primary Grades.* University of Chicago Press, 1928.

Brueckner, L. J., *Diagnostic and Remedial Teaching in Arithmetic.* Winston, 1930.

Buckingham, B. R., "Significance, Meaning, Insight — These Three." Ginn and Co. (Reprint from *The Mathematics Teacher*, January, 1938.)

Buswell, G. T., "Deferred Arithmetic." Ginn and Co. (Reprint from *The Mathematics Teacher,* May, 1938.)

Karpinski, L. C., *The History of Arithmetic.* Rand McNally, 1925.

Lee, J. M., and Lee, D. M., *The Child and His Curriculum.* D. Appleton-Century, 1940.

Miller, Arthur L., *Curriculum in Arithmetic for Lutheran Schools.* Concordia, 1937.

Morton, R. L., *Teaching Arithmetic in the Primary Grades.* Silver Burdett, 1937.

Morton, R. L., *Teaching Arithmetic in the Intermediate Grades.* Silver Burdett, 1938.

Morton, R. L., *Teaching Arithmetic in the Upper Grades.* Silver Burdett, 1939.

National Council of Teachers of Mathematics. 10th Yearbook, *Teaching Arithmetic.* New York: Bureau of Publications, Teachers College.

National Council of Teachers of Mathematics, 11th Yearbook, *Mathematics in Modern Education.* 16th Yearbook, *Arithmetic in General Education,* 1941. New York: Bureau of Publications, Teachers College.

Smith, D. E., *The History of Mathematics*. Ginn, 1923—25, Vols. I and II.

*Twenty-Ninth Yearbook*, National Society for the Study of Education. Public School Publishing Co., 1930.

*Thirty-Eighth Yearbook*, National Society for the Study of Education. Public School Publishing Co., 1939.

Wilson-Stone-Dalrymple, *Teaching the New Arithmetic*. McGraw-Hill, 1931.

# VI. SOCIAL SCIENCE

## INTRODUCTION

The Social Science area has been divided into Primary Social Studies, Geography, History, and Civics. Except in the Primary Social Studies section, Geography, History, and Civics have been treated as separate subjects, though the highest possible degree of correlation is recommended.

A number of unified social studies textbooks are available, and it is likely that some of these are used locally. The integrated course does not make for a difference in purpose or intent, but only in the arrangement of materials. Therefore the general aims and Christian viewpoint underlying the subjects in this area remain the same, whether they are taught separately or in the form of an integrated course.

## 1. Primary Social Studies

(Geography, History, Civics, Health, Safety, Science, Nature, Character, Manners. Grades 1—4)

### A. GENERAL OBJECTIVES

1. Increase of the small child's understanding and appreciation of life and material things that surround him.

2. Increasing consciousness of the Creator's presence, rule, and care in everything.

3. A better understanding of himself and his needs.

    a. An elementary understanding of his social and physical needs.

    b. Proper Christian behavior and good manners.

    c. Good habits of health and safety.

4. Acquaintance with some of the simpler laws of nature, natural phenomena, and causes that underlie certain common ex-

periences; and the formation of simple concepts of history and government.

5. An elementary understanding of the influence of environment upon man's life and work.

## B. DISCUSSION OF OBJECTIVES

### Combination of Subjects

Combining a number of subjects in a single social studies course for the primary grades does not mean that these areas are confused, but rather that they do not receive individual recognition on the school program and that the class is not always aware of a distinction between the various areas. Child interest and ability justify this treatment. The small child does not think in terms of subjects, but in terms of facts learned. He is interested in life — human, plant, and animal life — and in the universe as it affects the simple life he understands.

### Purpose of the Social Studies

The purpose of the primary Social Studies is to give the child some understanding of the chief social groups of which he is a part and, in some measure, of the world about him, and to have him begin to see himself in the proper relationship to his surroundings. The earth created and preserved by God as the home of man; all good gifts created by God for the benefit of man and to be used according to His will; home, school, church, and community as institutions designed for man's benefit and proper use — these are concepts which the child should acquire early.

### Understanding of Needs

To understand his place in the world, the child must know himself and his social, spiritual, and physical needs. The religious instruction helps him to see that he is a sinner, that Jesus is his Savior, and that he must live according to the rules of conduct established by God. This is fundamental for Christian character growth. The Social Studies provide many opportunities for building habits of Christian conduct and citizenship upon the foundation which has been laid in the religious instruction, because the subject matter of the Social Studies deals largely with relationships in which attitudes and right action are important.

### Good Manners

The term *good manners,* as distinguished from Christian conduct, refers to actions and behavior which are not in themselves moral or immoral, but which are socially desirable. The instruction and training in good manners is carried on incidentally at all times.

## Other Instructional Content

There is no agreement on the exact content for the social studies course. It is evident that some of the simpler laws of nature, natural phenomena, and simple cause-and-effect relationships should be taught.

Elementary concepts of history and government may be established on the basis of biographical incidents of great men and on the basis of discussions of the United States flag, national holidays, and the like.

## Influence of Environment

From the study of life among the Indians, Dutch, Chinese, and others the child acquires simple historical and geographical concepts and begins to see the influence of environment upon social and economic activity. The same understandings grow also out of a study of the local community and a consideration of the changes in environment and in the mode of living over a period of years. A study of the changes since grandfather was a boy will fascinate most children.

## Opportunities for Stressing the Christian viewpoint

The teacher will expand the following list of opportunities for stressing the Christian viewpoint:

1. The wonders of the universe. (The power and greatness of God.)
2. Food, clothing, shelter. (Gratitude to God for all good gifts; First Article; Fourth Petition.)
3. Home, school, church. (Third and Fourth Commandments.)
4. Life, health, safety. ("I am fearfully and wonderfully made," Psalm 139:14; God rules the lives of His children; Fifth Commandment requires observance of principles of health and safety; First Article; Fourth Petition.)
5. Study of life in other lands. (Gratitude for the comforts we possess by God's grace; tolerance, good will toward other peoples; compassion and help for them in their bodily needs; interest in their spiritual welfare.)
6. Life and occupations in the local community. (Honesty and Christian co-operation necessary; our dealings with fellow men to be in conformity with the Second Table of the Law.)
7. Christian conduct and good manners. (The Ten Commandments.)

## C. PRACTICAL SUGGESTIONS

**Sourcebooks**

Social studies, health and safety, and science readers supply material which is selected largely for its social usefulness. They appeal to the child's interests and answer his recurring questions of how and why. The Christian viewpoint must in all cases be supplied by the teacher.

Purchase of these books by the pupils would be costly. Since they may be used again and again in a supplementary reading program, it is suggested that the school purchase the texts.

**Time**

The amount of time devoted to the social studies program will vary with the type of school and the number of classes taught by the teacher. Where the teacher is responsible for a number of grades, much of the material may be covered in silent reading periods. If sufficient time and materials are available to the school, a half hour daily is suggested for reading and discussion in the social studies.

Field trips should be undertaken as much as possible during school hours.

## D. SUGGESTED COURSE CONTENT [1]

The course content listed below is merely suggestive. The teacher will add or omit as the needs of his pupils require. It is clear that it will be impossible to teach everything that would be of interest to children of this age. For this reason also textbooks differ rather widely in their choice of materials. The subject matter is not nearly so important as the ways of thinking and the habits and attitudes which are developed. Especially important is the development of the Christian viewpoint.

### GRADE I

1. *Home and Family:* The beginning of family life in the Garden of Eden; members of a family must be kind and helpful toward one another; how they can help one another; problems of the home in securing food, clothing, and shelter; family worship.

2. *The School:* The congregation supports the school that children may learn God's Word and will thoroughly; work and play in the Christian school; care of school property; working together; fair play, taking turns.

3. *The Church:* Established by God to care for man's spiritual

---

[1] Those desiring to teach Health and Safety Education and General Science as separate subjects in the primary grades, will find these subjects outlined more in detail on pages 174—177 and 193—202.

needs; diligent church attendance; proper behavior in church, both during services and at other times.

4. *The Community:* Acquaintance with the neighborhood and farm; the farm as a source of food supply; appreciation of the work done for us by people in all occupations; transportation and communication between home and the community and neighboring communities.

5. *The Seasons:* Study the characteristics of each season at the proper time.

*Summer:* Make a list of summer activities; discuss some of the flowers, fruits, vegetables, animals, and birds of summer; reasons for type of clothing in summer; the glories of summer as God's gifts.

*Autumn:* Plant bulbs for spring growth; if possible, observe squirrel's storing food for the winter and migration of birds; study fruits of autumn, pumpkins, apples, etc.; fix the idea of God's care for all creatures.

*Winter:* Observe winter animal activity; encourage pupils to feed birds; discuss winter sports and engage in winter play activities; study animals of cold regions, polar bears and others; observe trees and shrubs in winter, show why they shed their leaves; reasons for heavier clothing in winter.

*Spring:* Observe the lengthening days, the development of buds and flowers; have children make a garden if possible; discuss wind and rain; study birds and their nests; insects, bees, moths, and others; show God's care of all creatures from the First Article.

6. *Health and Safety:* Teach the need of cleanliness at home and in school; personal cleanliness of body and clothes.

Discuss care of colds; care in protecting self and others against colds; see that proper care is exercised in school. Observe health laws of the community.

Teach good food habits, eating fruits, vegetables, drinking milk. Observe the habits of children and help in giving training.

Discuss teeth-building foods and care of teeth; show how to brush teeth properly; encourage visits to the dentist; show how the work of the school physician and nurse aid the child.

Discuss time to go to bed, time to arise, and necessity of fresh air during the night.

Teach habits of safety on the street and in public conveyances; safety at home; care with hot water, matches, scissors, knives.

7. *Conduct and Good Manners:* Train in helpfulness and obedience, respect for superiors (Fourth Commandment); friendliness and kindness (Romans 12:10); pity for the sick and needy (Fifth Commandment); all the virtues required by the divine Law; also Thank you, Please, Excuse me, and the common amenities of life.

## GRADE II

1. *Protection:* The work of police and fire departments, traffic officers; duty of co-operation with these officers; Christian attitude toward them; fire alarm, fire drill in school.

2. *Communication and Transportation:* Writing and mailing letters, postage, postmen in city and country, others who handle the mail in the post office and mail car; parcel post; radio; newspaper; telephone.

Engineer, fireman, and conductor on the train; workers in the railroad station; care of the tracks; people who serve us on bus, streetcar, airplane; show how the means of communication and transportation serve the Church.

3. *Recreation:* Parks and playgrounds; games, fair play; library service, reading for recreation; Christian and unchristian amusements.

4. *Weather:* Air and wind, wind direction; how wind causes weather changes; clouds and rain; temperature and the thermometer; the sun and weather; how the weather affects activities and human well-being; Fourth Petition a prayer for good weather; Christian attitude in disagreeable weather.

5. *Living Things:* Plants and animals; how they grow; their need of food, air, and sunshine; their harmfulness or benefit to man; their creation at the beginning.

6. *Land and Water:* The earth's surface, plains, mountains, valleys, etc.; lakes, oceans, streams; simple map study of land and water; use of land and water.

7. *Sun, Moon, and Stars:* Importance of sun to life; how the moon gets its light; telling time and direction by sun; the milky way; the big dipper; why the stars do not shine during the daytime; the wonders of creation.

8. *Health and Safety:* Good habits of eating; production and distribution of food; God the Giver of all food, Ps. 145:15.

Care in using fire, electric appliances; safety in play, on the street, and on conveyances; what to do in case of injury.

Care of the eyes, ears, mouth, skin, hair, nails; sufficient rest, exercise; walking and sitting habits.

9. *Conduct and Good Manners:* See Grade I; good manners at the table, in company; practice of good habits under the guidance of the teacher.

10. *Our Country:* The Flag and its meaning; national holidays; obedience to the Government, Rom. 13:1.

## GRADE III

1. *Life in the Country:* The farm, country roads, country stores; the work of the farmer; use and care of animals and machinery; church and school life in the country; country recreation.

2. *Life in the City:* Streets, blocks, numbering of houses; streetcars and busses; mail delivery compared with rural delivery; different kinds of work; parks and recreation.

3. *Life of People in Other Lands:* Suggestions: Chinese, Eskimos, Indians, Arabs, Dutch, Swiss, people in Bible times; study their manner of living, their food and clothing; tolerance for other peoples; interest in the spiritual welfare of strange peoples.

4. *Other Geographical Concepts:* Plains, mountains, jungles, deserts, rivers, lakes, oceans; how wind and water change the earth: erosion, dust storms, river deltas; how to save the soil.

5. *Biographical Incidents:* Washington, Lincoln, Franklin, Luther, Walther, others; illustrate love and devotion to country by their example.

6. *Plant and Animal Life:* Land and water plants; their growth and protection.

Land and water animals; their habits of living; how they protect themselves; how they obtain food; care of their young; God's care of all creatures.

7. *Making Man's Work Easier:* Using our muscles; animal power; wheels, levers, pulleys, engines, electricity. (Gen. 1:28: "Subdue the earth.")

8. *Health and Safety:* Necessity of food, rest, sunshine, fresh air, and exercise for growth.

Care of the teeth; the functions of stomach, intestines, blood.

Structure of the body: bones, muscles, posture. (Ps. 139:14: "I am fearfully and wonderfully made.")

Protection against contagious diseases; immunity and immunization; protecting others when we are ill by not handling their things, sneezing into their faces, etc.; looking after the health and safety of others. ("Help and befriend them in every bodily need." Fifth Commandment.)

Safety at home; riding a bicycle; at picnics and outings.

9. *Conduct and Good Manners:* See Grades I and II.

## GRADE IV

Science, as well as Health and Safety Education, should be treated as separate subjects beginning with the fourth grade. (See suggestions under these headings.) Training in character and good manners will continue to accompany all teaching. The learning in the Social Studies should center about history, geography, and citizenship as it pertains to the local community.

As a course suggestion the teacher is referred to the text *Ten Communities.*[2] By a study of ten representative communities the authors of this text seek to develop geographical, historical, and citizenship concepts which will help the pupils to understand contemporary society. The material is related to the child's own community through comparisons at the end of each chapter. Methods of research into the geographical and historical aspects of the local community are indicated. This research is adapted to the level of the children for whom the text is intended.

The suggestion that *Ten Communities* be used as basic material is not meant to imply that other material might not be used as profitably. It is unlikely, however, that better choices will be made.

The ten communities treated in the text are: Williamsburg, Va.; New London, Conn.; Atlanta, Ga.; Brazoria, Tex.; Waterloo, Iowa; San Francisco, Calif.; Seattle, Wash.; Greeley, Colo.; Gary, Ind.; and New York City.

## E. CORRELATION POSSIBILITIES

Correlation is carried to its extreme in the fusion commonly practiced in teaching the Social Studies in the primary grades.

Demarcation between a number of different school subjects disappears almost entirely. But the designation of *Correlation* is still justified in certain instances:

*Religion.* Every application of Scripture or the Catechism to establish the Christian viewpoint or induce Christian conduct is a correlation with religion.

*Church History.* Stories from the life of Luther, Walther, Wyneken, and others to teach historical concepts, or stories that aid in gaining an understanding of church life and work.

*Reading.* It is possible to make the Social Studies course to the third grade (possibly to the fourth grade in one-room schools) largely part of the reading program. Various supplementary readers are used under this plan.

*Music.* See *Music Reader* and *Select Songs* for songs of country, home, school, church, nature, seasons.

*Art.* Scenes depicting the wonders of Creation; pictures of animals and birds; pictures of historical interest, Luther, Washing-

---

2) Paul R. Hanna, et al., *Ten Communities.* Scott, Foresman and Co., 1940.

ton, Lincoln, others; the Flag from the standpoint of art; transportation and communication pictures; creative art work.

*Field Trips.* Study of the near community to observe life and occupations; sources of food, clothing, shelter; animal and bird life and habits; nature in general; mines and quarries if convenient.

## F. EVALUATING OUTCOMES

In evaluating the results of his work in the Social Studies, the teacher will ask himself questions such as the following:

1. What understanding do my pupils exhibit of human life and work; of animal life and habits; of plants and their growth; of the universe? Their understanding on these points can be measured objectively. A more important question is: How much interest do the pupils take in the life about them?

2. What evidence is there that they recognize and revere God as the Creator, Preserver, and Ruler of all things, and that they trust in Him as their Provider?

3. Do they have an elementary understanding of the effect of the environment upon the manner of living?

4. Are they aware to a limited extent of the changes which man has made in the world?

5. Do they practice fundamental health and safety rules?

6. Is their conduct Christian; are they well mannered, respectful to superiors, helpful, kind, co-operative, concerned about the physical and spiritual welfare of others?

7. Do they seem to enjoy being in a Christian school, among Christian people?

8. Do the pupils take part in healthful play?

9. Are they willing to take responsibility for tasks within their ability?

### Selected References

*Caution:* The listing of these references is not to be interpreted as a blanket approval of every statement the books may contain. They are included here because they will aid the teacher in planning his course in the primary Social Studies.

Beauchamp, Wilbur L., and West, Joe Young, *Science for Children.* Scott, Foresman, and Co., 1938.

Beauchamp, Wilbur L., Blough, Glenn O., and Melrose, Mary. *Teacher's Manual* for *Discovering Our World;* Books One, Two, Three. Scott, Foresman and Co., 1938, 1939, 1941.

Carpenter, Harry A., et al., *Adventures in Science Series,* Grades 1—3. Allyn and Bacon, 1940.

Frasier, George Willard, Dolman, Helen, and Van Noy, Kathryne, *The*

*Scientific Living Series,* Pre-Primer to Book III. Teacher's Manual. Singer, 1937, 1938.

Gross, Herbert H., *Curriculum in the Primary Social Studies.* Concordia, 1941.

Hanna, Paul R., et al., *Social Studies Series.* Scott, Foresman and Co., 1935 to 1940.

Krug, Amelia C., *Good Manners for Boys and Girls.* Concordia, 1937.

Krug, Amelia C., *A Child's Story of the World and Its People.* Concordia, 1941.

Wilder, Kate Eleanor, *Pussy Letters.* M. A. Donohue and Co., 1929.

State, local, or District Course of Study.

## 2. Geography

### A. OBJECTIVES

1. An elementary acquaintance with the universe and particularly with the earth and its peoples.

2. A deep and growing sense of awe and gratitude for God's creation, preservation, and rule of the world as the temporal home of men. (God's kingdom of power.)

3. The realization

   a. That, through the fall of Adam, man has brought the curse of God upon the earth, and made it a place of sorrow, obstacles, and hard labor.

   b. That man's natural powers to subdue and rule over the earth are greatly weakened.

   c. That man's limited success in this respect is due solely to the grace of God.

4. The understanding that God maintains and rules the world primarily for the sake of His elect and maintains and extends therein His Kingdom of Grace.

   a. A growing interest in the extent and location of the Christian Church on earth.

   b. A particular interest in the geographical aspects of the work of the Lutheran Church.

5. An understanding of the effects of natural environment upon man and his means and mode of living.

6. An appreciation of the need of an economic use and conservation of natural resources.

7. A recognition of the interdependence of men and nations, and of the mutual advantages of honest and peaceful trade among the peoples of the earth.

8. The ability to use geographic tools, such as maps, atlases, and the like, and the habit of employing them in securing geographical information.

# B. DISCUSSION OF OBJECTIVES

## Acquaintance with God's Creation

Geography is the study of the earth and its life. The Christian child learns that the earth and man, as well as all visible and invisible creatures, are works of God, created about 6,000 years ago. Step by step he increases his acquaintance with the visible part of the great universe. He learns that the earth is the center of the universe and that the firmament and all heavenly bodies were created to serve the earth and its peoples. The child learns also to appreciate the effect the heavenly bodies, particularly the sun and moon, have upon the lives and efforts of man. He learns that the orderly operation of the universe under the rule of God will continue "while the earth remaineth." Gen. 8:22. At the same time he learns that at God's own appointed time the earth will pass away. 2 Pet. 3:7-10. The realization of the transience of all earthly things is necessary for a proper perspective with regard to material things.

## Attitude toward God's Creation

The Lutheran teacher of geography considers the cultivation of the proper attitude toward God and His glorious creation of paramount importance. He seeks to imbue the child with a profound awe for the Creator, Preserver, and Ruler, so that he will be impelled to praise God and the wisdom and power of His creation, preservation, and rule.

The teacher realizes that geography textbooks and other material used in our schools are not written from a Christian viewpoint, and he does all in his power to counteract the theories and principles that in any way minimize or deny the work of God. He knows also that advanced studies in this field may lead the growing child still further astray. Therefore, with all the pedagogical power at his command, the Lutheran teacher must prepare and fortify the child against such later assaults upon his belief in God.

## Realization of Man's Limitations

The Christian child will learn to realize that as a result of man's fall into sin his God-given powers to subdue the earth have been greatly weakened; his knowledge has become limited; and his best works have been rendered imperfect. The cursing of the ground as a punishment of sin has increased the difficulty of his task.

The child will also be led to appreciate God's mercy in sustaining and upholding him and all creatures in this sinful world, and in crowning his daily tasks with measures of success. In true humility, he will realize his shortcomings and look to God for all that he needs. "The eyes of all wait upon Thee; and Thou givest them their meat in due season. Thou openest Thine hand and satisfiest the desire of every living thing." Ps. 145:15, 16.

### Interest in the Geographical Aspects of the Church

The Christian child learns that God rules the world primarily with the preservation and extension of His Kingdom of Grace in view. The Great Commission, "Go and teach all nations," indicates this purpose. On the basis of this fundamental realization the teacher seeks to stimulate an active and growing interest in the extent and location of the Christian Church on earth, with special emphasis on the geographical aspects of the work of the Lutheran Church in all parts of the world.

### Understanding of Effects of Man's Environment

The child will be shown that environment is a part of God's providence. God has created zones of temperature and a great variety of climatic conditions; He has created land and sea, the mountains, valleys, and rivers; He has provided vegetation, animals, and minerals, according to the environment. All these environments have their natural effects upon man, upon his occupation, and upon his living; the products of one environment supply the lack of others.

Important geographical objectives are a realization of the divine wisdom of this arrangement; recognition of the general effects which temperature, climate, and location have upon men and the works, lives, and industry of men; a sympathetic attitude with respect to the problems of people whose environment has brought about a culture and outlook upon life different from one's own; and appreciation of the advantages of, and ability to cope with, the problems of one's own environment.

### Appreciative Use of God's Gifts

The Lutheran teacher will follow the example of the Savior (John 6:12) in teaching thrift in the use of natural resources. He will show the child that he must not waste the overabundance of God's gifts. The child will discover from Bible stories that misuse and waste of earth's riches lead to punishment and withdrawal of such gifts (Luke 15:13-16). On the other hand, he will enjoy more and more of these resources if he puts them to proper use.

Thus, in the study of geography, the child will learn that our Government by law aims to insure the conservation of our

natural resources. Forests and minerals are preserved and protected, game life is shielded, and citizens are taught to appreciate
and conserve what they have that future generations may not
be deprived of essential products.

### Recognition of Human Interdependence

Through his study of geography, the child will learn to recognize more and more how dependent he is upon other peoples and
nations. He will see that a great measure of his comfort and
happiness is due to our country's far-reaching trade with other
nations. He will learn that discoveries and inventions have brought
all nations closer together, and that serious disturbances in one
are likely to affect the welfare of the entire world.

The child will learn to appreciate the opportunities for mutual
assistance among all nations, realizing that the only basis for fair
trade and commerce is adherence to the fundamentals of the
divine Law. While he is not directly concerned with international
trade and is unable to grasp its far-reaching implications, an
elementary understanding of its nature and operation should be
sought for its citizenship value.

### Skill in the Use of Geographic Tools

Skill in the use of geographic tools is necessary for the immediate learning of facts, establishing of perspectives, and acquiring
of graphic conceptions, and it is needed throughout life for an
intelligent understanding of current events. The ability to interpret maps is necessary for a proper understanding of news and
reports in papers and magazines. Skill in the handling of globes,
charts, and atlases frequently is a valuable asset in obtaining
useful or necessary information. Certainly, also, efficient use of
these geographic tools makes possible a better understanding of
the extent and needs of the far-flung work of the Church. For
these reasons their independent and habitual use should be sought.

## C. DIVISION OF TIME AND MATERIALS

The formal study of geography is usually begun in the fourth
and continues through the eighth grade.

Classes may be combined, and the various sections of the
course treated alternately on a two-year basis. Thus, if fifth
and sixth grades are combined, United States geography may
be taught one year, and Canada, Mexico, and Latin America
the second.

The time required for the teaching period may vary from
20 to 30 minutes a day for the whole year; or, where the schedule

is crowded in a one-room school, the time may be cut to three periods a week. If the class periods must be few, the teacher may suggest readings or provide exercises to supplement the class instruction.

## D. COURSE SUGGESTIONS

### Intermediate Grades (4—6)

In the fourth or fifth grade a more detailed study of our own country is begun. A text or workbook is essential. The manner in which the United States is studied depends upon the text. Modern texts usually treat our country by regions rather than by groups of States, although a combination, or fusion, wherever possible, is desirable.

The study of Canada is sometimes closely correlated with the study of the United States because of similarities in regions and occupations. Because of political unity the possessions of the United States are next treated.

The study will also include Latin America. Mexico and Central America would logically be first, since they are immediate neighbors. The islands of the West Indies would be included. The rest of Latin America includes the countries of South America. Latin America has many problems which are similar to ours, and the study of these will help the child to overcome any strangeness which he may feel toward these Latin American neighbors.

The child of the sixth grade will be ready for the study of Europe. Political upheavals on the continent should not hinder the child from gaining a real enjoyment from the study of this particular phase. Europe presents a colorful array of physical factors and a great variety of occupations. This continent should be of special interest to the child because most of his ancestors once lived on this continent.

The British Empire may constitute a unit by itself. The study of this unit affords an insight into factors of world-wide trade and interdependence of nations and colonies. This unit will also develop in the child a concept of the world as a whole and how the parts of the world are interassociated.

The studies of Asia and Africa should not be curtailed in favor of lengthy units of the continents already mentioned. These continents, no longer dark and forbidding, are studied with great interest by the pupils. Here pictures and conditions are revealed that mystify and intrigue children of Western civilization. The teacher must be careful, however, to keep the children in sympathetic understanding of Eastern civilization, lest they lose sight of the fact that all races and peoples are creatures of the same God, who has offered them the same means of earthly existence.

Finally, in the study of these continents, the child should be kept conscious of our mission work throughout the world.[1] He must realize that the work of the Church is not bound by political areas or geographical barriers. He will learn that also our Lutheran Church is active in the fulfillment of Christ's command "Go ye into all the world, and preach the Gospel to every creature." Mark 16:15. A well-balanced geography course achieves the twofold purpose of fitting the child into his proper station in life and of bringing him to the realization that this world is just a huge scaffold used in the building of Christ's invisible Church.

### Suggested Course Content

*A. Peoples of Other Lands*

Discuss the efforts of the Church to extend God's kingdom in all the world: Alaska, Africa, etc. Tell mission stories, or have pupils read them.

1. How people live in cold countries.
2. How people live in hot climates.
3. How people live in mountainous countries.
4. How people make a living along the seashore.
5. Children of other lands: Swiss, Norwegians, Dutch, Arabians, Chinese, etc.

*B. The United States, Canada, and U. S. Possessions*

Include study of our Church; home missions; schools; colleges and seminaries. The teacher should make notations in his textbook of the opportunities for stressing the work of our Church as carried on in the various parts of the United States, its possessions, and Canada.

*C. Latin America*

While teaching the geography of Latin America, show how the Lutheran Church is represented in the various countries.

*D. European Continent*

Show the extent of the Lutheran Church in Europe; geographical locations important in the Reformation; population of northern countries of Europe (Denmark, Norway, Sweden, and Finland) almost wholly Lutheran.

*Note:* Europe may be studied by sections or by countries; or it may be treated according to races of which there are predominantly three: Latin, Teutonic, and Slavic. Under Latin would come Italy, France, Spain, Portugal. The Teutonic countries include Germany, the Netherlands, most of Belgium, Denmark, Switzerland, Norway, and Sweden. The Slavic peoples are found mostly in Poland, Russia, in the Balkans, and in the Baltic States.

1) Ask Department of Publicity and Missionary Education for descriptive booklets.

## E. The British Empire

As this unit is taught, the Missouri Synod churches in England, the Lutheran Church in Nigeria, Lutheran missions in India, the Ev. Lutheran Synod of Australia (and New Zealand) receive consideration.

## F. Asia

In the study of Asia, the Lutheran Church in China and India will receive attention. A thorough study of the Holy Land will aid Bible History instruction.

## G. Africa

The Lutheran Church in Nigeria will be studied if this has not been done in connection with the British possessions.

## Advanced Grades (7—8)

The present conception of a geography course adheres neither to a strictly one-cycle or two-cycle plan. In the advanced grades some of the material is reviewed, especially that dealing with our own country. Additional material is used to supplement facts already learned in order to cement concepts of greater importance and provide for different outlooks. In the suggested content for these grades we find the study of the United States in its relationship to the other countries of the world. Now that the child has become acquainted with the entire world in its basic factors, he can compare the position of his country with that of others. He will gain a sympathetic understanding of the will of our people to trade with their neighbors, and learn to realize how the welfare of our nation depends upon mutual good will.

In addition to this study, the whole world geography may be reviewed in the light of industry. Each industry is studied on the basis of world endeavor. For instance, lumbering is world wide. The child will see how lumbering is carried on the world over, from the primitive methods employed in uncivilized countries to the most modern way of civilized nations. This study will show that all peoples have common necessities, which they try to supply in the manner prescribed by their conditions.

Here again the Christian child should be trained to evaluate the opportunities for the extension of God's kingdom. He should acquire a spirit of interest for the work of our Church in the various regions of the world and be able to see how God opens the door for the preaching of His Gospel in various places.

### SUGGESTED CONTENT

a. *The United States among the Nations*

  1. The People Who Founded Our Nation
  2. The Lands to Be Developed
  3. The Climates of the United States

4. The Use of Farm and Grazing Lands
5. The Natural Resources of the U. S.
6. The Growth of Foreign Trade
7. The Development of Commerce
8. The Interdependence with Other Nations

b. *The World at Work*

1. The Climates of the World
2. Life in the Pasture Lands
3. Life in the Great Forests
4. The Chief Farming Regions
5. The Life of the Fishermen
6. The Life of the Miners
7. The Work of the Builders
8. Power and Manufacturing
9. Trade, Transportation, and Communication
10. Distribution of Peoples
11. The Earth as a Whole
12. The Earth in the Universe

## E. CORRELATION POSSIBILITIES

*Religion.* Maps and their symbols as well as other geographical concepts are constantly employed in the study of sacred history.

*Reading.* Children are fascinated by news reports, the stories of travels, descriptions by eye witnesses, and especially books in which children of other lands are treated, if they are given the geographical background.

*Language.* Oral and written composition topics may be taken from the field of geography. Exercise for development and solution of geographical problems improves organized thinking.

*Spelling.* Modern spellers have many names of countries, cities, places, and physical regions in their vocabularies. These names and terms may sometimes be isolated for special drills. Examples: mountain, island, peninsula, Atlantic Ocean, India.

*Arithmetic.* Many problems of reasoning concern themselves with geographical factors, such as measures of distance, wind velocity, area of farm land, length of rivers, and the like.

*History.* In history we learn why people settled in certain sections of a country or continent, why wars are fought, why certain peoples and nations combine or trade with one another. Geography and history are closely related, because all history takes place in, and is affected by, geographical environment.

*Civics.* An understanding and application of geographical factors is an important part of good citizenship. In order to understand the workings of our Government, a knowledge of geography is necessary. For instance, the Department of the Interior looks after our natural resources; laws are passed to conserve our soil and forests; the Department of Agriculture deals with problems of geography.

*Health and Safety.* Such topics as climate, latitude, and altitude are closely allied with certain phases of health study. The community in its drive against disease and accidents must take into account geographical factors, such as swamps, rivers, hills, vegetation, and others.

*General Science, Agriculture.* Such basic facts as uses of minerals, elements, and soils which affect man's living are better understood in the light of geography.

*The Arts.* There is frequent opportunity for drawing and painting scenes in nature, such as trees, birds, animals, mountain views, the seashore, rivers, and the like. Clay modeling may be developed in the making of relief maps or plastics which show a river system, the results of erosion, etc. The drawing of maps, either freehand or copied, develops the habit of exactness and precision.

Handwork of various kinds serves as a teaching aid and as a motivating factor.

In music the songs of various lands add a personal touch of interest. Many folk songs treat of geographical features, such as rivers, lakes, ponds, winter, spring, storms.

The possibilities mentioned are only samples. The list may be expanded according to the need.

### F. EVALUATING OUTCOMES

On the basis of the objectives listed at the beginning of this subject a number of questions regarding the values received by the child are in order. The following may be considered:

1. Does the child's knowledge of the universe, particularly of the earth and its people, measure up to the norms of standard tests?

2. Does the child really stand in awe of his Creator?

3. Does he sense the magnitude of God's creation, preservation, and government?

4. Does he realize how man, together with his fellow men, works hard to subdue the earth, as God commands him? Does he see the difficulties in his way because of greed, selfishness, and sin in general?

5. Does he show that he appreciates his place in his own environment, being conscious of God's Commandment "Love thy neighbor as thyself"?

6. Does he recognize his environment as his first interest and consider himself an active, living part of it? Does he take an interest in improving the environment?

7. Does he give evidence that he understands the use of geographical symbols and knows how to interpret them?

8. Does he show an interest in the world about him through voluntary reading and discussion?

9. Does he evince a spirit of discovery, to go out for himself and see how the world lives?

10. Does he acknowledge the fact that this world has its origin in God and that nothing was made without God?

11. Does he show a willingness to make use of his geographical knowledge for the glory of God and the welfare of his neighbor?

### Selected References

*Classroom Teacher, The,* Volumes VIII and XI. The Classroom Teacher, Inc., 1928.

Crawford, Claude C., and McDonald, L. P., *Modern Methods in Teaching Geography.* Houghton Mifflin, 1929.

Morrison, Henry C., *The Curriculum of the Common School.* University of Chicago Press, 1940, pp. 134—206.

Reed, Homer E., *Psychology of Elementary School Subjects.* Ginn and Co., 1938, pp. 398—504.

*The Teaching of Geography.* 32nd Yearbook of the N. S. S. E. Public School Publishing Co., 1933.

Thralls, Zoe A., and Reeder, Edwin H., *Geography in the Elementary School.* Rand McNally and Co., 1931.

Wesley, Edgar B., *Teaching the Social Studies.* D. C. Heath and Co., 1937.

Manuals accompanying textbooks.

State, local, or District Course of Study.

## 3. History

### A. GENERAL OBJECTIVES

1. Acquaintance with major historical developments, especially in the history of our own country.

2. Understanding of some of the influences which helped to mold American civilization and government.

3. Recognition of the fact that God rules individuals and nations, and a grateful appreciation of His wise direction of the course of history.

4. Enlightened patriotism and citizenship in our country.

5. The understanding that history presents a pattern of human experience whereby men may judge their present and future course, and the ability to apply the lessons which history teaches.

6. A wholesome respect for the past and its achievements, with a commensurate humility about oneself and the present.

7. An abiding interest in history and current events, and the ability and desire to benefit others by one's own historical understanding.

## B. DISCUSSION OF OBJECTIVES

1. *Acquaintance with major historical developments, especially in the history of our own country.*

a. The first objective of the history teacher must be to teach pupils history. Content is important. Meanings can grow only out of knowledge of historical fact, properly understood and interpreted.

b. History must be seen in its important movements, with the individual episodes furnishing the details of a larger pattern. For example: The fact that Lewis and Clark explored the Northwest is in itself of no great importance, but the fact that their expedition prepared the way for the westward movement gives it meaning; again, Eli Whitney's invention of the cotton gin would be a minor matter were it not for the part it played in the industrial revolution. There is little justification in the history course for detail which does not contribute to the understanding of the larger setting.

c. In order to give his pupils the larger concept of history, the teacher requires a sound historical background. He needs to be well versed in the history of his own country, first of all. But in order to understand national history, he must be acquainted with the history of mankind, and especially with that part of ancient and European history which has a direct bearing on that of our own country, and he must recognize its importance and meaning. Only to the extent that he himself sees beyond the mass of historical detail will he be able to convey to his pupils the wider meaningful view.

2. *Understanding of some of the influences which helped to mold American civilization and government.*

The pupil should learn to recognize some of the influences which contributed to American civilization and government. The following are examples: The settlement and development of America primarily by the Protestant nations of Northern Europe; the Reformation as one of the sources of our present civil and religious liberty; the inheritance of some knowledge of self-government and democracy on the part of the English settlers; and the frontier life which fostered a spirit of independence and initiative.

Where the textbook fails to point out these influences, the teacher should emphasize their importance.

*3. Recognition of the fact that God rules individuals and nations, and a grateful appreciation of His wise direction of the course of history.*

God's hand in history is not always evident to man. It must be understood that God rules human affairs according to moral and physical laws which He Himself has established. Yet the most enlightened among human beings does not know enough about the operation of these laws perfectly to understand the present or reliably to predict the future. God sees the whole panorama, man only a small part of the total picture. Much of God's dealing with mankind must, therefore, always contain an element of the unknown for the finite mind. But the fact that God rules is never in doubt. "He ruleth by His power forever; His eyes behold the nations." Psalm 66:7. "Thine, O Lord, is the greatness and the power, and the glory, and the victory, and the majesty; for all that is in the heaven and in the earth is Thine; Thine is the kingdom, O Lord, and Thou art exalted as Head above all." 1 Chron. 29:11.

The fact that the depraved will of man is opposed to the will of God and at times apparently frustrates the divine purpose does not indicate failure of God's rule. It points, rather, on the one hand, to the patience and mercy of God toward rebellious mankind (Deut. 4:31) and, on the other, to His unfailing justice according to which He visits punishment upon transgression (Hos. 8). To man it may seem as if God's rule has collapsed, but the Christian realizes that in the history of nations, as of individuals, God often turns apparent evil to a good purpose (Gen. 50:20), though man may be unable to understand God's ways (Is. 55:8,9).

Therefore the pupil must learn also to recognize God's dealing with individuals and nations as wise, gracious, and just. According to this view, adversity and national disaster serve as a punishment for the wicked and as a trial for the believers. In the end it will work out for the benefit of God's children, serving the purpose for which God still permits the world to exist. The most important thing for the individual is to come to the knowledge of His Savior and to faith in Him. Granting this, the most important thing for the world must be the building of Christ's Church on earth. God's rule of men and nations must, therefore, be primarily concerned with the protection and propagation of the Church. It will help the child more fully to appreciate God's wise and gracious rule if he is led to see how God has kept His promise through the ages: "The gates of hell shall not prevail against it (the invisible Church)." Matt. 16:19.

4. *Enlightened patriotism and citizenship in our country.*

Patriotism and good citizenship are built upon intellectual and spiritual foundations. They presuppose right understandings and attitudes. Among the more important of these are:

a. Knowledge of the history of our country, its settlement and development.

b. The realization that history is a course of events directed by Almighty God.

c. Appreciation of the blessings enjoyed by the citizens of our country as free and undeserved gifts of God's grace.

d. The realization that our civil and religious liberties were purchased at great cost, and that they can be preserved only by means of the utmost vigilance and sacrifice.

The highest type of patriotism and citizenship shows itself in obedience to authority in keeping with the Fourth Commandment; and in the exercise of the rights and duties of citizenship in accordance with Biblical principles.

Love for country; Christian obedience; unflinching loyalty; intelligent and wholehearted effort toward the preservation and improvement of a truly democratic society; readiness to serve the country in war or peace; prayer for the temporal and spiritual welfare of the country and its people; love, tolerance, and sympathy for the neighbor; exercise of all other rights and duties of citizenship honestly and intelligently; in short, "seeking the peace (welfare) of the city," Jer. 29:7; all these should be emphasized in the history instruction, as well as in the special civics course, as the essence of patriotism and citizenship.

5. *The understanding that history presents a pattern of human experience whereby men may judge their present and future course, and the ability to apply the lessons which history teaches.*

Both in the moral field and in purely civic affairs, history stands as a pattern of human experience whereby the present and the future of the country may be judged and charted. History is to a people what experience is to the individual. God indicates as much for the moral field when He says: "Righteousness exalteth a nation, but sin is a reproach to any people." Prov. 14:34. This the child should learn to understand early, for without it much of the meaning of history will be lost to him. But he should also learn to recognize, at least in an elementary way, that in law, in finances, and in other matters of policy, history has its lessons for future prosperity and well-being. "Days should teach, and multitude of years should teach wisdom" (Job 32:7) may well be applied to the whole course of human history. The fact that often man fails to read accurately the teachings of history does not alter the truth.

6. *A wholesome respect for the past and its achievements, with a commensurate humility about oneself and the present.*

In view of the achievements of present-day civilization, particularly in the field of science as it affects inventions, communication, transportation, and prevention and cure of disease, it is easy for the child to underrate the civilization and culture of the past. It is important, therefore, to create in the child a wholesome respect for the literature, the statesmanship, the architecture, the engineering works, the musical compositions, and other cultural achievements of bygone centuries.

Moreover, whatever is excellent in the civilization of today, still owes its quality largely to the foundation laid in the past, and there again largely to the civilizing influence of the Christian religion and to the burning missionary zeal of its adherents. This fact should be used to foster humility, in place of the sinful pride that accompanies much of human achievement. In the Christian school, all progress and achievement are to be regarded in the spirit of Samuel F. B. Morse, who after the successful completion of the telegraph said: "What hath God wrought!"

7. *An abiding interest in history and current events, and the ability and desire to benefit others by one's own historical understanding.*

The course in history will not have been successful in the individual case unless the child has developed an interest in history and current events. This interest is possible only on the basis of the understanding and attitudes discussed above. When it is once aroused, history and current events will acquire meanings which vitally affect life and conduct of the child and the adult. The person will better understand his environment both near and remote, he will be able to read newspapers and periodicals with greater intelligence and discrimination, to converse more intelligently about historical matters, to influence constructively the warped viewpoints of friends and acquaintances, and, in general, to wield a greater measure of Christian influence.

### Opportunities for Developing the Christian Viewpoint

Events in Biblical and in secular history may be utilized in developing the Christian point of view. A few examples to illustrate are listed below, but the teacher will expand this list according to the need:

1. The rise and fall of Israel, Rome, and other empires ("Righteousness exalteth a nation, but sin is a reproach to any people." Prov. 14:34).

2. The period preceding the birth of Christ ("God uses the ungodly for the purpose of working out His own design. God uses the Egyptians in making Israel a great nation; the Philistines, to punish Israel and bring them to repentance; the Assyrians, to destroy the ten tribes for rejecting the Gospel; the Babylonians, to punish Judah in order to bring the members of this tribe to repentance and preserve them as the bearer of His Promise; the Persians, to restore the kingdom of Judah; the Greeks, to build up a great civilization and, under Alexander the Great, the champion of Greek culture, to spread this civilization over the Orient, thereby giving the world a universal language; the Romans, with their law and order, especially the good Roman roads, to preserve and spread this Greek culture over the Mediterranean world — all this in preparation for the greatest event in history, the birth of Christ. For just when man has built up the highest civilization to glorify himself and has fallen so low as to worship his dead fellow man as a god, God in His Son humbles Himself and becomes man to redeem this lost and hopeless creature").[1]

3. Persecution of the early Christian Church (also tribulations of the Christians serve God's plan, for through the persecutions the borders of the Church were enlarged).

4. The abuses under the Church-State misrule of the Middle Ages (even in this dark period, God preserved His Church according to His promise, Matt. 16:18; culminated in the Reformation and led to an era of unprecedented religious revival and helped to secure rights and liberties never before achieved by the common man).

5. The invention of printing (came just in time for the spreading of the Gospel as restored in the period of the Reformation).

6. Invention of radio (serves as a powerful means for spreading the Gospel in all parts of the world).

7. Devastating wars; business depressions (God's punishment of pride, greed, and sin in general; a certain warning to heed the lessons of history for present and future prosperity and well-being).

8. The destruction of the Spanish Armada, 1588 (broke the power of the chief Catholic nation and gave Protestant countries a free hand in colonizing the New World).

9. American discoveries by Columbus and other Spanish explorers confined to the South (permitted free sway to Northern European countries in developing the best part of the continent as a stronghold of civil and religious liberty).

---

1) H. R. Klatt in *Lutheran School Journal,* August, 1924, p. 293.

10. Lutheran influence upon early history of our country: The Muehlenbergs; Pennsylvania Lutherans under General Herkimer at Oriskany, N. Y.; the bodyguard of Washington composed mainly of Lutherans; the Lutherans in New York, Georgia, Pennsylvania, and New Jersey in colonial times (the blessings that a country derives from the services of loyal Christians).

11. Adoption of the American Constitution (gratitude for the guarantee of religious liberty).

## C. METHOD; DIVISION OF TIME AND MATERIALS

### Method

Whatever the method, it must be devised to achieve the aims of the course. Mere memoriter work involving disconnected episodes is practically useless and soon forgotten, because it does not produce such understandings, habits, and skills as are necessary to make history a live, interesting, and functional subject. It is self-evident that the mere assignment of a given number of pages, with subsequent questioning on the content, does not constitute history instruction.

In order to select a suitable method, the teacher should be acquainted with a number of procedures. Under *Selected References* a number of titles are suggested for study on the part of the teacher. Morrison presents the Unity-Mastery Technique; Sieving brings a valuable summary of this method; Reed outlines a comparison of methods and procedures; Kelty submits a combination of the worth-while features of many methods, particularly of the Unit-Mastery and the Activity-Unit-of-Work plan.[2] Other teacher's manuals, as also State courses of study, often contain suggestions as to methods of teaching.

### Division of Time and Materials

The amount of time devoted to the study of history will depend upon the requirements made by the local educational authorities, upon the type of school, and upon the conception of history either as a separate subject, or as part of an integrated social studies course. Suggestions for time allotments will be found in the sample schedules appearing elsewhere in this book.

Because of the somewhat different aims and viewpoints of history and geography, these subjects are given separate treatment

---

2) Kelty's procedure is outlined carefully also in the Teacher's Manual for *The Beginnings of the American People and Nation*. Ginn and Co., 1936, pp. 1—39. There are two editions of this Manual dated 1936. The one numbered 536.7 contains the section on method.

beginning with the fifth grade. In the primary grades, history needs are met in the social studies course or by means of supplementary reading activities. *A Child's Story of the World and Its People* [3] is recommended for supplementary reading in fourth grade. If group reading is impractical, pupils should read the book individually in preparation for intensive history study in fifth grade.

In one- and two-room schools, fifth and sixth, and seventh and eighth grades may be combined, each on a two-year alternation plan. The courses for the fifth and seventh grades are then taught in one year and those for the sixth and eighth grades the next. In two-room schools divided on a three-five basis, fourth and fifth grades may form the first group, and sixth to eighth grades the second. In no case does the school program allow for more than two class divisions in history in any one room.

## D. COURSE SUGGESTIONS

### Grade V

Fifth grade history centers about the discovery and early settlement of our country. It is preferably biographical in form. The study will become a fascinating experience for most pupils if interesting persons and dramatic incidents are properly utilized. The choice of material in most standard books is good, but needs to be supplemented with characters and incidents of special interest to Lutherans.

The fifth grade material offers excellent opportunity for achieving some of the important aims in history: the foundation and course of American civilization and government molded chiefly by Protestant nations; appreciation of the benefits of a democratic form of government; the influence of Lutheran ideals in establishing freedom of religion and conscience; respect for the courage and vision of the past; lessons in citizenship, such as love of country, courage, tolerance, ambition for work and worth-while things, and willingness to serve the country in war or peace.

The following list indicates the characters about whom the history of American discovery and colonization is generally woven. Notations in parentheses indicate those that ought to be added in Lutheran schools.

    a. Christopher Columbus (Martin Luther)

    b. John Cabot

---

3) Amelia C. Krug, *A Child's Story of the World and Its People.* Concordia, 1941.

c. Ponce de Leon, Balboa, De Soto, Americus Vespucius, Coronado, Magellan

d. Sir Walter Raleigh, Sir Francis Drake

e. Captain John Smith

f. Captain Henry Hudson (Danish Lutherans on Hudson Bay, 1619)

g. Captain Miles Standish (John Eliot, the Apostle to the Indians)

h. Lord Baltimore

i. Roger Williams

j. King Philip

k. Peter Stuyvesant (Lutheran beginnings in New York)

l. William Penn (Lutherans in Delaware and Pennsylvania; Henry Muehlenberg)

m. General James Oglethorpe (The Salzburg Lutherans in Georgia)

n. La Salle

o. George Washington (Pennsylvania Lutherans under General Herkimer at Oriskany, N. Y.; Washington's Lutheran bodyguard; The Muehlenbergs)

p. Benjamin Franklin

q. Daniel Boone

r. General George Rogers Clark

In many textbooks the account is carried beyond the colonial period. Among the favorite characters of the latter period are: General Rufus Putnam, Eli Whitney, Thomas Jefferson, Robert Fulton, General William Henry Harrison, General Andrew Jackson, Samuel F. B. Morse, General Sam Houston, Captain Robert Gray, Captain Sutter, Abraham Lincoln, Theodore Roosevelt, Woodrow Wilson, Calvin Coolidge. The time available will dictate whether any or all of this material can be covered in the grade.

### Grade VI

In the sixth grade the Old World background of American history is studied. Care is necessary in the choice of textbooks, because in many of them the crassest form of evolution is taught. Others give too much prominence to mythology; still others attach too much importance to the Church of the Middle Ages, minimizing the influence of the Reformation.[4]

---

4) One of the best texts, from the Lutheran point of view, is *The Gateway to American History,* by Thomas Bonaventure Lawler (Ginn and Co., 1936). It is free from evolution and gives due place to Biblical history.

The period of history covered in this grade offers rich opportunity to stress and develop the Christian viewpoint:

a. The Church was preserved through the stress of the centuries.

b. The Reformation the outstanding historical event since the time of Christ; its influence upon the character of America; its providential coincidence with the invention of printing. (Where the text gives inadequate treatment to the Reformation, the teacher will supply additional materials.)

c. God uses individuals to rule secular affairs for the protection and propagation of His kingdom: Frederick, Elector of Saxony, and other Christian rulers.

d. Fall of Greece and Rome due to a moral decline; a warning to every individual and people today. "Righteousness exalteth a nation, but sin is a reproach to any people."

e. Corruption of the Church of the Middle Ages the cause of its loss of vitality and influence over lives of people.

f. Crusades, discoveries, conquests, all utilized by God to spread the Christian religion, indicating that in His mercy He often turns to good the folly or evil devices of men.

The following topics may be considered for inclusion in a course featuring the Old World Background:

1. The Ancient Egyptians
2. The Hebrews in Palestine
3. The Babylonians, Persians, and other People of the Near East
4. The Greeks
5. Alexander the Great
6. The Romans
7. The Rise and Spread of Christianity: Its Influence
8. The German Invasion of the Roman Empire
9. The Huns, Vandals, and Lombards
10. Justinian the Great
11. The Franks and Charlemagne
12. The Holy Roman Empire
13. The Rise of Feudalism
14. The Story of England
15. The Northmen
16. The Magna Carta
17. The Rise of Monasticism
18. The Spread of Mohammedanism
19. The Crusades
20. The Renaissance: Reformation

21. Marco Polo
22. Prince Henry the Navigator
23. Columbus
24. Spanish and Portuguese Explorations
25. French Explorations
26. The Reformation
27. Religious Wars: The Spanish Armada
28. Beginnings of American Colonization

### Grades VII and VIII

The history of the United States is taught in seventh and eighth grades. The course is introduced by way of review with a unit or two dealing with the Old World background and the colonization of America. This is followed with the history of the country to the present.

Where both seventh and eighth grades are in one room, the subject matter may be easily divided to provide for a two-year alternation course.

The textbook should be free from unwholesome propaganda and should present neither an intensely nationalistic nor internationalistic point of view. The instruction must be designed, in spite of the admitted faults and shortcomings of our form of government, to engender genuine love for the country. Material with a citizenship value is emphasized. The social, economic, and cultural factors are stressed, rather than the wars.

The pupils should have access to and be taught how to use supplementary materials, other texts, reference books, etc. They should make a beginning in judgment of contradictory viewpoints of different authors.

Lutheran influence is noted, and important events in Lutheran Church History are correlated. For this purpose the *Church History Inserts* [5] will be helpful.

### Suggested Course Content

*Unit One:* What the Old World Gave the New
   1. American beginnings in Europe
   2. How the search for trade led to the discovery of America
   3. Exploration and settlement

*Unit Two:* Colonization and Rivalry for North America
   1. Life in the English colonies
   2. The struggle for supremacy on the North American continent
   3. Northern European ideals in religion and politics

---

5) Published by the Department of Publicity and Missionary Education and supplied free of charge to Lutheran schools.

*Unit Three:* The Birth of a Nation

    1. The colonies before the Revolutionary War

    2. Conflict and independence

    3. Articles of Confederation and the Constitution

*Unit Four:* Growth of the New Republic

    1. The new government in operation

    2. Development of the West

    3. Winning the respect of European nations

*Unit Five:* Sectional Strife

    1. Jacksonian democracy

    2. Advance to the Pacific

    3. Division over the question of slavery

    4. The Civil War

*Unit Six:* The Industrial Revolution

    1. The rise of rapid transportation and communication

    2. Changed ways of living

    3. Problems of business, labor, agriculture, and government

    4. The influence of immigration upon American history

*Unit Seven:* The United States and World Problems

    1. The United States becomes a world power

    2. World War I

    3. Later international relations

*Unit Eight:* Social and Economic Change

    1. Confusion of the postwar era

    2. New directions of government enterprise

    3. World War II

## E. CORRELATION POSSIBILITIES

A few correlation possibilities are listed below merely to indicate opportunities.

*Church History*

General — The protection of the Church, not its support, has always brought great blessings upon a nation.

Good roads, order, and general stability of Roman Empire — Show how these aided the spread of Christianity.

The Reformation — Civil and religious liberty, freedom of thought, and other blessings we prize are directly traceable to the Reformation.

Use also *Church History Inserts* — Publicity Office, Missouri Synod.

*Reading*

A generous amount of historical material is incorporated in the reading course, especially above the primary grades. In one-room schools, with a crowded daily program, it should be possible to teach part of the history course in connection with the reading program.

*Language*

In composition, drama, and debate, topics of historical interest may be utilized.

*Geography*

Settlement of our country — reasons for choice of certain locations; how geography influenced the history of particular regions.

Westward Movement — Show how the Great Central Plain facilitated the movement.

Settlement of the West — Show influence of gold and other mineral deposits upon history; the growth of cities at gateways to the West: Denver, Salt Lake City.

*Civics*

Declaration of Independence — Far-reaching influence upon life and government.

Struggle for adoption of Constitution — Appreciation of rights and duties of citizens.

Sacrifices in connection with struggle for independence and at other times — Patriotism, love of country, unselfish service.

*Health and Safety Education*

Building of the Panama Canal; growth of large cities — Public health and sanitation.

The development of industry — Provisions for safety of workers.

*Science and Agriculture*

Biography of great inventors, Morse, Bell, Wright Brothers, Edison, others — Part played by science in the development of the country.

Transportation, Communication — As above.

Growth of the Middle West — Part played by agriculture. Agriculture the basic industry.

*Music and Art*

Patriotic songs, or songs with a historical setting, may often be used in connection with the history course. See *Music Reader, Select Songs,* or other song books for suggestions.

Works of art depicting historical scenes may be used. Examples: Pictures of famous Americans; Boughton, "Pilgrims Going to Church"; Rothermel, "Landing of the Pilgrims"; Leutze, "Washington Crossing the Delaware"; Bonheur, "Oxen Ploughing"; Trumbull, "Signing the Declaration of Independence."

Creative efforts in art to depict stirring scenes of history.

## F. EVALUATING OUTCOMES

To evaluate the success of his history instruction, the teacher will frequently refer to the aims of the subject and to the suggestions given under the Course for the respective grade levels. A detailed check list of objectives (understandings, desires, attitudes, habits) based on the course is suggested. This would make for purposeful teaching and indicate in a measure the progress of the class toward the values which are to result from the instruction. The list would be constructed around the following larger questions:

Does the child understand the significance of the more important movements and developments, especially in the history of the United States?

Does he understand some of the important influences which helped to mold American government and culture?

Does he realize that history is guided by God for the welfare of the Church and that all benefits enjoyed in Church and State are from God?

Does he understand how the Lutheran Reformation influenced the course of civil history, and the Church's place in history in general?

Does he manifest patriotism and loyalty?

Does he respect his government's authority, also in so-called little things?

Does he assume the citizenship duties which may be expected of him?

Does his obedience and service seem to proceed from the right motives. (Obedience to Fourth Commandment, Biblical principles underlying obedience and service?)

Is he able to read in history some of the lessons it teaches?

Is he humble both in respect to personal and national achievements?

Does he show a healthy interest in history and current events?

Has he mastered the subject matter satisfactorily?

Does he recognize the Christian school as a great constructive force in maintaining national strength and integrity?

## Selected References

Bailey, D. C., *A New Approach to American History.* Revised by E. T. Smith. University of Chicago Press, 1931.

Fredrick, Robert Wendell, and Sheats, Paul H., *Citizen Education through the Social Studies.* Row-Petersen and Co., 1936.

Johnson, H., *The Teaching of History in Elementary and Secondary Schools with Applications to Allied Studies.* Macmillan, 1940 (Revised).

Kelty, Mary G., *Learning and Teaching History in the Middle Grades.* Ginn and Co., 1936.

Kelty, Mary G., "The Supervision of History." Chapter VIII in *The Supervision of Elementary Subjects;* W. H. Burton, editor. D. Appleton-Century, 1929.

Knowlton, D. C., *Making History Graphic.* Chas. Scribner's Sons, 1925.

Morrison, Henry C., *The Practice of Teaching in the Secondary School.* University of Chicago Press, 1931.

Mitchell, Elene, *Teaching Values in New-Type History Tests.* World Book Co., 1930.

Reed, Homer E., *Psychology of Elementary School Subjects,* pp. 398—454. Ginn and Co., 1938.

Sieving, E. C., "The Teaching of History." *Lutheran School Journal,* October, 1933, pp. 49—68; Nov. 1933, pp. 97—110.

Stolper, B. J. R., and Fenn, Henry C., *Integration at Work.* Teachers College, Columbia University, 1939.

Wayland, John W., *How to Teach American History.* Macmillan, 1921.

Weaver, R. B., and Hill, H. C., *United States History by Units.* W. F. Quarrie and Company, Chicago, 1933.

# 4. Civics

## A. OBJECTIVES

1. The proper Christian foundation for citizenship.
   a. The realization that a true Christian life according to the Ten Commandments, applied to all human relationships, forms the proper foundation for good citizenship.
   b. The realization that righteousness is the strength, and sin the downfall of a nation (Prov. 14:34).
   c. The desire personally to live according to God's Commandments, and to convince others of the same need.
   d. The realization that all government is instituted by God, and that obedience to constituted authority is required of every citizen (Rom. 13:1).
   e. Frequent, fervent prayer for those in authority (1 Tim. 2:1-3).

2. An elementary understanding of American civic life and government.

3. A grateful appreciation of, and the determination to preserve, the advantages enjoyed as a citizen of the United States.

4. Willing acceptance of the duties and sacrifices attending citizenship.

## B. DISCUSSION OF OBJECTIVES

### The Proper Christian Foundation for Citizenship

The child is taught that citizenship embraces all the relationships of men which affect the weal and woe of a people united under the same government. The term citizenship means more than membership in a state or nation, more than obedience to the government; it means membership and proper conduct in human society in general. Neighbor to neighbor, consumer to producer, employee to employer, buyer to seller, and inferior to superior relationships are as much included as the relationship between subject and government.

In all these human relationships, it is *righteousness* that exalts a nation, and sin that reproaches a people. The Christian child is, therefore, impressed with the fact that a true Christian life according to the Ten Commandments, applied to all human relationships, is the proper Christian foundation for good citizenship. Such a life means, first, the proper relationship to God, and, second, the proper relationship to all fellow men. "Whatsoever makes a man a good Christian, also makes him a good citizen." — Daniel Webster.

The Christian child is taught also that such righteousness is not merely an ideal, or something desirable, but is required by God of all men; of everyone in his own station. The child must understand that such righteousness is the result of obedience to God; and that it proves itself also in obedience to the ordinances of man which are not contrary to God's Word.

Since the end of the Law is love out of a pure heart, the love of God and the love of man constitute the deciding factor in citizenship.

This foundation is, in the Lutheran School, laid down in the religious instruction and the entire course of Christian training; but in the subject of Civics, particular application to civic life is made.

It is true that also the non-Christian may achieve a high degree of civic righteousness through conformity with the natural law of God. Such righteousness may satisfy the demands of the Government and human society, and temporal benefits may accrue because of it, but it does not meet the requirement of God. The Christian child learns that "Without faith it is impossible to please God." Heb. 11:6.

## Understanding Civic Life and Government

The child must be brought to realize that all government and authority is instituted by God (Rom. 13:1) and that the purpose of government is to protect right and to punish evil (Rom. 13:3, 4). It is important, however, that the concept of citizenship be not limited to the sphere of law and government, but that the child be made aware that he is a citizen at all times and in all life situations. To be able to put the principles and attitudes underlying good citizenship into practice, he must understand both present-day life and government. He must be brought to understand, at least in an elementary way, the operation of the larger and smaller groups of which he is a part, such as the home, school, church, neighborhood, the larger community, and the State, — he must learn why they operate as they do, what their purpose and need is, and what part he as a Christian is to play in making all these co-operative enterprises successful.

The instruction will include both those citizenship situations with which the child is presently and actively concerned, and those which lie in the future, but which he is able to understand in principle. Examples of the latter: Safe driving, making a livelihood, voting, holding office.

## Appreciation of the Advantages Enjoyed and Determination to Preserve Them

Appreciation of the advantages enjoyed as American citizens rests on two factors: First, the realization that all blessings in home, Church, and Nation are wholly undeserved by reason of our sinfulness and are altogether due to the grace of God; second, that these blessings are important both for individual and collective well-being. The first of these will be adequately stressed in religious instruction and recalled frequently; the second will be explained and applied both in the Civics course, and throughout the school life as occasion arises.

The advantages enjoyed by the American citizen are stressed and their importance both for individual and national well-being emphasized. We are allowed to move about and choose our home at will; we may engage in the occupation of our choice; we have police and fire protection; we are permitted to attend the church and school of our choice; to speak and write our thoughts; to attend meetings and assemblies which we feel we should attend; to vote without being instructed how to cast our ballot; and to express our opinions to Congressmen, Senators, the President, and other Government officials on important matters.

Together with the civil and religious rights enjoyed by American citizens, the material advantages are emphasized. Many families who were poverty stricken in their homelands, often perhaps the parents or grandparents of the children in school, are able to provide for an honest and decent living here, and except in extraordinary times, every willing and able-bodied citizen can provide the necesities of life for himself and his family by honest labor.

The realization that all these benefits were achieved under great sacrifices on the part of heroic men and women of the past helps to increase the spirit of gratitude and appreciation for all we have.

At the same time the pupil must learn that sin and corruption are threatening to destroy all that we value most dearly. The greed, selfishness, pride, and rampant ungodliness in general must be recognized as influences which are undermining our national life and integrity. This is necessary to guard against a blind pseudo-patriotism which accepts everything American as unqualifiedly good.

A sincere appreciation of all benefits as gifts of God, a recognition of the weaknesses which endanger our national existence, frequent, fervent prayer for a continuance of blessings, eternal vigilance as the price of liberty and happiness, and the determination to bend every effort toward the preservation of the advantages which we enjoy by virtue of our American citizenship, — all these must go hand in hand in the good citizen. This must become increasingly clear to the child.

### Willing Acceptance of Duties and Sacrifices

The blessings enjoyed by American citizens center largely about various rights or liberties. The child is impressed with the fact that liberty does not mean freedom from obligation, or license; that liberty operates only in the sphere of non-injury to the fellow citizen; that the preservation of liberty may require great sacrifices; that liberty demands obedience to God and to superiors in home, school, or Nation; that it requires moral conduct in all situations — honesty, faithfulness, honor, respect, humility, industry, helpfulness, mercy, fortitude, patience, purity in thought, word, and deed, and every other virtue that is part of the Christian life and of good citizenship; that liberty invariably imposes duties.

Among the duties owed specifically to the Government are diligent efforts toward self-support, willing payment of taxes for all legitimate government operations, readiness to fight and die in the defense of the country, intelligent voting for good government, obedience to all laws that are not contrary to Scripture, support of the government in its efforts to suppress crime and vice, untiring vigilance in matters of legislation and conduct of government, prayer for those in authority (refer to petition for government in General Church Prayer), and such other duties as may devolve upon the citizen.

The course in Civics, supported by the general influence of the school, is directed toward creating a *willing* acceptance of all these duties. Only as this attitude prevails, will the moral expectation of men and women of the next generation enable them to do their part in preserving the liberties enjoyed in America today.

It is the teacher's responsibility to make sure that the child's acceptance of the duties of citizenship rests on the right basis. Evident motives are appreciation of blessings and the desire to preserve them. More important is the fact that the Law of God imposes specific rules of conduct in all life situations. Therefore the training for acceptance of citizenship duties finds its answer in effective religious instruction and attendant Christian training throughout the life of the child.

## C. DIVISION OF TIME

Civics in the primary and intermediate grades is correlated with religion and other school subjects. Probably only one formal course in Civics is taught in the elementary school, most probably in the upper grades. The time requirement will approximate 20 to 30 minutes per day for a semester, or, if preferred, the same amount of time three days per week for an entire school year.

## D. THE COURSE

### I. Primary and Intermediate Grades (1—6) *

Because of its intimate relationship to all life and learning, Civics is not taught as a separate school subject in the primary and intermediate grades. With a set of supplementary citizenship or social studies readers, much teaching can be done in the reading period. As suggested under *E. Correlation,* every school subject offers frequent opportunities for incidental teaching; the religious instruction for direct teaching of Christian citizenship. Continued training in good citizenship is provided in all work and play situations.

### II. Upper Grades (7—8)

In seventh and eighth grades a modern Civics text is introduced. This is necessary to give the pupils an organized knowledge of society in general, and of the State in particular, and to

---

* See also course in Primary Social Studies, pp. 128—137.

review and emphasize those values upon which the appreciation and willing acceptance of the duties and responsibilities of American citizenship are based.

Local conditions will decide whether the course will be concentrated in one semester with four or five class sessions per week, or whether it will be extended over a longer period of time with fewer weekly recitation periods. From the pedagogical viewpoint the former is probably the more desirable.

Presumably no textbook will treat civics and citizenship adequately from the Christian viewpoint, and the teacher will need to supplement the text at many points, as suggested in the outline below.

### Suggested Content

a. *Living Together*

1. Various local communities.
2. Political communities.
3. Communication and transportation.
4. Social and political interdependence of present-day life.
5. Necessity of co-operation in community life.

b. *The Christian Home*

1. The home established by God. Gen. 1:27, 28; Gen. 2:21-24.
2. The father the head of the home. Eph. 6:4.
3. Dangers threatening the Christian home.
4. Laws that support the home.
5. Responsibility of all members of the family for the spiritual and economic welfare of the home.
6. Obedience of children. Fourth Commandment.
7. Christian homes the best safeguard for individual and national well-being.

c. *The School*

1. The need and benefits of education.
2. Kinds of schools: Public, private, parochial.
3. Support and control of the schools.
4. Appreciation of the benefits of the parochial school.
5. The Christian child's attitude toward school life and work.
6. The Christian school a training institution for right living.

d. *The Church*

1. The Church instituted by Christ. Matt. 28:19, 20.
2. The organization and function of the Christian Church. Refer to Catechism, Ques. 184—193.
3. The permanence of the Church as compared with other institutions. Matt. 16:18.
4. Freedom of religion the greatest American blessing.
5. The importance of the Church in individual and national life.

*e. The Civil Community*

   1. Origin of citizens in the community (nationality, country, etc.).
   2. Tolerance toward those with different backgrounds and ideas.
   3. How an alien becomes a citizen.
   4. Government in the civil community.
   5. Rights and duties of citizens.

*f. Community Health*

   1. Health a gift of God.
   2. Conditions necessary for good health.
   3. Maintenance of health part of good citizenship. Fifth Commandment.
   4. Disease prevention.
   5. Caring for the health of workers.
   6. Community play and recreation.

*g. Protection of Life and Property.* Fifth and Seventh Commandments

   1. The problem of safety.
   2. Fire Prevention.
   3. Accidents in home and community.
   4. Protection of right and punishment of evil by constituted authority. 1 Pet. 2:14.
   5. How children can help to protect life and property.
   6. Christian education and training as the best defense against danger to life and property. Matt. 5:13-16.

*h. The Unfortunate Members of Society.* Is. 58:7; 1 John 3:17

   1. The orphans
   2. The blind and deaf.
   3. The poor and needy.
   4. The feeble-minded and mentally afflicted.

*i. Earning a Living*

   1. Earning a living the duty of every able-bodied person. 2 Thess. 3:10.
   2. The reward of the industrious workers. Prov. 10:4; 13:11; 31:10-31.
   3. Choosing one's work.
   4. Workers in various occupations.
   5. Conservation of natural resources.
   6. Attitude toward wealth and material benefits. Prov. 11:28; 1 Tim. 6:17; Ps. 62:10.
   7. Principles to be observed in acquiring material goods. The Seventh Commandment.
   8. Wise saving and spending. 1 Tim. 6:18; Luke 16:9.

*j. Business and Labor*

   1. Proper attitudes of employers and employees. Eph. 6:5-9.
   2. Problems between employers and employees.
   3. Government supervision of industry and labor.

k. *American Ideals of Government*

1. Various types of government.
2. The United States a representative democracy.
3. The meaning and guarantees of constitutional government.
4. The States and the Union.
5. Territories and Possessions.

l. *The Branches of the United States Government*

1. The principle of checks and balances.
2. Congress: How the laws are made.
3. The President: How the laws are enforced.
4. The Courts: How the laws are interpreted.

m. *State and Local Government*

1. How the States are governed. Special reference to own State.
2. Subdivisions of States: County, city, smaller community.
3. Voting privileges and duties.
4. Elections.
5. Political parties. Value of two-party system.
6. Legislation and law enforcement in State and its subdivisions.
7. State and local courts.
8. The individual's responsibility for law and order.

n. *Meeting the Costs of Government*

1. Why governments need money.
2. Taxes and how they are collected.
3. Other sources of government revenue.
4. Government indebtedness.
5. The citizen's duty with respect to assignment and payment of taxes. Seventh Commandment. Matt. 22:21.

o. *The Citizen's Personal Relationship to All Constituted Authority*

1. The citizen and his duties toward his fellow men individually.
2. The citizen's intercession for those in authority. 1 Tim. 2:1.
3. The citizen entitled to all benefits guaranteed by the Government.
4. The citizen as a worthy, moral, respectable person.
5. The citizen's co-operation with the Government in prosperous and perilous days.
6. The citizen seeking the "peace of the city" at all times.
7. The rewards of good citizenship. Eph. 6:2,3.

## E. CORRELATION POSSIBILITIES

*Religion.* All religious instruction prepares for good citizenship.

*Reading.* Any lesson in which honesty, kindness, helpfulness, courage, or any other virtue is stressed, is directly concerned with citizenship training. The conception of the entire subject of

Reading implies citizenship values: Viz., reading for enjoyment, edification, or utility.

*Language.* Oral and written composition topics, or topics for debate, may be taken from the field of Civics occasionally. The training in exactness of thought and expression in itself has citizenship value.

*Spelling.* The spelling vocabulary contains many of the words used in the Civics course. Words that need defining often require indirect citizenship applications. Examples: Obedience, honesty, faithfulness, love, legislature, law, Church.

*Arithmetic.* Arithmetic cannot be taught in a Christian school without occasional reminders that all computation is to be used for honest purposes, in accordance with the Seventh Commandment. New arithmetic texts contain many problems having to do with social relationships, and these teach, at least indirectly, citizenship values.

*Geography.* Topics such as transportation, communication, conservation of resources, business and commerce, and others may be used to show the need of co-operation among the members of a group. Tolerance toward others and other citizenship values should grow out of such instruction.

*History.* Biographies of great Americans lend themselves well to illustrate unselfish love of country, a spirit of sacrifice, trust in God, and other qualities of good citizenship. The Declaration of Independence and the Constitution are used to emphasize the principles upon which our form of government is founded. Stories of pioneers illustrate the difficulties under which our way of life was established and increase appreciation of blessings enjoyed. This is particularly true in respect to the early Lutheran pioneers and the establishment of our Church.

*Health and Safety Education.* Health is necessary to perform fully the duties of the citizen. Protection of one's own health and that of others, in keeping with the Fifth Commandment, is one of the most important citizenship duties.

*General Science.* The good citizen has an intelligent understanding of the world about him. Science is an aid in attaining that. An understanding of some of the principles of science will also enable a person to render more efficient service in "subduing the world." Gen. 1:28.

*The Arts.* Everything that makes man more appreciative or broadens his experiences along desirable lines, makes him a better citizen. Patriotic songs and works of art, for example, have particular value inasmuch as they inspire and give expression to the love of country. Creative art work to illustrate citizenship in action can be made to serve valuable training purposes.

These are merely examples to indicate correlation possibilities. The teacher will expand this list to meet the particular needs of his pupils.

## F. EVALUATING OUTCOMES

The teacher will judge the child's progress on the basis of the aims of the subject. Care must be exercised, for many of the citizenship values are of an intangible nature, and a great deal of subjective judgment is necessarily involved. Wherever there is doubt, the child should be favored in the evaluation. The following questions may be considered:

1. Has the child an elementary understanding of American civic life and government?

2. Does he understand the destructive influence of sin upon personal, community, and national well-being? "Sin is a reproach to any people." Proverbs 14:34.

3. Does he show evidences of the righteousness that is the foundation of good citizenship: Reverence, obedience, honesty, loyalty, industry, and others? (The Ten Commandments.)

4. Does he recognize the Christian school as a great constructive force in establishing and maintaining national integrity? (Genesis 18:19.)

5. Does he accept the duties of citizenship as definitely imposed by God? (Romans 13:1-7; Matt. 22:21; 1 Tim. 2:1-3; the Moral Law.)

6. Does he give evidence that he appreciates the blessings enjoyed as a citizen of the United States? (Observe his expressions, his behavior when the Flag is raised, his attitude during the singing of patriotic songs, the use he makes of his privileges, the exercise of his responsibilities, his respect for the rights of others, and similar situations.)

7. In general, does he conduct himself as one expects of a sincere Christian and of a person who has the best interests of his home, school, church, community, and country at heart?

## Selected References

The Bible.

United States and State Constitutions.

Gross, Herbert H., *Curriculum in Christian Citizenship for Lutheran Schools.* Concordia, 1942.

State, Local, or District Course of Study.

Textbooks in Civics and Citizenship.

# VII. SCIENCE

## 1. Health and Safety Education

### A. OBJECTIVES [1]

1. A distinctly Christian viewpoint of the subject of health and safety, principally the realization

    a. That man, as originally created by God, was physically perfect, healthy, and safe;

    b. That through his fall into sin he became subject to disease, danger, death, and damnation;

    c. That, therefore, health and safety measures are a necessary means of defense against the ravages of sin;

    d. That it is man's duty to seek the health and safety of others, as well as his own, by every possible means (Fifth Commandment);

    e. That man is dependent upon God for any measure of success in achieving health and safety.

2. Knowledge of principles and practices upon which safe and healthy living depends.

3. Good health and safety habits.

4. A wholesome influence upon the home and community in matters of health and safety.

5. The health and happiness of future generations.

### B. DISCUSSION OF OBJECTIVES

**Fundamental Concepts**

The Christian child learns that man, as originally created by God, was physically perfect, healthy, and safe; that only through his fall into sin he became subject to disease, danger, and death; that the greatest enemies to his physical as well as to his spiritual welfare are the devil, the sinning world, and his own corrupt flesh; that health and safety measures are a means of defense against the ravages of sin.

While seeking his physical health and safety, the Christian child must be kept conscious of the fact that he is wholly dependent upon God and God's good and gracious will for any measure of success; that "in Him we live and move and have

---

1) *Note:* Excepting the first, these objectives are essentially those adopted by the Joint Committee on Health Education of the National Education Association and the American Medical Association. Current textbooks and courses are designed to carry out these four aims. With the addition of the first, the subject of health and safety education is converted into a distinctly Christian branch of learning.

our being," Acts 17:28; that primary dependence upon self-help is idolatry. Therefore he is taught to commend himself, his health and safety in body and soul, to God; he is taught to pray for health and protection, to trust in the Lord for these blessings, according to God's will, and to receive them gratefully. In the First Article and the Fourth Petition he has a confession and prayer concerning health, safety, and a happy life that transcends all values of health and safety measures.

The Christian child must be taught that in spite of his observance of health and safety rules, he may, in God's own time, suffer sickness or accident, and death will surely overtake him. Therefore he must learn to bow under the benevolent will of God.

But he is also taught that, under God, he must certainly look after his own health and safety as well as the health and safety of others, realizing that it is criminal and a sin against God to be neglectful in this respect. (Fifth Commandment.) The Christian who confesses with the Psalmist, Ps. 139:14: "I am fearfully and wonderfully made," [2] becomes at the same time responsible for the care of the gift of his marvelous body.

### Health Principles and Practices

Health instruction must provide the pupil with an understanding of the principles and practices upon which safe and healthy living depends. This is comparatively simple. It is much more difficult to furnish sufficient motivation for healthful practices, for the price of careless and dangerous habits is likely to seem remote and unreal to the healthy child. The most important task of the teacher is to exercise the child constantly in good health and safety habits until he is mature enough to understand the scientific sanctions underlying these practices.

The physical environment of the school must be of a nature to avoid contradiction between precept and obvious practice, or the formation of desirable attitudes and habits will be hindered. The building equipment, heating, lighting, seating, drinking water, sanitation, playground and equipment, school hours, assignments of home work, and every other feature of the school must be arranged with the requirements of the pupil's health and safety in view.

---

2) "No machine has ever been constructed so efficient as man himself. Where can we find a pump as perfect as the human heart? If the boss treats it right, it stays on the job for more than 600,000 hours, making 4,320 strokes and pumping 15 gallons an hour. We have no telegraphic mechanism equal to our nervous system; no radio so efficient as the voice and the ear; no camera as perfect as the human eye; no ventilating plant as wonderful as the lungs, nose, and skin; no electrical switchboard can compare with the spinal cord. Isn't such a marvelous mechanism worthy of the highest respect and the best care?" — Floyd Parsons in the *Reader's Digest* (March, 1935, p. 61).

Among the important tasks in health education is the fostering of wholesome attitudes, or good mental hygiene. Comfortable and pleasant physical environment is an aid in this respect. More important is the social and learning atmosphere. A cheerful teacher, who understands the emotional life of children and treats their problems and failures sympathetically, who is fair and honest in all respects, who is kind even when he must punish, who directs the interests and activities of his pupils into healthy channels, who is a friend to the friendless, who knows how to reduce friction between pupils to a minimum, who, above all, deals with all his pupils in keeping with their high estate as children of God and points them to their Savior, works in the interest of mental hygiene most effectively.

### Influence on Home and Community

Some of .the instruction and training given by the school will be carried into the homes automatically by the pupils, but the school is not content with this incidental learning. It seeks consciously and systematically to influence the family and the community through its health program, especially in cases where carelessness and neglect at home counteract the work of the school.

·The presence of at least one parent when the child is physically examined; the subsequent discussion 'of the child's condition between physician and parent; the explanation of school health and safety objectives; the discussion in the voters' assembly and in parent groups of the needs of the school from the standpoint of health; emphasis on health and safety principles and habits in school exhibits and programs; and other means help to create a sympathetic attitude on the part of parents and patrons of the school, and offer opportunities for family and community education.

The fifth objective has in view the health and happiness of future generations. This will become a reality in the measure in which the preceding aims are achieved.

### Opportunities for Stressing the Christian Viewpoint

Below are listed a few opportunities for stressing the Christian viewpoint. The teacher will find others.

1. Definition of health. (Condition of body as near to perfection as possible under sinful condition of man.)

2. Illness. (Imperfections of body due to fall of man. A reminder of death.)

3. Desirability of health and safety. (Personal happiness and Christian service of others.)

4. Necessity of guarding against sickness and accident. (Fifth Commandment.)

5. Marvelous intricacies of human body and its functions. (Man is "fearfully and wonderfully made." Ps. 139:14.)

6. Protecting the health and safety of others. (This is not only good citizenship, but "Thou shalt love thy neighbor as thyself.")

7. Fresh air and breathing. (The perfect wisdom and providence of God in creating the inexhaustible body of air about the earth which constantly renews itself and makes life possible.)

8. The sun as the life and health giver. (Goodness of God, who made one creature for the benefit of others.)

9. Food and drink. (An appreciation of God's goodness in providing for all living things will help provide a motive for the proper use of food and drink. "Do all to the glory of God.")

10. Scientific discoveries in regard to health and healthful living. (All these are a part of God's commission to man to subdue the earth.)

11. Healthy appearance: Real and natural beauty. (These are not a matter of sinful pride, but of gratitude and glory to God.)

12. Example of how some pictures may be used: A picture showing the destruction of habit-forming drugs by the police may be properly interpreted by the question, "What higher reason has the Christian for avoiding these drugs than the mere fact that the law forbids their use?"

## C. DIVISION OF TIME AND MATERIALS

Schools generally will not devote more than one hour per week to formal health instruction. In one-room schools the amount of time available may be reduced to 30 or 45 minutes. Where as much as nearly an hour per week is available, it is better to divide the time into two recitation periods; where less than 40 minutes, one longer period is to be preferred to two or more shorter ones.

Two-room schools will not organize more than three classes in health education. Third and fourth, fifth and sixth, and seventh and eighth grades may be combined, and the work prescribed for the grades in the local course of study or textbook alternated.

In one-room schools incidental teaching is carried to the third grade. It may be combined with the social studies. The formal teaching of health is limited to one class weekly. Some ingenuity on the part of the teacher will be necessary in arranging the instruction materials. In view of the similarity of the basic materials in grades five and six, and again in grades seven and eight, a two-year alternating plan seems the most desirable. The subject taught is the same for all grades, but grades seven and eight, on the basis of the more extensive subject treatment in their textbook, will be required to do additional work. The two higher books of a three-book series lend themselves best to this arrangement. In addition, teachers may utilize valuable instructional materials often supplied free of charge by State or City Departments of Health or Education, or films and slides for visual education.

If possible, the classroom instruction should be supplemented by means of a physical education period. This should provide for orderly games and play in which all pupils who are physically able take part.

## D. COURSE SUGGESTIONS

### Primary Grades (1—3)

In the primary grades the emphasis is on the establishment of good health and safety habits. Stimulation of the desire for good health habits and frequent and intelligent repetition of the activities which are to become habits are important.

Most of the health teaching on the primary level is done incidentally. Or it may be combined with the Social Studies Course. See Social Studies for the Primary Grades, pages 128 to 137. Health and safety readers may be used profitably for supplementary reading activities.

The desire to avoid disease, pain, and harm, as also to live a pleasant and happy life, naturally serve as motives for doing healthful things, but the teacher must stress God's command (Fifth Commandment) as the most important reason for guarding and preserving the health.

The list of objectives given below is merely suggestive. Detail in all instances will be supplied by the classroom teacher.

### Outcomes

1. Recognition that we owe our health and safety to God.
   a. That God takes care of us.
   b. That He gives us everything we need to keep healthy, safe, and happy. (First Article.)
   c. That He can cure us of sickness and save us from death. (Bible History.)
   d. That God gives children their own protecting angels. Matt. 18:10.
   e. That He has given them parents, teachers, the Government (policemen, firemen), doctors, dentists, and others for their protection.

2. A realization that sickness, harm, and all kinds of unhappiness are often our own fault, due to carelessness; and that this is a sin.

3. Evidence of trust in God and gratitude to Him, and, as a result, freedom from fear and worry as well as conscientious guarding against sickness and danger.

4. Thankful appreciation of angel protection.

5. Strict and willing obedience to parents and other superiors for our own health and safety.

6. Careful avoidance of everything that might harm someone else. (Fifth Commandment.)

7. The knowledge and belief that God will deliver us from all evil, sickness, and danger when we die, and will then make us perfectly happy, healthy, strong, safe, and free from all fear in heaven, forever and ever.

### Important Health Habits

a. *Cleanliness and Neatness*

1. To keep bodies and clothes clean.

2. To wash face, ears, and neck regularly.

3. To wash hands after going to the toilet, before eating, and otherwise when necessary.

4. To bathe regularly and frequently.

5. To care properly for hair and nails.

b. *Food*

1. To learn the necessity of eating wholesome foods, such as milk, eggs, meat, vegetables, and fruit.

2. To avoid eating between meals.

3. To drink from four to six glasses of water per day.

4. Not to eat foods that have fallen to the floor or ground, or to trade bites.

5. To keep foods away from flies, dust, and dirt.

6. To avoid coffee, tea, and alcohol.

7. To eat slowly, chew food thoroughly.

8. To wash raw fruits and vegetables before eating them.

9. To eat candy only after meals.

c. *Rest and Exercise*

1. To sleep from 11 to 12 hours every night in a dark, well-ventilated room.

2. To rest a little after the noon meal every day.

3. To engage in quiet activities before going to sleep.

4. To see the need of daily bodily exercise.

5. To spend four hours out of doors every day, weather permitting.

### d. Protection against Disease

1. To use own towels and wash cloths.

2. To drink without touching drinking fountain with mouth, or from individual cup.

3. To keep hands away from the eyes, nose, and mouth.

4. To learn the need of fresh air, sunshine, work, play, and rest for healthy growth.

5. To go to the toilet at regular times.

6. To cover mouth and nose when coughing or sneezing.

7. To wear clothing suited to the temperature, both indoors and out.

8. To take proper precautions against taking cold.

9. To read with the book in right position, with the light coming over the left shoulder.

10. To sit and stand in good posture.

### e. Teeth

1. To visit a dentist for proper attention to the teeth.

2. To learn that good teeth are necessary for chewing, talking, a good appearance, and general health.

3. To exercise teeth properly by chewing food and brushing them.

### f. Safety

1. To observe safety rules in crossing streets and in riding on busses and street cars. (Safety Patrol.)

2. Not to run into the street.

3. To play safe in games.

4. To be careful with dangerous objects, matches, scissors, knives, gasoline, kerosene, electrical equipment, etc.

5. To obey safety rules in riding a bicycle.

### g. Good Manners

1. To be helpful and obedient to parents, and well-behaved generally. (Fourth Commandment.)

2. To be friendly and kind to everyone. (Rom. 12:10.)

3. To be helpful to the sick and needy. (Fifth Commandment.)

4. To be honest and truthful. (Eighth Commandment.)

5. To develop self-control, patience, self-reliance, and courage.

6. To realize the importance of obedience to God for general well-being.

### Intermediate Grades (4—6)

The habits and attitudes established in the primary grades must be strengthened and new ones developd. An additional aim is to supply some elementary knowledge of the reasons which underlie good health and safety habits. These reasons are given in simple and general terms, and detailed scientific explanation is omitted. The study of the organs of the body and their functions is begun in an elementary manner in the fifth and sixth grades.

In the formal lessons the aim is to establish intellectual and emotional foundations for thought and action. The materials emphasize attitudes, knowledge, and habits. Incidental teaching is continued, both in respect to individual and group needs. The Christian viewpoint must constantly be evident in the attitudes of teacher and pupils and become more fully developed.

The topics below are suggestive of the work of the intermediate grades. All good health texts for these grades cover approximately this area, except the Christian objectives listed, and the arrangement of the textbook and the local course of study will be taken into consideration.

### Outcomes

1. Recognition of sin as the fundamental cause of sickness and danger.

2. Recognition of the temptations of the devil as attempts to destroy health, safety, and happiness.

3. Realization that the body is the temple of God. (1 Cor. 6:19, 20.)

4. Appreciation of man's dependence upon God's mercy in all bodily needs. (Explanation of First Article.)

5. Realization that the body and all its organs are marvelous evidences of God's wisdom and providence.

6. Realization that it is murder to harm one's own or another's body or soul through neglect, recklessness, or sinful living. (Fifth Commandment.)

7. Recognition of the value of prayer in attaining and preserving health and safety. (Fourth Petition.)

8. Confidence in the face of the certain prospect of death.

### Suggested Course Content

*a. Nutrition*
1. Fats
2. Carbohydrates
3. Proteins
4. Minerals
5. Vitamins
6. Water
7. Malnutrition
8. Food allergy

*b. Rest and Exercise*
1. The healing power of sleep.
2. Amount of sleep needed at different ages.
3. Requisites for restful sleeping. (Dark room, quiet, relaxation.)
4. Work and play as health builders.

*c. The Digestive System*
1. The organs of the digestive system.
2. Getting rid of body wastes.
3. Rest after meals.
4. The teeth.
   a. Importance to health.
   b. Structure.
   c. Care of the teeth.
   d. Foods that build healthy teeth.

*d. Cells*
1. How body cells grow.
2. Food needs of the body cells.

*e. Bones and Muscles*
1. Structure of bones and muscles.
2. How bones and muscles grow.
3. Relation between bones and muscles.
4. Food, exercise, and rest in bone and muscle growth.
5. Good posture.

*f. The Skin, Nails, and Hair*
1. Structure and function of skin, nails, and hair.
2. Care of the skin, nails, and hair.

*g. The Lungs and Breathing*
1. The need of fresh air.
2. Structure of nose and lungs.
3. Mouth breathing. (Tonsils and adenoids.)
4. Ventilation.

h. *The Blood and Circulation.*

    1. The circulatory system and its function.

    2. Importance of right food to build red corpuscles.

i. *Special Sense Organs*

    1. The eyes.

        aa. Structure

        bb. Care of the eyes.

        cc. Good light from proper direction.

        dd. Protecting the eyes from disease and accident.

    2. The ears.

        aa. Structure of the ears.

        bb. Hygiene of the ear.

j. *The Nervous System*

    1. Structure of the nervous system.

    2. Function of the nervous system.

    3. The value of work, rest, and recreation in maintaining a healthy nervous system.

    4. Habit formation: Necessity, usefulness, manner.

    5. The part of vitamin B in the nervous system.

k. *Communicable Diseases*

    1. Germs and bacteria.

    2. Methods of avoiding germ infection.

    3. Colds: How to prevent them and keep from spreading them; care while ill.

    4. The work of Louis Pasteur, Edward Jenner, and others.

    5. Vaccination, immunization, immunity.

*Note:* Special instruction when communicable diseases are prevalent is valuable, because of the evident motivation for learning at such times.

l. *Safety*

    1. Safety on streets and highways: Crossing streets, riding a bicycle, coasting, traffic laws.

    2. Safety in the home: Fire prevention, working with tools, machinery, farm animals, etc.

    3. Safety in recreation: Vacation, boating, fishing, swimming, camping, sunburn, poison ivy, etc.

m. *Clothing and Shoes*

    1. Different materials for different purposes.

    2. Importance of clothes that fit.

*n. Tea, Coffee, Alcohol, Drugs*

1. Harm to sleep and digestion.

2. Crowding out of wholesome foods.

3. Danger on highways. (Alcohol.)

4. Sinfulness of harming body through excessive use.

**The Course for the Higher Grades (7—8)**

In grades seven and eight the physiological and scientific basis underlying the practice of good health and safety habits is more fully laid. This is necessary that the habits may be practiced intelligently and effectively. Incidental teaching, frequent health inspection, and continued training in health and safety habits still go hand in hand with formal teaching. The Christian viewpoint becomes more firmly fixed. Care must be exercised not to glorify the human side of scientific achievement, but to interpret them in the light of Gen. 1:28.

**Outcomes**

1. Nearer perfection of the Christian objectives named for the primary and intermediate grades.

2. Interpretation of all scientific achievements in the field of health and safety in the light of Gen. 1:28 ("and subdue it") to the glory of God.

3. Sense of responsibility for the health of others: community health. ("Thou shalt love thy neighbor as thyself.")

4. Realization of the importance of faith and trust in God for happiness, contentment, and mental health in general.

5. Joyful anticipation of complete perfection and safety in heaven. (Seventh Petition.)

### Suggested Course Content

*a. Review and Expansion of Work in Previous Grades*

1. Nutrition.
2. Rest and exercise.
3. The digestive system.
4. Cells.
5. Bones and muscles.
6. The skin, nails, and hair.
7. The lungs and breathing.
8. The blood and circulation.
9. Special sense organs.
10. The nervous system.
11. Communicable diseases.
12. Safety.
13. Clothing.
14. Tea, coffee, alcohol, tobacco, harmful drugs.

b. *Shelter, Heat, and Light*

    1. Brief history of the improvement of human shelter.

    2. Heating and ventilating.

        aa. Relative merits of different heating systems.

        bb. Home and school heating.

        cc. Temperature and humidity.

        dd. Air conditioning.

    3. Proper lighting.

        aa. History of artificial lighting.

        bb. How to achieve good lighting.

c. *Buying Food and Planning Meals*

    1. Discretion in buying food: Saving.

    2. Planning and serving well-balanced meals.

    3. Good habits of eating: Table etiquette.

    4. Care in the handling of food: Refrigeration, flies, dirt.

d. *Protection of Milk and Water Supply*

    1. Dangers of impure drinking water.

    2. Safe water in city and country.

        aa. Sources of safe water.

        bb. Making impure water safe.

    3. Safe milk from farm to table.

        aa. Diseases of cattle: Testing.

        bb. Milk-borne diseases.

        cc. Pasteurization of milk and milk products.

e. *Home Sanitation*

    1. Keeping home and community clean everybody's duty.

    2. Removal of body wastes: Outdoor toilets.

    3. Proper washing of dishes.

    4. Care of beds and bedding.

    5. Laundering clothes.

f. *Community Health*

    1. Diseases caused by insect carriers: Typhus, bubonic plague, malaria, yellow fever.

    2. Tuberculosis: Tuberculin tests; X-ray; prevention and cure of the disease.

    3. The conquest of smallpox and diphtheria.

    4. Quarantine and isolation.

    5. Medical inspection of school children.

    6. Every individual's responsibility for guarding the health of others.

*g. Home Safety*

1. Emergencies: First aid for sprains, bruises, broken bones, profuse bleeding (tourniquet), etc.

2. Preventing falls: Small loose rugs, ice on steps, poorly lighted steps, etc.

3. Fire prevention.

4. Scalds and burns.

5. Asphyxiation.

6. Care in handling electrical equipment.

7. Artificial respiration.

8. Treating and dressing wounds to prevent infection.

9. Keeping small articles out of the reach of babies and small children.

*h. Mental Health*

1. Result of nervous strain.

2. Necessity of facing facts courageously.

3. Interests and pleasant activities.

4. Hobbies: Independent work during leisure time.

5. Trust in God necessary for mental health.

### E. CORRELATION POSSIBILITIES

*General.* Healthful environment in the schoolroom and on the playground; training in health and safety habits.

*Religion.* The course in religion lays the basis for correct attitudes in matters of health and safety. It plays a vital part in establishing mental health.

*Reading.* Health and safety readers provide valuable supplementary reading material. Or individual selections in the basic reader dealing with principles of health and safety are utilized.

*Language.* Written and oral composition offer opportunities for treating problems of health and safety.

*Geography; History.* The study of certain regions and their development, Cuba, the Panama Canal Zone, or larger cities, for instance, offer opportunities for studying sanitation and public health problems.

*Civics.* Observance of health and safety measures are taught as a necesary part of good citizenship.

*General Science.* Most science texts contain chapters on the structure of the body, on sanitation, and the conquest of disease. These should be utilized to supplement the course in health and safety.

*Music.* Especially with young children, "My Clean Hands" [3] and similar selections are utilized.

*Art.* Posters and pictures pertaining to health and safety. Creative art efforts in illustration of health principles.

## F. EVALUATING OUTCOMES

The objectives of Health and Safety Education supply the basis for a list of desirable outcomes. The teacher will evaluate the success of his work according to questions such as the following:

1. Have the pupils acquired a sound basis for safe, healthy, and happy living?

   a. Have they a distinctly Christian viewpoint of health and safety? (See first *Objective* and *Outcomes* under primary, intermediate, and higher grades.)

   b. Have they acquired a knowledge of bodily structure and function, and the ability and habit to care for their bodily needs?

   c. Are they careful at work and play, at home, in school, and on the street? Do they exercise judgment with sharp or otherwise dangerous objects?

   d. Are they concerned about the health and safety of others? Do they do all in their power to prevent injury or harm to others? Are they interested in community welfare in matters of health and safety?

   e. Do they observe the fundamental health rules pertaining to cleanliness, food, rest, and exercise? In short, has healthful and safe living become habitual with them?

   f. Do they show poise and mental balance? Are they fair, open-minded, sincere, happy, contented?

2. Do the school surroundings meet health and safety requirements?

   a. Is the building construction safe?

   b. Do heating, lighting, and ventilation facilities measure up to accepted standards?

   c. Are adequate toilet facilities provided?

   d. Is the drinking water safe?

   e. Are pupils properly seated with respect to light, height of seat and desk?

   f. Is the playground space and equipment adequate for the number of pupils enrolled?

---

3) *Select Songs,* No. 294. Concordia.

3. Is the school health program adequate for the needs?

a. Is the length of the school day suited to the ages of the children? Recess periods properly distributed?

b. Are playground activities supervised?

c. Is the noon lunch supervised and made pleasant? Is a hot lunch available?

d. Are health examinations given by a competent physician, either to all children periodically, or to those who are referred to the doctor by the teacher or nurse as needing special attention? Are the children weighed and measured regularly?

e. Are the parents present at these examinations, and are the results fully discussed with them?

f. Are the services of a school nurse or other public-health nurse available for supervising the health of the school children?

g. Are good health records kept by the school?

### Selected References

Bancroft, Jessie, *Games for the Playground.* Macmillan, 1921.

Edgerton, Avis E., "Social Consciousness — A Major Objective in Health Education." *Elementary School Journal,* January, 1939, pp. 357—362.

*Health Education.* Report of Joint Committee on Health Problems in Education (N. E. A. and American Medical Association). National Education Association, 1941 (Revised).

Krug, Amelia C., *Games and Playground Supervision for Lutheran Schools.* Concordia, 1937.

Missouri *Courses of Study,* 1937. Pp. 1061—1267.

Morrison, Henry C., *The Curriculum of the Common School.* University of Chicago Press, 1941. Pp. 639—662.

Neilson, N. P., and Van Hagen, Winifred, *Physical Education for Elementary Schools.* A. S. Barnes and Co., 1930.

Reed, Homer B., *Psychology of Elementary School Subjects.* Ginn, 1938. Pp. 529—559.

State, local, or District Course of Study.

Manual accompanying textbook.

## 2. General Science

### A. OBJECTIVES

1. A growing knowledge and appreciation of God's majesty, power, wisdom, providence, and love as manifested in the order and detail of Creation.

2. A growing understanding of some fundamental concepts inherent in the physical and biological sciences.

3. A growing recognition of the effect which natural phenomena and environment have upon man's mode of living.

4. Grateful and economical use of the gifts of God in nature and intelligent conservation of natural resources.

5. Development of new vistas of interest in God's Creation, resulting in a broader outlook on, and a fuller enjoyment of, the same.

6. The ability to reason logically toward the solution of the problems of life that lie outside the realm of faith.

7. The willingness and habit to subject human reason to the revealed Word of God.

## B. DISCUSSION OF OBJECTIVES

### Knowledge and Appreciation of God's Majesty, Power, Wisdom, Providence, Love

Science, rightly understood, glorifies God; unscientific speculations destroy faith in God. To create right attitudes and to guard the pupil in his faith, revelation must be brought to bear upon science. Correct attitudes toward God's Creation and the scientific achievements of men are expressed in the following passages of Scripture:

"The heavens declare the glory of God." Psalm 19:1.

"Marvelous are Thy works." Psalm 139:14.

"Oh, give thanks to Him that by wisdom made the heavens." Psalm 136:5.

"O Lord, Thou preservest man and beast." Psalm 36:6.

"How excellent is Thy loving-kindness, O God." Psalm 36:7.

"What hath God wrought!" Numbers 23:23.

Simple daily happenings, such as day and night, sunrise and sunset, changes from fair to rainy weather, and the changes of the seasons may be used to point to God, who rules, regulates, and directs these natural manifestations for the benefit of man. The infinite size of the universe, many amazing natural phenomena, the creation of rational man, and the bountiful provisions for man's preservation indicate the magnitude of God's majesty, power, wisdom, providence, and love, and help to move the pupil to an attitude of awe at the abundance and variety which God has provided in nature, all for the benefit of man. Thus is laid the foundation of knowledge and appreciation necessary for a Christian viewpoint with regard to science, the present needs of the child are met, and he is prepared to withstand possible anti-Christian attacks by science teachers in secondary schools which he may attend later.

## Growing Understanding of Fundamental Science Concepts

The purpose of the science course is not to produce scientists, but to teach pupils to understand in an elementary way the physical world about them. They should know how science influences the life of the average person and how it prepares him for successful living in modern society. An elementary knowledge of science can spell the difference between a successful and an unsucessful housewife in such matters as the purchase of food and clothing, and in the care of mechanical and electrical devices. It may spell the difference between an intelligent and an ignorant citizen with respect to transportation, communication, housing, lighting, sanitation, and other matters with which everyone ought to be familiar. This implies that the course must consist of the science of the home, the shop, the city, and the farm.

The instruction must be made practical and applied to the child's problems, so that he will learn to care for growing plants and pets, repair an electric bell and other simple household appliances, handle simple tools, replace a burnt-out fuse, remove spots from clothing, and take care of many similar everyday needs. These practical applications of science will captivate the child's interest and serve a utilitarian purpose at the same time.

The teacher is not expected to know all the answers to these problems in advance, but he grows with his pupils as they discover the new world of the why and how of things. With a good textbook as a guide, the average teacher can become successful in the teaching of general, practical science.

## Recognition of the Effect of Environment upon Man's Mode of Living

Winds, atmospheric conditions, products and materials at hand, and physical conditions in general determine largely the way of life in a given region. The pupil's own community is rich in opportunities for teaching the limitations and the potentialities which are offered by environment. This is the starting point for a general appraisal of environment as a factor in determining customs and habits throughout the world.

At the same time the pupil learns that environment is not static, but subject to change for better or for worse. Man either exhausts earth's resources, or he replenishes them and increases their usefulness through proper husbandry and through the application of proper scientific methods. Gen. 1:28.

Understanding the environment is both a social studies and a science objective. In the social studies the emphasis is on people throughout the world and on their interdependence; in science.

improvement of the environment by the use of reason and scientific procedure is stressed. In both, the social studies and science, dependence upon God in all things and gratitude for His blessings are important objectives.

## Use of God's Gifts and Conservation

Science has been defined as a method of thinking and acting. In itself science is neutral, neither good nor bad. But the products of science have great potentialities for good or evil. Science instruction must, therefore, be concerned with the development of attitudes which will insure the right use of natural resources and of scientific discoveries.

The first requirement for such use is absolute humility in the face of scientific achievement. "What hath God wrought!", Samuel F. B. Morse's first message over the telegraph, indicates the spirit that should be sought. The person with this attitude will seek only the constructive use of scientific discoveries and inventions. He will seek to prevent their use for wanton destruction or for other sinful purposes.

The second requirement is gratitude for all good gifts of God, both the natural gifts and those resulting from the inventive genius of man. The attitude of gratitude is necessary to insure the economical use of God's gifts and the determination to conserve natural resources for future generations.

## Development of New Vistas of Interest

Science material appeals to most pupils and requires little motivation. Modern science texts, generally speaking, provide fascinating reading and often arouse the desire to learn more. The teacher should seek to recognize and encourage special interests of his pupils for an enrichment of their knowledge and a broadening of their horizons. Elementary science should be utilized to the fullest extent to indicate to pupils the possibilities the subject holds for future progress and enjoyment. The course in science may well lead to a lifelong vocation or avocation if the teacher is able to recognize talents and inclinations and to direct them into utilitarian or recreational channels.

## The Ability to Reason Logically Toward a Solution

The ability to reason logically is often called the scientific method of thinking. This ability is necessary in the solution of everyday problems. The method is learned by practicing it.

Logical thinking requires a step-by-step procedure of

1. Realizing a problem.

2. Finding and recalling facts that seem to bear upon the problem.

3. Seeking relevant facts.

4. Weighing the evidence for or against a given conclusion.

5. Testing the conclusion.

6. Generalizing the conclusion.

Logical thinking requires the suspension of judgment until all the facts are supplied, complete intellectual honesty, and submerging of personal bias. All this runs counter to the mere emotional treatment of problems, which is too prevalent. Only a healthy and disciplined mind can be interested in absolute truth and seek mastery over snap judgment and prejudice. The nature of science materials and conclusions demands logical thinking. It is believed that practice in scientific thinking in many situations, with constant application to the simple problems of life, will tend to make such thinking habitual.

The teacher will best succeed in training his pupils in logical thinking if he works with them, guiding them in thinking about the simple facts of the world and training them in the use of reliable methods of observation, study, and experimentation which will be of value to them throughout their lives.

### Subjection of Reason to the Word of God

Application of the scientific method is valuable in all matters that lie outside the realm of faith and Christian conduct. When God's Word speaks, reason must submit.

With the materially minded, human reason becomes a fetish, or god, which is expected to solve all problems. Since reason cannot be applied to the supernatural, the materialist concludes that the supernatural does not exist.

The Christian teacher must, first of all, himself become intimately acquainted with Scripture and its applications in order to know when reason must be silenced. Then he must seek to develop the same understanding in his pupils and aid them in developing the conviction that wherever a conflict occurs between the Word of God and human reason, the latter is in error. This understanding is developed in the religious instruction, but it is emphasized systematically in the science course until it becomes habitual with his pupils to subject reason to revelation.

The limitations of man and his reason may be illustrated by pointing to evident errors of reason and man's inability to understand many common things, such as the growth of grass and the like; or man's limitations may be effectively impressed by means of Bible passages such as Eccl. 8:17: "Then I beheld all the work of God, that a man cannot find out the work that is done under the sun, because though a man labor to seek it out, yet he shall not find it; yea, farther; though a wise man think to know it, yet shall he not be able to find it."

## C. PRACTICAL SUGGESTIONS

**Time Allotment**

In the primary grades, science may be taught incidentally, especially in connection with reading and Primary Social Studies.[1] Beginning with the intermediate grades, definite time should be set aside for the subject.

An organized science course may be substituted for health and safety education, nature study, and conservation, which are often allotted separate time on the school program. Or, it may be possible to allot some of the time usually spent on reading and language to science. In the latter case purposeful reading and language activity assume special importance.

The science course must be adapted to the time available. Efforts to crowd and hurry the instruction defeat its purpose. Less time for science means fewer science units. The opportunity to observe, experiment, and discuss under any given topic should not be curtailed.

**Experiments** [2]

1. Experiments provide a motivating force for the pupil to associate himself intimately with immediate problems. This stimulates interest and attention and makes for intelligent learning.

2. Choosing materials for experimenting, setting up the necessary apparatus, performing the experiment, making or verifying conclusions, applying the results of the experiment to the problems of daily life require thought and give practice in logical thinking.

3. The pupil should be tested for his understanding of every experiment that has been performed. This testing may take various forms. For example: A brief concise written report, a drawing or sketch illustrating the procedure and the result, or a few test questions.

4. Simple experiments may be performed by the pupils them-

---

1) See pp. 128—137.

2) For a demonstration of method and experiments see Glenn O. Blough, "An Elementary Science Group at Work." Scott-Foresman and Co. (Booklet sent free upon request.)

selves. Delicate equipment or dangerous ingredients should never be handled by the inexperienced.

5. All ingredients should be carefully and permanently labeled.

6. Generally speaking, pupils may follow textbook instructions in experiments.

7. As much as possible, children should be given practical experiences in caring for plants, flowers, pets, trees, gardens, and the like.

### Field Trips [3]

Field trips, hikes, and school journeys are useful means of instruction if wisely planned and properly managed. They offer actual experiences with native materials. Visits may be made to gardens, fields, markets, zoos, lakes, ponds, and industrial plants, animals, birds, and insects, and such phases of industrial life as the children can understand. The success of these activities depends largely upon the following factors:

1. Preliminary survey of the territory to be visited, a list of available materials to be studied in connection with the trip, careful planning of the route, and the means of transportation to be used, if any.

2. Permission of the owner or representative of the place to be visited if it is private property.

3. A guide sheet containing questions to be answered, needed hints, directions, or suggestions for each pupil.

4. An understanding with the pupils that any conduct unbecoming to a Christian boy or girl will not be tolerated.

5. A checkup in the form of a written report, an oral quiz, or handing in of the guide sheet with questions properly answered.

### Materials and Equipment

Science can be taught successfully with comparatively inexpensive equipment. Many experiments may be performed with simple equipment, such as are found in most kitchens or pantries, materials obtained from free sources,[4] materials furnished free of charge by school patrons connected with chemical plants, or products of the local environment. Some of the common helpful materials are listed below.

---

3) See G. H. Reifschneider, "Field Trips, School Journeys, Excursions." *Lutheran School Journal,* March, 1941, p. 309; April, 1941, p. 358.

4) See Alwin R. Roschke, "List of Free and Inexpensive Materials for Schools." *Lutheran School Journal,* June, 1941, p. 452.

1. Basic textbook.

2. Other instructional materials, such as reference sets, books, and pamphlets.

3. All kinds of visual aids, charts, maps, drawings, photographs, models, films, pictures, and the like, many of which may be collected from newspapers and magazines.

4. Collections of living and nonliving things from the local environment. These may include vegetables, fruits, roots, bulbs, plants, seeds, fish, tadpoles, insects, and the like, which are displayed in the "science corner," or museum, aquarium, terrarium, or insect cage. To be of value, these displays require class study and discussion and periodical changing.

5. A microscope.

6. Window box or outdoor garden, bird bath, bird houses, etc.

7. Sand table, construction materials.

8. Bulletin board, nursery and seed catalogs, compass, thermometer, weather vane, and the like.

## D. COURSE SUGGESTIONS

Science is comparatively new in the elementary school curriculum. There is, therefore, no general agreement as to course content. In the past, science was usually taught under the name of nature study and frequently consisted of a haphazard consideration of unrelated facts. Today science is conceived more in terms of experience, attitudes, interpretations, and ways of thinking. Science is reality, and children should be given every opportunity to experience with their senses and thus to become aware of God's handiwork and of the contributions which men of science have made through their ability to use the laws and principles which God has placed in nature.

Research studies seem to indicate that children's interests in science vary little between elementary and junior high school ages, the difference being rather a wider and deeper aspect of concepts.

Below are listed guiding principles that serve as a basis for selecting content materials or content areas of the modern science course:

1. The subject matter is chosen from all fields of science and should include astronomy, physics, biology, and other physical science subjects.

2. The materials take into account the environment of the

children, their interests and abilities, and lead them from the known to the unknown.

3. The subject matter shifts the emphasis from mere fact learning to the use of factual materials in the interpretation of life and the individual's adjustment to his environment.

4. The course in science forms a progressive, unified plan, broad and comprehensive enough to enable the child to make generalizations that are concerned with the important aims of science education as presented from the Christian viewpoint.

5. Seasonal materials are included.

6. The course is built around the following areas of content:
   a. The universe, or beyond the earth.
   b. The earth and its inhabitants.
   c. Conditions that are necessary to life.
   d. Physical and chemical forms.
   e. Man's efforts to control his environment.

Most science textbooks contain large amounts of material which is objectionable from the Christian viewpoint, and, therefore, many teachers hesitate to introduce them. For this reason the course in science is outlined in much greater detail than the course in most other school subjects. This material may be used as the basis of the course and supplemented with reading from various sources as the teacher may direct. The course is divided into seven units each for the primary, intermediate, and upper grades. It is not necessary to cover all the units nor to carry out every unit in detail. Adjustments must be made to the needs of the local school and community. Seasonal materials should be studied in season. This will necessitate division of certain units.

The following division indicates how the units may be arranged for a three-year course on the basis of an autumn, winter, and spring program.

### Primary Grades

|  | Autumn | Winter | Spring |
|---|---|---|---|
| I Year | I | II | III |
| II Year | III | IV | I |
| III Year | V | VII or VI | V or IV |

### Intermediate Grades

|  | Autumn | Winter | Spring |
|---|---|---|---|
| I Year | I | II | IV or I |
| II Year | III | VI | V |
| III Year | VII or V | VII | III or VII |

## Upper Grades

|  | Autumn | Winter | Spring |
|---|---|---|---|
| I Year | IV | I | III |
| II Year | V | II or VI | IV |
| III Year | III | VII | V |

## Primary Grades (1—3)

In the primary grades, the emphasis is on very simple concepts. No attempt is made to explain causal relationships, because the pupils are not sufficiently mature to understand these. The course is built around phenomena of the natural environment with which the pupil can become acquainted by personal observation. The teacher's task is to arouse the curiosity of the child and to make him aware of the wonderful handiwork of God's Creation. Most of the materials will be presented by the teacher by means of stories or by discussion and observation activities. Science readers are valuable aids.

### I. The Seasons

A. *Problems to be Studied*

1. How do we change our ways of living according to the season?

2. What happens to animals and plants as the seasons change?

3. How does God provide for us through the seasons?

B. *Understandings to be Developed*

1. *Spring:*
   a. Days become warmer and longer.
   b. Plants begin to grow.
   c. Animals become more active: Birds return, animals wake from their winter sleep.
   d. The farmer plants and sows his seed; gardens are made.
   e. Holidays in spring: Easter, Resurrection Day.

2. *Summer:*
   a. Summer comes after spring.
   b. Days grow longer, nights shorter.
   c. Plants experience greatest growth: Trees, flowers, grass.
   d. Animals are active: Butterflies, birds, insects, squirrels, others.
   e. Man's activities during the summer: Farmer, city dweller.
   f. Holidays in summer: Fourth of July, Independence Day; vacation time.

3. *Autumn:*

    a. Autumn, or fall, follows summer.

    b. The days grow shorter, cooler; nights longer.

    c. Plants begin to die: Flowers, leaves, grass.

    d. Animals are less numerous and active: Birds migrate, some animals begin winter sleep. (Hibernation.)

    e. Activities of man: Farmer harvests crops; fruits and vegetables are canned and stored; a store of warmer clothing and fuel is laid up.

    f. Holidays in autumn: Harvest festival and Thanksgiving to give thanks to God for His blessings; Reformation Festival; Armistice Day.

4. *Winter:*

    a. Winter comes after autumn.

    b. Days are shorter; nights longer than in autumn.

    c. It is colder than in autumn: Water freezes, snow falls.

    d. Animals in winter:

        (1) Some animals sleep through the winter.

        (2) Many birds have gone to warmer lands.

        (3) Most insects are not active in winter.

        (4) Some animals live on stored food.

        (5) Food is hard to find. Feed especially the birds.

    e. Plants in winter:

        (1) Many have died in autumn.

        (2) Some cannot grow because water in soil is frozen.

        (3) Some keep alive because food is stored in seeds, stems, buds, and roots.

    f. Man's activities in winter:

        (1) Needs warm clothing.

        (2) Must heat houses.

        (3) People cut and store ice in some places.

        (4) Eat stored food or send for it to the South.

    g. Holidays in winter: Christmas, the birthday of Jesus; birthdays of Washington and Lincoln, great men of our country.

## II. The Weather

*A. Problems to be Studied*

1. What are some of the changes in weather from day to day?

2. Why are changes of weather necessary for the welfare of human, animal, and plant life?

3. Who makes the seasons and weather to change at the proper time?

B. . *Understandings to be Developed*

1. Wind causes weather changes.

   a. Wind is moving air; is everywhere.

   b. Wind has force; it can be felt, is sometimes strong, sometimes quite weak.

   c. Some winds are warm, some are cold.

   d. Weather vane shows wind direction: clouds and smoke likewise.

2. Moisture causes weather changes.

   a. There is moisture in the air.

   b. When the air becomes cool, drops of water form.

   (1) Clouds, rain, fog.

   (2) Sleet, hail, ice, snow, frost.

3. The sun causes weather changes.

   a. Heat comes from the sun.

   b. The sun warms the earth.

   c. When clouds cover the sun, the earth becomes cooler.

   d. At sundown the earth becomes cooler.

4. The thermometer tells us how warm or how cold it is.

5. God made the sun, the wind, and the clouds. He gives light and warmth and regulates weather so that crops grow and people can live.

### III. Living Things on the Earth

A. *Problems to be Studied*

1. How does God provide for the various kinds of animals?

2. Why do different kinds of plants grow in different places?

3. Of what use are animals and plants to man?

B. *Understandings to be Developed*

1. Animals are living things.

   a. There are many different kinds of animals, all properly provided for by God.

   b. Some animals live on land: Horse, cow, dog, cat, etc.

   c. Some live in the water: Fish, whale, seals, etc.

   d. Some live on the land and in the water: Geese, frogs, beavers, etc.

   e. Some live in the air and on land: Birds, insects.

   f. Animals differ greatly in size: Elephant, weasel, snail.

   g. Animals differ greatly in appearance: Some are fur-covered, some have scales, some feathers.

   h. God provides for the animals. Psalm 136:25; Psalm 147:9.

2. Plants are living things.

    a. Some plants grow on land: Trees, flowers, grasses, vegetables, grains, shrubs.

    b. Some plants grow in water: Water-lily, etc.

    c. Plants multiply in different ways: Potatoes by their roots; carrots by seeds; etc.

    d. Different parts of plants have different work to do.

        (1) Roots take water and food from the soil.

        (2) Stem sends water and food to branches and leaves.

        (3) Leaves prepare the food for the plant to use.

        (4) Flowers produce seeds; serve for the enjoyment of man.

        (5) Seeds are the beginning of new baby plants.

    e. Plants and animals are very useful to man.

        (1) Plants furnish food: Vegetables, grains, fruits, nuts.

        (2) Animals furnish food: Milk, meat, eggs.

        (3) Animals and plants furnish clothing: Cotton, wool, silk, flax, furs, hides.

        (4) Animals and plants furnish shelter: Lumber, hides for tent coverings.

        (5) Animals help man with his work: Horses, dogs, oxen, elephants.

        (6) Animals and plants help man to be comfortable and to enjoy life: Shade trees, pets, canaries, birds in general.

        (7) God made plants and animals for man: First Article; Fourth Petition; Gen. 1: 28, 29.

### IV. The Sun, Moon, and Stars

A. *Problems to be Studied*

    1. How does the sun help life on earth?

    2. How does the sun help us to keep time?

    3. In what way do all the lights of heaven benefit us?

B. *Understandings to be Developed*

    1. God created the sun, moon, and stars on the fourth day. "And God made two great lights; the greater light to rule the day, and the lesser light to rule the night; He made the stars also." Gen. 1: 16.

    2. The universe is so great that we cannot imagine its size. This shows the power and greatness of God.

    3. The sun looks like a great ball of fire. It gives light and heat.

4. The sun tells time and direction.
   a. It rises in the East in the morning.
   b. It is noon when the sun is high overhead.
   c. It sets in the West in the evening.
   d. The time between night and sunrise is dawn.
   e. The time between sunset and night is twilight.
   f. God directs the sun to rule the day. *Note:* Joshua, a great man of God, once commanded the sun and moon to stand still, and they did so. This was a miracle. Josh. 10:12-14.

5. The sun casts shadows.
   a. As the sun rises, the shadows become shorter.
   b. At noon the shadow is very short.
   c. As the sun sets, shadows lengthen.

6. The moon looks like a great white ball.
   a. It rises in the East, goes down in the West.
   b. It can be seen best at night, but also during the day.
   c. The moon receives its light from the sun. Its light is reflected sunlight.
   d. Sometimes the moon is full and round (full moon); sometimes it is narrow like a sickle (new moon).
   e. The moon of all lights in the sky is nearest to the earth.
   f. There is no man in the moon, as some people say.
   g. God directs the moon to rule the sky.

7. The stars are the lesser lights in the sky.
   a. Stars are suns; they have their own light.
   b. Stars look small because they are so far away.
   c. Stars often form pictures (constellations) in the sky.
      (1) North Star, Pole Star, guide for sailors.
      (2) The Big Dipper points to the North Star.
      (3) The Little Dipper, Cassiopeia, Orion, the Milky Way.
   d. God used a star to direct the Wise Men to the Christ child. Matt. 2:2.

### V. The Surface of the Earth

A. *Problems to be Studied*

   1. How can people travel about on earth?

   2. In what way are different parts of the earth and sea useful to man?

   3. Why does the surface of the earth change sometimes?

   4. What can we do to keep the earth useful to man?

B. *Understandings to be Developed*

1. "And God called the dry land earth; and the gathering of the waters called He seas." Gen. 1:10.

2. How the earth's surface is made up.
   a. Of land forms.
   b. Of different kinds of water bodies.
   c. The outside of the earth is called its surface.
   d. Under the land and water are layers of rock.

3. The earth can be shown as a globe. It is round.
   a. Men have traveled around the earth by airplanes.
   b. Men have traveled around the earth in ships.

4. Maps help us to see the earth in its proper form.
   a. We can see only a small part of the earth itself at one time.
   b. Maps show the different land and water forms.
   c. Directions on maps: The top of the map is *north;* the bottom is *south;* the right is *east;* the left is *west.*

5. There are many different kinds of land forms.
   a. *Valleys* are lowlands between hills; usually small streams or large rivers flow through them.
   b. *Mountains* are the highest parts of the earth's surface. The Rockies, Mt. Sinai, Mt. Ararat (Ark).
   c. *Hills* are smaller raised parts of the earth's surface, not so high as mountains.
   d. *Plains* are large areas of level or nearly level land: Our western prairies.
   e. *Deserts* are places with very little rainfall. Israel traveled through the Desert.
   f. *Swamps* or *marshes* are places where the land is very wet.
   g. The *North Pole* and the *South Pole* are places always covered with ice and snow.

6. Most of the earth's surface is made up of water.
   a. To show the proportion, a circle may be drawn on the board and cut into four parts.
   b. The globe shows waters in blue; land forms in various colors.
   c. The largest bodies of water are called *oceans:* Atlantic and Pacific.
   d. *Seas* are somewhat smaller than oceans. Famous seas mentioned in the Bible: Red Sea, Dead Sea, Sea of Galilee.

e. *Lakes* are smaller inland **bodies** of water.

f. *Ponds* are much smaller **than lakes**. They are usually found in meadows or woods, in low places.

g. Rivers and streams are *moving* bodies of water. They always move downhill.

h. Many large and small streams empty into other streams or lakes or oceans.

i. Some famous rivers: Mississippi, Ohio, Missouri. In Bible lands: Nile, Jordan.

7. The parts of a stream.

a. The beginning is its *head;* the end is its *mouth;* the channel is its *bed;* the sides are its *banks.*

b. Streams sometimes have *waterfalls.* These are places where the water drops from a high to a low point.

c. Streams cause *floods* when the waters overflow their banks.

d. Oceans, lakes, and seas have *shores* and *beaches.*

   (1) Shores are the sides of lakes or oceans.

   (2) Beaches are low sandy shores; used for bathing.

8. The surface of the earth sometimes changes.

a. The *wind* changes the surface of the earth.

   (1) Winds pick up loose soil and carry it away.

   (2) Winds cause dust storms.

   (3) Winds deposit the soil in other parts of the earth.

   (4) Farmers sometimes have to move when the wind blows the top soil from the land.

b. *Moving water* changes the surface of the land.

   (1) Moving water carries away top soil.

   (2) Moving waters make gullies, ditches, gulches.

   (3) As moving waters slow down, soil is dropped, and it often forms islands in streams.

   (4) Conservation: Farmers and other people who live along streams can save soil by planting crops, grass, or trees to hold it in place.

   (5) Moving waters form soil by breaking rocks into small pieces.

   (6) Small rocks in streams are called pebbles or gravel; they are made smooth by water rubbing one rock against the other. (David took "five smooth stones out of the brook" for his sling and killed Goliath. 1 Sam. 17:40.)

## VI. Making Our Work Easy

A. *Problems to be Studied*

    1. How do we use natural forces to make our work easier?

    2. How do machines make our work easier?

    3. How can electricity help man?

    4. How does man use fire to make his work easier?

B. *Understandings to be Developed*

    1. God has given man reason and skill to discover the laws of nature and thus to make his work easier. "My reason and all my senses." First Article.

    2. Man has learned to use natural forces to help him do his work more easily.

        a. Man must depend upon his muscles for much of his work: Pushing, pulling, lifting, or turning things.

        b. Man has tamed and harnessed animals to help him: Horses, dogs, elephants, etc.

        c. Man has learned to use the wind for some of his work: Moving boats, turning windmills for grinding grain or pumping water.

        d. Water helps man with his work: Moving heavy objects, like logs, turning factory wheels, carrying boats.

        e. Heat that comes from burning fuel is used to do some of our work: Blast furnaces, etc.

    3. Man has invented machines to make his work easier.

        a. We use *levers* to lift things and for other purposes: Scissors, pliers, nutcrackers.

        b. We use *wedges* to split things apart: Hatchet, ax, etc.

        c. *Wheels* help us to move things about more easily: Wagon, automobile, bicycle.

        d. *Pulleys* help to lift or pull things: Flag on flagpole, pulley on tow truck, pulleys to lift hay into barn.

    4. Electricity helps man by giving him light and running his machines.

        a. Most of our electricity comes from generators in power-houses.

        b. Electric light bulbs are turned on by a switch or by pressing a button.

        c. Some machines run by electricity: Clocks, sewing machines, street lights, cook stoves, washing machines, carpet sweeper, toasters, stop-and-go signs, telephone, fan, radio, electric doorbell.

        d. Electricity can be stored in batteries.

5. Man can use fire to make his work easier when he keeps it under proper control.

    a. To make a fire, we need a combustible material. (Material that will burn.)

    b. A fire must have air in order to burn.

    c. To put out a fire, we must cut off its air supply or take away the combustible material.

    d. Burning things give off heat.

    e. We use heat to cook our foods, heat our homes, burn rubbish, etc.

6. All inventions and discoveries are to be used to the glory of God. 1 Cor. 10:31.

### VII. Magnets

A. *Problems to be Studied*

1. What will magnets do?

2. How can we make magnets?

3. When do magnets push on each other, and when do they pull on each other?

4. How does a compass work?

B. *Understandings to be Developed*

1. There are several kinds of magnets: Lodestone, bar, horseshoe (U-shaped), the compass.

2. Magnets pull some things toward them.

    a. Magnets will pull or pick up only iron or steel objects.

    b. A magnet pulls hardest at each end.

    c. Magnets will pull through paper, water, air, wood, or glass, but they will not pick up these items.

3. We can make magnets.

    a. A piece of iron will become a magnet if it is held against a magnet.

    b. A piece of steel stroked with a magnet will remain magnetized for a long time after the magnet has been removed.

4. A magnet can push or pull another magnet.

    a. The two ends of a magnet are called poles: North pole, south pole.

    b. Unlike poles pull on each other; like poles push each other away.

    c. We do not know why this happens; it is one of the mysteries man has not been able to find out; it shows the wonders of God's Creation.

5. A magnet can be used as a compass.
    a. In a suspended magnet that turns freely the same end
       will always turn north, and the opposite end will point
       south.
    b. The needle of the compass is a magnet.
    c. A compass is used to find directions: Guiding ships,
       piloting airplanes, traveling where there are no roads.
    d. The magnet is one of the great gifts of God.

## Intermediate Grades (4—6)

Pupils in the intermediate grades are capable of a somewhat
broader view of the world and of understanding simple cause-and-
effect relationships. This permits the expansion of the concepts
begun in the primary grades.

For a natural growth in knowledge and understanding, training in exact observation, sense experiences, simple experiments,
and the reading of suitable materials are emphasized. The
almighty, loving, and all-wise God, who directs, rules, and preserves the world, is always kept in the foregound. The beautiful
order of nature, the marvelous regeneration of species, and provision for the needs of life, all of which are handiworks of God,
demand this. Emphasis upon economy in the use of God's gifts
follows naturally from the foregoing.

### I. Man, Some Plants, and Some Animals Live in Communities

*A. Problems to be Studied*

1. Why do we find some plants usually living in groups or
communities?

2. Why do many animals live in communities?

3. What animals live together at some times and not at others?

4. What are some advantages and disadvantages of community life?

*B. Understandings to be Developed*

By observing plant and animal communities, we can get
a better understanding of the wisdom of the Creator in establishing communal living for man.

1. Many plants live in groups.
    a. Living close together gives some plants protection:
       Elderberry bushes, briars, sumac.
    b. Plants of the same kind require similar conditions for
       growth.
    c. Plants that live in groups both help and hinder each
       other: Weeds or other plants growing in wrong place;
       trees give shade to certain plants that require it or
       rob others of sunlight and hinder their growth.

2. Many animals live in communities.
    a. Some insects live in highly organized communities: Ants, bees.
    b. Some mammals live in communities: Beavers, muskrats, prairie dogs.
    c. Grazing animals live in herds: Antelope, reindeer, buffaloes, wild horses.
    d. Some birds are usually found in flocks: Golden plovers, bobolinks, humming birds, wild ducks, wild geese, blackbirds.
3. Some animals live together at some times, but not at others.
    a. Most birds migrate in flocks: Bluebirds, robins.
    b. Some birds live together to rear their young: Robins, wrens, pigeons, barn swallows.
    c. Some animals hunt together: Musk oxen, wolves, lions, pelicans, buzzards.
4. People live in communities.
    a. We depend upon other people in many ways.
    b. Community life requires co-operation with one another.
    c. Because of man's sinful condition laws are necessary in human communities.
    d. Each member of a community has certain responsibilities toward his fellow men: Help to maintain outward decency and order; prevent crime; help to prevent accidents; prevent diseases from spreading; prevent fires. The Christian owes it to his fellow men to teach them the way to salvation.

### II. Light Enables Us to See Things

A. *Problems to be Studied*

1. When was the first light created?
2. From what different sources do we get light?
3. Do most things around us reflect any light?
4. What happens to light rays when passing from one substance to another?
5. Do some materials absorb more light than others?

B. *Understandings to be Developed*

1. God created light on the first day. Gen. 1:3.
2. He also created special heavenly bodies to give light: Sun, moon, stars. Gen. 1:14-19.
3. Some objects produce light directly.
    a. Most of our light comes from the sun.
    b. Light may be obtained by burning fuels: Match, candle, lamp.

  c. We can get light from electricity: Glass bulb, flashlight.

  d. Light travels through space in a straight line.

 4. Light is reflected by many objects.

  a. Objects can be seen because they reflect light.

  b. Some objects reflect more light than others: Smooth, shiny, and highly polished objects.

  c. Mirrors reflect light rays.

  d. Dust and water particles scatter light rays in the air.

 5. When light rays pass from one substance to another, the rays may be bent.

  a. Light rays sometimes bend when passing from water into the air.

  b. We use lenses to bend light rays: Eye glasses help some people to see better; eye hygiene.

  c. Some rays are bent more than others when light passes through a prism. Show spectral colors by means of a prism.

 6. Some substances absorb more light than others.

  a. Some objects absorb light and change it to heat: Dark cloth lying on white snow; light-colored clothes are cooler than dark-colored clothes when worn in the sunlight.

  b. The color of an object depends upon the light that is not absorbed. A dress is blue or red because the dye absorbs all colors with the exception of either the blue or the red.

### III. Plants Need Flowers to Produce Seeds

*A. Problems to be Studied*

 1. What parts of a flower are necessary to produce seeds?

 2. In what manner is pollen carried from one flower to another?

 3. What happens after fertilization has taken place?

*B. Understandings to be Developed*

 1. To produce seeds, most flowers of the common plants require two parts: Stamens and pistils.

  a. Stamens produce pollen (flower dust).

  b. The pistil holds and produces the seeds.

  c. Stamens are the male part of the flower, the pistils are the female parts.

  d. Most flowers have pistils and stamens.

  e. In some plants, pistils and stamens are to be found in separate flowers.

2. Pollen for fertilization is carried in several ways.

    a. Insects carry pollen to flowers: Bees, moths, butterflies.

    b. The wind carries pollen to some flowers: Corn.

3. Seeds grow after fertilization has taken place.

    a. Pollen grains grow downward through the pistil.

    b. Eggs at bottom of pistil are fertilized by pollen. A new seed is thus produced.

    c. If nothing unusual happens, seeds may grow into new plants.

    d. God has produced the miracles by which plants can produce their own kind.

### IV. All Animals Have Young

A. *Problems to be Studied*

1. In which verses of Genesis 1 do we find the creation of animal life?

2. Do all animals have parents?

3. What animals lay eggs?

4. How do mammals care for their young?

B. *Understandings to be Developed*

1. God created all animals in the beginning and gave them power to have young, when He said: "Be fruitful and multiply, and fill the waters in the seas, and let the fowl multiply in all the earth." Gen. 1:22.

2. All animals have parents.

    a. Some baby animals resemble their parents: Dog, cat, horse, cow, bird.

    b. Some baby animals do not resemble their parents: Moths, butterflies, frogs, bees.

    c. Baby animals grow up: Puppies, kittens, calves.

3. Some animals lay eggs.

    a. Some animals deposit their eggs in water: Frogs, fish, toads.

    b. Some animals lay their eggs on land: Turtles, snakes.

    c. Birds make nests and hatch their young: Robins, chickens, ducks.

    d. Insects lay eggs in many places: Stagnant pools (mosquito); moths on trees (cocoons).

4. Some animals bring their young into the world alive (mammals).

    a. The young grow in the mother's body.

    b. Mammals nurse their young.

 c. Mammals care for their young in many ways: **Keep** them clean, protect them, feed them.

 d. Some animals have one baby at a time: Cow, horse.

 e. Some animals have a number of young at a time: **Cat —** kittens; dog — a litter of puppies.

 f. Animals are creatures of God, and God wants us to be kind to them.

### V. Some Insects are Harmful and Some are Useful

*A. Problems to be Studied*

 1. Why are some insects harmful?

 2. Which are some harmful insects?

 3. In which ways are some insects useful?

 4. Which insects are useful to man?

 5. How can harmful insects be destroyed?

*B. Understandings to be Developed*

 1. Some insects are harmful. They eat plants, fruits, seeds; carry diseases; eat meats; live on other bodies; live in the home of man if permitted.

 2. Some harmful insects: Mosquito, flea, body lice, housefly, cockroach, grasshopper, boll weevil, Japanese beetle, potato beetle, aphid, scale insects.

 3. The harmfulness of insects had its beginning in the fall of man. Before that time everything was very good. Gen. 1:31.

 4. Some insects are helpful: Eat harmful insects; help scatter seeds; carry pollen; provide food for other animals (for fish and birds); produce food for man; · feed plants (Venus flytrap); produce clothing material.

 5. Some helpful insects: Dragon fly; praying mantis; ladybird beetle; lac insects; honey bee; bumblebee; silkworm.

 6. Harmful insects are best destroyed by spraying them with chemicals or by destroying their breeding places.

### VI. How Sounds are Made

*A. Problems to be Studied*

 1. What is sound?

 2. How does sound travel?

 3. What is an echo?

 4. What are some characteristics of most sounds?

 5. Why do we *hear* sounds?

*B. Understandings to be Developed*

    1. Sound is the rapid vibration of any object.

        a. The human voice can make sounds by the vibration of the vocal chords.

        b. Animals can make sounds by the vibration of their wings or by air sacs in the throat.

        c. Objects that produce sounds: Tuning forks, rubber bands, musical instruments, etc.

    2. Sound travels by vibration through the air in all directions.

        a. Sound travels through liquids, solids, gases.

        b. Sound travels at the rate of 1,100 feet per second, or about a mile in 5 seconds.

        c. Objects through which sound travels are called conductors. Water, the earth, wood, and metals are sound conductors. Water carries sound four times faster than air.

        d. Gases are poor conductors of sound. Solid things are better, because they carry sounds farther and faster.

    3. Echoes are reflected sound waves.

        a. Echoes are produced when sound waves strike a solid object and bounce back.

        b. Echoes are a hindrance to hearing in auditoriums, schoolrooms, theaters, and public halls. They can be overcome by hanging curtains to break the sound waves.

    4. The three chief characteristics of most sounds are pitch, loudness, and quality.

        a. Pitch is the highness or lowness of a sound. Highness has fast vibrations; lowness has slow vibrations.

        b. Loudness of the sound depends upon the size of the sounding body and the distance the moving body vibrates.

        c. Quality is the difference in sound.

        d. Musical instruments produce sounds.

            (1) Some use strings or wires to produce tones: Violin, guitar, harp, mandolin.

            (2) Some use wind to produce tones: Organ, harmonica, clarinet, oboe, cornet, bugle, trombone.

            (3) Some produce tones by striking: Piano, xylophone.

        e. All musical sounds have pitch and tone with regular vibrations.

        f. Noises are disturbing because they do not have regular vibrations. Avoid them.

5. We hear when sound waves coming to the ear cause the eardrums to vibrate.

    a. Nerve endings in the eardrum carry the sound vibration to the brain.

    b. The brain then tells us what type of sound it is.

    c. It is important that our eardrums be protected against punctures, noises that are too loud, and infections.

    d. God gave us our sense of hearing so that we may gladly hear and learn His Word. "So, then, faith cometh by hearing and hearing by the Word of God." Rom. 10:17.

    e. The radio, which carries sound over great distances, is used to proclaim the Gospel.

### VII. Conservation of Natural Resources

A. *Problems to be Studied*

1. What is meant by conservation?

2. What are our chief natural resources?

3. In what way are we failing to conserve our resources?

4. How can we practice conservation?

B. *Understandings to be Developed*

1. Conservation is the wise and effective use of our natural resources not only for today, but tomorrow.

    a. Man is the cause of much waste and ruthless destruction of some of our natural resources.

    b. Man is responsible to God for the proper use of the gifts received from God.

    c. Man depends upon natural resources for his food, clothing, shelter, and power.

2. Some of our most important natural resources are the forests, the soil, coal, and other minerals, wild life (birds and other animals).

    a. Our forests are being used up at a rapid rate.

        (1) Man cuts trees to obtain lumber, paper, etc.

        (2) Fires destroy forests; in 1940 the loss in forest value by fire was $450,000,000.

        (3) Careless campers fail to put out fires.

        (4) Harmful insects destroy forest trees; in 1940 the loss by insects amounted to $100,000,000.

    b. Our soil has lost much of its fertility.

        (1) Failure to add fertilizer is one cause.

        (2) Failure to rotate crops causes loss of fertility.

        (3) Erosion of the top soil by water and wind is a cause.

c. Coal and mineral resources are wasted.
  (1) By inefficient mining or manufacturing methods.
  (2) By inefficient heating plants.
d. Wild animals and certain wild plants are often wantonly destroyed by man.
e. Societies, such as the National Association of Audubon Societies, have done much toward the preservation of wild life.
f. The Government has established 70 game preserves, sanctuaries and havens of protection for birds, fish, and other wild life.
g. Most States limit the hunting and fishing seasons.
h. The American Humane Society teaches kindness to animals. Its objects are:
  (1) To regulate the abuses in cattle transportation by railroads.
  (2) To treat wild animals in captivity kindly and intelligently.
  (3) To treat cage birds and pets affectionately.
  (4) To regulate traps to reduce the suffering of captured victims.

3. The Christian considers it his duty to help in the conservation of natural resources, because God's gifts must not be squandered.
  a. Forests can be preserved by replanting trees, treating trees for diseases, spraying insects, preventing fires.
  b. Soils can be preserved by using proper fertilizers, by crop rotation, contour farming, planting trees and grass to anchor the soil.
  c. Coal and mining resources can be conserved by more efficient mining methods; better heating equipment; the use of substitute fuels.
  d. Wild life of field and forests can be protected by the enactment and enforcement of proper laws; willing obedience to these laws on the part of everyone; kindness to animals (Prov. 12:10).

## Upper Grades, 7 and 8

The course of study for the upper grades is designed to broaden and develop the background of the pupils in useful understandings. The average pupil in these grades is able to profit from the study of more remote topics, such as electricity, heat, air, water, rocks, minerals, science as an aid to man, and the fundamental differences between man and animals from the Christian viewpoint.

Observation still plays an important role, but learning through experimentation becomes more important, because understandings of basic scientific principles underlying natural phenomena are necessary for solving many environmental problems which confront man. Because of greater reading proficiency in the upper grades, the amount and usefulness of reading for purposes of solving science problems under discussion and study is increased.

As time permits, pupils should be given opportunity to perform demonstrations or experiments of their own. In many instances it may not be feasible to permit much individual experimentation because of a lack of equipment, time, and room space. Where that is the case, most experiments may have to be performed by the teacher. This may be done with the aid of one or more pupils.

### Christian Objectives

1. A growing intelligent conception and understanding of the phases of nature that affect our mode of living.

2. A growing appreciation of the manifold provisions God has made for man in nature.

3. A growing appreciation of the role physical forms and processes play in God's provision for man.

4. A growing recognition of the role chemical forms and processes play in God's provision for man.

5. A growing recognition of man's superior position as the foremost of God's living creatures.

6. A growing recognition that superstitions concerning natural phenomena are due to a lack of faith in the Creator and failure to understand natural causes and effects.

### I. Man and Other Creatures

A. *Problems to be Studied*

    1. What is the origin and nature of man?

    2. In what way are man and animals different?

    3. In which way is man superior to animals?

B. *Understandings to be Developed*

    1. Man's creation is recorded in Gen. 1 and 2.

        a. Only God could record the origin of man.

        b. The account of man's origin is genuine, trustworthy.

        c. In creating other creatures, God spoke; creatures appeared.

        d. In creating man, God took counsel, "Let us make man."

    e. Man's origin was not due to blind chance, but was a planned act of God.

    f. Other creatures were created by the word of God; man was formed. Gen. 2:7.

    g. Man is the foremost of all living creatures.

    h. Man was made in the image of God. Gen. 1:27.

    i. Man has an immortal soul. Gen. 2:7.

    j. Man was to share heavenly joys with God; man sinned.

2. There are many differences between man and animals.

    a. Man walks erect, with eyes toward heaven; most animals walk stooped, with eyes cast toward the earth.

    b. Man has speech; animals only make sounds.

    c. Man has reason — with senses, understanding, will, and memory; animals have instinct — an unconscious, involuntary, unreasoning prompting to action.

    d. Man can counsel, plan, judge, compare, resolve; animals cannot think; the Creator has done their thinking for them.

    e. Man advances in knowledge, discovers new truths or laws of nature, and perfects himself; animals cannot advance.

    f. Man admires, praises, worships; animals are not capable of such emotions.

3. Man is superior to animals, because he has a mind that enables him to understand and to adjust himself to his environment.

    a. Man was created by God to have dominion over the creatures.

    b. Animals are to furnish man with goods and clothing, and serve as beasts of burden.

    c. Man named the animals at God's direction.

    d. Before the Fall, man's dominion was complete.

    e. Since the Fall, creatures have rebelled against man's dominion.

    f. Man must force animals into subjection and service.

    g. Examples of man's inventive mind: the use of steam, electricity, aviation, printing, telephone, telegraph, radio, photography, phonograph, typewriter, linotype, tools and machinery to make work easier, better means of transportation and communication, etc.

    h. Examples of man's creative mind.

        (1) The Seven Wonders of the Ancient World: The Pyramid of Cheops; the Great Walls of Babylon; the Statue of Zeus; the Temple of Diana at Ephesus; the Tomb of Mausolus; the Colossus of Rhodes; the Lighthouse of Pharos.

(2) Modern wonders: Empire State Building; Boulder Dam; Panama Canal, etc.

(3) Art — "The Last Supper," Da Vinci.

(4) Music — *The Messiah,* Haendel; Organ, chorus.

(5) Sculpture — great statues: Black Hills Monument; Lincoln Monument; wood carvings in churches, and so forth.

### II. How Science Has Aided Man

#### A. Problems to be Studied

1. What is science?
2. What are some of the branches of science?
3. How do scientists work?
4. How has science overcome "superstition"?
5. How has science aided man?

#### B. Understandings to be Developed

1. Science is organized knowledge.
   a. Knowledge has been accumulated by careful observation, experiment, and reasoning.
   b. Ancient Greeks probably some of first to observe and investigate; Archimedes — lever and fulcrum; Pythagoras — apparatus to study vibration of strings.
   c. Early Babylonians and Egyptians developed a fairly accurate calendar.
   d. Early Greek astronomers: Ptolemy, Aristarchus.
   e. In 16th century — Copernicus, Galileo, Newton, Joseph Henry (United States), Ampère (France), Faraday (England).
   f. Before end of 18th century, science began to attack disease.
      (1) Edward Jenner (1797) — vaccination against smallpox.
      (2) Pasteur — successful in treatment of rabies.
      (3) Dr. C. F. Finley — discovered cause of malaria.
      (4) Ronald Ross — discovered that mosquitoes are cause of yellow fever.

2. The branches of science are divided into different groups of information.
   a. Biology is the study of living things.
   b. Physics is the study of inanimate matter and energy.
   c. Chemistry is the study of materials, what they are made of, and how they act.
   d. Botany is the study of plants.
   e. Zoology is the study of animals.
   f. Physiology is the study of how our bodies function.

g. Bacteriology is the study of microscopic plant life.

h. Astronomy is the study of heavenly bodies.

i. Geology is a study of the composition of the earth's surface and its structure.

3. The work of scientists is to solve problems.

    a. Scientists attempt to solve problems by a definite, orderly method of procedure.

    b. Scientists employ the *scientific* method to solve problems.[5]

    c. Scientists depend upon accurate measurements to weigh and to measure things; use scientific instruments that are more sensitive than our senses to help them in their work: scales, analytical balances, microscopes, telescopes, thermometers, X ray, stethoscope, etc.

    d. Scientists cannot solve all problems.

        (1) Before the Fall, man's mind was perfect.

        (2) Since the Fall, it is fallible.

        (3) Scientists cannot answer the most vital questions except by hypothesis.

        (4) A hypothesis is a *human* explanation or a probable answer of a cause or an effect.

        (5) Many hypotheses are contrary to God's Word: Evolution, origin of the earth, of life, of coal, of oil, of fossils, of the missing link. Reconstructed animals in museum are often products of the imagination.

4. Superstition in man is due to a lack of faith in the Creator, who made, rules, and preserves all; also a failure to understand one's environment.

    a. Primitive peoples ascribe misfortunes such as storms, diseases, and famines to evil spirits.

    b. Primitive peoples try to appease evil spirits by magic rites.

    c. Even in civilized countries people believe in "luck," "magic charms," "jinxes," astrology, "tea leaf readings," and so forth.

    d. Natural phenomena are due to natural causes or a series of causes.

    e. In a natural event we see an application of an established law of God applied many times. Miracles go beyond natural laws.

    f. Moses, Aaron, and Old Testament prophets performed miracles as well as Jesus and some of His disciples.

5) See J. E. Potzger, "The Scientific Method." *Curriculum in Science,* Appendix II, p. 41.

5. Science has brought about many changes in our daily life.
   a. Science has made work easier through the inventions of machines.
   b. Improved means of communication and transportation are products of science.
   c. Living conditions have been bettered.
   d. Methods of farming and food production have been improved.
   e. Science has taught man conservation of natural resources.
   f. Vast stores of energy have been tapped.
   g. Better understanding of the human body is evident.
   h. Better safeguards against disease and pain have been worked out.
   i. Science has taught man effective ways of solving many of his problems — scientific method.
   j. It has taught man to recognize that human reason cannot answer all questions.

### III. Air and Its Importance to Man

A. *Problems to be Studied*

   1. What are some of the properties of air?
   2. In which way does man use air?

B. *Understandings to be Developed*

   1. Air has certain properties or characteristics.
      a. It is a real substance.
      b. It occupies space.
      c. It has weight.
      d. It completely surrounds the earth.
      e. Air that surrounds the earth is called *atmosphere*.
         (1) The lower layer is called *troposphere,* about eight miles in height.
         (2) The upper layer is called *stratosphere,* above the troposphere.
         (3) Aviators tell us that the air "thins out" very rapidly above three miles.
         (4) Maximum height attained by man (by three Russians in 1934) is 13.7 miles.
         (5) Maximum height attained by unmanned sounding balloon was 21 miles.
      f. Air is present in water and porous materials, such as wood, soil, rock.

g. Air exerts great pressure.

    (1) Air pressure helps to explain many common phenomena.

    (2) Air pressure is 15 pounds per square inch at sea level.

    (3) Air pressure can be measured by a barometer. (Toricelli in 1640 was first to prove atmospheric pressure.)

    (4) Instruments used to measure air pressure are mercury barometer, aneroid (dry) barometer, altimeter (aviation).

    (5) Air becomes lighter as the altitude increases.

    (6) Air pressure is a great factor in changes of weather.

    (7) Air is essential to living things.

    (8) Air in motion is wind.

h. Air is a mixture of several gases: oxygen, nitrogen, carbon dioxide, water vapor, helium, argon, neon, krypton.

    (1) Oxygen makes up one fifth of the air, is invisible, tasteless, odorless; supplies body cells with oxygen, thus supporting life; is found in most materials; necessary to make things burn (combustion).

    (2) Nitrogen makes up almost four fifths of the air; is colorless, tasteless, odorless; necessary to support life; does not support combustion.

    (3) Carbon dioxide is a gas made up of carbon and oxygen, produced when carbon is burned alone; .03 of air is carbon dioxide; is tasteless, odorless, colorless; given off from human and animal lungs; used by plants; used in making "soda water"; fire extinguisher.

    (4) Water vapor in the air is due to evaporation of waters from oceans, lakes, and rivers; condensation of water vapor in air changes into rain, snow, hail, fog, dew, or frost.

    (5) Other gases in smaller amounts: helium, noninflammable and used in balloons and dirigibles; argon, used to fill incandescent lamps; neon, to make neon advertising signs.

2. Man uses air in many ways.

  a. Soda straw — liquid enters place in straw where air is removed.

b. Medicine dropper — rubber forces air out, permitting liquid to take up space where air was.

c. Vacuum sweeper — uses air to remove dust.

d. Vacuum bottle — has two thin walls with air removed between them.

e. Drainpipe cleaner — used to clean sinks.

f. Suction cup — used for attaching small articles to a smooth surface, such as glass.

g. Lift pump, force pump, and siphon are used to convey liquids.

h. Compressed air is used in airbrakes on trains; bicycle and automobile tires; for pneumatic tubes used to send cash in department stores; submarines; door checks; hair drying machines; paint gun; sand blasting.

i. Man uses heavier-than-air craft to fly through space.

j. Air is necessary to our well-being.

    (1) Air in our houses is kept clean by frequent ventilation.

    (2) Air should be kept at about 65—70 degrees for comfort in the house.

    (3) It is important to keep the garage door open when starting a car (carbon monoxide gas).

    (4) Avoid breathing air containing any poisonous gases.

k. Air is necessary for combustion (burning).

    (1) Burning requires a fuel, a continuous supply of air, and sufficient heat to start the fuel burning.

    (2) Combustion is a rapid form of oxidation as in ordinary burning; slow oxidation — decaying of wood, the rusting of iron.

    (3) Spontaneous combustion is a self-starting fire due to slow oxidation. Caused by leaving oily or paint-covered rags in poorly ventilated closet or small room; green hay when stored too early; soft coal heaped in high piles.

    (4) Annual U. S. fire losses are one half billion dollars in property and 10,000 to 15,000 lives.

    (5) Fires can be put out (a) by water, (b) by smothering, (c) by using fire extinguisher. Real purpose is to shut off supply of air.

    (6) Fires can be prevented by (a) removing fire hazards, (b) care in use of matches, (c) making buildings fireproof, (d) improving fire and water supply departments.

l. At times air can be a great destructive force. Tornadoes, hurricanes, typhoons, and monsoons are violent types of windstorms.

m. Man has used air to sail his ships and drive his windmills.

### IV. Water and Man's Use of It

A. *Problems to be Studied*

1. What are some of the characteristics of water?
2. Why is water important?
3. How are our homes supplied with water?
4. How is used water removed from our homes?

B. *Understandings to be Developed*

1. Water has certain characteristics which make it of great value to man.

    a. Water covers about three fourths of the earth's surface.

    b. Water is a chemical compound of hydrogen and oxygen ($H_2O$).

    c. Water is found in the soil, in the air, and in living things.

    d. Water is a substance because it occupies space.

    e. Water has weight.

    f. Water will take the shape of the container that holds it.

    g. Water is colorless, odorless, and tasteless.

    h. Water can occur in different states: ice, solid; steam, gas.

2. Water is necessary for all living things.

    a. Water is necessary for plants, animals, and man.

    b. God provided Israel with water in the desert.

    c. Water is used to perform a baptism.

    d. Water is used to cleanse our bodies.

    e. Water is called the "universal solvent," because it will dissolve practically everything to some extent.

    f. Water is necessary for washing our clothes and cooking our food.

    g. Water may be either "hard" or "soft."

        (1) "Hard water" is water containing certain dissolved minerals.

        (2) "Soft water" is water containing no dissolved minerals; *rain* water is "soft water."

        (3) "Hard water" can be softened by using soap. But washing soda is six times more effective than soap and more economical.

    h. Water transports much of the commerce of the world, moves objects, turns mill wheels.

3. Our homes are supplied by water from lakes, streams, springs, and wells.

    a. Wells are simplest means of obtaining water for a home in the country.

    b. Towns and cities require large amounts of water at all times.

    c. Towns and cities employ three methods of obtaining their water supply.

        (1) The pumping system — pumps water from a large body of water to a higher level.
            Examples: Cleveland, Chicago, Buffalo, and Milwaukee obtain water from Great Lakes; St. Louis from Mississippi River.

        (2) The gravity system — used by a city located near a mountain area; water flows into the cities from sources above them because of the pull of gravity. Example: Los Angeles receives its water from Owen's Lake.

        (3) Combination of pumping and gravity system is used by New York City on account of tall buildings.

    i. Water is brought to homes by means of mains and pipes, and its flow is controlled by faucets.

    j. Our water supply must always be kept safe for drinking.

    k. In the country, human and animal excrements may contaminate water supply.

    l. Surface drainage in the country may carry typhoid germs, intestinal diseases, and parasites, such as hookworm and tapeworm.

    m. Cities insure their water supply by

        (1) Aeration, spraying water into the air to kill harmful bacteria by exposing them to sun light.

        (2) Filtration to remove impurities.

        (3) Storing it in settling basins.

        (4) Adding certain chemicals.

4. Water is used as a flushing agent to remove wastes from our homes.

    a. Waste and sewage disposal is fairly simple for the country and small communities but quite a problem for large cities.

        (1) In the country, cesspool is used, a ten-foot covered hole into which wastes are deposited, there decomposed by bacteria; the water drains into the soil; this is dangerous to near-by well or spring.

(2) Septic tank, modern apparatus for sewage disposal.

(3) Cities build large sewage disposal plants, which dispose of waste efficiently; sludge turned into valuable fertilizer.

(4) Cities near the ocean often send their sewage through pipes ten or twenty miles out to sea.

b. A constant and adequate water supply depends partly on adequate forests.

(1) Forest trees hold twice as much water in the soil as open ground covered by grass and bushes.

(2) Shade prevents excessive evaporation from soil.

(3) Roots hold soil firmly together, and this soil holds much water.

(4) Forests help prevent floods.

### V. Rocks and Minerals

A. *Problems to be Studied*

1. What are the important classes of rocks and their uses?

2. What is the difference between a rock and a mineral?

3. What are some of the common minerals and their uses?

4. What are some of the most common rocks and their uses?

5. What are some common metals obtained from mineral ores and their uses?

6. What are fossils and their origin?

B. *Understandings to be Developed*

1. Rocks are usually grouped into three classes (1) igneous, or "fire formed"; (2) sedimentary, or "deposited"; and (3) metamorphic, or "changed."

a. Igneous rocks were probably formed as the result of tremendous heat — lava, pumice, obsidian, granite, basalt, trap rock.

b. Sedimentary rocks are always formed in strata or layers — sandstone, limestone, shale, conglomerate.

c. Metamorphic rocks are formed from either sedimentary or igneous rocks owing to mighty upheavals of heat and pressure; usually formed in mountainous regions — gneiss, quartz, marble, slate, soapstone.

2. Rocks and minerals are different in composition:

a. Rocks are usually mixtures of two or more minerals not chemically combined.

b. Minerals may be either a single element or a compound of two or more elements chemically combined.

3. Some common minerals and their uses.
   a. Quartz — found in sand and sandstone.
   b. Feldspar — is present in granite; pottery clay.
   c. Calcite — found in limestone and marble.
   d. Mica — found in thin sheets; used as isinglass in stoves and lanterns, insulation for electrical equipment.
   e. Talc — called soapstone, softest mineral; used to make soap, paper, lubricants, toilet powder.
   f. Asbestos — a fibrous material; used as insulation for high-pressure steam packing, fireproofing, brakelining, heat and electrical equipment.
   g. Galena — source of lead; paint, type, bullets, plumbing.
   h. Salt (sodium chloride) — a condiment and preservative; dairy, meat packing, chemical and glass-making industries.

4. Some common rocks and their uses.
   a. Limestone — building construction, fertilizers, glass, railroad beds, highways, cement, lime, and iron smelting.
   b. Marble — building construction, monuments, sculpture, church altars and pulpits.
   c. Sandstone — building construction, sidewalks.
   d. Slate — blackboards, electrical switchboards, sinks, roofs, mantels, floors.
   e. Granite — building construction, monuments.
   f. Diamonds — cutting, drilling, engraving tools for hard surfaces, jewelry.

5. Some common metals and their uses.
   a. Iron — steel; alloyed with other metals for use in tools, machinery, automobiles, airplanes, stoves.
   b. Copper — electrical equipment, coins, roofing, window screens, ship bottoms, gutters on houses.
   c. Aluminum — high voltage transmission wires, kitchen utensils, automobiles, railway trains, paints, telescopes, airplanes.
   d. Gold — most beautiful, but least useful; coins, jewelry. David before his death collected between two to three billion dollars worth of silver and gold to build the Temple.
   e. Silver — coins, jewelry, silverware, silvering expensive mirrors.
   f. Mercury — thermometers and barometers, mercury vapor lamps, explosives; as a tin alloy used to silver cheaper mirrors.

6. Fossils are the solidified or petrified remains of plants and animals frequently found in sedimentary sandstone or limestone; are probably remains of the Flood.

### VI. Electricity and Some of Its Uses

A. *Problems to be Studied*

1. What is the nature of electricity?

2. In which three ways may electricity be produced?

3. What are some of the characteristics of an electric current?

4. How does man use electricity in the home?

5. How is electricity used in industry?

B. *Understandings to be Developed*

1. Electricity is a form of energy.

    a. Earliest scientific knowledge of electricity — Thales, a Greek (600 B. C.), rubbed amber with woolen cloth to attract bits of paper.

    b. Benjamin Franklin — suggested positive and negative charges.

    c. Electron theory — an atom is composed of a nucleus of positive electricity and a proton surrounded by negative electricity, called electrons.

    d. Man does not definitely know what electricity is.

2. Electricity may be produced in three ways: (a) by rubbing, or friction; (b) by chemical action; (c) by magnets.

    a. Rubbing, or friction, is termed static electricity; "like" charges repel, and "unlike" charges attract each other; lightning is static electricity — more dangerous to stand under an isolated tree than in a grove; lightning rods offer some protection to homes and other buildings.

    b. Electricity produced by chemical action is termed galvanic.

        (1) Simple electric cell — copper plate, zinc plate, and sulfuric acid; not practical, current weakens.

        (2) Dry cells — carbon plate, zinc plate, and ammonium chloride; of practical value because dry cell does not use much space. Used in flashlights, doorbells, electrical toys, radio sets, etc.

        (3) Storage cells — two lead strips in battery jar and diluted sulfuric acid; must always have their plates covered with distilled water, otherwise will be ruined. Used in automobiles, radio sets, powerhouses, submarines, telephone exchanges.

        (4) Hydrometer — battery-testing equipment.

c. *Magnetic* or *dynamic* electricity is used in part by using magnets.

    (1) Electromagnet — foundation of nearly all electrical inventions; made by winding insulated wire around a soft-iron bar or cylinder, called the core; is only an electromagnet while current flows through. Used in doorbell, telegraph, telephone, motor, dynamo, radio, electric hoisting crane.

3. An electric current is electricity in motion.

    a. A *circuit* is the path of a current from its source through its medium of conduction and back to its source.

    b. A *short* circuit is produced when electricity does not follow the intended path, but a shorter one.

    c. A *closed* circuit is one that stops the flow of electricity.

    d. Electricity can be controlled by switches and push buttons, thus breaking or completing a circuit.

    e. Fuses — offer protection against short circuits or overloading a circuit with too many electrical appliances running at one time.

    f. Copper and aluminum are probably the best conductors.

4. Electricity gives us power, heat, and light.

    a. Some electrical devices used in our homes:

        (1) Electric bell.      (5) Electric ironing machine.
        (2) Vacuum cleaner.    (6) Electric refrigerator.
        (3) Electric fan.       (7) Electric sewing machine.
        (4) Washing machine.

        *Note:* Most of these are driven by motors.

    b. Some electrical devices depend upon the heating effect of electric currents:

        (1) Electric iron.      (4) Electric stove.
        (2) Electric heater.    (5) Electric heating pad.
        (3) Electric toaster.

        *Note:* These devices use wires that are poor conductors and thus become hot.

    c. Electric lights are the result of an electric current passing through a poor conductor, causing it to become so hot that it gives off light.

    d. Means of communication make use of electricity:

        (1) Telegraph.      (4) Radio.
        (2) Telephone.      (5) Talking pictures.
        (3) Ocean cables.    (6) Television.

    e. Some means of transportation depend upon electricity:

        (1) Automobile.      (3) Electric locomotive.
        (2) Trolley car.      (4) Electric ship.

## VII. Heat and How Man Uses It

A. *Problems to be Studied*

   1. What is the nature of heat?

   2. What are some of the sources of heat?

   3. What is the "molecular theory"?

   4. How does heat affect solids, liquids, and gases?

   5. How does heat travel?

   6. How do we use heat in our homes?

B. *Understandings to be Developed*

   1. Heat is a form of energy.

      a. Heat can move objects — kinetic energy.

      b. Heat has weight.

      c. It cannot be seen.

      d. It is not a liquid, gas, or solid.

   2. Heat can be obtained from various sources.

      a. The sun is our chief source of heat.

         (1) It helps us to keep warm.

         (2) It helps plants to grow.

         (3) Plants store up sunlight energy in the form of starch, sugar, and other substances.

      b. All energy, when it acts upon matter, produces heat.

         (1) Chemical action — acids burn skin; wood decays; sulfuric acid put on zinc.

         (2) Friction — sliding down rope quite rapidly will burn hands; matches are ignited by friction.

         (3) Compression — inflating a tire makes the pump warm because air is compressed; metal pounded with a hammer becomes hot.

         (4) Electricity — electric current passing through a thin wire will generate heat.

         (5) Burning of fuels — most important source of heat controlled by man.

   3. The molecular theory is a possible explanation to interpret what heat is.

      a. All matter is believed to be made up of minute particles called atoms.

      b. The small particles are always moving.

      c. Between the particles are spaces.

      d. The constant moving of the molecules we call *heat*.

e. The *faster* the molecules move the *hotter* an object becomes, the *slower* the molecules move, the *cooler* an
object becomes.
*Note:* This explanation is only a theory, which *seems*
to be true, and we cannot prove it absolutely.

4. Heat affects the size of solids, liquids, and gases.
  a. Solids, liquids, and gases *expand* when they are heated.
  b. Solids, liquids, and gases *contract* when they are cooled.
  c. Expansion and contraction are due to the increase or
  decrease of molecular movement.
  d. Man uses instruments to register temperatures:
    (1) Mercury and colored liquids are used in ther-
    mometers to indicate temperature.
    (2) Fahrenheit thermometer (most common in use)
    has a freezing point of 32° and a boiling point
    of 212°.
    (3) Centigrade thermometer (scientific purposes) has
    a freezing point of 0° and a boiling point of 100°.
    (4) Clinical thermometer (doctor, hospitals) used to
    determine body temperature (98.6 F.).
    5. Thermostats and automatic heat control depend
    upon heat expansion and contraction.
  e. Solids may be changed to liquids by heating; the change
  will depend upon the temperature. Substances have
  definite melting and freezing points. Ice becomes water;
  butter, paraffin, chocolate, lead, and wax will melt
  when heated.
  f. Liquids may be changed again to solids by cooling them.
    (1) Water changes to ice when cooled at 32° F.
    (2) Other substances that become solids again when
    cooled are paraffin, wax, lead, and chocolate.
  g. Liquids may be changed to gases by adding heat to them.
    (1) When a liquid becomes a gas, it evaporates.
    (2) Evaporation can be hastened by raising the
    temperature.
    (3) Not all liquids have the same rate of evaporation;
    ether and alcohol evaporate faster than water.
  h. Gases can be changed to liquids by cooling them.
    (1) When steam is cooled, it condenses into water.
    (2) When impure water is distilled, solid substances
    will remain, and clean water will result.
    (3) Moisture in the air condenses; pipes in the base-
    ment "sweat" in summer; glass containing ice
    water will "sweat."

5. Heat travels in three ways: **(1) by** conduction, **(2)** by convection, **(3)** by radiation.

    a. Conduction — occurs when **heat** travels from one molecule to another in a solid. When cooking a meal, the heat from the stove passes through the utensil into the food by *conduction*.

        (1) Some substances are better conductors of heat than others.

| GOOD CONDUCTORS | POOR CONDUCTORS | |
| --- | --- | --- |
| Silver | Water | Air |
| Copper | Wood | Paper |
| Aluminum | Glass | Silk |
| Iron | Cotton | Granite |
| Zinc | Wool | Brick |
| Brass | Limestone | Plaster |

    b. Convection — occurs when heated particles move and produce a current; convection currents are the cause of all winds and ocean currents. Rooms in our houses are heated by *convection* currents.

    c. Radiation — occurs where heat radiates from a body without heating the intervening space. The sun's heat reaches the earth and warms the surroundings by *radiation*.

Summary:

Heat travels through metals by conduction.

Heat travels through liquids and gases by convection.

Heat travels through space by radiation.

6. We heat our homes by using various fuels.

    a. Wood was once our only source of heat.

    b. Coal is obtained from mines.

        (1) Soft, bituminous, coal is 75% carbon; has high fuel value; gives off much smoke; used chiefly in industry.

        (2) Hard, anthracite, coal is 90% carbon; has high heat yield; little smoke or ash, ideal for the home; more expensive.

    c. Coke is made from soft coal by driving off the gaseous compounds; excellent fuel; intense, steady heat; no smoke, little ash; used also to extract iron from ores in blast furnaces.

    d. Oil is obtained from petroleum; clean and convenient but expensive; used in ships, locomotives, and houses.

e. Natural gas is obtained chiefly from oil wells; is cheap; superior to artificial gas; used for cooking and heating, making of steel, pottery, brick, and glass.

f. Coal gas is artificial gas made from coal; is more expensive; used in regions where natural gas cannot be obtained in homes and industries.

g. Other fuels of less importance are peat and charcoal.

h. We heat our homes by using various types of heating systems.

　　(1) Open fireplaces — earliest heater in the home; not very economical, because it consumes fuel wastefully and heats only small portion of room; provides good ventilation.

　　(2) Stoves — in use for about 200 years; today we use coal, gas, kerosene, and gasoline stoves; many modern stoves equipped with automatic time and temperature controls.

　　(3) Central heating systems — employ one heating system for entire dwelling or building.

Types of heating systems:

　　aa. *Hot-air furnace* — depends upon convection currents; advantages: easy and economical to operate; disadvantages: carries dust and waste to rooms and does not give equal distribution of heat on a windy day; air becomes too dry if humidifier is neglected.

　　bb. *Hot-water furnace* — depends upon convection currents and radiation; advantages: uses fuel economically and maintains an even temperature; disadvantages: expensive to install; no provision for fresh air.

　　cc. *Steam heat* — heats by means of convection currents and radiation; advantages: highly efficient, best for large buildings; disadvantages: expensive to install; no provision for fresh air; hard to control during mild weather.

　　dd. Gas heaters and oil-burning systems are now efficient, cleaner, convenient, easily regulated, but too expensive for most people.

7. Ventilation in the home is important.

a. It is necessary that we provide for a constant circulation of fresh air.

b. A certain amount of moisture must be maintained; relative humidity should be 50% to 60%.

c. The average temperature for comfort should be between 65° F. and 70° F.

## E. CORRELATION POSSIBILITIES

Correlation of science with other school activities and subjects is especially important in small schools where classes must be combined, but it enriches the instruction in any kind of school because of the close relation of science to all areas of life. The examples of correlation possibilities listed below are intended merely to be suggestive.

*Religion:* The following science concepts may well grow out of religious instruction, as indicated:

1. The account of the Creation (origin and propagation of human, plant, and animal life).

2. Feeding of the Five Thousand (conservation, economy, thrift).

3. Joseph in Egypt (effects of a famine on mankind due to abnormalities of natural laws).

4. First Article (preservation of man and of animal and plant life).

5. The account of the Creation (man made in God's image, the foremost among visible creatures, with dominion over other inferior creatures by virtue of his reason).

6. The promise of the rainbow as a reminder that there would be no more general flood (God's love and mercy toward man. God keeps His promises).

7. God made the laws of nature, and He is the Ruler of them. He sets them aside for His own purposes. Examples:

    a. Joshua, by God's direction, tells the sun to stand still. Josh. 10:12-14.

    b. The sun returns ten degrees backward for Hezekiah. 2 Kings 20:9.

    c. The sun darkened at the crucifixion. Luke 23:44.

    d. The waters of Jordan divided for Joshua, Josh. 3:15-17; for Elijah, 2 Kings 2:8; for Elisha, 2 Kings 2:14; the waters of the Red Sea divided for Moses and Israel, Ex. 14:21, 22.

    e. Elisha causes iron to float. 2 Kings 6:1-7.

    f. The unnatural occurrence of Peter's draught of fishes. Luke 5:4-11.

    g. The specially created star to lead the Wise Men to Jesus. Matt. 2:2.

    h. The feeding of Israel in the desert for forty years with manna. Ex. 16:4; 14:31-35.

    i. The fall of Jericho's walls. Josh. 6.

    j. In general, all miracles.

*Arithmetic:* Arithmetic is largely a science course. Problems along scientific lines, counting, measuring, numbering, determining values of materials and products, keeping records or charts are applications of scientific thinking and should be so understood by the pupils. Telling time, pointing out directions, and many other topics occurring commonly in arithmetic textbooks are science topics.

*Reading:* Science is learned through reading, and much of the science course may be taught in connection with the reading program. Most basic readers contain useful science materials, and the supplementary reading program can be planned to include science stories about animal life, plant life, the earth, weather, insect life, and health, as well as biographies of men of science which stress their contributions to human welfare.

Other training consists in teaching the scientific use of materials, how to use books, how to select pertinent details from the mass of materials, and the like.

*Language:* Science, like every other subject in the curriculum, having its own vocabulary, involves language skill. As correlative science activities in language, these are suggested as useful: Making a vocabulary chart of newly learned science words; composing rhymes and riddles of plants or animals for identification, or poems praising God for the wonders of nature; oral reports on readings, experiments, observations; written reports on similar terms; finding poems on plants or animals; writing letters for information on certain scientific subjects, or for exhibits of natural or manufactured products; keeping a science notebook; and similar activities.

*Art:* Drawings and paintings: Freehand drawings of nature subjects; record charts of the arrival of birds in spring, the first appearance of flowers, leaves, buds, etc.; maps of local or distant areas showing location of certain plants, minerals, or other natural phenomena; mottoes and posters on the conservation of natural resources; diagrams of experimental science equipment; the coloring of outline pictures or stencils of plants and animals. Titles expressing Christian sentiments should be encouraged for the productions.

Handwork: Making a scrapbook of scientific articles or pictures of current interest; collecting pictures which illustrate scientific principles or achievements; constructing a sand table illustrating different types of wild-life habitat; making rock, mineral, or seed collections, bird-egg and bird-nest collections, pressed flower booklets, leaf charts,[6] blue-print leaf designs, plastic plaques of leaves or flowers; setting up an aquarium or terrarium; building cages for animals for observation; making a model of Noah's Ark of construction paper or plywood; making star maps, not too detailed; making a weather vane; constructing a feeding rack or bath for birds, bird houses, or planting a window box; making an insect cage, an insect spreading board, or insect display boxes; making and painting fruits and vegetables modeled from clay; paper cutting of snowflakes, fruits, vegetables, etc.; establishing a science museum.

*Geography:* Frequent reference is made to natural resources in regional studies; areas of useful minerals, rocks, and animal and plant life are located. The geographic distribution of these items is studied together with man's exploitation and use of them.

*History:* Biographical sketches of some of the great men of science who were also humble Christians; effects of scientific discoveries and inventions upon the mode of living, the methods of church work, warfare, etc. *Examples:* Vitamins, foods, rubber, sanitation, airplanes, radio, automobile, etc.

*Current Events:* Post on bulletin board current articles and pictures from newspapers and magazines, or call attention to them. Because many of the articles on science in these sources are written for popular consumption and often cannot be trusted for scientific accuracy, care must be exercised. At times these articles present opportunity for evaluation with respect to truth or untruth, overstatement or understatement, and the like.

## F. EVALUATING OUTCOMES

Both objective and essay-type tests have their place in evaluating science outcomes. Standardized achievement tests are valuable particularly in checking subject matter and content. Attitudes must be determined, at least in part, by observation and by tests which permit spontaneous pupil expression. Among the important questions which should be considered in evaluating outcomes are these:

1. Does the pupil see God's majesty, power, wisdom, and love in Creation?

    a. In the order, detail, and magnitude of Creation.

    b. In the preservation of man, animals, and plants.

    c. In the operation of the laws of nature.

    d. In the infinite variety in nature.

---

6) See J. E. Potzger, *Curriculum in Science for Lutheran Schools,* p. 3, for suggestions on chart making.

2. Does he regard himself and the universe, including all plant and animal life, as creatures of Almighty God? Does he disavow the doctrine of evolution?

3. Does he realize that the laws of nature are not immutable, but that God can set them aside at will? Can he name examples where this was done?

4. Does the pupil credit also the minor phenomena and happenings in nature to God's rule and direction?

5. Has the pupil grown in understanding of his physical environment? Does he take an interest in the natural phenomena of his own surroundings?

    a. The influence of natural environment upon his mode of living.

    b. The influence of scientific achievement upon his life.

    c. The science of home, shop, factory, farm, and the like.

    d. Plant and animal life.

6. Has the pupil a desire to improve the conditions of his natural environment? Does he understand that, according to Gen. 1:28, it is his duty to contribute to the improvement of his surroundings and to that of the world in general?

7. Does he receive gratefully and use properly the blessings of God bestowed in nature? Is he thrifty and economical in their use?

8. Does he put scientific discoveries and inventions to constructive and beneficial use, encouraging others to do likewise?

9. Has the pupil developed individual interests in science which give promise that they may lead to a vocation or an avocation?

10. Does he read independently to increase his knowledge in the field of science?

11. Does he of his own initiative undertake experiments to solve problems?

12. Is the advanced pupil able to attack a problem and follow it step by step to its conclusion?

    a. Recognizing and visualizing the problem.

    b. Recalling facts which may help in the solution.

    c. Selecting pertinent facts.

    d. Weighing the evidence.

    e. Stating the conclusion.

    f. Testing the conclusion.

13. Does the pupil in all his reasoning bow under the revealed Word of God?

14. Is he able to construct simple equipment which is useful in the study of nature and science: Window boxes, feeding racks for birds, electric circuits, charts, and the like?

### Selected References

Bruce, Guy V., *World of Water and Air*. Book I. 1938; *Heat, Fire, and Fuel*. Book II. 1938; *Magnetism and Electricity*. Book III. 1939. Newark: New Jersey State Teachers College.

Croxton, W. C., *Science in the Elementary School*. McGraw-Hill, 1937.

Dau, W. H. T., *The Testimony of Science*. Concordia, 1928.

De Vries, John, "Developing Christian Character through Science Teaching." *Christian Home and School Magazine*, November, 1941, p. 8 ff.

Eifrig, C. W. G., *Our Great Outdoors*. 2 Vols. Rand McNally, 1928.

Garrison, C. G., *Science Experiments for Little Children*. Scribner's, 1939.

Graebner, Theo., *Essays on Evolution*. Concordia, 1925.

Graebner, Theo., *Evolution*. Northwestern Publishing House.

Graebner, Theo., *God and the Cosmos*. Grand Rapids: Wm. B. Eerdmans Publishing Co.

Handrich, Theo. L., *Every-Day Science for the Christian*. Concordia, 1938.

Herget, J. F., *Questions Evolution Does Not Answer*. Cincinnati: Standard Publishing Co.

Lynde, C. J., *Science Experiments with House Equipment*. Scranton: International Textbook Co., 1937.

Lynde, C. J., *Science Experiments with Inexpensive Equipment*. Scranton: International Textbook Co., 1939.

Miller, A. H., *Science in the Grades*. River Forest, Ill.: Miller Publishing Co.

National Society for the Study of Education, *Thirty-First Yearbook*. Part I. "A Program for the Teaching of Science." Public School Publishing Co., 1932.

Potzger, J. E., *Curriculum in Science for Lutheran Schools*. Concordia, 1931.

Scott, H. N., *Essential Experiments in General Science*. Parts I and II. Beckley-Cardy, 1937.

Underhill, Orra E., *The Origins and Development of Elementary-School Science*. Scott-Foresman, 1941.

Zim, Herbert S., "Development of a Program of Elementary Science." *Elementary School Journal*, May, 1940, pp. 657—669.

State, District, or local Courses of Study.

Manuals accompanying textbooks.

# VIII. FINE ARTS

## 1. Music

### A. OBJECTIVES

1. The ability to sing easily and naturally with an attractive tone of voice and correct pitch.

2. The ability to read music fluently.

3. The ability to recognize and appreciate good vocal and instrumental music, especially the chorale and other church music by Lutheran composers.

4. An acquaintance with outstanding religious and non-religious vocal and instrumental music for personal appreciation and enjoyment.

5. Truly devotional participation in congregational or other forms of church singing; in general, the use of song in the worship and praise of God and for the edification of self and others.

6. The desire to grow in the knowledge and appreciation of that which is worth while and edifying in music.

### B. DISCUSSION OF OBJECTIVES

**Proper Tone Production**

The foundation of good singing is proper tone and pitch. These, in turn, depend chiefly on a discriminating ear. Therefore, ear training must go hand in hand with, or even precede, voice training. "A good ear for music," that is, in this case, an ear that can distinguish a pleasing tone from a faulty tone or a higher pitch from a lower pitch, is fundamental. The monotone or conversational singer is one who has not learned to hear differences of pitch and to raise or lower his tones; one who produces unpleasant tones has not learned to use his voice to best advantage or to appreciate the difference between good and bad tone production by his sense of hearing. Proper tone production must be the aim in all grades of the school and with all pupils, regardless of age or present ability to sing. For details the teacher is referred to the *Manual* of the *Music Reader* and the *Curriculum in Music*.

**The Reading of Music**

This objective has to do with a technique of learning to sing a given selection or the various voices of a part song. One way to learn these is "by ear." It is a learning by rote, a procedure most suitable for the primary grades. The other way is to sing by notes, a procedure possible and practical from the third grade upward. Music reading is an important objective because of its practical value in school and throughout life. Even if the teacher should not engage in elaborate part singing or children's chorus work, he should teach his pupils the technique of note reading and all the mechanics that go with it, in order that they may learn melodies with so much greater facility and exactness. For details the teacher is referred to the guides already indicated.

### Appreciation of Good Music

The child hears music daily. Into his home the radio brings music of every description, much of it with a bad influence upon the listener. The child must learn, first, to distinguish between edifying and degrading music; second, to appreciate the kind of music which elevates the soul and spirit, whether that be religious or classical music.

Appreciation of good music and recognition of its ageless character grow only out of an understanding of its quality and value. They come to the one who lives with good music. The child must therefore be given opportunity to sing and hear Christian, and specifically Lutheran, hymns, and other worth-while songs; to feel the comfort, peace, joy, and satisfaction they impart; and to experience how repeated hearing and singing endear both words and music.

As appreciation of the quality and value of music and the desire to sing the best in music develop, proper discrimination in the choice of music heard over the radio and wise selection of music for his own library will become easy and natural for the child.

### Acquaintance with Outstanding Music

The Lutheran child will become acquainted with outstanding musical compositions, especially those written by great Lutheran composers. He will learn that such masters as Bach and Mendelssohn have contributed a great share of the music which today ranks highest in the fields of religious and classical musical literature. By means of well-planned music appreciation hours in the classroom the child will learn many of these gems of music.

Specifically, the average child is capable of building up a repertory along the following lines:

a. Knowledge of the hymns sung commonly in the church services.

b. Songs of a secular nature: Country, nature, etc.

c. Songs or instrumental selections which he cannot himself perform, but which he can recognize and enjoy.

d. A special repertory of songs or other selections which are his own in a special sense and which he uses frequently.

The child should also become acquainted with the purposes, aims, and lives of a selection of great composers.

### Devotional Participation in Church Singing

The Christian child must be prepared for active participation in the joint worship of the church. As a member of the singing Church, the Lutheran child should be trained in the habit of singing the hymns and joining in the liturgical parts of the divine service.

To participate wholeheartedly in the musical part of the church service, the child must feel the need of musical expression in the house of God. He is made mindful of the expression of David "Let us sing unto the Lord a new song" and "Sing praises unto Him." He should appreciate the fact that music expresses the feelings of sorrow, repentance, trust, and joy. To this end the teacher should direct the child's attention especially to the content and meaning of the chorale, hymns, and liturgy. (For an explanation of the Common Service see Course in Church History, pp. 76—79.) The child will learn that in the singing of hymns, as in all worship, mere lip service is not enough, but that the heart must be in it.

### Desire for Growth in Musical Knowledge and Appreciation

The desire for further growth does not exist apart from musical knowledge and appreciation. The former is achieved with the latter. The teacher's main task is to advise or to direct the desire. This may mean the further training of a gifted voice, learning to play an instrument, singing in the church choir, or other useful activity.

The child should be sure that his ambition is not based upon selfish motives, but upon the humble desire to use his gifts in the service of God and man. This ideal should constantly be held before the child, especially when his skill is utilized in church services and school programs.

### C. DIVISION OF TIME

Singing is taught in all grades. In the primary grades no definite time need be set aside, but several short singing periods may be held daily. In the intermediate and upper grades the singing period should be definitely established on the program. A short period of fifteen minutes a day brings better results than two or three longer periods a week.

In one-room schools all grades may sing at the same time, but it will be necessary to give special attention to the beginners.

## D. COURSE SUGGESTIONS

### Primary Grades (1 and 2)

There is sufficient time in these grades to teach a number of simple hymns, chorales, and secular songs. These are taught by the rote method. Uniform tone and pitch are emphasized. Every normal child has the latent ability to sing, and those who have difficulty are given individual attention. The children are taught to sing softly and to listen to their neighbors while singing. A great deal of patience is required until uniform tone and pitch are attained, but the reward will be direct results and a solid foundation for future progress. The following content is suggested:

1. Songs to be used for morning devotions.
2. Songs for the children's Christmas service.
3. Simple songs for school programs.
4. Seasonal songs and songs of the church year.
a. A Mighty Fortress Is Our God.
b. Glory Be to Jesus.
c. Let Me Learn of Jesus.
d. Seeing I am Jesus' Lamb.
e. I Know that My Redeemer Lives.
5. Songs learned in the Memory Work.
6. Nursery rhyme songs.
7. Songs listed in the *Music Reader* for these grades.

### Intermediate Grades (3—6)

In these grades the co-ordination of eye and ear should begin. Use should be made of the song material which the children have acquired in the primary grades. The development of sight reading and the recognition of symbols must be slow but sure. Children should learn to read music in grades three and four. The movable *do* system is an example of a simple method for teaching singing at sight in all signatures.

Once sight reading has been developed and true tone and pitch is maintained, the class is ready for part singing. The teacher makes a selection of the better voices for parts other than the melodies. Testing of the voices is necessary to place the children according to their voice ranges. At first the range of the music must be limited, but as the voices develop, the range is extended to fit the needs of song arrangements.

Care must be taken not to strain voices beyond their natural abilities. Proper tone production is possible only if the voice is kept in its natural range and volume.

Our chorales and hymns provide more than sufficient material for the singing lessons.  Suggested content:

1. Songs learned in the Memory Work.

2. Songs for Christmas, Lent, and Easter.

3. Seasonal songs of a secular nature: Fall, winter, etc.

4. Patriotic songs.

5. Folk songs of American and Old World origin.

6. Well-known songs of great composers.  See *Music Reader* and *Select Songs* for religious and secular numbers.

7. Hymns for divine services.

### Advanced Grades (7 and 8)

If the proper foundation has been laid in the lower grades, the advanced grades will be ready for much part singing.  Preparation of multiple-part songs should culminate in actual renditions in church services and school programs.

Much part singing is justified only when pupils are able to read music at sight quite fluently.  With many other important school subjects on the program for advanced grades, much time is wasted by teaching three- or four-part songs by rote.  It would be better in such cases to concentrate on melodies and a greater variety of song material.

Music appreciation will grow to some extent out of the learning of worth-while songs.  Separate periods may be devoted to this phase of the music program where time permits.  A record player or radio is valuable for this purpose.  Where these instruments are lacking, it is more difficult to acquaint the children with the better types of classical composition.  The teacher may play such numbers himself or call upon gifted pupils to play certain pieces that illustrate the lesson.

In schools of two to eight rooms a joint period may be devoted to the rehearsal of hymns for the church service.  Also music appreciation classes may be held jointly to save time.  There may also be opportunity for visiting artists to give school programs.

Programs arranged by the school for the benefit of the congregation or the public provide additional opportunity for good singing and music cultivation and appreciation.

*Note:* In the one-room school part singing can best be accomplished if the children of the lower grades sing the familiar melody voice, and the higher grades are used for the other parts. In that manner the voices of the entire school can be used in the chorus.

**Suggested Course Content** (See *Music Reader*)

1. Increase of chorale and hymn repertory.

2. Additional songs of American song literature.

3. Patriotic and national songs.

4. Multiple-part arrangements of seasonal church hymns.

5. Program songs (school festivals, church services, and graduation exercises).

6. Famous songs of great composers.

## Music Appreciation

The course in music appreciation must be planned by the teacher according to the time and equipment available. Suggestions are given below:

1. Lives and works of great composers.

a. Johann Sebastian Bach.

b. Martin Luther.

c. Paul Gerhardt.

d. Johannes Brahms.

e. Joseph Haydn.

f. Friedrich Haendel.

g. Felix Mendelssohn.

h. Others, as time may allow.

2. Recordings (if record player available).

a. Great composers.

b. Famous songs.

c. Christmas music.

d. Contemporary American composers.

e. Folk songs.

f. Types of different music.

g. Types of rhythm.

3. Radio programs (if radio is available).

## E. CORRELATION POSSIBILITIES

*Religion:* The use of sacred songs, chorales, and memorized hymns in the singing lesson helps to vitalize the religious instruction and to make the religious life of the child more expressive. As the knowledge of religious songs is increased, a wider selection of hymns for the morning devotion is made possible.

*Reading:* The content of all songs and melodies helps to broaden the vocabulary of the child. Many new expressions and words are learned through the reading and singing of the hymn content.

*Language:* Correct expression in songs helps the child to express himself better. Analyzing contents of hymns leads to good summarizing and visualization of a whole theme. Proper interpretation of songs is a result of good understanding of words and expressions.

*Spelling:* The child is led to see on repeated occasions the spelling of words in song texts. Constant repetition of songs will help to establish the word pictures. Writing hymns from memory is a good spelling aid.

*Arithmetic:* There are frequent opportunities for the use of calculation, such as the life span of notable composers and artists, duration of hymn melody from time of writing to present time, also numbers of particular rhymes, of the metrical schemes, such as 8, 7, 8, 7, found over a hymn melody. Time in music — whole, half, quarter notes, etc. — may serve as a study of the comparative value of fractions.

*History:* The history of music portrayed in elementary form parallel to world and United States history will answer for the child the why and wherefore of the melodies and lyrics that have been written. For example, the Negro folk songs are a product of pre- and post-Civil War days; the hymns of Luther are largely a result of the time in which he lived; our best patriotic songs grew out of the struggles of the new nation. These and other songs may be sung as the respective periods in history are studied.

*Civics:* Patriotic sense and civic duty is expressed admirably in our patriotic and national song literature. Such songs are the expression of a sincere patriotic heart, and selections should be sung as part of the Civics course.

*Health and Safety:* Health songs are especially useful in the primary grades; posture and correct breathing.

*Geography:* Songs of other lands and regional songs of America help to visualize climes, peoples, and countries. Some songs treat of streams, rivers, mountains, and seasons.

*The Arts:* Pictures of great artists may be studied in music appreciation. Scenes from their lives also help to understand the times in which their music was written. Biblical pictures recreate certain situations in which music was used, such as David and his harp, and the like.

Certain scenes portrayed in hymns may be drawn or pictured by the children.

The teacher will expand this list as time and need indicate.

## F. EVALUATING OUTCOMES

The following questions may serve as a guide to determine how far the aims of the music program are being carried out in the school:

1. Does the voice of the child readily blend with the voices of his companions in the singing group?

2. Is the child able to sing in accurate pitch?

3. Has everything possible been attempted to help the monotone and conversational singer overcome his trouble?

4. Are all children of unequal talents given equal opportunity for advancement in singing skill?

5. Has singing become a freewill expression properly led into Christian channels of appreciation and selection?

6. What does the child know of the background of our Lutheran song and music literature?

7. Has the child learned to distinguish between edifying and debasing music?

8. Does the child carry over his knowledge of music into spontaneous appreciation of beautiful music?

9. Does the child feel a desire, or have a taste, for more and more of the Christian music that should become his own expression?

10. Finally, does the child show that he wants to continue in the growth of musical knowledge; actively participate in the worship of the church; and, if well gifted, lend his talents for special work of the church?

### Selected References

Backer, E. D., *Music in Our Schools.* E. D. Backer, Dr. Martin Luther College, New Ulm, Minn.

Christiansen, F. Melius, *School of Choir Singing.* Minneapolis: Augsburg Publishing House, 1916.

Hardy, T. M., *How to Train Children's Voices.* Philadelphia: Theo. Presser Co.

*Lutheran Hymnal.* Concordia, 1941.

Music Department, *Lutheran School Journal.*

Grundmann, J., and Schumacher, B., *Music Reader for Lutheran Schools.* Concordia, 1933.

Grundmann, J., and Schumacher, B., *Manual for the Music Reader for Lutheran Schools.* Concordia, 1933.

Polack, W. G., *The Handbook to the Lutheran Hymnal.* Concordia, 1942.

Stinson, Ethelyn Lenore, *How to Teach Children Music.* Published under the auspices of the Child Research Clinic of the Woods Schools. Harpers, 1941.

Theiss, J. A., and Schumacher, B., *Select Songs.* Concordia, 1922.

Zurstadt, H. M., *Curriculum in Music for Lutheran Schools.* Concordia, 1936.

State, local, or District Course of Study.

# 2. Art Education

## A. OBJECTIVES

1. The realization

a. That beauty and the aesthetic sense are creations of God, meant for His praise and honor.

b. That the artistic taste and ability of man are corrupted by sin, and in need of correction and development.

c. That natural man uses art for the gratification of his vanity and sinful lusts.

d. That Christians must condemn and avoid such abuse of art, and instead devote art to its God-given purpose.

2. An elementary understanding of the principles underlying art and the ability to apply them.

3. The ability to discern and appreciate the beauty of form and color as revealed in God's work of creation and in the works of man.

4. An artistic attitude and practice in the ordinary things of life, such as personal appearance, pleasing arrangement of objects, home decoration, and beautification of surroundings.

### Definition of Art as a School Subject

Webster gives ten definitions of art. Essentially, art means skill, or something that requires skill. In that sense, handwriting is an art. So is letter writing, conversation, cooking, housekeeping, carpentry, surgery, or the ability to think logically, speak effectively, and sing beautifully.

But art education, as a special branch of learning in the elementary school, means only *a study of the theory and practice of taste in the expression of beauty in form and color.* It leaves out the expression of beauty in tone, speech, and movement.

Form and color, or the expression of beauty in form and color, then, are the chief concern of this subject; and this involves a study of the theory and practice of *taste* (aesthetics). Form and color of *objects* is meant. Form here means more than the shape of a single object; it refers also to a group of objects, as in a picture. The same is true of color.

The subject approaches the theory and practice of taste from two angles — the *receptive* and the *expressive.* In simple terms, this means that pupils, on the one hand, view, study, and appreciate what is truly artistic, and, on the other, express their own taste and ability in productive or reproductive work. On the *receptive* side the pupils are led to study masterpieces of art in form or color, or both, such as plants, flowers, animals, man, and natural scenery; paintings, sculpture, architecture, landscaping, home decorations (often beautifully shown in magazine advertisements), good photographs and pictures of all kinds, comparisons of the inartistic with the artistic (such as remodeled rooms or homes), and the like. Pupils will learn what makes forms or colors artistic (the theory or principles underlying art). The *expressive* side leads to such simple activities as drawing, sketching, molding, cutting, arranging, building, or anything else that has to do with artistic form; it leads to coloring, painting, decorating, or anything else that has to do with beauty in color.

## B. DISCUSSION OF OBJECTIVES

The primary and immediate object of the study of art in school is to develop the child's aesthetic sense, which he possesses by nature as a precious gift of the Creator, and to lead him to appreciate beauty in form and color, wherever found, as likewise a precious gift of the Creator, meant for the praise and honor of His holy name. The object is not to produce masters in the art of drawing, painting, and the like. The more remote and ultimate objects are: The pleasure and practical value derived from a cultivated taste in the ordinary things of life; possible further development in some branch of the field of art; the standing ability and desire to promote beauty in the service of man and to the honor and praise of God as well as to discourage, avoid, and condemn the use of art for the gratification of vanity and lust.

Our objectives begin with the statement that the child should, in this course, learn to realize four facts: First, that beauty and the aesthetic sense are creations of God, meant for His praise and honor. Art does not have its origin in man or in the devil, but in God. "All things beautiful" are of God; and so is the sense to appreciate and admire them, or the human ability to produce works of art. It follows, therefore, that art is meant for the glorification of God. This the Christian child must be taught to realize.

In the second place, he must understand that the original artistic taste and ability of man is corrupted by sin and in need of correction and development. This can readily be demonstrated by the lack of artistic taste and ability on the part of the pupils themselves; by the fact that most adults are not much better situated, many showing poor taste (say, in choosing the colors of paint for the house) and still poorer ability in producing artistic things; that manufacturers and business firms, church and home decorators, and wealthy individuals employ experts to do their designing, landscaping, and the like. This general weakness has its origin in the fall of man. Art and the artistic sense is not lost to man, but it is weakened, like his reason.

This leads to the third realization: That natural man, the unbeliever, uses art for the gratification of his vanity and sinful lusts. Attention is called to the illustration of filthy magazines and their covers, to commercialized art in general, to the movies, to scant and unbecoming dress, to unchaste statues, to advertising and money-making, to offensive comic strips, etc. And this leads to the important realization that Christians must condemn and avoid such abuse of art, and instead devote art to its God-given purpose. The child must be led to judge between right and wrong, and this includes personal adornment. He must learn not to be "conformed to the world," but to devote art to its God-given purposes, for example, in general Christian modesty and chastity, in modesty of dress and personal grooming, in decorating the walls of his house with Biblical and chaste pictures, in exterminating from his heart the very love of the world and its ways in art, in confessing the Lord and His righteousness before the world in his every artistic endeavor, and in giving thanks and praise to God for all the beauty which He has given or with which He has surrounded us. In the first objective of this course we have the spiritual and moral aspect of the subject, by which the teaching in Christian schools should distinguish itself from that in other schools.

In the last three objectives it is pointed out that the child should learn to understand, apply, and benefit by art as such. Through the study of the principles underlying works of art he will learn why one object, or group of objects, is artistic, and another is not. He will learn correct form, grouping, and coloring. In his simple school activities, he is taught how to apply those principles to his own reproductions. Both are to build up his aesthetic sense, so that he may discern what is beautiful in God's creation and in the works of man (not merely the great masterpieces of painting, for example, but every other artistic effect wrought by man). Finally, he is to become artistic himself and bring his artistic sense to bear on his person, home, and other ordinary things in life. To achieve this, he must be encouraged to pursue varied creative art activities.

## C. PRACTICAL SUGGESTIONS

**Method**

The dictation-demonstration method, by which the teacher tells the pupils what to do and shows them how to do it, is suitable for primary children, but it has serious disadvantages in the higher grades.

With a suitable textbook older children who are well able to read can proceed almost independently, because the book out- lines a step-by-step procedure and provides for review and self- help opportunities. Thus the teacher is enabled to devote his time to supervision and individual criticism and help. The *Ele- mentary Art Series* [1] is designed for a maximum of pupil inde- pendence in the intermediate and upper grades. It was written with the needs of the busy, and ofttimes inexperienced, teacher especially in mind.

### Time

The time which can be devoted to art will vary in different schools. In many cases only one half hour per week will be available. In such instances it is best to present the lesson at the beginning of the week, and to discuss principles and techniques. The pupils will do their work in art after they have completed their assignments in other subjects or outside school hours. Papers are collected and evaluated on Friday.

With a longer time allotment more work, and perhaps all of it, can be completed during school time and under the supervision of the teacher.

### Materials

Large, cheap paper (wall paper cut into convenient sheets serves well), a good grade of wax crayolas, and some colored construction paper constitute a minimum list of materials. A good art course is possible with this equipment.

Crayola, pencil paints, chalk, and scratch paper have several advantages: They are economical in price; they can be used in short periods of 20 to 30 minutes; and they are available at all times to the pupil without serious class disturbance.

Paints are more costly and require longer periods for efficient use. They can be added as the teacher gains experience, if sufficient time is available for their use.

### The Problem of Art Appreciation.

Great masterpieces of painting, sculpture, architecture, and landscaping may be studied directly to stimulate art appreciation, particularly in communities where excursions make a first-hand study of these works possible. The study of plant and animal life in its relation to art may be undertaken similarly by means of field trips and excursions.

---

1) By W. W. Bloom and H. C. Gruber. See *Selected References.*

Classroom art appreciation lessons must be confined to the study of reproductions of great paintings, outstanding pictures and photographs, including pictures of home decorations and the like.

The Christian teacher utilizes great religious pictures which, besides illustrating the basic principles of art, provide opportunity for the inculcation of important religious truths.

The teacher must not allow himself to be confused by the wealth of material available. Rather, where no art library exists, he should begin in a small way to collect and file materials for purposeful and economical use, remembering that the qualitative, and not so much the quantitative, aspect is important.

**A Selection of Famous Religious Pictures** [2]

Boughton, "Pilgrims Going to Church."

Brown, "Washing the Feet of the Disciples."

Corregio, "Holy Night."

Clementz, "Golgotha."

Da Vinci, "The Last Supper."

Giovanni, "Our Lord on the Mount of Olives."

Hassam, "Church at Old Lyme."

Hofmann, "The Boy Christ."

Hofmann, "Christ and the Rich Young Ruler."

Hofmann, "Christ Blessing Little Children."

Hofmann, "Christ in the Temple."

Hofmann, "Christ in Gethsemane."

Millet, "The Angelus."

Muncacsy, "Christ before Pilate."

Plockhorst, "The Entry into Jerusalem."

Rubens, "The Crucifixion."

Uhde, "The Welcome Guest."

---

[2] This list is brief and incomplete, but it indicates the variety of religious subjects that might serve for art appeciation lessons. Other religious pictures, as also famous paintings of a nonreligious nature, are described in any good encyclopedia under *Painting* and related topics. Reproductions of, or descriptive literature on, masterpieces may be obtained from Concordia Publishing House, St. Louis, Mo.; F. A. Owen Publishing Co., Dansville, N. Y.; Mentzer, Bush and Co., Chicago, Ill.; Perry Picture Co., Malden, Mass.; Practical Drawing Co., Dallas, Texas; and others.

## How to Study a Great Painting

1. Display the picture.

2. Create a favorable situation. Introduce in as interesting a manner as possible. A story about the author, extraordinary circumstances under which the masterpiece was produced, special seasonal appeal of the painting, as Hofmann's "Christ in Gethsemane" during Lent, and similar approaches are helpful.

3. Let pupils study the picture silently for a short while.

4. Have pupils state what they consider the idea the artist wishes to convey. This calls for recognition of principal character or characters, or principal features, and their place in the production.

5. Make sure that pupils understand how the artist accomplishes his purpose. Discuss grouping, figures in foreground, figures in background, filling of space, contrasts, design, color, light, shading, etc.

6. Call attention to points of particular beauty that have escaped the pupils.

7. Compare with other pictures the class has studied.

8. Have pupils summarize. This may take the form of a story, especially in the case of younger children.

9. In the case of a religious picture, always close with a spiritual note (not a lecture or sermon).

## D. COURSE SUGGESTIONS

A suitable textbook series [3] furnishes the rough outline of the course to be followed. If the textbook sequence does not provide for the features listed below, it is modified or supplemented to include them at the appropriate time and in the appropriate place:

1. The seasons and seasonal interests, with appropriate reference to God's plán in the creation and preservation of the world: Gardening, harvest, etc.

2. Church festivals and special religious observances: Christmas, Easter, Reformation, Thanksgiving, etc. Posters, religious scenes, study of masterpieces, and room decorations are particularly suitable.

3. Patriotic days, observances, and symbols: Flag, Decoration Day, Independence Day, etc. Posters, scenes, designs, room decorations, and construction projects are suggested.

4. Local needs and special events: Church or school anniversary, outstanding local civic events, and the like.

---

3) See suggestions under *Selected References*.

5. If possible and practical, field trips or excursions to study works of art directly: Paintings, sculpture, architecture, nature in its relation to art, and the like.

6. Sketching, modeling, decorating, or selected handwork.[4]

7. Incidental, but constant, training in art appreciation and artistic expression as indicated in the *Discussion of Objectives*.

## E. CORRELATION POSSIBILITIES

The correlation of art with the rest of the school program makes it a live and interesting subject. Under *D. Course Suggestions,* some important correlation possibilities are mentioned. These are of primary importance. Additional suggestions follow:

Correlation with reading, history, language, etc., is possible through story illustrations, slogans, posters, and the like. Special units which trace the development of transportation, homes, furniture, etc., are valuable in the social sciences.

The number of illustrations in standard dictionaries and the publication of special picture dictionaries for younger children indicate the practical value of art in spelling and vocabulary studies. Graphic illustrations will be used by the teacher wherever they are helpful in these studies.

Simple pictures are also very practical in arithmetic, especially in the lower grades, in the development of number concepts. For example: Two trees and two trees (expressed graphically) are four trees.

## F. EVALUATING OUTCOMES

The outcomes of art are difficult to evaluate, especially the graphic representations and creative work. As the teacher becomes thoroughly familiar with *particular principles* and techniques, evaluation becomes less difficult and more objective. He will know what skills and perfections to look for and how to rate them. The filling of space, good contrasts, balance, and pleasing color harmonies are the more important criteria for evaluating papers.

Accurate objective tests can be prepared on the principles, fundamentals, and art appreciation facts which have been taught. Such tests may be true-false, completion, multiple-choice, or matching tests, or a combination of types.

Interest in works of art of various kinds indicates that some degree of appreciation has been achieved.

The distribution of grades will follow a bell curve, the same as that used in grading other work, in classes that are sufficiently large to make this method of grading reliable.

---

4) For suggestions see *Integrated Handwork for Elementary Schools,* by Louis V. Newkirk. Listed under *Selected References.*

## Selected References

BOOKS FOR THE TEACHER

Bloom, W. W., and Gruber, H. C., *Elementary Art Series*. St. Louis: Bloom and Gruber, Publishers, 1941. (Also available at Concordia Publishing House.)

Bloom, W. W., and Gruber, H. C., "Art in the Primary Grades." *Lutheran School Journal*, Dec., 1941, pp. 160—164.

Deffner, E., and Diesing, A. E., *Curriculum in Art for Lutheran Schools*. Concordia, 1932.

Horne, Joicey M., *The Art Class in Action*. Longman's, 1941.
Covers all phases of art experience, and particularly handcraft projects, for Canadian schools.

Lemos, P. J., *The Art Teacher*. Worcester: The Davis Press, Inc., 1935.

Neale, Oscar W., *World-Famous Pictures*. Lyons and Carnahan, 1933.

Newkirk, Louis V., *Integrated Handwork for Elementary Schools*. Silver-Burdett, 1940.
This book is valuable for the teacher who wishes to include handwork in his art program. The author 1. defines handwork; 2. shows its relation to industrial arts, fine arts, social studies, English, science, arithmetic, reading; 3. discusses and illustrates the use of integrated handwork as a teaching procedure; 4. suggests equipment and proper school facilities for handwork techniques; and 5. explains and illustrates methods of doing the more common types of handwork. The book contains 342 pages and numerous illustrations.

N. S. S. E., "Art in American Life and Education," *Fortieth Yearbook*, Public School Publishing Co., 1941.

Tangerman, Elmer J., *Design and Figure Carving*. McGraw-Hill, 1940.

Todd, J., and Gale, N., *Enjoyment and Use of Art in the Elementary School*. University of Chicago Press, 1933.

Williams, Lida B., *Picture Studies from Great Artists*. Hall and McCreary, 1922.

State, local, or District course of study.

TEXTBOOKS

Bloom and Gruber, *Elementary Art Series*. (See above.)
*Concordia Art Books* (with Manual). Concordia.

# IX. THE KINDERGARTEN

## A. STATUS AND NEED OF THE KINDERGARTEN

In spite of the fact that the percentage of American children attending kindergartens is comparatively small,[1] the kindergarten appears to be firmly established as an American educational institution, especially in the larger cities.

Generally speaking, there is no difference in purpose between the kindergarten and the higher school grades, except that formal reading is not attempted in the kindergarten. The fact that the activities differ from those in higher grades indicates merely recognition of the truth that education does not necessarily consist of book learning.

Where parents have the time, the ability, and the inclination to devote themselves to the proper training of their children, and this is certainly the foremost duty of all parents, there is little need of the kindergarten. Its value is more apparent in the case of those children who are handicapped by undesirable home conditions. Generally such children profit from a year of efficient pre-school education. In these cases it is as important for the kindergarten teacher to instruct parents in the proper rearing of their children as it is to supply educative experiences for the children, since the training of the children will prove effective only when the parents work with the teacher.

It is sometimes difficult to win for the Lutheran school, children who have attended a public kindergarten, because parents prefer not to have their children change schools. For this reason some congregations find it advisable to add a pre-school class to their parochial school. This obviates the necessity of a change in schools after the kindergarten year and removes one of the problems in the way of enrolling the congregation's children.

## B. OBJECTIVES OF THE KINDERGARTEN

1. *Aid to parents in providing for the proper spiritual, physical, emotional, social, and intellectual development of the child.*

*Note:* The parents are responsible for the education of their children, and it is not educationally desirable to take very young children away from the influence of the parents. The kindergarten is justified only in so far as it helps parents in performing

---

1) Dorothy Walter Baruch in 1939 estimated the number enrolled at 645,000, as compared with 9 million children not receiving a pre-school education. In *Parents and Children Go to School.* Scott, Foresman, and Company, 1939, p. 410.

more successfully their duty of providing a Christian training for their children. Frequent conferences with parents are necessary to achieve this. For this reason parents are encouraged to visit the kindergarten in session.

2. *Provision for an easy, gradual transition between the home and school environment.*

*Note:* For the small child this transition is likely to be much more important than the average adult realizes. The kindergarten provides an intermediate stage in which the departure from home life is not too abrupt, both because the kindergarten ordinarily is in session only a half day and because the kindergarten environment is more informal than that of the classroom.

3. *Instruction in simple truths of God's Word.*

*Note:* This includes the telling and discussion of Bible stories, application of Biblical truth to the child's life, and constant training in Christian behavior. The same educational principles apply as in all Christian education and training.

4. *Provision for the health of the child.*

*Note:* Some of the children come from homes where the health needs of the children have been adequately provided for; others have a background of unhygienic conditions and physical neglect. A careful physical examination at entrance with at least one parent present, regular health inspection on the part of a physician or nurse, training in health habits, suggestions to parents, and a second thorough examination before promotion to the first grade constitute the health work of the kindergarten.

5. *Development of emotional balance and a sense of security.*

*Note:* When parents lack emotional balance, when there is quarreling in the home, or when children are not wanted in the home, they feel insecure and useless. They are nervous and restless and often present other behavior problems. The teacher must show a special measure of love and kindness to these children, thus making them feel useful, wanted, and secure. When mistreatment, neglect, or coddling have given the child a warped outlook upon life, the performance of simple tasks and duties in the kindergarten, with a balance of success and failure, constitutes a valuable training toward emotional balance. Important in this connection is the nurture of trust in God in all situations, and dependence upon God in the performance of difficult tasks.

6. *Aid in social adjustment through companionship with other children of the same age.*

*Note:* Children at the age of five years desire the company of others of the same age. Some of them have been denied this privilege in their homes, and consequently they do not know what it means to take turns, talk with equals, consider the rights of others, practice following or leading, play alone or with others, or settle differences as Christian children must. The wise teacher provides opportunity and guidance for learning in these respects.

7. *Development of a background of experiences, concepts, and language ability needed for normal progress in school.*

*Note:* This includes religious experiences (hearing God's Word, prayer), sensory contacts (seeing, hearing, touching), simple musical experiences, experiences with nature (animals, earth, water — also simple stories about them), play activities with many different kinds of apparatus and materials, story telling, answering of children's questions, opportunities for muscle development in play and work activities, and the like.

## C. ACTIVITIES, EQUIPMENT, METHODS

It is possible here only to state the general purposes of the kindergarten, not to outline a detailed procedure or curriculum. The latter would require a volume. The kindergarten teacher is advised to choose two or more titles from the list of *Selected References* and to give them thorough study. In this way even the teacher untrained in kindergarten technique will gradually widen her background and improve her instruction and guidance.

Religious instruction, worship, and Christian training are of first importance in the Christian kindergarten. In all other activities the teacher will exercise discriminative judgment and choice, being careful to adopt only that which is in keeping with the aims and ideals of the Christian school.

## D. OUTCOMES

At the end of the kindergarten year there should be evidences of outcomes such as these:

1. Pupils have learned to know their Savior, and to fear, love, and trust in Him.

2. They have acquired a measure of independence by living away from home for short periods of the day.

3. They have been thoroughly examined physically, perhaps show improvement in health through corrections, and have learned simple health habits. Unless previously immunized against diphtheria and vaccinated against smallpox, these preventive measures may have been taken during their kindergarten year.

4. The parents have learned to understand their children better and have learned important principles of child care and child training.

5. The children have learned to meet simple problems more practically and calmly.

6. They have learned to get along better with others.

7. The children have developed meaningful concepts of life about them, together with an enlarged vocabulary, and thus have developed a foundation for reading.

8. They have grown in auditory discrimination for language improvement.

9. Through the reading of stories on the part of the teacher and the examination of books they have developed a liking for books.

10. Through practice in muscle co-ordination by means of planned or spontaneous physical activity a foundation for writing has been laid.

11. Through incidental dealing with numbers, size, and spatial relationships a foundation for arithmetic has been laid.

12. The children have learned a number of simple prayers and religious and secular songs.

### E. DAILY PROGRAM [2]

8:30— 8:40 Morning Worship.

8:40— 9:10 Bible story period. Learning of appropriate memory gems: Hymns, prayers, Bible texts.

9:10—9:30 Self-chosen activity: Play with apparatus or toys, clay modeling, painting, picture books, and the like.

9:30— 9:40 Recess and toilet. Washing hands, preparation for lunch.

9:40— 9:55 Luncheon period: Milk or fruit, table manners, pleasant conversation.

9:55—10:00 Rest period.

10:00—10:30 Conversation: Discussion of health habits, nature study, safety, and the like.

10:30—11:00 Music and language: Stories, songs, rhymes, dramatizations.

11:00—11:30 Varied group activities: Games, outdoor play, excursions.

11:30 Closing song or prayer. Dismissal.

---

2) This program is merely suggestive and will likely need modification and adaptation to local needs. Books discussing the kindergarten generally contain acceptable programs, except that most of them lack provision for religious instruction. This must be placed first on the program and less important activities omitted to provide time for it. *Living with Our Children* by Gertrude Doederlein contains time plans especially prepared for Lutheran kindergartens. See note under *Selected References*.

## Selected References

Baruch, Dorothy Walter, *Parents and Children Go to School.* Scott, Foresman and Co., 1939.

Doederlein, Gertrude, *Living with Our Children.* Minneapolis: Augsburg Publishing House, 1941.

Doederlein, Gertrude, Art Packets for *Living with Our Children.* Packet No. 1 and Packet No. 2. Augsburg, 1941.

Foster, Joesphine, and Headley, Neith E., *Education in the Kindergarten.* American Book Co., 1936.

Froebel, F., *Pedagogics of the Kindergarten.* D. Appleton and Co., 1895.

Juvenile Literature Catalog. Concordia Publishing House.

Bulletins dealing with the kindergarten. U. S. Office of Education, Washington, D. C.

State, local, or District Course of Study.

### Notes on Selected References

Miss Doederlein is the kindergarten teacher in St. Luke's Lutheran School, Chicago, Ill. Her book is intended for fathers and mothers of small children who are interested in developing Christian character in the very young. Materials and methods are supplied. Her book contains "suggestions as to how to direct the child's activities; how to develop true appreciation of Bible stories, good pictures, books, music, poetry; how to cultivate an awareness of the love of God for him, to instill early in the child the wish and need to worship through prayer, praise, and thanksgiving." Selections of religious verse, simple songs on the level of the pre-school child, Bible stories in child language, suggestions for activities of various types, samples of time plans (daily schedules) which provide time for religious activities, and other helps are contained in the book. The Bible stories require careful evaluation on the part of the teacher, because the author has permitted her imagination rather free reign at times.

Baruch and Foster cover all phases of the kindergarten and list many references for additional reading.

Dr. Baruch stresses particularly the possibilities of parent education, as the title of her book indicates. Both volumes contain valuable lists of literature and music selections suitable for the kindergarten as well as lists of equipment required for successful operation of the kindergarten. Teachers will not go as far in the matter of sex education as Dr. Baruch suggests.

# X. THE DAILY PROGRAM

The following pages contain a variety of Daily Programs, prepared by teachers either directly connected or well acquainted with the types of schools represented, one-room, two-room, three-room, and four-room schools. A number of important considerations with respect to the Daily Program are listed below:

1. The purpose of the Daily Program is to regulate the study periods and the seat work of the pupils as well as the recitation in the various subjects.

2. The Daily Program is a guide for the pupil as well as for the teacher. For this reason it should be prominently posted.

3. The Daily Program should be followed unless there is a good reason for deviation from the time schedule.

4. The Program must be flexible enough to allow for adaptations when this becomes desirable.

5. Owing to local conditions, number and size of classes, variation in the time of opening and close of school, and other factors, it is impossible to design a program that will fit all schools. Therefore each school must study its own needs and possibilities and adapt the program accordingly.

6. While the principal is often made responsible for an adequate Daily Program in each room, study of the program needs of the entire school by the teaching staff is profitable.

7. The program of every schoolroom should be checked for possible improvement at least once a year during the vacation period.

8. In the one-room school an extraordinarily small number of pupils in a class, or high average ability of the group, may make it possible to shorten the recitation period for one class for the benefit of others who need more attention.

9. If the pastor is able and willing to take over the religious instruction in Grades 6 to 8 in the one-room school, the teacher can arrange his program for more effective work with the rest of the pupils in the most important school subject.

## APPROXIMATE TIME ALLOTMENT SCHEDULE

### One-Room School

| Subject | Daily | Weekly |
|---|---|---|
| Religion | 70 min. | 350 min. |
| Language Area | 115 min. | 575 min. |
| Arithmetic | 60 min. | 300 min. |
| Social Studies | 45 min. | 225 min. |
| Science and Health | 25 min. | 125 min. |
| Fine Arts Area | 15 min. | 75 min. |
| | 330 min. | 1,650 min. |

## TIME ALLOTMENT BY SUBJECTS AND GRADES

### One-Room School

| | Daily | Weekly |
|---|---|---|
| **Religion, 70 minutes** | | |
| Devotion | 5 min. | 25 min. |
| Bible History, or Catechism | 25 min. | 125 min. |
| Bible History, Primary Grades | 10 min. | 50 min. |
| Recitation | 20 min. | 100 min. |
| Bible Study or Church History | 10 min. | 50 min. |
| **Language Area, 115 minutes** | | |
| Reading, Grade One | 25 min. | 125 min. |
| Reading, Grade Two | 15 min. | 75 min. |
| Reading, Grade Three | 15 min. | 75 min. |
| Reading, Grades Four to Eight | 15 min. | 75 min. |
| Spelling, All Grades | 20 min. | 100 min. |
| Language, Grade Two | 5 min. | 25 min. |
| Language, Grades Three to Eight | 20 min. | 100 min. |
| **Arithmetic, 60 minutes** | | |
| Arithmetic, Grade One | 5 min. | 25 min. |
| Arithmetic, Grade Two | 10 min. | 50 min. |
| Arithmetic, Grade Three | 10 min. | 50 min. |
| Arithmetic, Grade Four | 10 min. | 50 min. |
| Arithmetic, Grade Five | 10 min. | 50 min. |
| Arithmetic, Grade Six | 10 min. | 50 min. |
| Arithmetic, Grades Seven and Eight | 5 min. | 25 min. |
| **Social Studies, 45 minutes** | | |
| Social Studies, Grades Three and Four | 10 min. | 50 min. |
| Social Studies, Grades Five and Six | 15 min. | 75 min. |
| Social Studies, Grades Seven and Eight | 20 min. | 100 min. |
| **Science and Health, 25 minutes** | | |
| Science or Health, Grades Three and Four | 10 min. | 50 min. |
| Science or Health, Grades Five to Eight | 15 min. | 75 min. |
| **Fine Arts Area, 15 minutes** | | |
| Singing, Penmanship, or Drawing | 15 min. | 75 min. |
| | 330 min. | 1,650 min. |

# The Daily Program

## One-Room School

| Time | Min. | Monday | Tuesday | Wednesday | Thursday | Friday |
|---|---|---|---|---|---|---|
| 9:00 | 5 | Devotion | Devotion | Devotion | Devotion | Devotion |
| 9:05 | 35 | — | — | Bible History and Catechism in alternate units | — | — |
| 9:40 | 20 | Memory Work | Memory Work | Memory Work | Memory Work | Memory Work |
| 10:00 | 15 | Handwriting | Music | Handwriting | Music | Handwriting |
| 10:15 | 15 | Reading, A and B. Grade 1, blackboard printing or drawing. | Reading, A and B. Group A alternate with Group B. Group not reciting prepare reading. | | — | Grades 2—4 prepare reading. |
| 10:30 | 15 | — | — | Recess | — | — |
| 10:45 | 15 | Reading, Grades 1 and 2. Divide time as needed according to individual interests. | | Need not be the same each day. Grades 3—6, arithmetic. | | Grades 7 and 8 read or study items according to individual interests. |
| 11:00 | 35 | Arithmetic. Alternate 3 with 4, and 5 with 6. | | Divide time as needed. Grades 7 and 8 prepare arithmetic lesson. | | Grades 1 and 2 reading seatwork to correlate with the new assignment or previous lesson. |
| 11:35 | 10 | Numbers, Grades 1 and 2. Grades 3—8 continue with previous assignment. | | | | — |
| 11:45 | 15 | Arithmetic, Grades 7 and 8 (combine or alternate). Grades 1 and 2 number seatwork. | | | | Grades 3—6 read or study items according to individual interests. |
| 12:00 | 60 | Noon Hour | — | — | — | — |
| 1:00 | 20 | Spelling, Grades 2—8. Use some combination and alternation plan. Grade 1, drawing or construction work. | | | | Grades not reciting prepare spelling. |
| 1:20 | 30 | Social Studies, B and C. Divide time according to requirements, and other types of profitable activities. A, prepare social studies. | | | Grades 1 and 2 writing | Church History and Bible Study (all grades) |
| 1:50 | 10 | Reading, Grade 1. Grades 2—8 continue previous assignment. | | | | |

# The Daily Program

## One-Room School

(Continued)

| Time | Min. | Monday / Tuesday / Wednesday / Thursday / Friday |
|------|------|--------------------------------------------------|
| 2:00 | 30 | *Social Studies, A. Grade 1, reading seatwork to correlate with assignment or previous lesson. Grade 2, reading seatwork and study reading. Grades 3—6 prepare social studies according to previous assignment. |
| 2:30 | 15 | Recess |
| 2:45 | 15 | Reading, Grades 3 and 4. Divide time as needed. Grade 1, silent reading (picture reading during first months). Grades 5—8, general study period. Prepare reading. |
| 3:00 | 10 | Reading, Grade 2. Grade 1, blackboard printing, or sentence building. Grades 3—8 prepare language or science. |
| 3:10 | 15 | Language, A and B. Alternate B with A. The group not reciting has definite language assignment. Grades 1—4, language seatwork or construction work. Grades 3 and 4 may read supplementary materials. |
| 3:25 | 15 | Language, C and D. Alternate C with D and divide time as needed. The group not reciting has definite language assignment. Grades 5—8 prepare science or health. |
| 3:40 | 20 | Art, all grades. **Science, A and B. Alternate A with B. Group not reciting prepares science. Grades 3 and 4, silent reading period, or art assignment. Grades 1 and 2, writing period and sand table assignment. |
| 4:00 | | Closing |

Note: A represents Grades 7 and 8; B Grades 5 and 6; C Grades 3 and 4; D Grades 1 and 2.

* Determine the time required to study the units of the social studies (history, geography, and civics) and divide the time accordingly.

** The health units are included in the science area.

## The Daily Program — Morning

### Grades 5—8

| Time | Min. | Monday | Tuesday | Wednesday | Thursday | Friday |
|---|---|---|---|---|---|---|
| 9:00 | 5 | Devotion | Devotion | Devotion | Devotion | Devotion |
| 9:05 | 35 | Religion | Religion | Religion | Religion | Religion |
| 9:40 | 20 | Memory Work | Memory Work | Memory Work | Memory Work | Memory Work |
| 10:00 | 30 | Language, A; B, prepare lang. | Language, B; A, prepare lang. | Remedial Language Work; Pupil's choice | Language, A; B, prepare lang. | Language, B; A, prepare lang. |
| 10:30 | 15 | | | Recess | | |
| 10:45 | 15 | Reading, 5 | Word Study, 5 | Reading, 5; Grades 6, 7, 8 prepare arithmetic | Check Silent R., 5 | Reading, 5 |
| 11:00 | 15 | Arithmetic, 8 | Arithmetic, 8 | Arithmetic, 8; Grades 5, 6, 7 prepare arithmetic | Arithmetic, 8 | Arithmetic, 8 |
| 11:15 | 15 | Arithmetic, 7 | Arithmetic, 7 | Arithmetic, 7; Grades 5, 6, 8 prepare arithmetic | Arithmetic, 7 | Arithmetic, 7 |
| 11:30 | 15 | Arithmetic, 6 | Arithmetic, 6 | Arithmetic, 6; Grades 5, 7, 8 prepare arithmetic | Arithmetic, 6 | Arithmetic, 6 |
| 11:45 | 15 | Arithmetic, 5 | Arithmetic, 5 | Arithmetic, 5; Grades 6, 7, 8 prepare arithmetic | Arithmetic, 5 | Arithmetic, 5 |
| 12:00 | 60 | | | Noon Hour | | |

## The Daily Program — Afternoon
### Grades 5—8

| Time | Min. | Monday | Tuesday | Wednesday | Thursday | Friday |
|---|---|---|---|---|---|---|
| 1:00 | 10 | Church History | Bible Reading | Church History | Bible Reading | Church History |
| 1:10 | 20 | Literature, 8<br>Silent Reading, 7 | Literature, 7<br>Silent reading, 8 | Literature, 8<br>Silent reading, 7 | Literature, 7<br>Silent reading, 8 | Check Silent R.<br>7 and 8 |
| | | | Grade 5 prepare reading. Grade 6, spelling | | | |
| 1:30 | 15 | Reading, 6 | Word Study, 6<br>Grade 5 prepare spelling; | Reading, 6<br>7 and 8 study geography, | Check Silent R.<br>history, or civics as needed | Reading, 6 |
| 1:45 | 25 | Civics, A<br>Study period, B<br>Pupil's choice | Geography, A<br>B, study geography | Geography, B<br>A, study geography | Geography, A<br>B, study geography | Geography, B<br>A, study geography |
| 2:10 | 10 | Spelling, B | Spelling, B | Spelling, B<br>Grades 7 and 8 prepare their spelling | Spelling, B | Spelling, B |
| 2:20 | 10 | Spelling, A | Spelling, A<br>Grades 5 and 6 read or study | Spelling, A<br>according to individual needs or interests | Spelling, A | Spelling, A |
| 2:30 | 15 | | | Recess | | |
| 2:45 | 25 | History, A<br>B, study history | History, B<br>A, study history | History, A<br>B, study history | History, B<br>A, study history | History, A<br>B, Reading or study period |
| 3:10 | 30 | Art | *Science, A<br>B, study science | Science, B<br>A, study science | Science, A<br>B, study science | Science, B<br>A, study science |
| 3:40 | 20 | Music | Handwriting | Music | Handwriting | Music |
| 4:00 | | | | Closing | | |

Note: A represents grades seven and eight. B represents grades five and six. The subject materials of the grades are to be alternated.

* Alternate the units of science and health according to the requirements of the course.

# The Daily Program
## Grades 1—4

| Time | Min. | Grade 1 | Grade 2 | Grade 3 | Grade 4 |
|------|------|---------|---------|---------|---------|
| 9:00 | 5 | Devotion | Devotion | Devotion | Devotion |
| 9:05 | 35 | Religion | Religion | Religion | Religion |
| 9:40 | 20 | Memory Work | Memory Work | Memory Work | Memory Work |
| 10:00 | 10 | Writing | Writing | Writing | Writing |
| 10:10 | 20 | Reading | Study reading | Special activities in area of Religion | |
| 10:30 | 15 | - - - - - Recess - - - - - | | | |
| 10:45 | 15 | Reading seatwork | Reading | Study reading | Study reading |
| 11:00 | 20 | Handwork | Reading activity | Reading | Study reading |
| 11:20 | 20 | Number seatwork | Arithmetic activity | Reading activity | Reading |
| 11:40 | 20 | Numbers | Arithmetic | Library | Library |
| | | Flexible time division | | | |
| 12:00 | 60 | - - - - Noon Hour - - - - | | | |
| 1:00 | 15 | Reading | Study reading | General study period | General study period |
| 1:15 | 15 | Reading seatwork | Reading | Study arithmetic | Study arithmetic |
| 1:30 | 30 | Library | Library | Arithmetic | Arithmetic |
| | | | | Flexible time division | |
| 2:00 | 15 | - - - - - Music - - - - - | | | |
| 2:15 | 15 | Writing | Spelling | Spelling | Spelling |
| 2:30 | 15 | - - - - - Recess - - - - - | | | |
| 2:45 | 15 | Language | Language | Prepare language | |
| 3:00 | 20 | Language activity | Language activity | Language | Language |
| 3:20 | 15 | Social Studies or Science | | Social studies activity | |
| 3:35 | 20 | Social studies activity | | Social Studies or Science | |
| 3:55 | 5 | - - - - - Closing - - - - - | | | |
| **Mondays** | | | | | |
| 3:20 | 35 | - - - - - Art - - - - - | | | |

# The Daily Program

## Grades 7 and 8

| Time | Min. | |
|------|------|---|
| 9:00 | 5 | **Devotion** |
| 9:05 | 35 | **Religion** |
| 9:40 | 20 | **Memory Work** (10 minutes each) |
| 10:00 | 15 | **Music** |
| 10:15 | 15 | **Recess** |
| 10:30 | 30 | **Language** (combined or 15 minutes each) |
| 11:00 | 45 | **History** (2) **Geography** (2) **Civics** (1)* |
| 11:45 | 15 | **Art** (3) **Handwriting** (2) |
| 12:00 | 60 | **Noon Hour** |
| 1:00 | 45 | **Science** (combined, or Grade 7, 20 min., Grade 8, 25 min.) |
| 1:45 | 30 | **Arithmetic** (15 minutes each) |
| 2:15 | 15 | **Recess** |
| 2:30 | 15 | **Arithmetic** or **Reading,** or any other subject, as needed |
| 2:45 | 30 | **Reading** (15 minutes each) |
| 3:15 | 30 | **Spelling** (15 minutes each) |
| 3:45 | 15 | **Bible Reading** (3) **Church History** (2) |
| 4:00 | | **Closing** |

* Note: Grades may be combined and History taught four days a week during the first semester, Geography the second semester. Civics may be taught one day a week the entire year. If preferred, one subject may be taught at a time until completed.

# The Daily Program

## Grades 4, 5, 6

| Time | Min. | Subject |
|------|------|---------|
| 9:00 | 5 | Devotion |
| 9:05 | 35 | Religion |
| 9:40 | 20 | Memory Work |
| 10:00 | 15 | Arithmetic, Grade 6 (4 and 5 prepare Arithmetic) |
| 10:15 | 15 | Arithmetic, Grade 5 (4 and 6 prepare Arithmetic) |
| 10:30 | 15 | Recess |
| 10:45 | 15 | Arithmetic, Grade 4 (5 and 6 prepare Arithmetic) |
| 11:00 | 15 | Reading, Grade 6 (4 and 5 prepare Reading) |
| 11:15 | 15 | Language, Grades 5 and 6 (combined class) 4 prepare Language |
| 11:30 | 15 | Language Grade 4 (5 and 6 prepare Language) |
| 11:45 | 15 | Bible Reading (3) Church History (2) |
| 12:00 | 60 | Noon Hour |
| 1:00 | 30 | Spelling, Grades 4, 5, 6 (Grades not reciting study Spelling) |
| 1:30 | 15 | Reading, Grade 5 (4 and 6 prepare Reading) |
| 1:45 | 15 | Reading, Grade 4 (5 and 6 prepare Reading) |
| 2:00 | 15 | History, Geography (Social Studies) Grade 6 4 and 5 prepare Social Studies |
| 2:15 | 15 | History, Geography (Social Studies) Grade 4 5 and 6 prepare Social Studies |
| 2:30 | 15 | Recess |
| 2:45 | 15 | History, Geography (Social Studies) Grade 5 4 and 6 prepare Social Studies |
| 3:00 | 25 | Science (including Health) Grades 5 and 6 4 prepare Science |
| 3:25 | 10 | Science, Grade 4 (5 and 6 prepare Science) |
| 3:35 | 10 | Art (1) Handwriting (4) |
| 3:45 | 15 | Art (1) Singing (4) |
| 4:00 | | Closing |

# The Daily Program

## Grades 1, 2, 3

| Time | Min. | Recitation | Study Period |
|------|------|------------|--------------|
| 9:00 | 5 | Devotion | |
| 9:05 | 30 | Bible History | |
| 9:35 | 25 | Memory Work | |
| 10:00 | 5 | Relaxation | |
| 10:05 | 5 | Health Inspection | |
| 10:10 | 20 | Reading, Grade 1 | Spelling, Grades 2 and 3 |
| 10:30 | 15 | Recess | |
| 10:45 | 15 | Singing | |
| 11:00 | 10 | Handwriting | |
| 11:10 | 15 | Numbers, Grade 1 | Reading and Workbook Grades 2 and 3 |
| 11:25 | 15 | Reading, Grade 2 | Number Work, Grade 1 |
| 11:40 | 20 | Reading, Grade 3 | Number Work, Writing Grade 2 |
| 12:00 | 60 | Noon Hour | |
| 1:00 | 15 | Spelling, Grades 2 and 3 | Reading seatwork Grade 1 |
| 1:15 | 25 | Social Studies | |
| 1:40 | 20 | Reading, Grade 1 | Number Busy Work Grade 2 Arithmetic, Grade 3 |
| 2:00 | 30 | Arithmetic, Grades 2 and 3 | Writing and Library Grade 1 |
| 2:30 | 15 | Recess | |
| 2:45 | 20 | Remedial Reading Grades 1 and 2 | Written Language Grade 3 |
| 3:05 | 20 | Language, Grade 3 | Language Workbook Grade 2 Workbook, Grade 1 |
| 3:25 | 15 | Health, Grades 1, 2, 3 | |
| 3:40 | 15 | Art, Handwork, Grades 1, 2, 3 | |
| 3:55 | 5 | Closing | |

# The Daily Program

## Grades 1 and 2

| Time | Min. | Grade 1 | Grade 2 |
|---|---|---|---|
| 9:00 | 5 | Devotion | Devotion |
| 9:05 | 30 | Bible History | Bible History |
| 9:35 | 20 | Memory Work | Memory Work |
| 9:55 | 10 | Handwriting | Handwriting |
| 10:05 | 5 | Health Inspection | Health Inspection |
| 10:10 | 20 | Reading | Study Reading |
| 10:30 | 15 | - - - - - Recess - - - - - | |
| 10:45 | 15 | Reading seatwork | Reading |
| 11:00 | 20 | Number Work | Reading activity |
| 11:20 | 20 | Complete number work (Workbook) | Arithmetic |
| 11:40 | 20 | Handwork | Arithmetic seatwork |
| 12:00 | 60 | - - - - Noon Hour - - - - | |
| 1:00 | 20 | Reading | Reading preparation |
| 1:20 | 20 | Reading seatwork | Reading |
| 1:40 | 20 | Singing | Singing |
| 2:00 | 15 | Writing | Writing |
| 2:15 | 15 | Library | Spelling |
| 2:30 | 15 | - - - - - Recess - - - - - | |
| 2:45 | 20 | Remedial Reading | Remedial Reading |
| 3:05 | 15 | Language | Prepare Language |
| 3:20 | 15 | Language activity | Language |
| 3:35 | 25 | Social Studies Science, Health | Social Studies Science, Health |
| 4:00 | | - - - - - Closing - - - - - | |

# The Daily Program

## Grades 3 and 4

| Time | Min. | Grade 3 | | Grade 4 |
|------|------|---------|---|---------|
| 9:00 | 5 | **Devotion** | | **Devotion** |
| 9:05 | 35 | **Religion** | | **Religion** |
| 9:40 | 20 | **Memory Work** | | **Memory Work** |
| 10:00 | 15 | **Handwriting** | | **Handwriting** |
| 10:15 | 15 | **Remedial Work** or **General Study Period** | | **Remedial Work** or **General Study Period** |
| 10:30 | 15 | – – – – – | **Recess** | – – – – – |
| 10:45 | 30 | **Reading** | | Preparation of Reading lesson, or silent reading |
| 11:15 | 30 | Reading seatwork, silent reading | | **Reading** |
| 11:45 | 15 | **Music** | | **Music** |
| 12:00 | 60 | – – – – | **Noon Hour** | – – – – |
| 1:00 | 20 | **Spelling** | | **Spelling** |
| 1:20 | 25 | **Arithmetic** | | Prepare Arithmetic |
| 1:45 | 20 | Prepare Arithmetic | | **Arithmetic** |
| 2:05 | 25 | **Language** * Study Language | | Study Language **Language** |
| 2:30 | 15 | – – – – – | **Recess** | – – – – – |
| 2:45 | 20 | **Social Studies** or **Science** | | Study Social Studies or Science |
| 3:05 | 25 | Study Social Studies or Science | | **Social Studies** or **Science** |
| 3:30 | 25 | Art (Tues. and Thurs.) **Library Hour** (Mon., Wed., Fri.) | | Art (Tues. and Thurs.) **Library Hour** (Mon., Wed., Fri.) |
| 3:55 | 5 | – – – – – | **Closing** | – – – – – |

* Grades 3 and 4 may alternate. Prepare assignment on day not reciting.

# The Daily Program

## Grades 5 and 6

| Time | Min. | Grade 5 | Grade 6 |
|------|------|---------|---------|
| 9:00 | 5 | Devotion | Devotion |
| 9:05 | 35 | Religion | Religion |
| 9:40 | 20 | Memory Work | Memory Work |
| 10:00 | 15 | Study Science | Science |
| 10:15 | 15 | Science | Study Arithmetic |
| 10:30 | 15 | – – – – – Recess | – – – – – |
| 10:45 | 20 | Study Arithmetic | Arithmetic |
| 11:05 | 25 | Arithmetic | Study Reading |
| 11:30 | 15 | Bible Study (3)<br>Church History (2) | Bible Study (3)<br>Church History (2) |
| 11:45 | 15 | Music | Music |
| 12:00 | 60 | – – – – Noon Hour | – – – – |
| 1:00 | 20 | Study Reading | Reading |
| 1:20 | 20 | Reading | Study Geography |
| 1:40 | 15 | Study Geography | Geography |
| 1:55 | 15 | Geography | Study Spelling<br>or Language |
| 2:10 | 10 | Study Spelling | Spelling |
| 2:20 | 10 | Spelling | Study Language |
| 2:30 | 15 | – – – – – Recess | – – – – |
| 2:45 | 15 | Study Language | Language |
| 3:00 | 15 | Language | Study History |
| 3:15 | 15 | Study History | History |
| 3:30 | 15 | History | Study Science |
| 3:45 | 15 | Penmanship (2) Art (3) | Penmanship (2) Art (3) |
| 4:00 | | – – – – – Closing | – – – – |

# The Daily Program

## Grades 7 and 8

| Time | Min. | Grade 7 | Grade 8 |
|---|---|---|---|
| 9:00 | 5 | Devotion | Devotion |
| 9:05 | 35 | Religion | Religion |
| 9:40 | 20 | Memory Work | Memory Work |
| 10:00 | 30 | Prepare Science or Health<br>Science | Science or Health<br>Prepare Arithmetic |
| 10:30 | 15 | - - - - - Recess | - - - - - |
| 10:45 | 45 | Prepare Arithmetic<br>Arithmetic | Arithmetic<br>Prepare Literature |
| 11:30 | 15 | Bible Study (3)<br>Church History (2) | Bible Study (3)<br>Church History (2) |
| 11:45 | 15 | Music | Music |
| 12:00 | 60 | - - - - Noon Hour | - - - - |
| 1:00 | 40 | Prepare Literature<br>Literature | Literature<br>Prepare Geography |
| 1:40 | 30 | Prepare Geography<br>Geography | Geography<br>Prepare Spelling<br>or Language |
| 2:10 | 20 | Prepare Spelling<br>Spelling | Spelling<br>Prepare Language |
| 2:30 | 15 | - - - - - Recess | - - - - - |
| 2:45 | 30 | Prepare Language<br>Language | Language<br>Prepare History<br>or Civics |
| 3:15 | 30 | Prepare History or Civics<br>History: Civics | History: Civics<br>Prepare Science |
| 3:45 | 15 | Penmanship (2) Art (3) | Penmanship (2) Art (3) |
| 4:00 | | - - - - - Closing | - - - - - |

# GENERAL COURSE OF STUDY

### for

# LUTHERAN ELEMENTARY SCHOOLS

---

## SUPPLEMENT

# Lutheran Elementary Schools

## HISTORY

The Lutheran elementary school as well as popular education in general had its source in the conviction of Dr. Martin Luther and like-minded contemporaries that the education of the masses is a necessity for the welfare and freedom of a people, and for the perpetuation of the great institutions of God for such welfare and freedom — the home, the Church, and the state. As little as Luther would countenance churches and schools that purveyed impure doctrine, so little would he countenance a popular education that is wholly secularized or unchristian. "I would certainly advise no one," he said, "to place his child where the Word of God does not rule; for everything must perish that does not pursue the Word of God unceasingly." Luther cared little whether schools were called Lutheran; in fact, he wanted no church or school to be named after him; but he insisted that schools, both higher and lower, should be Christian schools and their teaching in accord with the Bible.

With its beginning in the Reformation, more than four hundred years ago, the Lutheran school has followed Lutheranism the world over: To Austria, Hungary, Sweden, Norway, Denmark, Russia, Finland, Iceland, Australia, Canada, the United States, South America, and perhaps others; in recent decades it has also spread to China, India, and Africa. It exists among Negroes, Mexicans, and other nationalities in our own country. The first Lutheran school to be established on American soil was French (1564), the second Swedish (1638).

Since the discovery of America by Columbus, 450 years have passed; since the first permanent English settlement, 335 years; since the establishment of the first Lutheran school by the Swedes in Delaware, over 300 years; since the establishment of the American public schools, a little over 100 years. Thus the Lutheran and other parochial and private schools antedate the public schools by more than 200 years.

When the Salzburgers came to Georgia in 1734, uniting with the colony of General Oglethorpe, they immediately established a Christian school for their children and in time built up a system of schools. John Adam Treutlen, the first governor of Georgia, was a product of one of these schools.

Henry Melchior Muehlenberg, the "patriarch of the Lutheran Church in America," who arrived in Pennsylvania in 1742, was instrumental in organizing hundreds of churches and schools. His sons, Frederick, Henry, and Peter, all of whom played important parts in the Revolutionary War, received their early training in Lutheran parochial schools.

Lutheran schools of Scandinavian, German, and Dutch origin flourished in New York, Pennsylvania, Delaware, New Jersey, Maryland, the Carolinas, Virginia, and Georgia in the early days of American history. They date back to colonial days and form an integral part of the history of our country.

The elementary schools of the Evangelical Lutheran Synod of Missouri, Ohio, and Other States (Missouri Synod) date back to the decade between 1830 and 1840, when a number of Lutheran congregations were organized in Midwestern States and established Christian schools for their children. The first of these schools are older than the public school systems in most States. Among these early schools still in operation are Immanuel, Cole Camp, Missouri (1834); Zion, Addison (Bensenville), Illinois (1837); St. Paul's, Fort Wayne, Indiana (1837); St. John's, Marysville, Ohio (1839); the schools established by the Saxon immigrants in St. Louis and in Perry County, Missouri, in 1839; and those established by the Bavarian Lutherans in the Saginaw Valley in Michigan in 1845. The oldest school in the Missouri Synod is that of St. Matthew's, New York. This congregation was established in 1664 under a charter granted by Governor Nicolls and joined the Synod in 1886. Its school has been maintained uninterruptedly since 1753.

## STATISTICS (MISSOURI SYNOD)

Statistics for 1940 list 1,259 schools, 71,151 pupils, and 2,247 teachers. Nearly 9,000 of the pupils are from non-Lutheran homes. These figures do not include the number in foreign mission fields, but only those of the United States, Canada, and South America. They divide as follows:

United States _____ 1,123 schools — 66,679 enrollment
Canada _____ 13 schools — 306 enrollment
Argentina _____ 24 schools — 804 enrollment
Brazil _____ 99 schools — 3,668 enrollment

## STATISTICS: OTHER LUTHERAN BODIES, 1940

|  | Schools | Enrollment | Teachers |
|---|---|---|---|
| Joint Synod of Wisconsin _____ | 150 | 10,083 | 309 |
| Norwegian Synod _____ | 9 | 193 | 9 |
| Slovak Synod _____ | 5 | 224 | 5 |
| Colored Missions _____ | 43 | 2,440 | 56 |
| American Lutheran Church (1939) _____ | 34 | 1,942 | 68 |

## TEACHER TRAINING

Plans to begin teacher training at the log cabin college in Perry County, Mo., in 1843, failed to materialize. Systematic Lutheran teacher training in America was begun in 1846, when Dr. Wm. Sihler and Pastor Wm. Loehe established a seminary for pastors and teachers at Fort Wayne, Indiana. In 1855 a separate teacher-training seminary was opened at Milwaukee, Wisconsin, in which six enrolled the first year. Two years later this institution was combined with that at Fort Wayne, and in 1864 the teachers' seminary was transferred to Addison, Illinois, where it remained until 1913.

Today the Missouri Synod maintains two teachers' colleges with full high-school and college courses — one at River Forest, Illinois, and the other at Seward, Nebraska. All but a small percentage of the teachers are graduates of these institutions and as such are eligible for State certification. They are mostly men who have chosen teaching as their lifework. This makes for a stable teaching force. For the professional growth of teachers, District and local conferences are provided, and the teachers' colleges conduct summer schools. Also the theological students in the seminaries at St. Louis, Mo., and Springfield, Ill., receive some pedagogical training, because ministerial candidates often serve temporarily as supply teachers and some of the pastors in small parishes are called upon to teach in the parochial schools of their congregations. In 1940, 211 teaching pastors, 58 ministerial candidates, and 34 ministerial students were active as teachers in parochial schools.

The teachers of the Joint Synod of Wisconsin receive their training at Dr. Martin Luther College, New Ulm, Minnesota; those of the Norwegian Synod at Bethany Lutheran College, Mankato, Minnesota.

## MAINTENANCE

The Lutheran schools are parochial schools in the full sense of the term, since they are established and maintained by congregations by means of the freewill offerings of the members. There are a few interparish schools, and there seems to be a growing tendency toward this arrangement, especially in some of the larger Lutheran centers.

## SUPERVISION

Locally the Lutheran school is supervised by the pastor and the congregational Board of Education.

The Synod is divided into thirty-two Districts, which again are subdivided into circuits. The Circuit Visitor, who is elected to his office by the synodical District, supervises not only the congregations, but also the schools in his circuit.

Each of the Districts has its own Board of Christian Education. Nine of the larger Districts have full-time superintendents, who visit the schools and promote Christian education in general.

In Districts that have no superintendent the schools are periodically visited by members of the Board of Education or by special school visitors appointed by the Board, who work in conjunction with the Circuit Visitor.

The Synod itself elects a general Board of Christian Education and employs a full-time Secretary of Schools and an assistant.

## PUBLICATIONS

The Synod, through Concordia Publishing House, St. Louis, Missouri, publishes all the religious books used in the schools and some other texts. Textbooks from other sources are carefully evaluated, and only modern books are introduced. Professional books, curriculum studies, and educational tracts, as well as the *News Service,* a monthly promotional bulletin, are published in the interest of Lutheran schools.

The *Lutheran School Journal,* a professional magazine for teachers, has been published without interruption since September, 1865.

---

## The Call of the Teacher

*Note:* Below is reprinted the official form of the *Diploma of Vocation* which is issued to a teacher when called by a Lutheran congregation.

### DIPLOMA OF VOCATION

In the name of the Holy Trinity, God the Father, Son, and Holy Ghost. Amen.

Having called upon the Lord, our God, for guidance, and in the exercise of the authority with which He has vested His Church on earth, we

_____ Evangelical Lutheran Congregation

of _____,

in lawful meeting assembled on _____, have resolved to call a parochial school teacher. We have elected to this sacred office

Mr. _____, of _____.

Pursuant to this election, which was held in the fear of God, and with due observance of the order laid down by Him, we herewith extend to our teacher-elect this

## SOLEMN CALL

We ask our teacher-elect, for Jesus' sake to take charge of the office of parochial school teacher in our midst as speedily as practicable and faithfully to discharge the same in all its parts, in accordance with the Word of God, and so as to fulfill the detailed conditions as hereinafter specified.

We pray God and the Father of our Lord Jesus Christ to convince our teacher-elect by His Holy Spirit that the call which we herewith extend to him is a divine call, to conduct him safely into our midst, and to bless his sacred ministrations among us, to the glory of His name, to the salvation of our children's souls, and to the advancement of His glorious kingdom.

## OBLIGATIONS OF THE TEACHER

We authorize and obligate our teacher-elect to instruct the children entrusted to him in the Word of God as contained in the canonical writings of the Old and New Testaments, and professed in the confessional writings of the Lutheran Church, diligently and faithfully, basing such instruction on the Small Catechism of Dr. Martin Luther;

to teach them thoroughly also the common elementary school branches from the Christian point of view;

to maintain Christian discipline in the school, serve the congregation as an example by his Christian conduct, earnestly endeavor to live in brotherly unity with his pastor and such other teachers as may at any time be in the service of the congregation, submit to the supervision of the pastor, and by the grace of God do everything within the limits of his calling that is possible for him to do toward the upbuilding of the school and for the general advancement of the kingdom of Christ;

according as the circumstances of the congregation may require, to perform the office of organist, director of the choir, leader in young people's work, secretary of the congregation, or reader in the divine services, as specified in the letter accompanying this document.

## OBLIGATIONS OF THE CONGREGATION

On the other hand, we obligate ourselves to receive our teacher-elect as a servant of Jesus Christ unto our children, to accord him the honor and show him the love which we owe him as such, and to support his work among us with our diligent and faithful prayers;

by peaceable conduct, and in every other way possible, to render the discharge of his duties easy for him, to send our children to school both punctually and regularly, and to aid him in the maintenance of Christian discipline in school;

to provide for his decent maintenance according to our
ability, and to that end to pay him promptly and regularly a
_____ salary of _____.

_____ Evangelical Lutheran Congregation
of _____.

Signed this _____ day of _____, A. D. _____, in
the name of the congregation by its officers.

_____    _____

_____    _____

_____    _____

_____

## Policy Regarding Children of Non-Members

Two classes of children of non-members are represented in
Lutheran schools: A. Unchurched children; B. Children belonging
to other churches (other Lutheran congregations or other denominations). The policy with respect to these groups is outlined below.

### A. Unchurched Children [1]

1. Mission work by the parochial school should be materially
augmented and carried out with all the vigor at our command.

2. No undue or unwise restrictions should be placed upon the
school's mission endeavors or upon mission children and their
parents, such as

a. Discouragement of school canvasses.

b. Charging a high tuition to mission children.

c. Making school attendance dependent upon the child's decision to be confirmed Lutheran or upon his attendance at church
or Sunday school.

3. Mission children should be retained in school as long
as they

a. Submit to and accept Christian instruction and training the
same as every other pupil.

b. Do not willfully and despite proper instruction and admonition conduct themselves so as to become a menace to the
spiritual welfare of other children.

c. Give evidence, the same as other children, of progress in
their Christian education and of the hope of saving their souls.

4. A continued effort is to be made to convince these children

---

1) Outline based on Policy adopted by Synod's Board of Christian
Education, April 16, 1934.

that they should attend and support only the Church of the pure Word and unadulterated Sacraments, and to avoid all false churches and Sunday schools — the same as is done with our own children.

5. Contributions by unchurched children are to be left entirely voluntary, but the children are to be trained, the same as our own, to realize their duties toward church and school, and to contribute as a matter of conviction.

6. Congregations should look upon any added expense of such mission work as a great opportunity rather than an undesirable burden.

7. Where congregations are unable to carry alone the necessary extra expense caused by the attendance of unchurched children, synodical Districts should gladly lend their financial assistance, considering such mission expenditures money well invested.

### B. Members of Other Churches [2]

1. There must be no proselyting, and therefore children from other churches can come only unsolicited.

2. Parents belonging to other churches, but desiring to enroll their children in the Lutheran school, should be asked to gain the consent of their pastor.

3. Our responsibility begins when such children are entrusted to the school for Christian instruction and training, and this responsibility continues as long as they remain for that purpose.

4. So long as the children are not members of the Lutheran Church, they are guests in the school (Sunday school, etc.); the pastor of the church in which parents and children hold membership is their pastor; and the school's responsibility consists only in giving a Lutheran school training and all that it implies. The same principle applies to children of sister congregations, though these are of the same faith.

5. These children are held to submit to the instruction and training of the school, the same as our own children.

6. The school shall not change its character, course, discipline, or doctrinal stand in deference to such children, their parents, or their church.

7. The testimony against error and false churches shall in no way be diminished in deference to these children, or out of fear that the parents may take them out of school. Special attention, if necessary privately, shall be given children who might be affected by such testimony and would not understand. Parents should be informed of this policy at the time of enrollment.

---

2) Outline based on Policy adopted by Synod's Board of Christian Education, May 17, 1941.

8. Until we can expect it on the basis of conviction and personal decision, we should not insist that these children attend the Lutheran church services or Sunday school as a condition for school attendance. Legalistic methods are always out of order. But we certainly may and should in the proper evangelical manner seek to win such children for the truth through the one opportunity voluntarily offered us.

9. Children of other denominations shall be refused admittance to our schools, or be dismissed therefrom, on exactly the same conditions on which all other children are refused or dismissed.

10. It is fair to suggest to the parents of other denominations the per capita cost of the school as a fair freewill offering, just as it is fair to ask this of sister congregations or parents belonging to sister congregations.

11. In general, these children should be treated with the same consideration accorded the same type of children in our Sunday schools, Saturday schools, summer schools, and weekday religious instruction, or that is accorded adults that come to us for instruction while still members of other churches (or of lodges).

---

# The School Library

**Purposes**

1. To assist in teaching pupils to read.

2. To supplement, verify, or correct the textbook when that is necessary or desirable.

3. To direct pupils in the selection of reading materials for information, edification, and recreation.

4. To encourage a profitable use of leisure time.

### Suggestions for Library Equipment

1. Open shelving for books; filing cabinet for pictures and pamphlets.

*Specifications for Shelving*

| Lower Grades | Intermediate and Upper Grades |
|---|---|
| 3 feet 6 inches high (counter height) | 5 feet 2 inches to 6 feet high |
| 3 feet long | 3 feet long |
| 8 to 10 inches deep | 8 inches deep |
| 12 inches deep for magazines and picture books | 12 inches deep for magazines |
| Adjustable shelves | Adjustable shelves |
| Capacity, about 75 books | Capacity, about 125 books |

2. Library table, at least 3 by 6 feet, and at least four chairs.

*Specifications for Tables*

| Long | Round |
|---|---|
| 24 to 28 inches high | 4 to 5 feet in diameter |
| 36 inches wide | 24 to 28 inches high |
| 60 to 78 inches long | |

3. A collection of at least 500 carefully selected books, magazines, and pamphlets.

4. One approved, authentic reference encyclopedia.

5. Dictionary (Webster's *New International,* if possible, otherwise Webster's *Collegiate,* which satisfies most needs).

6. A sufficient number of Children's dictionaries (Recommended: Webster's *Elementary Dictionary,* a dictionary for boys and girls; Thorndike's *Century Junior Dictionary*).

7. At least two supplementary readers for each child in grades one to four (Science, health, social studies, citizenship, art, history).

8. Three or more Christian children's magazines (*Child's Companion, Young Lutherans' Magazine, Concordia Messenger*).

9. A children's newspaper on the order of *Current Events* or *My Weekly Reader.* (Great care is necessary in the introduction of any general children's literature. Every issue should be examined by the teacher before being made available to the children.)

10. Books in the following fields: * Religion, Church History and Missions; Civics; Science, Industry, Invention; Practical Science; Fine Arts; Literature; Geography, Travel, Nature; History, Discovery, Exploration; Biography; Fiction (including good fiction with a Christian background); Easy books for slow readers (including Bible story books); Supplementary Readers.

11. Pamphlets, pictures, and clippings properly indexed and filed.

12. Texts in the various school subjects by different authors. (These are separate from the main library and may be kept in storage cabinets, to be used at direction of teacher.)

13. A complete cataloguing, circulation, and charging system.

## Other Suggestions

1. If no separate room is available, locate the library in an attractive corner of the schoolroom. In any case it is probably best to supply each room with a smaller library of its own.

---

* See Concordia *School Reference* and *Juvenile Literature Catalogs* for suggestions.

2. Classify books according to some practical plan, perhaps the Dewey Decimal System.

3. Discard or rebind badly worn books.

4. Secure State or Federal bulletins useful in the elementary school (List of Federal bulletins obtainable from Superintendent of Documents, Washington, D. C.).

5. Take advantage of free or inexpensive material furnished by travel and other commercial agencies (for a list of these materials see *Lutheran School Journal,* June, 1941, p. 452).

6. Co-operate with public library.

7. Take advantage of any State or county rental plan, library in County Superintendent's office, Bookmobile, or other services available.

8. Secure a specified annual appropriation for library purposes from the congregation or societies within the congregation.

9. Select books carefully for a well-balanced library.

### Selected References

American Library Association. Catalogs. and Bulletins.

Beck, G. Herm., "The Elementary-School Library." *Lutheran School Journal,* March, 1933, p. 299.

Beust, Nora E., *500 Books for Children.* Bulletin No. 11, 1939, U. S. Office of Education, Washington, D. C.

*Demcobind,* A Manual for Repairing Books. Demco Library Supplies, Madison, Wis.

*Inexpensive Books for Boys and Girls.* American Library Association, 520 N. Michigan Ave., Chicago, Ill.

*Juvenile Literature Catalog.* Concordia Publishing House.

Kammeyer, Elise, "The Library in the Elementary School." *Lutheran School Journal,* December, 1936, pp. 156—162.

Kidd, D. M., *Bookcraft.* Gaylord Bros., Inc., Syracuse, N. Y.

*Manual of Suggested Procedure for the Organization of a Small Rural School Library.* Superintendent of Public Instruction, Springfield, Ill. (It is likely that most State departments of education supply similar materials.)

*School Reference Catalog.* Concordia Publishing House.

Sears, Minne E., compiler, *Children's Catalog.* H. W. Wilson Co., 950 University Ave., New York, N. Y.

State, local, or District Course of Study.

State Reading Circle or Elementary School Library List.

State Department of Education.

# Records and Reports

## I. Need of Records from the Standpoint of the School

A. To chart the child's spiritual, social, academic, and emotional growth with a view to understanding his problems and improving the instruction.

B. To preserve important information, which without records would be lost when the pupil passes from one grade to the next.

C. To facilitate understanding and co-operation between parents and teachers for the improvement of discipline and for more effective pupil guidance.

D. To aid in finding the explanation of problem behavior, truancy, and failure in academic work.

E. To help in discovering special abilities in music, art, and the like.

F. To help identify specially gifted children, who are capable of additional work, as well as mentally slow or retarded children, who require special methods of instruction or a minimum assignment of subject matter.

G. To furnish an incentive to the teacher for developing pupil character.

H. To be able to furnish accurate information when higher schools of learning, public agencies and institutions, or employers inquire into the school history of pupils or former pupils.

## II. Need of Records and Reports from the Standpoint of the Parents

A. To inspire confidence in the teacher who is able to refer to records and report accurately on the standing of each child.

B. To supply parents with information about their children which they ought to have but often do not have.

C. To aid in providing parents with a basis for constructive development of the child.

## III. Need of Records and Reports from the Standpoint of the Pupil

A. To serve as an incentive for diligence and honest effort.

B. To indicate the direction pupils must follow for self-improvement and constructive development.

C. To make possible a follow-up in the case of physical defects that need correction.

## IV. Elements of a Good Record System

A. A good record system is comprehensive, simple, and flexible, with no essentials omitted and no useless information included. It is vital and meaningful in all its parts.

B. It is a cumulative system in which each entry adds to the developing picture of the child as a whole. It charts the progress of all phases of the child's development, intellectual, emotional, religious, social, and physical. It "is a depository of several types of information and a drawing together of usable and comparable data spread over a period of years and put into a common setting." [1]

C. It supplies not so much a record of the past as a guide for future dealings with the child.

D. It makes possible tactful and diplomatic dealing with parents who have learned that school records represent an honest effort to become intimately acquainted with the child for the purpose of assisting in his development.

E. A good record system deals principally with the positive phases of the child's growth.

F. Records and reports that serve their purpose are always in such condition that an experienced teacher can at any time determine from them the status of the school and of the individual child.

## V. Caution in the Use of Records

A. The child's welfare is always the first consideration. Therefore it is necessary to guard against misuse and misinterpretation in the case of confidential information. If it is necessary to record such information, it should be kept under lock and key.

B. Petty infringements of school regulations are never made a matter of permanent record.

C. The past should not be overemphasized. It is more constructive to take the child where he is at present and to work for improvement now and in the future.

D. Information must ordinarily not be obtained at the risk of arousing antagonism.

## VI. Types of Records

A. *Pre-school Children.* A record of the children within the congregation who are nearing school age, containing name, address, birthday, and names and church connection of both parents or guardian. In large congregations a card record may be desirable; in smaller congregations the names of the children with all necessary information may be recorded on a single sheet which is filed for ready reference.

---

1) Walter D. De Krock, "A Proposed Cumulative Record System for the Christian Schools of America." *Christian Home and School Magazine,* April, 1941, p. 8.

B. *Permanent Cumulative Record.* **This** is a permanent record of every child in school, which provides space for the following information: Name, address, birthday, name and church connection of parents or guardian, schools previously attended, date of entrance, date of leaving school and reason, attendance, punctuality, behavior, habits and attitudes, achievement, health, baptism, confirmation, scores on standardized tests, and space for unclassified data or special remarks.

The requirements of this record are adequately met by the *Eight-In-One-Record,*[2] or the *S-B Cumulative Record.*[3]

C. *Daily Pupil Record.* The daily record provides space for the names of the pupils in the class, space for recording grades of the pupils, and for keeping a record of absence and tardiness. The averages from the daily record are recorded on the permanent record quarterly or at other stated intervals.

D. *Daily Lesson Plan.* This need not be an expensive commercial record, but may be any loose-leaf book, with large ruled pages on which a record of every lesson is kept. This includes the aim of the lesson, subject matter taught, method of presentation, and assignment. This information is entered as the lesson is being planned and prepared, and later the sheets are filed as part of the permanent record of the school.

E. *Pupil's Transfer Card.* This is filled out and signed by the principal when a pupil wishes to enter another school.[4]

F. *Diploma.* This may take the form of a diploma, certificate of scholarship, or certificate of graduation.[5]

G. *Health Reports.* Health inspections are generally made by the State or City Department of Health, and the blanks recommended by these agencies are used.

H. *Reports to Parents.* The traditional formal report card indicating merely achievement in subject matter is not sufficient. Various types of reports are indicated below.

1. *Requirements of Reports.*

a. They convey objective, easily understood information about the child's progress in subject matter, social adjustment, health habits, and Christian character.

b. Not to discourage the poorly gifted child, they give credit

---

2) Klemp, E., and Huedepohl, Elmer H., *Eight-In-One Record.* Concordia Publishing House.

3) Schmieding, Alfred, and Beck, G. Herman, *S-B Cumulative Record.* Concordia Publishing House.

4) See "Concordia Pupil's Transfer." Concordia Publishing House.

5) See "Diploma." Concordia Publishing House.

for honest effort and make possible grading according to the pupil's ability.

c. They are varied in type according to the need.

d. In addition to the regular reports, a report is made to the parents at any time it would be helpful in the educational development of the child.

e. An exact record of the report is kept at school.

2. *Types.*

a. *Personal Conferences.* These constitute the ideal report. They provide for an exchange of ideas between teacher and parents and for the discussion of means and procedures whereby the child's progress and growth might be aided. Through them the teacher learns much about the background and nature of the child. These conferences are more feasible in smaller schools, but even in larger schools parents can be invited to discuss special problems concerning the child's welfare.

b. *Informal Essay-Type Report. Letters.* These can be made much more meaningful than the conventional report card. In the informal report the child is treated as an individual and judged on his own ability to perform, whereas in the formal report card he is compared with others. Some schools issue the essay-type report alternately with the formal report.

The essay-type report, or letter, contains a descriptive analysis of scholastic achievement, a statement of difficulties the child might have, and suggestions for improvement. Spiritual and social aspects of the child's character are discussed frankly yet charitably and are accompanied by suggestions to the parents for more effective training of the child, when this is necessary. The discussion centers about specific traits, not too many at a time. Space is provided on the card or letter for comment by the parents. Samples are added below.

c. *Formal Report Cards.* Formal report cards, issued at regular intervals, furnish a comparison of the child's work with that of the class, at the same time making allowance for differences in ability. They can be made more vital and individual than they have been in the past. In the measure in which that is done they will contribute toward a better understanding between parents, teacher, and child and thus assist in pointing the way toward more effective child training. A sample report is added below.

d. *Health Reports.* These are made ordinarily after examination by the school physician or nurse on such blanks as the State, city, or county health service provides.

## Samples of Informal Reports

### No. 1

............................ LUTHERAN SCHOOL

St. Louis, Mo.

Report of ............................................ Grade ............ Date ............................

To Mr. and Mrs. ............................................

*Comment on Character:* You will be glad to hear that John conducts himself as a Christian boy should. He is kind, thoughtful, and considerate of others, and it is evident that the Christian training you are giving him at home is effective. At times I observe in John a tendency toward carelessness in lesson preparation. If we pay particular attention to this weakness and insist on thoroughness and exactness in all his work at home and at school, I am sure we shall be able to help him overcome this fault.

*Comment on Scholarship:* John's work in general is satisfactory and, in some instances, above the average. He takes particular interest in history and geography and ranks among the best in the class in these subjects. His tendency toward carelessness shows itself especially in the written work in arithmetic and language, which for that reason lacks neatness and accuracy at times. I am sure it would benefit John and the school if you could find time to supervise his written home work a little more closely.

Signature of Teacher ............................................

*Comment by Parents:* ............................................

............................................................................................

Signature of Parent ............................................

No. 2

............................ LUTHERAN SCHOOL
St. Louis, Mo.

Report of ................................. Grade .......... Date .....................

To Mr. and Mrs. ......................................

*Comment on Character:* Esther is having some difficulty in adapting herself to the social life of the school. I have been trying to determine the reason, but I am not sure at this time that I have found the cause. It does seem, however, that part of the trouble is an inclination toward selfishness. Too often she insists on having her own way, and when she cannot have it, she is dissatisfied and irritable. I suggest that in her training you emphasize Christian love of the neighbor and sharing with others.

I notice also that often she looks pale and tired. Perhaps she needs more rest. A tired person is much more likely to be irritable, as we know from our own experience.

I feel quite sure that she wants to do right, and no doubt we can help her overcome her difficulties if we can find the underlying cause. Would you care to arrange for a personal conference?

*Comment on Scholarship:* Esther's work in school is entirely satisfactory. She does not rest until she knows her lessons and can always be depended upon to complete her assignments. Her perseverance is commendable.

Signature of Teacher ...............................

Comment by Parents: ..........................................

.........................................................................

Signature of Parent ...............................

## Sample Report Card, Page 1

_____ LUTHERAN SCHOOL

St. Louis, Mo.

Report of _____

Grade _____ School Year _____ _____ Date _____

_____ _____Teacher

### Aims of the School

1. _Thorough instruction in the elementary school branches._
   a. Christian doctrine and Christian life.
   b. The secular subjects in the light of God's Word.

2. _Promotion of strength and growth in faith and in holy life._
   a. Due reverence for God, His Name, and His Word.
   b. Chastity and propriety in word and deed.
   c. Christian conduct at all times, in the school and on the playground.
   d. Due respect for, and cheerful obedience to, parents, teachers, government, and other superiors.
   e. Regular church attendance.

3. _Proper social adjustment of the pupil._
   a. Christian association with fellow men.
   b. Kind, friendly, and helpful attitude toward schoolmates.
   c. Due consideration for the feelings, good name, and property of others.
   d. Orderliness about the schoolroom, building, and personal belongings.
   e. Proper conduct in room, corridors, street, and on playground.
   f. Willing and honest work.

4. _Good habits of health and safety._
   a. Realization that health is a gift of God which must be appreciated and guarded.
   b. Cleanliness and neatness of body and clothing.
   c. Good sitting, standing, and walking posture.
   d. Obedience to health and safety authorities and rules.

*     *     *

"The fear of the Lord is the beginning of wisdom." Psalm 111:10.

(1)

## Sample Report Card, Page 2

### Habit and Attitude Report

Below are listed attitudes and habits for which pupils should strive. If there is no mark, this indicates that so far as the teacher can determine, the child is making satisfactory progress in the development of the attitude or habit in question. A check ( √ ) indicates unsatisfactory attitudes or behavior. If a child continues to be unsatisfactory in any habit or attitude, parents are urged to consult the teacher.

| Quarter | 1st | 2d | 3d | 4th |
|---|---|---|---|---|
| 1. Manifests reverent attitude toward sacred things: Word of God, divine services, etc. | | | | |
| 2. Respects parents, pastor, teachers, and all constituted authority, giving prompt and willing obedience | | | | |
| 3. Conducts himself as a Christian, also while not under the direct supervision of the teacher, in the classroom, cloakroom, on the playground, and on way home from school | | | | |
| 4. Respects the rights and property of others | | | | |
| 5. Is alert and interested in the work at hand | | | | |
| 6. Contributes ideas and suggestions in group work | | | | |
| 7. Is courteous, helpful, mannerly, co-operative | | | | |
| 8. Is active physically | | | | |
| 9. Works independently | | | | |
| 10. Displays initiative for worth-while undertakings | | | | |
| 11. Participates in class discussion | | | | |
| 12. Is regular and punctual in his school attendance | | | | |
| 13. Works quietly without disturbing others | | | | |

(2)

# Sample Report Card, Page 3

## Studies

| Quarter | 1st | 2d | 3d | 4th |
|---|---|---|---|---|
| Religion | | | | |
| Memory Work | | | | |
| Church History | | | | |
| Reading | | | | |
| Language | | | | |
| Spelling | | | | |
| Arithmetic | | | | |
| Primary Social Studies | | | | |
| Geography | | | | |
| History | | | | |
| Civics | | | | |
| Health and Safety | | | | |
| General Science | | | | |
| Music | | | | |
| Art | | | | |
| Handwriting | | | | |

## Attendance and Punctuality

| | | | | |
|---|---|---|---|---|
| Days in Quarter | | | | |
| Days Absent | | | | |
| Times Tardy | | | | |

### Key

A. Excellent Work              D. Below Average

B. Work Above Average          F. Failure

C. Average Work

(3)

## Sample Report Card, Page 4

### To Parents and Guardians

This folder contains two reports. The first (page 2) indicates the progress of your child in Christian living and in work and study habits. This is the more important part of the report, and therefore you will give it particular attention. For this part of the child's training and development the home and the school must co-operate and share the responsibility.

The second part of the report (page 3) covers the regular studies and indicates the efforts and attainment of your child.

Please examine this report thoroughly, sign it, and return promptly. Your signature does not indicate approval, but merely that you have inspected the report. If progress does not seem satisfactory, or if you have any questions concerning the report or the progress of your child, please confer with the teacher at a time when classes are not in session.

You are cordially invited to visit the school at any time.

### Parent's Signature

1st Quarter ........................................................................................

Comment ........................................................................................

2d Quarter ........................................................................................

Comment ........................................................................................

3d Quarter ........................................................................................

Comment ........................................................................................

4th Quarter ........................................................................................

Comment ........................................................................................

*Note:* Your child will work in Grade ....... during the next school year.

(4)

## VII. Concordia Records

1. Concordia Pupils' Roster and Record Card.
2. "K and H" Eight-in-One Record.
3. S-B Cumulative Record.
4. Nuoffer Class Records.
5. "K and H" Report Card.
6. Concordia School Report Card.
7. "Let us Co-operate" Warning Blanks.
8. Concordia Pupil's Transfer.
9. Diploma or Certificate of Scholarship.

### Selected References

De Kock, Walter D., "Proposed Cumulative Record System for the Christian Schools of America." *Christian Home and School Magazine,* March, 1941, p. 16; April, 1941, p. 8.

Evans, R. O., "Trends and Issues in Reporting to Parents on the Welfare of the Child in School." Teachers College, Bureau of Publications, Columbia University, 1938.

Foreman, Anna B., "A Report Card for Evaluating the Progress of the Whole Child." *Elementary School Journal,* November, 1940, pp. 195 to 205.

Hamalainen, Arthur E., "Evaluating Growth of Individual Children." *Elementary School Journal,* January, 1941, pp. 359—367.

Kraeft, W. O., "Records." *The Lutheran Teacher's Handbook,* pp. 105—125.

Kramer, A. H., "School Records and Reports." *Lutheran School Journal,* November, 1929, pp. 121, 122.

"Records and Reports." *Research Bulletin* of the National Education Association, Vol. V (1927), No. 5.

Voth, Walther H., "Informal Report Cards." *Lutheran School Journal,* December, 1938, pp. 156—159.

State, local, or District Course of Study.

---

# Educational Guidance

Educational guidance is not a new, mysterious technique to be performed by an expert for the classroom teacher. Guidance is rather implied in nearly everything the classroom teacher does in behalf of his pupils, and it can therefore not be separated from teaching. Pupils have been guided ever since there have been parents and teachers. But guidance has been emphasized increasingly in the recent past, and a better understanding of guidance techniques may have been developed.

A consecrated Christian teacher who understands child nature and loves children has the fundamental qualifications of a guidance expert for elementary school purposes. With an adequate knowledge of his pupils and their background, and a familiarity with certain necessary records and techniques, he will be able to point many a child to a happier, fuller, and more useful life. This is the purpose of guidance.

## Requirements for an Adequate Guidance Program

1. A Christian teacher who loves children, who understands child nature and child needs, and who knows how to apply the techniques of guidance.

2. Interest in the temporal and spiritual welfare of every pupil in school.

3. Close and sympathetic observation of pupil habits and behavior.

4. A personal record of every pupil.

5. Patient and sympathetic dealing with pupils who are in need of guidance.

6. Visits in the homes of pupils and tactful dealing to secure the continued co-operation of parents.

## Understanding the Pupil

Most pupil difficulties and advantages arise in the areas of

A. Family and cultural Background.

B. Health and physical Development.

C. Personal and social Development.

D. Attendance and scholarship record.

E. Religious and moral attitudes (pupil behavior).

Below are listed important points of information in these areas. An attempt is made to indicate how they contribute to an understanding of the child's difficulties and how the teacher may try to help solve the child's problems.

It will be seen that the regular school records and reports contain much information useful for guidance purposes.

*Note:* The following outline on guidance is based on M. W. Darlington, *A Teacher's Handbook for the Self-Appraisal of a Rural Elementary School.* University of Nebraska. Lincoln, Nebr. It has been adapted for Lutheran schools with the permission of the compilers.

## A. FAMILY AND CULTURAL BACKGROUND

1. Name, sex, birth date of pupil. (Information needed for classification of pupil; for records and reports.)

2. Full name of each parent or guardian. (Information needed for records and reports.)

3. Address and telephone number of parents or guardian. (Information needed in cases of emergency.)

4. Race, nationality, birthplace of parents, church affiliation. (Information needed for an understanding of pupil's background.)

5. Citizenship, economic and social status, and occupation of parents. Information may be useful in the following ways:

a. Amount of supplies the pupil can be expected to buy.

b. Understanding why a pupil borrows or misappropriates materials.

c. Reason for close supervision of school supplies, lunch baskets, school lunch supplies, play activities.

d. Special care to avoid ridicule of meager lunches.

e. Generous aid to poorer pupils if school provides lunch.

f. Friction between families in the community may be the cause for undesirable acts on the part of pupils in the schoolroom or on the playground.

g. May indicate to the teacher how he may appeal to the interest of the pupil.

h. May give the teacher an understanding of the parents' or child's attitudes toward society.

i. May indicate to the teacher how the home may be utilized in the education of the pupil, information of educational value that may be secured from parents, articles they can exhibit either at school or in their homes.

6. Marital status of parents: Whether living together happily or unhappily, divorced, separated, remarried, both parents living, or whether dominated by grandparents or other relatives.

a. May be the cause of pupil's maladjustment, worries, fears, outbursts, coverups, or his withdrawing from the school group.

b. May affect home responsibilities of pupil, such as cooking, caring for younger brothers or sisters, chores of various kinds. These duties may interfere with school work.

c. May be the cause of the pupil's peculiar attitudes toward the home, school, teacher, and others.

d. Makes it important for the teacher to compensate as much as possible for the child's difficulties at home by special kindness, encouragement, and comfort.

7. Number of older or younger brothers and sisters.

a. Will be an additional interest center to be used by the teacher.

b. May color the pupil's attitude toward other children, the school, the teacher.

c. Treatment he receives from brothers or sisters may affect his disposition, character, and habits.

d. May determine the amount of time and attention the pupil receives at home, also the amount of time and assistance in the activities of the school the teacher can expect of the parents.

e. If the pupil is the only child, he may have special difficulty in getting along with other children. The teacher will seek home co-operation to overcome such difficulty.

8. Marked talents or accomplishments of members of the family or relatives.

a. May be a resource that the teacher can use in school.

b. May be used as an incentive for the pupil.

c. May help the teacher to understand certain interests and aptitudes of the pupil.

9. Health status of the family.

a. May be cause of pupil's worry or undue responsibility.

b. May be cause of poor scholarship of pupil.

c. Because of illness or physical handicap of a member of the family the pupil may be subjected to many limitations or problems.

d. May affect the pupil's happiness or outlook on life. Sympathetic attitude on the part of the teacher and comfort from the Word of God will make it easier for pupil to bear his trials.

e. There may be infectious or contagious diseases present in the family. See if proper steps for correction are being taken.

10. Attitude of family toward school.

a. May influence pupil's school achievement.

b. May be cause of pupil's absence or tardiness.

c. May account for negative attitude toward religious instruction, toward teacher, school, or other pupils. Every effort should be made to solve difficulty.

11. Modern conveniences in the home.

a. May determine the health rules the pupil can practice.

b. May affect the amount of time he can devote to home study.

c. May account for the pupil's personal cleanliness and dress.

d. May account for the pupil's lack or abundance of enthusiasm and ambition.

e. May account for the child's maladjustment at school.

12. Cultural and educational resources of the home: Library, Christian and other good literature, radio, musical instruments.

   a. May account for the pupil's rich, or poor, background.

   b. May account for pupil's contributions to school activities.

   c. Will determine use of home materials in school.

   d. May determine teacher's suggestions to pupil concerning his leisure time.

   e. May determine type of home activities the teacher can expect.

   f. Gives teacher an idea as to the child's tastes, possible hobbies, interests, and ways of doing things.

13. Plans of the parents for pupil's future.

   a. May be basis of consultation between teacher and parents.

   b. Gives teacher an opportunity to discuss tactfully with parents the pupil's limitations and possibilities in a profession or occupation.

   c. May be used to develop pupil interest in school.

   d. May give the teacher an idea why pupil acts as he does.

14. Family activities such as excursions, trips to town, movies, visits, fairs, membership in, and attendance at, community organizations.

   a. Gives teacher an idea of pupil's experience and background.

   b. May be the cause of pupil being sleepy, irritable, etc.

   c. May determine pupil's interests.

## B. HEALTH AND PHYSICAL DEVELOPMENT

The greatest value of this type of information is that it provides the teacher with a basis for guiding the pupil's health program in school, for co-operating with the home in all health habits and practices, and for determining the school load and pressure, the pupil's limitations for concentrated study, and the type of school activities he may undertake.

1. Height and weight.

   If the child is either seriously underweight or overweight, the teacher should discuss the problem and corrective measures with the parents.

2. Vision.

   a. Make necessary adjustment for the pupil with respect to shades, position of pupil's desk, distance from maps and blackboard, lighting, and periods of rest to accommodate eye deficiency.

   b. Select reading material with clear, large print.

    c. On dark days, if proper lighting is unavailable, the teacher may lessen the amount of extensive reading and arrange for other activities.

    d. Watch for such symptoms as bloodshot, watery eyes; crossed or squinting eyes; twitching and continual blinking; frowning; headaches; and for such reactions as unnatural holding of reading material, lack of natural interest, and generally poor school achievement.

    e. The teacher should talk with parents about possible eye defects and advise them to take child to an eye specialist.

    f. Be alert to discover teasing of child with poor vision.

3. Hearing.

    a. The teacher should learn to recognize the pupil's ear defects by these symptoms: running ears, complaints of earache; inattentiveness, asking for repetitions, holding head to one side, extremely loud talking, poor scholastic record.

    b. Knowledge of hearing difficulty enables the teacher to provide a better seating position for the child.

    c. The teacher should protect pupil susceptible to ear trouble against window drafts and make sure that he dresses properly for outdoor play.

    d. The teacher makes such adjustments as plain lip movements, clear enunciation, speaking directly to pupil with hearing difficulty.

    e. The teacher should talk with parents about possible ear defects of the child and encourage them to take child to doctor.

4. Speech defects.

    a. Speech defects of a physical nature cannot be remedied by the teacher. They require the services of a specialist in that field.

    b. Such speech mannerisms as baby talk, loud or shrill talking, peculiar pronunciation, and careless enunciation may often be corrected by the teacher's sympathetic and patient understanding of the speech difficulty, together with continuous work with the pupil.

    c. In cases of stuttering or stammering, the teacher may lessen the pupil's tendency by avoiding undue excitement or tension in the pupil's activities, and by creating opportunity for a happy, calm pupil participation in activity. He will not countenance ridicule on the part of fellow pupils.

    d. The teacher may create a desire to speak correctly by setting a good example himself and by observing and encouraging good speech habits.

e. The teacher should seek the co-operation of the home in practicing good speech habits in and out of school.

5. Posture.

a. Try to discover the cause of poor posture: weariness, loss of sleep, overwork, malnutrition, excessive exercise, physical defects, sickness, carelessness, habit, ill-fitting clothes, improper seating facilities, or self-consciousness because of tallness.

b. Proceed to overcome any particular posture difficulty and enlist parents' help.

6. Physical abnormalities or deformities.

a. Keep children from teasing the afflicted person, or from overprotecting or overhelping him.

b. Make his experiences those of a normal pupil as much as possible.

c. Help the child accept his affliction as a cross from his kind and loving Father in heaven, to face reality in a natural, matter-of-fact manner, and to make the best of the situation.

7. Illness or injuries.

a. May account for poor scholastic progress or for maladjustment.

b. Make reasonable adjustments in school requirements and provide rest periods.

8. Tonsils and adenoids.

a. Bad tonsils and adenoids may be the cause of mouth breathing, habitual cough, susceptibility to colds and sore throat, and to other diseases. Condition may be such as to give pupil the appearance of dullness or inattentiveness.

b. Consult with parents for correction of condition.

9. Teeth.

a. Encourage proper care of teeth through meaningful health activities.

b. Suggest that parents provide for regular examination and care by dentist.

10. Immunizations.

Find out what vaccinations, inoculations, and diseases the pupil has had and, if necessary, plan a health program. In many cases, State or city health departments take care of the needs.

11. In general, instill in the pupil a desire for healthful living.

## C. PERSONAL AND SOCIAL DEVELOPMENT

The information under this topic will give the teacher an insight into the habits and behavior of the child, both in school and outside of school.

Although the parents are responsible for the pupils outside of school hours, the teacher is also concerned, because every experience of the child may affect him. The teacher should encourage and utilize in the regular school program as many of the child's out-of-school experiences as possible. If the teacher discovers undesirable activities or wasteful use of time on the part of a pupil, he may tactfully suggest and perhaps help to create an interest in desirable activities.

*Interest Inventories* may help to discover guidance possibilities.

1. Marked interests.

   Give encouragement and correlate with school work.

2. Special talents: Musical, artistic, athletic, inventive, literary, dramatic.

   a. Provide opportunities for use of talents.

   b. Correlate with other work.

3. Voluntary reading.

   a. Encourage voluntary reading.

   b. Guide it into desirable channels: This, for the Christian child, means to include Christian and other good literature.

   c. Utilize it for school activities.

4. Participation in home and school activities.

   a. If not a participant, find the reason.

   b. Provide opportunities for participation.

   c. Observe if pupil is temperate in participation.

5. Educational and vocational intentions of older children.

   a. May account for types of pupil interests.

   b. May be used as basis for advising pupils if teacher recognizes limitations and possibilities of pupils.

6. Employment of pupils outside of school hours: Home chores with or without pay, nature of other employment, time required, use of money earned, etc.

   a. May account for the fact that pupil accepts responsibility, is dependable, honest, thrifty, careful, and that he finishes tasks he begins.

   b. May have a direct bearing on pupil's school work, or may be the cause of his lack of interest, of being tired, etc. Investigate, and if outside work interferes, consult with parent.

   c. May be the basis for child interest in school in general.

7. Use of leisure time: amount given to play, reading, hobbies, movies, radio, etc.

a. May indicate special interests.

b. In the case of pupils making undesirable use of leisure time or not knowing how to use it, create some interests which may help to develop a beneficial use of leisure.

8. Playmates or companions.

a. Encourage companionship with Christian boys and girls.

b. Impress the Word of God "My Son, if sinners entice thee, consent thou not," Prov. 1:10, or similar passages.

c. Foster social situations which will be conducive to the formation of friendships between Christian children.

## D. ATTENDANCE AND SCHOLARSHIP RECORD

The grading systems and remarks on the records of pupils differ widely among teachers. Do not accept reports of former teachers as a blueprint of the child. However, the marks and grades indicate to some extent the pupil's past behavior and achievement and occupy an important place in pupil's guidance.*

1. Attendance and tardiness record with reasons for excessive absence or tardiness.

May lead to an understanding of causes and to steps for overcoming difficulties in this area.

2. Complete academic record.

a. Consists of achievement and diagnostic tests in basic subjects, records and reports, and teacher opinions and judgments.

b. May help in proper grade placement.

c. May aid in planning pupil's individual work.

## E. RELIGIOUS AND MORAL ATTITUDES (PUPIL BEHAVIOR)

In his daily contact with the pupil the teacher has the finest opportunity for guiding religious and moral development. The daily religious instruction is the foundation upon which the Christian teacher bases his efforts in training and guidance. He seeks the wholehearted co-operation of the home. It is difficult to develop Christian moral principles in school when the spirit of the home is contrary. Guiding the religious and moral development of the child requires the utmost in sympathetic understanding, love, and patience. The teacher's own example may be more effective than his words and devices.

Proceed slowly, tactfully, and wisely in all disciplinary matters and behavior problems. By all means discuss difficulties fully and

---

* See Records and Reports, pp. 279—289.

openly with the parent and the child. Remember also that children cannot be treated alike. Find the cause of a difficulty and treat it according to Biblical and sound educational principles.

1. Family attitude toward church, school, and Sunday school.
a. This may determine the child's favorable or unfavorable attitude toward religious instruction, toward the teacher, and toward the aims of the Christian school.
b. The content of the instruction, the method and manner of instruction, the religious atmosphere of the school, and the conduct of the teacher should be such that the pupil must at least respect them.
c. Dealings with the pupil as an individual must be of a nature to convince him that the school is seeking his welfare.

2. A critical evaluation of teaching procedures and other teacher demands of the pupil.
a. Will indicate if teaching method and materials are interesting and challenging.
b. Will indicate if teacher demands are unreasonable.
c. Will indicate if individual differences of pupils are given due consideration.

3. A critical evaluation of the teacher's habits and attitudes.
a. Am I a worthy example for my pupils to imitate and follow?
b. Am I seriously concerned about the spiritual and temporal welfare of every pupil under my care?
c. Am I perfectly fair and impartial in my dealings with members of the class?

### Behavior Problems

The teacher's procedure should be preventive rather than merely remedial. "An ounce of prevention is worth a pound of cure" applies to its fullest extent here. A sympathetic understanding of the pupil's difficulties is half the battle won.

1. When pupils display outbursts of temper, stubbornness, habits of pouting and sulking.

*Possible Causes*

a. Natural sinful condition of child which has not been corrected.
b. Merely a desire or habit.
c. Find that through such actions they get their own way.
d. Discover that it is one means of getting attention.
e. A reaction against the teacher's too heavy or too severe demands.
f. A reaction due to rejection or dislike by the group.

*Possible Remedies*

a. Show him that his behavior is not in keeping with the principles of Christian love for his neighbor. Earnest application of the Word of God.

b. Ignore the pupil's outburst.

c. Make results unpleasant.

d. Give pupil deserved attention and praise when he is doing worth-while things.

e. Try to keep the pupil occupied with something pleasant and useful.

f. Tactfully endeavor to draw him into the group as an accepted member.

2. When pupils are cruel to other children or to animals.

*Possible Causes*

a. Failure to realize the sinfulness of the action.

b. A socially or intellectually inferior pupil may show a sense of superiority in this way.

c. Another method of getting attention.

d. A compensation for thwarted desires.

*Possible Remedies*

a. Application of the Fifth Commandment: "We should fear and love God that we may not hurt nor harm our neighbor." "A righteous man regardeth the life of his beast." Prov. 12:10.

b. Make clear to him how kindness toward man and beast shows itself.

c. Let him know how it might feel if the tables were turned.

d. Try to find the cause of the difficulty.

e. Try to substitute opposite interests.

3. When pupils complain constantly.

*Possible Causes*

a. Selfishness.

b. Pains or ill health.

c. Method of getting what they want.

d. Method of getting attention.

e. Copying other complaining people, perhaps at home.

f. Result of organic difficulty.

g. Reaction against a poor environment.

*Possible Remedies*

a. "Oh, give thanks unto the Lord; for He is good." Ps. 118:1.
"Call upon Me in the day of trouble." Ps. 50:15.

b. A physical examination.

c. Try to determine when the pupil may be mimicking, and get his co-operation in solving the difficulty.

d. If he complains of being ill, make him comfortable; then divert the activity to something in which the pupil is intensely interested, but do not permit the "ill" pupil to participate at this time.

e. Guide pupil in serving others.

f. Make certain that you are not overworking the pupil at school or that his homework is not too heavy or too difficult.

g. Investigate the pupil's home environment and the cause, and discuss with the parents a suitable remedy.

4. When pupils are subject to certain fears.

*Possible Causes* and *Remedies*

a. Lack of trust in God. — "Cast all your care upon Him, for He careth for you." 1 Pet. 5:7.

b. Fear of failing in school. — Help the pupil to win confidence in himself by giving him tasks within his ability. Recognize his efforts and lead other pupils to recognize them.

c. Fear of other pupils. — Have pupil play in active games with other children. Sometimes have other children invite him to show them how to do a thing, how to play a game, or to play a game with them.

d. Fear of talking in class. — Respect the pupil's attitude at first, but call upon him as soon as he raises his hand. If he does not volunteer, ask his opinion occasionally, and guide the other pupils to ask him. Take advantage of any contribution he can make from his life experiences out of school.

e. Fear of going to and from school. — "He shall give His angels charge over thee, to keep thee in all thy ways." Psalm 91:11.
If pupil merely wishes companionship, encourage others to go his way with him. Find the real cause of the fear — perhaps a dog, a tramp, or some exacting adult.

f. Fear of doing the wrong thing. — Build up the pupil's attitude of self-confidence. Be extremely sparing, kind, and charitable in your criticisms of his work or oral contributions. Recognize his accomplishments, even though they may seem small.

g. Fear of appearing before an audience. — Encourage the pupil to make a little contribution, and gradually increase his contributions. Encourage him to participate in the activities of the school at all times.

h. Fear of teacher or parents. — Show the love which God demands of both teacher and pupil. Never frighten or threaten the pupil with your authority or that of his parents. Win the pupil's confidence through kindness and sympathetic understanding. Assign him some small task connected with the administrative duties of your desk.

5. When pupils are poor losers.

a. Show them that their trouble is lovelessness and selfishness.

b. Ignore their lack of good sportsmanship.

c. Praise pupils that are good sports.

d. Place emphasis on playing for fun rather than for score or for winning.

e. Let group approval have influence.

f. Handle the situation immediately — get pupil back into game or activity as soon as possible.

g. Try to establish a slogan for the school which will make for wholesome, correct spirit.

6. When pupils are too domineering.

a. "Thou shalt love thy neighbor as thyself." Matt. 22:39. Also Matt. 7:12.

b. Ignore "show off" tactics, and guide other pupils to do the same.

c. Give him some one thing to do within his ability.

d. Provide constructive outlet for his activity.

7. When pupils are selfish.

a. "Look not every man on his own things, but every man also on the things of others." Phil. 2:4.

b. Remind pupils of the many blessings for which they should be thankful.

c. Lead pupils to see that if they will lend their things, they may also borrow from others.

d. Emphasize sharing of public property, playground equipment, and other common belongings.

e. Insist that pupils take care of what they borrow and that they return it with thanks.

8. When pupils are very restless.

a. If possible, take care of any physical defect.

b. Be sure that your teaching and the schoolwork are as interesting, challenging, and meaningful as possible.

c. Make necessary seating adjustments.

d. Be sure that the school lighting, heating, ventilation, temperature, and humidity are as good as they can be made.

e. Provide sufficient activity for the child.

f. Determine whether pupils receive proper food and sufficient sleep.

9. When the pupil daydreams or is given habitually to idleness.

a. "In the sweat of thy face shalt thou eat bread." Gen. 3:19. "Go to the ant, thou sluggard; consider her ways, and be wise." Prov. 6:6.

b. Have enough meaningful activity for both bright and slow.

c. Provide interesting and challenging schoolwork, which will keep the pupil occupied because he wants to work.

d. Try to find out what is on the pupil's mind.

10. When pupils are usually late.

a. "Whatever thy hand findeth to do, do it with thy might; for there is no work, nor device, nor knowledge, nor wisdom, in the grave whither thou goest." Eccl. 9:10.

b. Ask parents to co-operate in improving home conditions or organization.

c. Insist that all schoolwork and other materials come in promptly.

d. Practice promptness in your own activities.

11. When children lie.

a. Eighth Commandment. Point out the sinfulness of lying.

b. Find any other cause of the lying, and remove it, if possible.

c. Get pupil to realize that he must think before he acts and must take the consequences for his act.

d. Encourage the pupil to talk about his problems with any adult in whom he has confidence.

e. Encourage pupil to avoid exaggeration and to aim for exactness in all he says.

f. Be perfectly truthful and above board in all dealings with the pupils.

12. When sex problems cause difficulty.

  a. As a preventive teach the Sixth Commandment earnestly, in the fear of God.

  b. As much as possible, see that the toilets do not become places for loitering or play.

  c. Deal individually with pupils who present problems.

  d. Secure the aid of the pupil's parents when necessary.

13. Unsatisfactory behavior in general.

  a. Sin must be treated as sin at all times, according to God's Word.

  b. Correction must be based on Biblical principles and on sound educational procedure. The two never clash.

  c. Prayer should be utilized. The teacher praying for and with his pupils for strength to do what is right and for God's mercy when sin has been committed, utilizes a power in guidance which is found in no school but a Christian school.

### Selected References

Buszin, P. T., "The Faith Life of Our Pupils." *Lutheran School Journal*, February, 1941, p. 248.

Darlington, M. W., *A Teacher's Handbook for the Self-Appraisal of a Rural Elementary School*. University of Nebraska. Lincoln, Nebr.

Dobberfuhl, M. E., "Some Prerequisites for Individual Soul Service." *Lutheran School Journal*, February, 1934, p. 241.

Edwards, S., "The Art of Guidance." *Journal of Religious Instruction*, February, 1942, p. 527.

Illinois Department of Education, *Educational Press Bulletin*, September, 1941, entire issue.

Jones, Arthur J., *Principles of Guidance*. McGraw-Hill, 1935.

Missouri Department of Public Schools, *A Handbook of Occupational Information and Guidance*, 1941.

Macomber, Freeman G., *Guiding Child Development in the Elementary School*. American Book Co., 1941.

Runge, J. M., "When Children Tell Lies." *Lutheran School Journal*, March, 1941, p. 314.

Schriefer, W. H., "How Can We Educate Our Pupils to Become Loyal Friends of Our Church and School?" *Lutheran School Journal*, June, 1932, p. 433.

Stellhorn, A. C., "Take This Child Away and Nurse It for Me." *Lutheran School Journal*, October, 1937, p. 77.

Wangerin, Adolph, "What the Modern Business World Expects of Our Pupils." *Lutheran School Journal*, April, 1930, p. 353.

Williamson, H. E., *How to Counsel*. McGraw-Hill, 1939.

## Standards for Rating Lutheran Schools

The purpose of including standards for rating is to supply some means whereby the teacher may evaluate not only the school with its equipment and general physical environment, but also his own person and his success as a Christian instructor.

### A. THE TEACHER

**Personal Qualifications**

1. Indicates Christian spirit by words and actions, as an example to pupils and congregation. 1 Tim. 4:12.

2. Is diligent student of God's Word.

3. Has pleasant disposition, is kind and pleasant toward children.

4. Is free from communicable disease. Observes the principles of healthy living.

5. Is neat in personal appearance.

6. Speaks with a well-modulated voice.

7. Meets people easily, courteously, and tactfully.

8. Is faithful, trustworthy, industrious, resourceful.

9. Seeks co-operation with co-workers in congregation, as becomes Christian leaders.

10. Uses good judgment in school and community relations.

11. Is open to suggestion, able to distinguish between principles and personalities.

12. Avoids undesirable habits and mannerisms.

**Efficiency of Instruction**

1. Is interested in his work.

2. Stimulates and utilizes pupil interest and initiative.

3. Secures class discussion and group co-operation.

4. Plans and prepares for his daily work carefully.

5. Pursues definite aims in his instruction.

6. Uses methods in keeping with stated objectives.

7. Is clear and definite in his assignments.

8. Encourages pupils in clear and objective thinking habits.

9. Assists pupils in evaluating their own work.

10. Makes teaching practical by application to life situations.

11. Provides opportunity for Christian service.

12. Succeeds in keeping several groups profitably occupied at the same time.

13. Understands the significance of learning readiness and takes it into account.

14. Disposes of routine matters economically.

15. Has daily workable program.

16. Supervises the activities and play of children outside the classroom.

**Professional Preparation**

1. Daily prepares for class with a view toward general professional growth.

2. Attends and is active at conferences, synodical conventions, circuit meetings, institutes.

3. Has attended school recently, preferably a synodical institution.

4. Receives and reads the *Lutheran School Journal* and at least one other professional magazine.

5. Reads several professional books each year.

6. Holds certificate required by State or is working to meet requirements.

7. Maintains contact with professional groups other than his own.

## B. THE PUPILS

1. Manifest reverent attitude toward sacred things: the Word of God, divine services, etc.

2. Respect parents, pastor, teachers, and all constituted authority, giving prompt and willing obedience.

3. Conduct themselves as Christians, also while not under the direct supervision of the teacher — in the classroom, in the cloakroom, on the playground, on the way home.

4. Respect the rights and property of others.

5. Are alert and interested in the work at hand.

6. Contribute ideas and suggestions in planning work.

7. Are courteous, mannerly, helpful, co-operative.

8. Are active physically.

9. Use their imagination in creative literary, art, and construction work.

10. Gather and utilize information intelligently.

11. Display initiative for worth-while undertakings.

12. Participate in class discussion.

13. Are regular and punctual in their school attendance.

14. Work quietly without disturbing others.

## C. THE BUILDING [1]

### General

1. Compliance with the State requirements in the matter of heating, lighting, ventilation, seating, water supply, and toilets. (Write State Department of Education.)

### Heating

2. Heating plant capable of heating building uniformly to temperature of 70 degrees Fahrenheit.

3. At least 200 cubic feet of air space and seventeen square feet of floor space per pupil in each room.

4. Window sashes in condition for easy adjustment.

5. Three or more windows with glass ventilator shields unless there is a mechanical ventilation system.

6. A humidifier in constant use while artificial heat is provided.

7. Fresh air, uniform temperature, and humidity maintained in the room.

### Lighting

8. Windows to left of pupil while seated.

9. Glass surface at least one fifth of floor space.

10. Double roller shades of light color on sides exposed to sun.

11. Shades adjusted to keep out direct sunlight, yet to admit a maximum of light.

12. Walls and ceilings painted in soft, light tints according to State specifications. Ceiling: light ivory or white; walls: not quite so light. Flat paint to avoid glare.

13. Windows frequently washed.

14. Indirect or direct electric lighting, or fluorescent lights.

### Seating

15. Single desks adjusted to size of pupils with aisles at least 24 inches between rows of seats. Spacing between desks and seats: Sizes 5 and 6, eight to nine inches; size 4, nine to ten inches; size 3, ten to eleven inches; size 2, eleven to twelve inches. Smaller pupils seated nearest windows. When new desks are purchased, they should be of the movable, adjustable type.

16. Desks kept refinished and in good state of repair.[2]

---

1) See Rating Scale for own State.

2) For an article containing practical suggestions for refinishing school furniture see *Lutheran School Journal*, April, 1930, pp. 368, 369.

## Water Supply

17. Water supply approved by State Department of Public Health.

18. Drinking fountains or covered cooler with faucet and individual drinking cups.

## Toilets

19. Indoor water flush-type toilets.

20. Outdoor toilets clean, well ventilated, light, at least 50 feet apart, with a tight board screen in front of entrance. A urinal in good repair in boys' toilet.

## Fire Protection

21. Fire extinguishers in working order.

22. Exit doors supplied with safety bars that open the door when pressure is applied.

23. Window guards hung so that they open readily from inside.

24. Fire escape if building is more than one story high.

25. Flue inspected annually.

26. Sweeping compounds kept in closed metal container.

27. Regular fire drills.

## Condition of Building

28. Building in good repair. Well painted.

29. Interior tastefully decorated.

30. Well lighted and ventilated cloakroom or lockers for pupils' clothing.

31. Suitable provisions for lunch containers.

32. Satisfactory janitorial service.

### D. EQUIPMENT

1. Flag pole. A large flag for all rooms. See State specifications.[3]

2. A teacher's desk and chair in good condition.

3. Blackboards to the front and right of children; slate or composition; at least three feet wide; 24 to 26 inches from floor for primary pupils.

4. A bulletin board; or a tack strip over the blackboard for the display of schoolwork.

5. Storage cabinet of sufficient size in each classroom.

6. First-aid kit; clock; thermometer; metal wastebasket.

7. Several folding chairs for visitors.

---

3) See p. 326 for references on proper display of flag.

8. Adequate library, book shelves, study table, and chairs in each schoolroom. Museum collection.

9. A modern reference set.

10. An approved dictionary (Webster's *Collegiate* sufficient) and several children's dictionaries.

11. Two or three children's magazines.

12. Supplementary readers as specified in the reading course.

13. A full set of textbooks for the teacher and texts for all pupils.

14. A globe about twelve inches in diameter.

15. Charts and maps: A set of geography maps of high quality; Concordia Picture Roll (for primary grades); map of the Holy Land; charts for the music readers; charts for the basic reader.

16. A musical instrument, preferably a piano; a radio or phonograph if possible.

17. Two or three good art pictures in each room.

18. A duplicating machine.

19. Lavatory facilities, preferably with running water; soap, mirror, paper towels.

## E. SCHOOL GROUNDS

1. A playground at least one half acre in size (100 to 200 square feet per pupil).

2. Playground fairly level and well drained, preferably surfaced.

3. Walks to entrance of school, well, and outbuildings.

4. Outbuildings in good state of repair; no unused outbuildings.

5. Grounds free of weeds, brush, rubbish, ashes.

6. Trees and shrubbery for beautification without sacrificing utility of playground.

7. Fences in good repair and painted.

8. Playground equipment: Balls, bats, backstop, volley ball, basket ball and goals, sandbox, horizontal bars, slides, swings. (*This list suggests merely types of equipment that may be considered. Instructional materials are more important than expensive playground equipment. The necessary equipment can often be constructed cheaply with the aid of a few interested congregation members.*)

## F. EXTERNAL RELATIONS

1. Regular reports to the congregation by the School Board or principal. (By the teacher in case of the one-room school.)

2. Parent evenings with planned program.

3. Visits in the home of parents.

4. Parents visiting school during regular instruction hours: Exhibit days, visiting days, parents' days.

5. All children of school age or the highest possible percentage enrolled.

6. School serving its purpose as mission agency by enrolling unchurched children.

7. Regular contributions on part of pupils for church and charitable purposes.

8. Pupils' record of church attendance satisfactory.

9. Regular faculty and board meetings held.

10. Cordial, Christian relationship and willing co-operation between teachers, pastor and teachers, faculty, board members, and parents.

11. Adequate and dignified publicity that stresses the distinctiveness and value of a Christian education.

12. Cordial relations with public school authorities.

13. Pupils of Lutheran school accepted on recommendation of teacher or principal when transferring to public elementary or high schools.

### Readings

Barr, A. S., "Systematic Study of Teaching and Teaching Efficiency." *Journal of Educational Research*, Vol. XXXII, May, 1939, pp. 641—648.

Hamalainen, Arthur E., "Evaluating Growth of Individual Children." *Elementary School Journal*, Vol. XLI, No. 5, Jan., 1941, pp. 359—367.

Herrick, John H., "Outcomes of Systematic Evaluation." *Elementary School Journal*, Vol. XLI, No. 4, Dec., 1940, pp. 257—268.

Jones, J. J., "Evaluation and Its Relation to the Program of Teacher Education." *Educational Research Bulletin*, Oct., 1940, pp. 391—396.

Kittrell, O. A., "Principles of Developing and Using Teacher Rating Scales." *American School Board Journal*, Vol. XCVI, June, 1938, p. 51.

Krause, L. W., "A Method of Noting and Evaluating Modern and Progressive Practices in a Classroom." *Elementary School Journal*, Vol. XLI, No. 7, Mar. 1941, pp. 521—532.

Thomas, F. W., "Criteria for Judging the Effectiveness of Teaching." *California Journal of Elementary Education*, Vol. VII, Feb., 1939, pp. 162—168.

Trow, W. C., "How Shall Teaching Be Evaluated?" *Educational Administration and Supervision*, Vol. XX, April, 1934, pp. 264—272.

Tyler, Ralph W., "The Place of Evaluation in Modern Education." *Elementary School Journal*, Vol. XLI, No. 1, Sept., 1941, pp. 19—27.

Rating Scales of State Department of Education.

See also references under *Related School Topics*, especially those under the heading "The Teacher," pp. 328, 329.

# Rules and Regulations for Lutheran Schools

### (A Guide)

## AIMS OF THE SCHOOL

_____ Lutheran School is organized in keeping with the Biblical principles expressed in Gen. 18:17-19; Deut. 4:9; Deut. 6:6, 7; Ps. 111:10; Prov. 22:6; Matt. 18:2-6; Matt. 28:19, 20; Mark 10:13-16; Eph. 6:4; John 21:15; and 2 Tim. 3:15.

These shall be the aims of the school:

1. Diligent teaching of God's Word according to divine command.

2. Protection of the pupil against the dangers of a purely secular schooling.

3. Provision for both the temporal and eternal welfare of the child by means of an integrated Christian education in a single environment, which substitutes for the combination of the public school and the Church's part-time agencies of religious instruction.

4. Thorough indoctrination of the pupil in the fundamentals of Christianity.

5. Daily Christian pupil-fellowship as one of the most powerful factors in building character and training in Christian living.

6. Stabilization and strengthening of the congregation and the Church generally through the training of a well-grounded, discerning laity and youth.

7. The maintenance of a single-minded, faithful ministry and teaching profession within the Church.

8. Support of parenthood and home life for the purpose of strengthening the very base of human society.

9. Christian citizenship grounded in obedience to God and His Word.

## MANAGEMENT OF THE SCHOOL

_____ Lutheran School is an institution of _____ Lutheran Church and is at all times under the control of this congregation, which is responsible for its management and maintenance. The calling of teachers, the adoption of a course of study and textbooks, and all major changes in the school must be carried out with the approval of the congregation.

## SUPERVISION OF THE SCHOOL

The school shall be under the supervision of the Board of Education, including the pastor, which shall act by authority of the congregation and in accordance with the rules and regulations laid down by it.

## SUPPORT OF THE SCHOOL

The school, as the congregation, shall be maintained by means of freewill offerings of the members of _____ Lutheran Church. With respect to children of non-members, the policy shall be as follows:

A. To parents belonging to sister congregations and other non-members who send their children unsolicited, the per capita cost of the school shall be suggested as a fair freewill offering.

B. Solicited mission children shall not be expected to pay until they have learned to see the value of the Christian education and training they receive and are ready to contribute to the maintenance of the school.

*Note:* It is impossible to suggest rules to fit every case. In general, the charging of tuition is discouraged. Yet it is realized that there may be instances where the school must depend for a part of its maintenance upon the collection of a fixed tuition.

In all cases the circumstances of the parents desiring to enroll children must be taken into consideration. The contribution of the per capita cost of the school is fair, particularly when a sister congregation arranges to send a large number of children to the school.

## THE COURSE OF STUDY AND TEXTBOOKS

The Board of Education and teaching staff shall be held to provide a distinctively Lutheran and Christian course of study, which shall state:

A. The aims and scope of the religious instruction, and

B. The aims and outlines of the secular school branches in the light of Scripture.

In the selection of textbooks three general criteria shall govern:

A. Their excellence from the educational standpoint.

B. In religious books, freedom from all error of doctrine and their distinctively Lutheran character.

C. In secular books, freedom from statements or illustrations that militate against the Word of God.

## GENERAL RULES

A. All rules and regulations pertaining to the school which have been approved by the congregation can be rescinded only by the congregation.

B. The discipline of the school must be in keeping with the principles of the Word of God.

C. The school calendar shall coincide with that of the public schools except for such departures as have the approval of the Board of Education.

D. The school day shall be opened with appropriate devotions consisting of hymn, Scripture reading, prayer, confession of faith, and the like. The sessions shall be closed with prayer, spoken or sung.

E. Promotion shall be based on the average yearly achievement of the pupil in the various branches of the curriculum, and on such other factors as the best interests of the pupil and the school may require.

F. Pupils shall be held to purchase their own textbooks in religion and to provide their own supplies apart from textbooks and workbooks. All texts and workbooks in the secular subjects may be purchased by the school and rented to the pupils at reasonable rates as determined by the Board of Education.

*Note:* Textbooks can be supplied most economically by the rental system where the congregation is unable to provide free textbooks. The rates vary from congregation to congregation, but many are able to supply the books at from $1.00 to $1.50 per pupil per year.

The suggestion that pupils purchase their religious texts is made because of the desirability of owning these books.

In some cases the school sells all books and supplies to the pupils, using the profits in the purchase of school equipment. In others a local merchant handles the books for the school.

G. A school library shall be maintained. Its management shall be in charge of the teachers or someone appointed by the staff. Funds for books may be obtained from such sources as have the general approval of the Board of Education.

H. Complaints and problems originating from parents are to be received and dealt with only outside the regular school hours and as a rule must be directed to the teacher involved. In case a settlement is not brought about, the principal, pastor, and Board of Education may in turn be appealed to.

I. There shall be no smoking on the school premises during the school day.

## REGULATIONS FOR THE BOARD OF EDUCATION

*A. Membership*

The Board of Education of _____ Lutheran Church shall be composed of the following members:

1. Voting: Six (or three) laymen, voting members of the congregation, chosen in a way that the entire personnel is not changed at any one time.

2. Ex officio: The pastor.

3. Advisory: The regularly called teachers of the parish school or the principal and the Sunday school superintendent.

### B. Meetings

The Board shall hold monthly (or quarterly) meetings on a fixed date, or oftener if circumstances require, all such meetings to be duly announced. The Board elects its own chairman and secretary and designates the person or persons responsible for the preparation of a program for each meeting.

### C. Duties of the Board

The duties of the Board of Education shall be as follows:

1. To organize, manage, and supervise all educational activities of the congregation:

    a. In school.

    b. In Sunday school.

    c. In other part-time agencies.

2. To meet regularly for the study and discussion of educational needs and problems of the congregation:

    a. To study educational conditions, accounting for every child connected in any way with the Church.

    b. To see that written records are kept of every child in the congregation, whether enrolled in school, Sunday school, or other part-time agencies, or receiving no religious instruction at all.

    c. To submit regular reports and recommendations to the voters' assembly for the external and internal improvement of the congregational educational agencies as they are needed.

    d. To execute such resolutions as the congregation may adopt in educational matters.

3. To determine by actual visits of the classes in the parochial school, as well as the part-time agencies:

    a. Whether the aims of Christian education are being achieved.

    b. Whether Christian discipline prevails.

    c. Whether the provisions of the course of study adopted by the congregation are carried out.

    d. Whether the relation between teacher and pupils is satisfactory.

4. To consider and act upon proposed changes in the course of study, textbooks, equipment, and existing school regulations, under the rules of the congregation.

5. To make recommendations to the congregation in the calling or appointment of teachers in the school and to pass upon the qualifications of teachers and officers considered for appointment to service in the part-time agencies.

6. To assist the teachers in their work by word and deed wherever possible and, if necessary, to remind them of their duty.

7. To look also after the temporal welfare of the parochial school teachers and make recommendations to the congregation concerning their salaries or living conditions.

8. To assist conscientiously in maintaining and increasing within the congregation the proper esteem of Christian education and the Lutheran school:

    a. By reports in congregational meetings.

    b. By soliciting pupils for the educational agencies, especially for the school.

    c. By admonishing parents who neglect their duty in the education of their children.

    d. By studying and utilizing the mission opportunities open to the congregational educational agencies.

9. To co-operate with the District Board of Christian Education to the fullest extent:

    a. By furnishing all reports requested.

    b. By considering seriously its recommendations for local adoption.

10. To foster the proper relationship between parents and teachers and the personnel of the various educational agencies.

11. To assist in maintaining proper order among the school children in the church services.

### RULES FOR PUPILS

A. All pupils enrolled in the school are subject to its rules and regulations.

B. Each pupil must be supplied with the books and materials required in his class.

C. No pupil may be excused from instruction in religion.

D. In accordance with the laws of the State, all pupils are held to regular and punctual attendance. All absences must be excused in writing by a parent. Pupils are not permitted to leave the school premises during recess or school hours without the permission of the teacher.

E. Pupils must enter and leave the schoolrooms and building as instructed by the teacher.

F. Pupils must appear in the classroom with clean hands, a clean face, and clean clothes. Also the desks must be kept in clean and orderly condition.

G. Pupils are not permitted to play outdoors before school opening in the morning. Playing with a hard ball or throwing snow balls on the school grounds is forbidden at all times.

H. Every pupil owes implicit obedience to his teacher, according to the Fourth Commandment. Pupils, however, have the right to appeal to their teacher when they believe they have received unfair treatment.

I. Waste materials of any kind must not be thrown on the floor or grounds, but into containers provided for that purpose.

J. Pupils who through carelessness or negligence cause damage to school property or to the property of a fellow pupil will be held to pay the amount of the damage.

K. Pupils who have satisfactorily completed the studies prescribed for the grades will be awarded a diploma by the school. The diploma may be withheld, however, for a general failure in conduct.

L. In general, pupils shall make every effort to conform their lives to the rules of God's Word.

## RULES FOR THE PASTOR

A. The pastor is the spiritual head of the school as well as of the entire congregation, and to him also with reference to the school children apply the words of Acts 20:28: "Take heed therefore unto yourselves and to all the flock over the which the Holy Ghost hath made you overseers to feed the Church of God, which He hath purchased with His own blood."

B. Inasmuch as the pastor, by virtue of his call, is made responsible for the spiritual care of all the members, including the children, he is especially charged with the following duties relative to the school.

1. To promote the school publicly and privately and to look after the attendance of the children of the congregation as well as of mission children.

2. In behalf of the congregation to supervise the school work and the maintenance of Christian discipline.

3. To assure himself that all secular instruction is subordinated to, and permeated by, the eternal truth of God's Word.

4. To assist and advise with the teachers in all matters pertaining to the welfare of the school and the attainment of its objectives.

C. If parents or others bring complaints to the pastor against any teacher, he shall direct them to the teacher involved. The pastor may deal in these cases only when they have failed of settlement as stated under *General Rules.*

## THE PRINCIPAL

The congregation shall designate one of its teachers as principal, who shall be responsible for the proper administration and supervision of the school. Ordinarily the principal shall be the teacher of the upper grade or grades.

*A. Position of the Principal*

1. The position of the principal shall be one not so much of authority as of helpfulness, service, and leadership. His entire activity shall center about the advancement of the best interests of the Christian school, its pupils, and teachers.

2. The principal is expected to set an example in his zeal for making the school a thoroughly effective agency for the Christian education and training of the congregation's children and such others as are enrolled in the school. That this object may be attained, he shall seek diligently the advice and co-operation of his fellow teachers, the pastor, and the congregational Board of Education.

3. In the discharge of his duties the principal shall be directly responsible to the Board of Education and ultimately to the congregation.

*B. Administrative Duties*

The administrative duties of the principal deal with all provisions that are necessary to provide conditions favorable to instruction, such as the general order, equipment, supplies, reports, records, sanitation, repairs, and the like.

1. The principal is responsible for the execution of all regulations adopted by the congregation and the Board of Education relative to the school.

2. He shall keep himself informed as to changing trends in religious and secular education and in textbooks, and make the necessary recommendations to his fellow teachers, the Board of Education, and the congregation, in order that the instruction may be maintained on a high level of efficiency.

3. As chairman of the teaching staff he shall plan and arrange for regular monthly meetings of the pastor and the staff for the consideration of educational topics and school problems.

4. He shall report regularly to the pastor, the Board, and the congregation (either personally or through the Board) on the progress and standing of the school. He shall prepare all reports for synodical officials as well as for county and State officials who are entitled to them.

5. He shall keep on file an accurate inventory of school equipment and recommend to the Board or congregation such repairs, replacements, or additions as become necessary from time to time. In case of current and minor needs he may make the purchases himself.

6. He shall be responsible for the direction of all extracurricular activities, such as children's services, children's programs, the collection of funds for charity, missions, or school purposes, fire drills, publicity, and any others that may be introduced. Even where the direction of these activities is delegated, he is coresponsible.

7. With the co-operation of his fellow teachers he shall provide for the proper supervision of the hallways, gymnasium, and playground.

8. He shall pass upon all promotions, demotions, admissions, and suspensions of pupils. All transfer cards to other schools are issued to him, and all transfer cards from other schools are examined by him.

9. He shall keep on file in his office all information of importance concerning the pupils of the entire school. This includes the usual information as to age, address, parents, school history, health record, church connections, baptisms, grades, transfers, dismissals.

10. He shall insist on proper hygienic conditions in and about the school, and to that end check the seating, heating, ventilation, lighting, condition of the toilets, and the general cleanliness of buildings and grounds.

11. He shall confer with the truant officer, doctor, nurse, agents, Red Cross representative, Board of Health, and the like in matters pertaining to the school.

12. He shall represent the school in the congregational Board of Education, the congregation, the synodical District, over against the public school, and the public.

13. In cases of neglect of duty, insubordination, lack of harmony, and refusal to co-operate among members of the staff, he shall adjust according to Matthew 18. If unsuccessful, he shall solicit the assistance of the pastor and, in case of necessity, refer them to the Board.

14. Before the opening of the school year, he shall prepare a calendar for the year and supply the pastor and all teachers with a copy.

*C. Supervisory Duties*

The supervisory duties of the principal deal with the supervision of instruction in all subjects, particularly that of religion, and the effective Christian training and discipline throughout the school.

1. The principal shall see that each teacher is supplied with an adequate course of study for all subjects and a daily program. With the help of the teaching staff the work of each grade is clearly outlined:

      a. That each teacher may know what is to be accomplished.

      b. That there may be co-ordination of methods and subject matter and, in general, unity of purpose throughout the school.

2. He shall visit, as frequently as possible, all classes while in session and keep a confidential record of his observations regarding efficiency of instruction, Christian training, and discipline. These he shall discuss with the classroom teacher subsequently and privately.

3. He shall keep himself informed on the progress of the classes in carrying out the schedule of work agreed upon and called for in the course of study, and assist teachers when difficulties arise.

4. He shall supervise the giving of standardized tests in all classes and provide for the study of results in a subsequent staff meeting.

5. He shall supervise the school library unless other regulations are agreed upon by the teachers.

6. He shall at all times be careful that his supervisory activities do not take an arbitrary turn, but that they remain humble efforts in which the principal, with the classroom teachers, seeks the glory of God and the salvation of the pupils.

## RULES FOR THE CLASSROOM TEACHER

A. It shall be understood that teachers meet the requirements laid down by Synod for its parochial school teachers and that they are capable of fulfilling the provisions of their call.

B. The teacher shall utilize opportunities for professional growth and ever seek to prepare himself better for his sacred calling. He shall emphasize growth in doctrinal understanding and knowledge, but maintain also the professional standard required of teachers in general.

C. Every teacher shall cheerfully co-operate with the principal and execute his instructions. He shall also welcome the visits of the principal in his class and act upon the principal's recommendations.

D. Complaints relative to the administration or janitorial service and requests for repairs, equipment, and the like shall be presented to the principal, or to the staff at a regular meeting.

E. The teacher shall be in his classroom one half hour before opening in the morning and fifteen minutes before opening at noon.

F. Each teacher shall be allowed one day a year on which he may visit other classes, either in his own or in another school. His own class may be dismissed if necessary.

G. Serious differences between teachers shall be settled according to Matthew 18:15-17. As a third party the principal or pastor may be taken into consultation. Extreme cases which thus have failed of settlement shall be referred to the staff and ultimately to the Board of Education for adjustment.

H. The classroom teacher is responsible for the instruction and discipline of his classes, but shall submit special cases of discipline to the principal. In keeping with his responsibility to his class the teacher shall be held:

1. To teach faithfully and effectively the subject matter prescribed for his grade (grades) in the course of study.

2. To maintain a discipline conducive to effective school work and in accordance with Biblical principles.

3. To keep an accurate record of the attendance, achievement, and deportment of the pupils, and to enter the yearly averages into the permanent records of the school.

4. To issue report cards at intervals determined by the Board of Education.

5. To recommend promotion to pupils having satisfactorily completed the work of a given grade.

6. To keep a record of special cases of pupil offenses and their correction, noting reasons for punishment and mode of procedure.

7. To assist in executing within his room, in the corridors, and on the playground all regulations of the school.

## CHANGES IN REGULATIONS

Changes in these regulations may be made with the approval of the Board of Education or the congregation.

## Selected References

Graebner, Th., *Handbook for Congregational Officers*. Concordia Publishing House, 1939, pp. 45—58.

Jacobson, Paul B., and Reavis, William C., *Duties of School Principals*. New York: Prentice-Hall, Inc., 1941.

*Regulations of St. John's Lutheran School*, Chester, Ill.

*Rules and Regulations for Trinity Lutheran School*, Sheboygan, Wis.

Stellhorn, A. C., *Congregational Boards of Education*. Concordia Tract 116.

Stellhorn, A. C., *Aims of the Lutheran Elementary School*.

Articles in the *Lutheran School Journal*:

> Gross, H. H., "The Duties of the Principal." January, 1936, p. 210.
>
> Jaeger, Herbert, "Duties of a Principal in a Lutheran School." February, 1933, p. 246.
>
> Kohn, W. C., "The Principal and Supervision." March, 1936, p. 315.
>
> Kraeft, W. O., "The Principal in the Lutheran School." December, 1930, p. 152.
>
> Miller, Arthur L., "Suggestions for Local Boards of Christian Education." October, 1940, p. 260; April, 1941, p. 353; June, 1941, p. 447.
>
> Sieving, E. C., "The Lutheran Principal as a Leader in Education." May, 1941, p. 403.

# Constitution for Lutheran School Associations *

### (Guide for interparish schools)

### Article I. Name

The name of this Association shall be the _____
Lutheran School Association of _____, _____.

### Article II. Purpose

The purpose of this Association shall be the maintenance of a joint or union Christian school for all children of the congregations holding membership in the Association, as also for such others as desire to make use of the facilities offered by the Association.

### Article III. Membership

All congregations in the _____ area affiliated with the Synodical Conference shall be eligible for membership in the Association in accordance with the rules and regulations of its Constitution and By-laws.

### Article IV. Organization

1. A Joint Board of Christian Education to direct and conduct the affairs of the Association shall be elected by all member congregations on the basis of one representative for every 50 com-

---

* See also Rules and Regulations for Lutheran Schools, pp. 310—320.

municant members or fraction thereof. The pastors of all congregations and the principal of the school shall be ex officio members of this Board.

2. All voting members of the member congregations shall be considered congregational representatives at the plenary meetings of the Association. (See Article VII. 2.)

### Article V. Authority

1. The authority of the congregations acting jointly as members of this Association shall be the same as that exercised ordinarily by individual congregations in their educational endeavors.

2. The Association shall have the right to call teachers, to acquire and hold property and equipment, and to engage in such other activities as may be necessary to conduct its work successfully.

### Article VI. Duties of Members

1. Every member congregation shall contribute toward the support and maintenance of the joint school in such a manner as the Association shall determine in its By-laws or its rules and regulations.

2. Every member congregation pledges itself to use its influence with the parents in its midst to the end that the children of school age who are within reach of the school attend the same.

3. Every member congregation shall be held responsible for the regular attendance of its representatives at the meetings of the Joint Board of Christian Education or the plenary meetings of the Association.

### Article VII. Meetings

1. The Joint Board of Christian Education shall meet on the _____ of every month during the school year to hear reports and transact such business as may be necessary. The members of this Board shall report on these meetings in their respective congregations.

2. An annual plenary meeting of the voting members of all member congregations shall be held on _____. The Joint Board of Christian Education shall be held responsible to prepare programs for these meetings which will provide time both for educational features and for necessary reports and business transactions.

3. Special meetings may be called by the officers of the Association.

### Article VIII. Dissolution

1. This Association shall not be dissolved as long as two congregations desire its continuance.

2. In case of dissolution the proceeds of the sale of all property owned jointly shall be distributed pro rata among the member congregations. Property owned by individual congregations shall in no way be affected.

### Article IX. Teachers

1. The teachers for the school shall be called and salaried by the Association, to which they shall be held responsible. Calls may be issued only in regular or special plenary meetings which have been duly announced in all churches of member congregations.

2. A congregation desiring special services of a teacher for organ or choir work, or such other duties as are commonly required of parochial school teachers, shall be privileged to engage one of the teachers for this purpose. Remuneration for these services shall be the responsibility of the congregation so engaging the teacher and shall not be counted in pro-rating costs for any given congregation.

### Article X. Officers

1. The Association in its annual meeting shall elect by ballot from among the members of the Joint Board of Christian Education previously certified a President, a Vice-President, a Secretary, and a Treasurer, each for a term of one year.

2. The members of the Joint Board of Christian Education shall be elected for a period of three years by the individual congregations. The officers of the Association shall serve also as officers of the Joint Board of Christian Education.

### Article XI. Duties of Officers

1. The President shall preside at all meetings of the Association and Joint Board of Christian Education and perform such other duties as are generally performed by such officers.

2. The Vice-President shall perform the duties of the President in the absence or disability of the latter.

3. The Secretary shall keep the minutes of the Association and the Joint Board, conduct the correspondence of the Association, and perform such other duties as are generally assigned to the secretary of an organization.

4. The Treasurer shall receive all moneys from the treasurers of the member congregations, the synodical Mission Boards contributing to the maintenance of the school, or any other contributions; he shall deposit all money to the credit of the Association in a bank designated by the Joint Board of Christian Education; he shall disburse such moneys only on written order by the chairman of the Association; he shall submit a complete report of receipts and expenditures at each regular meeting of the

Association and at the meetings of the Joint Board of Christian Education whenever required; and he shall render a detailed report in the annual meeting of the Board.

5. The Joint Board of Christian Education shall administer the affairs of the Association and its school and hold monthly meetings for the purpose of planning and directing its work. It shall be responsible to the Association and be guided by this constitution and the rules and regulations which may be adopted from time to time.

### Article XII. Removal of Officers and Teachers

All officers and teachers of the Association may be removed from office in accordance with Christian practice if they persist in false doctrine, an unchristian life, or unfaithfulness in their official duties.

### Article XIII. Schoolbooks

Besides the Holy Scriptures and Luther's Small Catechism, only such books shall be used for instruction in Christian doctrine as are in accordance with the Symbolical Books of the Evangelical Lutheran Church. In respect to secular texts, every care should be taken to select books that are free from false doctrine or that have been rendered innocuous by proper correction.

### Article XIV. Rules of Order

In the business meetings of the Association and of the Joint Board of Christian Education all questions of order shall be decided in accordance with Robert's Rules of Order, unless such rules are contrary to this Constitution.

### Article XV. Amendments

This Constitution may be amended by a vote of two thirds (⅔) at any regular plenary meeting of the Association, provided, however, that such amendment has been submitted in writing to all member congregations at least sixty days prior to the meeting at which the vote is taken or has been considered at a previous meeting of the Association.

## BY-LAWS

### Finances

1. The cost of maintaining the joint school shall be distributed pro rata among the various congregations according to their communicant membership.

2. The Joint Board of Christian Education shall appraise the value of the present school plant and agree on a fair rental; compute the actual cost of salaries, transportation service, light, fuel, and other expenses; and on the basis of the total annual cost apportion

the share of the participating congregations, with the understanding, however, that congregations which are unable to assume their proportionate amount may appeal to their respective Mission Board for the necessary financial assistance.

3. There shall be no tuition charges, either for members of participating congregations or non-members. All members shall be encouraged to contribute liberally toward the pro rata cost of their respective congregations, and non-members shall be informed of the per capita cost of the school and given opportunity for freewill offerings.

### Order of Business

1. Prayer. 2. Minutes. 3. Report of Committees. 4. Unfinished Business. 5. New Business. 6. Roll call. 7. Adjournment.

---

## Related School Topics *

The following bibliography of *Related Topics* supplements a number of topics discussed in this Course of Study and deals with others not touched upon. Most references are to the *Lutheran School Journal* and *The Lutheran Teacher's Handbook* by W. O. Kraeft (St. Louis: Concordia, 1929). The abbreviations *L. S. J.* and *Kraeft* are used throughout.

### Architecture

"Better School Architecture" (A. C. Stellhorn). L. S. J., May, 1930, p. 401; Feb., 1932, p. 252.

### Audio-Visual Education

"The Eyes Have It" (Ewald V. Nolte). L. S. J., Nov., 1941, p. 112.

"The Still Picture" (Ewald V. Nolte). L. S. J., March, 1942, p 303.

"Visual Materials in Religious Education" (W. H. Beck). Report of Midwestern Teachers' Conference, 1941, p. 51.

"Visual Materials, Handwork, and Activities in Religious Education" (W. H. Beck). L. S. J., March, 1942, p. 295.

*Proceedings of the Fifth Annual Southern Conference on Audio-Visual Education.* Southern Conference on Audio-Visual Education, 223 Walton St., N. W., Atlanta, Ga.

*Audio-Visual Aids to Instruction* (Harry C. McKown and Alvin B. Roberts). McGraw-Hill, 1940. Pp. XIV and 386.

*Radio and the Classroom.* Report of the Radio Commission of the Department of Elementary School Principals of the N. E. A. Washington: National Education Association, 1940, p. 98.

---

* For selected references in the various areas of instruction see the individual subjects and the Concordia *School Reference Catalog.* The latter contains also a general list of professional books for teachers.

## Board of Education

"Should Congregations Have One Board of Christian Education to Supervise All Agencies?" (W. H. Luke). L. S. J., May, 1931, p. 391.

"Topics for Discussion at Meetings of Congregational Boards" (P. T. Buszin). L. S. J., June, 1935, p. 433.

"Administration in the Lutheran Parochial Schools" (H. H. Gross). L. S. J., Jan., 1936, p. 207.

"Worthwhile Meetings of the Board of Education" (Arthur L. Miller). L. S. J., Oct., 1941, p. 58.

"Suggestions for Local Boards of Christian Education" (Arthur L. Miller). L. S. J., Feb., 1941, p. 260; Apr., 1941, p. 353; June, 1941, p. 447.

## Canvass

"Getting the Pupils." Kraeft, pp. 1—72.

## Children's Choir

"Children's Choirs." L. S. J., June, 1932, p. 467.

"Development of Tone in Children's Choirs" (Theo. Stelzer). L. S. J., March, 1939, p. 317.

"Organization of Vocal Groups" (Theo. Stelzer). L. S. J., Sept., 1940, p. 30.

"Building Tone" (Theo. Stelzer). L. S. J., May, 1941, p. 415.

## Children's Organizations

"The Religion of Boy Scouting" (H. C. Schillinger). L. S. J., Oct., 1940, p. 60.

"In Explanation" (H. C. Schillinger). L. S. J., Jan., 1941, p. 235.

"Lutheran Boys and Girls of America" (H. C. Schillinger). L. S. J., Sept., 1941, p. 22.

## Children's Services

"Liturgical Principles and Children's Christmas Services" (P. E. Kretzmann). L. S. J., Dec., 1931, p. 153.

"Children's Services, a Discussion of Principles and Samples." Kraeft, pp. 128—167.

## Discipline

"How I Obtain Proper School Decorum in the Primary School" (E. M. Pigoraz). L. S. J., April, 1928, p. 136; May, 1928, p. 161; June, 1928, p. 213.

"Christian Discipline" (K. J. Buchop). L. S. J., Sept., 1926, p. 337.

"Discipline Again" (A. C. Stellhorn). L. S. J., March, 1930, p. 319.

"The Place of Love in Discipline" (Geo. Jung). L. S. J., Dec., 1930, p. 173.

"Nagging-Ridiculing" (M. A. Bartlett). L. S. J., May, 1931, p. 415.

"Discipline in Our Schools" (F. Wolter). L. S. J., Dec., 1931, p. 169.

"Restraint, Discipline, Manners" (A. C. Stellhorn). L. S. J., March, 1936, p. 321.

### Extracurricular

"Extracurricular Activities in the Elementary School" (N. Robert Ringdahl). L. S. J., Jan., 1931, p. 226.

"Field Trips, Excursions, School Journeys" (G. H. Reifschneider). L. S. J., March, 1941, p. 309; April, 1941, p. 358.

"Social Functions, Entertainments, Picnics, Outings." Kraeft, pp. 174—244.

### Flag

"Pledge to the Flag." L. S. J., March, 1941, p. 323.

"Flag Code." L. S. J., April, 1941, p. 341.

"Saluting the Flag." L. S. J., May, 1941, p. 420.

*Manual for the Flag of the United States of America.*" F. A. Owen Publishing Co., Dansville, N. Y.  Price, 5 cents.

*Flag Code.*  Contains full directions for use of Flag.  The American Legion, Indianapolis, Indiana.  Free to schools.

### Free Materials

"List of Free and Inexpensive Materials for Schools" (Alwin R. Roschke). L. S. J., June, 1941, p. 452.

### Furniture

"Opportunity for a Little Manual Training."  Contains suggestions for refinishing school furniture (A. C. Stellhorn). L. S. J., April, 1930, pp. 368, 369.

### Graduation Exercises

"The School Commencement" (M. J. R.). L. S. J., May, 1939, p. 395.

"Vitalized Commencement Program" (H. D. Bruening). L. S. J., March, 1940, p. 306.

"The Lutheran Graduation." Kraeft, pp. 292—349.

"The School Commencement" (A symposium). L. S. J., May, 1942, p. 398.

### Home Work

"Home Work" (W. O. Kraeft). L. S. J., April, 1930, p. 360.

"Results of Study on Home Work" (W. O. Kraeft). L. S. J., Sept., 1930, p. 20.

"Pupils' Home Study" (Paul Denninger). L. S. J., Nov. 1930, p. 120.

"Home Work by Pupils" (Albert V. Maurer). L. S. J., Oct., 1940, p. 76.

### One-Room School

"The Lutheran One-Teacher School" (Theo. Kuehnert). L. S. J., Mar. 1936, p. 309; April, 1936, p. 351; May, 1936, p. 397; June, 1936, p. 438; Sept., 1936, p. 4; Oct., 1936, p. 55; Nov., 1936, p. 110; Dec., 1936, p. 151.

"Conservation of Time in the One-Teacher School" (Herman W. Teske). L. S. J., Nov., 1938, p. 109.

"Organizing Instruction in the One-Teacher School" (Fred H. Witte). L. S. J., March, 1941, p. 305.

"The Reading Program in the One-Teacher School" (Fred H. Witte). L. S. J., May, 1941, p. 408.

"Advantages of a One-Room School" (J. G. Gehner). L. S. J., June, 1941, p. 450.

## Orchestra and Band

"Orchestra and Band" (Northern Illinois District). L. S. J., June, 1941, p. 465.

"Strike Up the Band" (W. F. Bertram). *Concordia Messenger*, Oct., 1940, p. 220.

"School Orchestra or Band" (W. O. Kraeft). Kraeft, pp. 280—289.

## Parent-Teacher

"Parent-Teacher Associations" (J. F. Stach). L. S. J., Nov., 1939, p. 113.

"Dramatized Program for P. T. A." (Milton Marten). L. S. J., Nov., 1940, p. 115.

"Shall Our P. T. A.'s Federate?" (J. Arthur Koss). L. S. J., Jan., 1941, p. 211.

"Regional P. T. A. Organized" (L. C. Heidemann). L. S. J., Feb., 1941, p. 284.

"Parent-Teacher Organizations." Kraeft, pp. 255—280.

## Physical Education

"Suggestions for a Program of Physical Education in the Elementary School" (Wm. A. Hedtke). L. S. J., Oct., 1938, p. 68.

## Publicity

"Publicity, Why and How" (E. E. Foelber). L. S. J., Nov., 1927, p. 411.

"School Publicity" (S. J. Roth). L. S. J., Dec., 1932, p. 163.

"Promoting the Cause in the Local Parish" (Arthur Karl Piepkorn and Edwin Jacob: Pastor's Viewpoint; Carl W. Greinke: Teacher's Viewpoint; A. H. Ahlbrand: Layman's Viewpoint). L. S. J., Mar., 1940, p. 300; April, 1940, p. 342; May, 1940, p. 391.

"Advertising the School" (Theo. Kuehnert). L. S. J., Oct., 1941, p. 51.

"School Publicity" (Wm. A. Kramer). L. S. J., Oct., 1941, p. 62.

"Making Known the Work of the School." Kraeft, pp. 74—104.

## Public Relations

"The Status of the Lutheran Teacher in the Community" (Alvin Hitzemann). L. S. J., Nov., 1938, p. 116.

"Correct Status of Christian Citizens with Regard to the Secular State and Its Non-Religious Schools" (J. Herzer). L. S. J., June, 1925, p. 201; July, 1925, p. 248; Aug., 1925, p. 288.

## Records and Reports

"Records." Kraeft, pp. 105—125.

## School Papers

"An Excellent Medium to Provide for Pupil Activities and Experiences in Language Work" (Irma Beck). L. S. J., June, 1930, p. 442.

"School Papers in Review" (Wm. A. Kramer). L. S. J., March, 1941, p. 312.

"School Paper." Kraeft, pp. 247—255.

## The Teacher

### A. THE CALL OF THE TEACHER

"Our High Calling, and How to Become More Proficient in It." L. S. J., Jan., 1928, p. 3.

"Beruf und Amt eines Gemeindeschullehrers" (L. A. Heerboth). L. S. J., Oct., 1931, p. 49.

"The Call of the Teacher" (J. F. Boerger). *Building the Parochial School of Tomorrow*, p. 49.

### B. THE TEACHER AS A PERSON

"The Teacher as a Model for His School and Community" (W. C. Poll). L. S. J., Nov., 1930, p. 109.

"The Bible-Saturated Teacher" (P. E. Kretzmann): L. S. J., Feb., 1933, p. 241.

"The Teacher as a Person" (A. V. Maurer). L. S. J., Feb., 1940, p. 255.

"The Teacher's Ethics" (C. A. Buescher). L. S. J., May, 1941, p. 400.

"Workers in the Vineyard" (L. G. Bickel). L. S. J., June, 1941, p. 445.

### C. THE TEACHER AND HIS PUPILS

"The Teacher an Example to His Pupils" (J. H. Brase). L. S. J., Oct., 1925, p. 372.

"How Teachers Gain and Retain the Respect of Their Pupils" (J. Wambsganss). L. S. J., April, 1930, p. 363.

### D. THE TEACHER AND THE CONGREGATION

"The Teacher as Student and Literary Worker" (Herbert D. Bruening). L. S. J., Dec., 1927, p. 453; Jan., 1928, p. 11.

"Influence of the Lutheran Teacher within the Congregation" (L. E. Schilke). L. S. J., April, 1935, p. 337.

"The Work of the Lutheran Teacher Outside the Classroom" (A. W. Gross). L. S. J., June, 1936, p. 433.

### E. THE TEACHER AND THE YOUTH

"The Teacher's Social Intercourse with the Young People" (A. H. Miller, Jr.). L. S. J., Feb., 1924, p. 57.

"The Teacher as Leader in the Education of Future Builders of Homes, Churches, and Communities" (E. H. Engelbrecht). L. S. J., April, 1933, p. 352.

"The Lutheran Teacher and the Youth Program of the Church" (S. J. Roth). L. S. J., Dec., 1936, p. 145.

F. The Teacher as Missionary

"The Missionary Obligations of a Lutheran Teacher" (A. C. Stellhorn). L. S. J., Feb., 1931, p. 241.

G. The Teacher and the Community

"The Status of the Lutheran Teacher in the Community" (Alvin Hitzemann). L. S. J., Nov., 1938, p. 116.

H. The Teacher (All Christians) and the Public School

"Correct Status of Christian Citizens with Regard to the Secular State and Its Non-Religious Schools" (J. Herzer). L. S. J., June, 1925, p. 201; July, 1925, p. 248; Aug., 1925, p. 288.

# Directory of Publishers

### 1. Lutheran Publishers and Jobbers for Concordia Publications

*Concordia.* Concordia Publishing House, 3558 S. Jefferson Ave., Saint Louis 18, Mo.

*Augsburg.* Augsburg Publishing House, 425 S. Fourth St., Minneapolis 15, Minn.

*Augustana.* Augustana Press, Rock Island, Ill.

*Biehl.* Ferd Biehl, 1336 W. 7th St., Davenport, Iowa.

*Buckeye.* Buckeye Stationery Co., 1472 W. 25th St., Cleveland, Ohio.

*Gagern.* M. C. Gagern, 178 Southampton St., Buffalo, N. Y.

*International.* International Book Store, 2944 Gratiot Ave., Detroit, Mich.

*Kaufmann.* Ernst Kaufmann, 209 S. State St., Chicago, Ill.

*Kaufmann.* Ernst Kaufmann, 7—11 Spruce St., New York, N. Y.

*Klemm.* M. K. Klemm, 707 Lyon St., Saginaw, Mich.

*Lutheran Bible Church.* Lutheran Bible and Church Supplies, Inc., 82 W. Washington, Chicago, Ill.

*Lutheran Supplies.* Lutheran Bible and Church Supplies, Inc., 82 W. Washington St., Chicago, Ill.

*Northwestern.* Northwestern Publishing House, 935—937 N. 4th St., Milwaukee, Wis.

*Toledo.* Toledo Lutheran Publishing Co., 538 N. Erie St., Toledo, Ohio.

*Wartburg.* Wartburg Press, Columbus, Ohio.

### 2. Other Educational Publishers

*Allyn and Bacon.* Allyn and Bacon, 2231 South Park Way, Chicago 16, Ill.

*American.* American Book Co., 360 N. Michigan Ave., Chicago, Ill.

*Appleton-Century.* D. Appleton-Century Co., 35 W. 32d St., New York, N. Y.

*Augsburg.* Augsburg Publishing Co., Nashville, Tenn.

*Barnes.* A. S. Barnes and Company, 67 W. 44th St., New York 18, N. Y.

*Beckley-Cardy.* Beckley-Cardy Co., 1632 Indiana Ave., Chicago, Ill.

*Benson.* W. S. Benson and Company, Austin, Tex.

*Bobbs-Merrill.* Bobbs-Merrill Co., 729 N. Meridian St., Indianapolis 7, Ind.

*Columbia.* Columbia Press, Bloomington, Ind.

*Compton.* F. E. Compton and Co., 1000 N. Dearborn St., Chicago 10, Ill.

*Doubleday.* Doubleday and Co., Inc., 14 W. 49th St., New York, N. Y.

*Dutton.* E. P. Dutton and Co., Inc., 300 Fourth Ave., New York, N. Y.

*Eerdmans.* Wm. B. Eerdmans Publishing Co., Grand Rapids, Mich.

*Flanagan.* A. Flanagan Co., Chicago, Ill.

*Follett.* Follett Publishing Co., 1255 S. Wabash Ave., Chicago 5, Ill.

*Ginn.* Ginn and Co., 2301—2311 Prairie Ave., Chicago, Ill.

*Globe.* Globe Book Co., 175 Fifth Ave., New York, N. Y.

*Grolier.* The Grolier Society, School and Library Division, 2 W. 45th St., New York 19, N. Y.

*Hall-McCreary.* Hall and McCreary Co., 434 S. Wabash Ave., Chicago 5, Ill.

*Hammond.* C. S. Hammond and Co., 88 Lexington Ave., New York 16, N. Y.

*Harcourt.* Harcourt, Brace, and Company, 383 Madison Ave., New York, N. Y.

*Harper.* Harper and Brothers, 47 E. 33d St., New York, N. Y.

*Heath.* D. C. Heath and Co., 285 Columbus Ave., Boston, Mass.

*Holt.* Henry Holt and Co., 257 Fourth Ave., New York, N. Y.

*Houghton Mifflin.* Houghton Mifflin Co., 2 Park St., Boston, Mass.

*Iroquois.* Iroquois Publishing Co., Syracuse, N. Y.

*Johnson.* Johnson Publishing Co., 8 S. 5th St., Richmond, Va.

*Laidlaw.* Laidlaw Brothers, 320 E. 21st St., Chicago, Ill.

*Laurel.* Laurel Book Co., 325 Market St., Chicago, Ill.

*Lippincott.* J. B. Lippincott Co., 333 W. Lake St., Chicago 6, Ill.

*Little-Brown.* Little, Brown and Co., 34 Beacon St., Boston 6, Mass.

*Longmans.* Longmans, Green, and Co., 55 Fifth Ave., New York, N. Y.

*Lyons-Carnahan.* Lyons and Carnahan, 2500 Prairie Ave., Chicago, Ill.

*Macmillan.* The Macmillan Co., 60 Fifth Ave., New York, N. Y.

*Manual.* Manual Arts Press, Peoria, Ill.

*McGraw-Hill.* McGraw-Hill Book Co., 330 W. 42d St., New York, N. Y.

*McKnight.* McKnight and McKnight, 109 W. Market St., Bloomington, Ill.

*Mentzer-Bush.* Mentzer, Bush, and Co., 2210 S. Park Way, Chicago 16, Ill.

*Merrill.* Charles E. Merrill Co., 381 Fourth Ave., New York, N. Y.

*Midwest.* Midwest Book Co., 1811 Pershing Road, Lincoln, Nebr.

*Nelson.* Thomas Nelson and Sons, 385 Fourth Ave., New York, N. Y.

*Newson.* Newson and Co., 72 Fifth Ave., New York, N. Y.

*Noble.* Noble and Noble, 100 Fifth Ave., New York, N. Y.

*Nystrom.* A. J. Nystrom and Co., 3333 Elston Ave., Chicago, Ill.

*Owen.* F. A. Owen Publishing Co., Dansville, N. Y.

*Oxford.* Oxford University Press, 114 Fifth Ave., New York, N. Y.

*Page.* L. C. Page and Co., 53 Beacon St., Boston, Mass.

*Palmer.* A. N. Palmer Co., 2128 Calumet Ave., Chicago 16, Ill.

*Practical.* Practical Drawing Co., 1315 South Michigan Ave., Chicago, Ill.

*Public School.* Public School Publishing Co., 509 N. East St., Bloomington, Ill.

*Putnam's.* G. P. Putnam's Sons, 2—6 W. 45th St., New York, N. Y.

*Quarrie.* The Quarrie Corporation, Chicago, Ill.

*Rand McNally.* Rand McNally Co., 536 S. Clark St., Chicago, Ill.

*Row-Peterson.* Row, Peterson and Co., Evanston, Ill.

*Russell Sage.* Russell Sage Foundation, New York, N. Y.

*Sanborn.* Benjamin H. Sanborn and Co., 131 Clarendon St., Boston, Mass.

*Scott-Foresman.* Scott, Foresman, and Co., 623 S. Wabash Ave., Chicago, Ill.

*Scribner's.* Charles Scribner's Sons, 600 W. Van Buren St., Chicago 7, Ill.

*Silver Burdett.* Silver Burdett Co., 221 E. Twentieth St., Chicago, Ill.

*Singer.* L. W. Singer Co., 249 W. Erie Blvd., Syracuse, N. Y.

*Smith.* Turner E. Smith and Co., 441 W. Peachtree St., N. E., Atlanta, Ga.

*Southern.* Southern Publishing Co., 321 Santa Fe Bldg., Dallas, Tex.

*Southwestern.* Southwestern Publishing Co., 201 W. Fourth St., Cincinnati, Ohio.

*Teachers College.* Teachers College, Bureau of Publications, Columbia University, 525 W. 120th St., New York, N. Y.

*University of Chicago.* University of Chicago Press, 5750 Ellis Ave., Chicago 37, Ill.

*Wagner.* H. Wagner Publishing Co., 609 Mission St., San Francisco, Calif.

*Warp.* Warp Publishing Co., Minden, Nebr.

*Webster.* Webster Publishing Co., 1808 Washington Ave., St. Louis 3, Mo.

*Westminster.* Westminster Press, Philadelphia, Pa.

*Wheeler.* Wheeler Publishing Co., 2831 South Park Way, Chicago, Ill.

*Winston.* John C. Winston Co., 623—633 S. Wabash Ave., Chicago, Ill.

*World Book.* World Book Co., Yonkers-on-Hudson 5, New York, N. Y.

*Zaner-Bloser.* Zaner-Bloser Co., Columbus, Ohio.

*Zondervan.* Zondervan Publishing Co., Grand Rapids, Mich.

### 3. Leading Publishers of Tests for Elementary Schools

*Bureau of Publications,* Teachers College, Columbia University, New York City, N. Y. (All types.)

*California Test Bureau,* 3636 Beverly Blvd., Los Angeles, Calif. (All types.)

*Co-operative Test Service,* 15 Amsterdam Ave., New York City. (Junior high school tests.)

*Educational Test Bureau,* 720 Washington Ave., S. E., Minneapolis 14, Minn.

*Houghton Mifflin Company,* 2500 Prairie Ave., Chicago, Ill. (All types.)

*Psychological Corporation,* 522 Fifth Ave., New York City. (All types.)

*Public School Publishing Company,* Bloomington, Ill. (All types.)

*Scott, Foresman, and Company,* 623 S. Wabash Ave., Chicago, Ill. (Arithmetic tests.)

*Webster Publishing Company,* 1808 Washington Ave., St. Louis, Mo. (Arithmetic tests and classification test for beginners in reading.)

*World Book Company,* 2126 Prairie Ave., Chicago, Ill. (All types.)

### 4. Leading Educational Magazines

*Lutheran School Journal.* Concordia Publishing House, St. Louis, Mo. Price, $1.50.

*American School Board Journal.* Bruce Publishing Co., 540 N. Milwaukee St., Milwaukee 1, Wis. Price, $3.00.

*Childhood Education.* Association for Childhood Education, 1201 16th St., N. W., Washington, D. C. Price, $2.50.

*Christian Home and School Magazine.* National Union of Christian Schools, 10119 Lafayette Ave., Chicago, Ill.

*Clearing House.* Inor Publishing Co., 207 Fourth Ave., New York, N. Y. Price, $3.00.

*Education Digest.* P. O. Box 100, Ann Arbor, Mich. Price, $3.00.

*Education for Victory* (formerly *School Life*). U. S. Office of Education, Washington, D. C. Price, $1.00.

*Educational Method.* 1201 16th St., N. W., Washington, D. C. Price, $3.00.

*Educational Press Bulletin.* Room 100, Centennial Bldg., Springfield, Ill. Free to Illinois teachers.

*Elementary English Review.* C. C. Certain, Detroit, Mich. Price, $2.50.

*Elementary School Journal.* University of Chicago, Chicago, Ill. Price, $2.50.

*English Journal.* National Council of Teachers of English, 211 W. 68th St., Chicago, Ill. Price, $3.00.

*Grade Teacher, The.* Educational Publishers Corporation, Darian, Conn. Price, $2.50.

*Hygeia.* American Medical Association, 535 N. Dearborn St., Chicago, Ill. Price, $2.50.

*Instructor, The.* F. A. Owen Publishing Co., Dansville, N. Y. Price, $2.50.

*Journal of the National Education Association.* 1201 16th St., N. W., Washington, D. C. Price, $2.00, including membership in Association.

*Mathematics Teacher.* 525 W. 120th St., New York, N. Y. Price, $2.00.

*Progressive Education.* Progressive Education Association, 310 W. 90th St., New York, N. Y. Price, $3.00.

*School and Society.* The Science Press, North Queen St. and McGovern Ave., Lancaster, Pa. Price, $3.50, including membership. $5.00 to non-members.

*Social Education.* 204 Fayerweather Hall, Columbia University, New York, N. Y. Price, $2.00.

# INDEX

Administration 316—318

Advent, unit course, 37, 38

Aims: of Christian education 3; of the Lutheran school 310; see also *Objectives*

Altar 79

American government, influences in, 147

American life, dangers to, 163

Apology to Augsburg Confession 74, 75

Apostles' Creed 73

Arbuthnot, May Hill, on benefits of memorizing, 46

Architecture, school, 324

Arithmetic: 119—128; objectives 119, 120; discussion of objectives 120, 121; method, 121—123; drill theory 121, 122; incidental theory 122; meaning theory 122, 123; course suggestions 123—125; organization of materials 123, 124; problem solving 124, 125; grade placement, 125; correlation possibilities 125, 126; evaluating outcomes 127; selected references 127, 128

Art education: 240—247; objectives 240; definition of art 240, 241; taste in art 240, 241; discussion of objectives 241, 242; origin of art 241; purpose of art 241; misuse of art 242; method 242, 243; materials 243; time allotment 243; art appreciation 243 to 245; *Elementary Art Series* 243; famous religious pictures 244; course suggestions 245, 246; correlation possibilities 246; evaluating outcomes 246; selected references 247; textbooks 247

Athanasian Creed 74

Attendance 297

Attitudes, religious and moral, 297 to 303

Audio-visual aids 324

Augsburg Confession 74

Band 327

Baptismal font 79

Behavior: 297—303; problems 298 to 303

Bible: "place memory," 57; use of 56

Bible history: 22—34; objectives 22, 23; purpose of 23; discussion of objectives 23, 24; divine authority of 24; method 24—29; type lesson 26—29; course suggestions 29—32; schedules 16, 17, 30—32; primary grades 29; upper grades 29, 30; correlation possibilities 33; evaluating outcomes 33, 34; selected references 34

Bible passages, locating, 63

Bible reading: 55—68; objectives 55; importance of 55; types of 56, 57; course suggestions 58—66; method 57, 58; materials 58; time allotment 58; fifth grade 59, 60; sixth grade 60—64; seventh grade 64, 65; eighth grade 65, 66; correlation possibilities 66, 67; evaluating outcomes 67; selected references 68.

Bible text, use of in Bible history, 30

Bibliography 324—329

Board of education, local, 312—314, 325

Bobbs Merrill Readers 89, 93

Building 306, 307

Call of the teacher 272—274, 328

Candles 79

Canvass 325

Catechism: 9—22; objectives 9, 10; scope 10; instruction in 11; teacher of catechism 11, 12; preparation of lesson 13; type lesson 13, 14; course suggestions 14—21; primary grades 14; intermediate grades 14, 15; upper grades 15; schedules 17—21; correlation 21; evaluating outcomes 21; selected references 21, 22; Luther's 75; Large 75; Small 75

Children's books, 97

Children's organizations 325

Children's services 325

Choir, children's, 325

Christian education: aims 3 (See also *Objectives*); nature 3; results of 3

Christian life 2, 23

Christian viewpoint: primary social studies 130; history 150—152; citizenship 161; health and safety education 170—173; science 185

Church bells, ringing of, 80

Church, geographical aspects of 139

Church history: 68—84; objectives 68; fundamental concepts 68; function of 69, 70; method 70;

www.ingramcontent.com/pod-product-compliance
Lightning Source LLC
Chambersburg PA
CBHW021215090426
42740CB00006B/235

*9 780758 652638*